EMANON

MEMORIES OF EMANON   VOL 1

Manga by
SHINJI KAJIO & KENJI TSURUTA

Translation by
DANA LEWIS

Lettering and Touchup by
**SUSIE LEE AND BETTY DONG
WITH TOM2K**

DARK HORSE MANGA

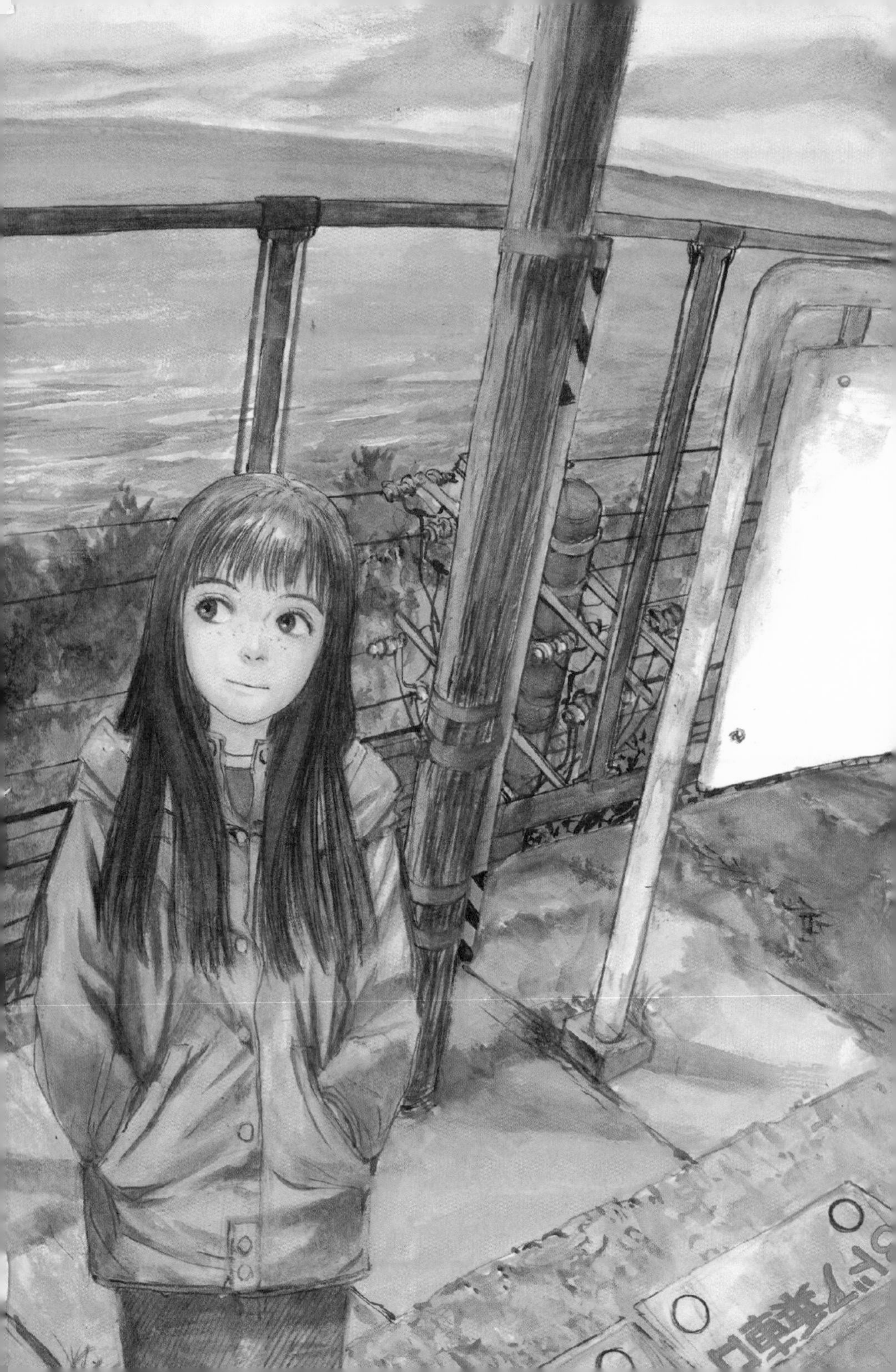

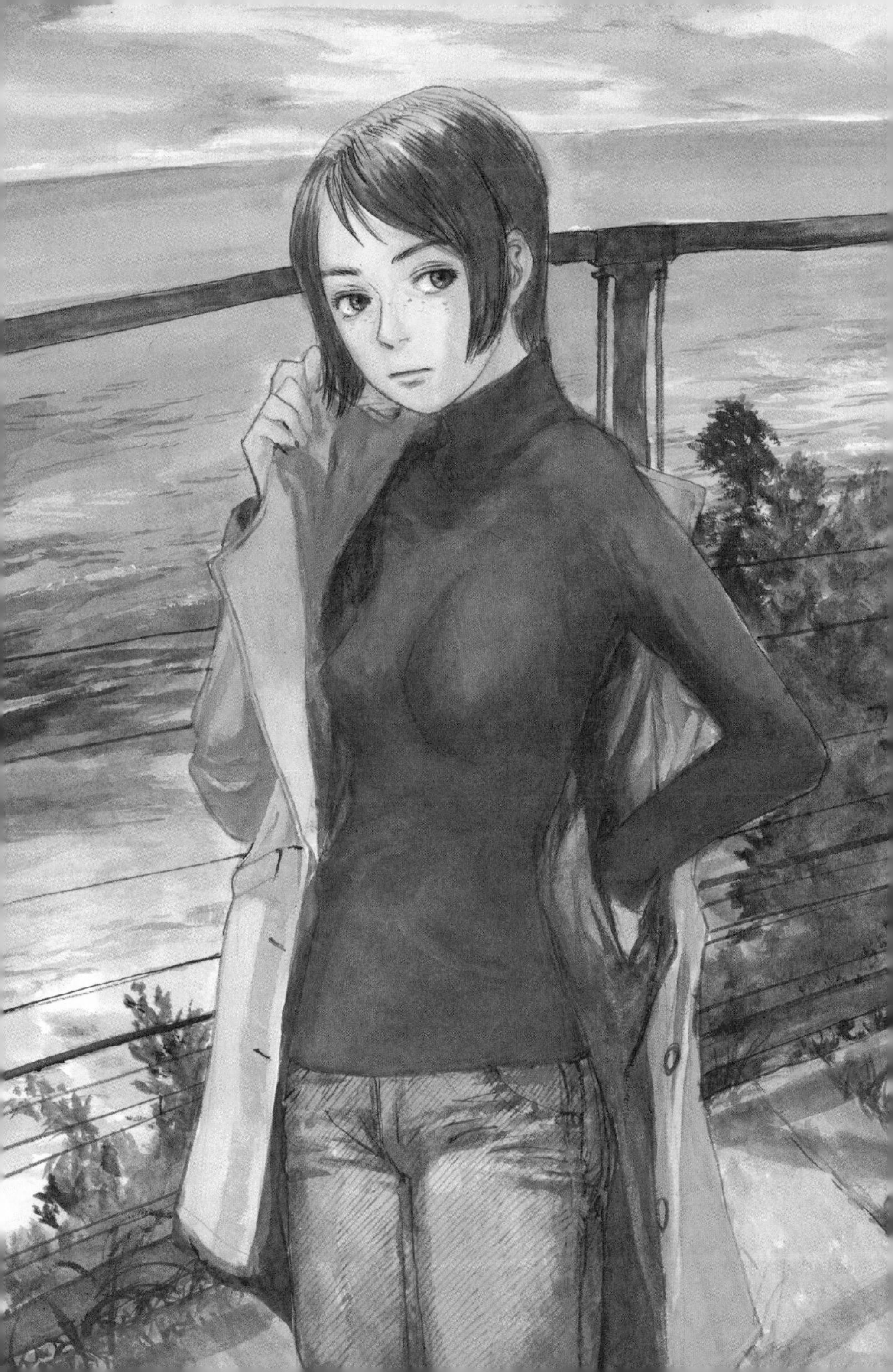

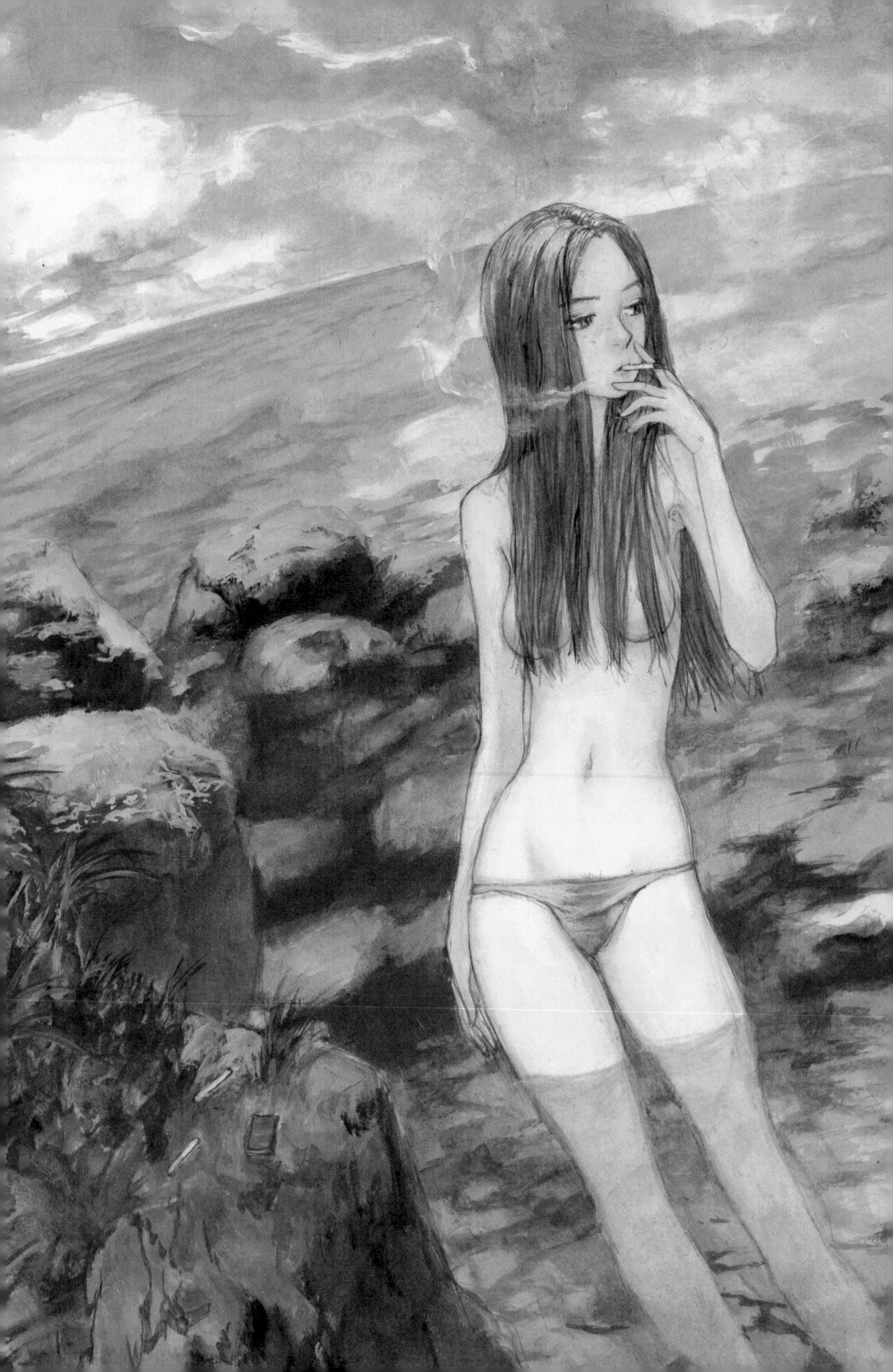

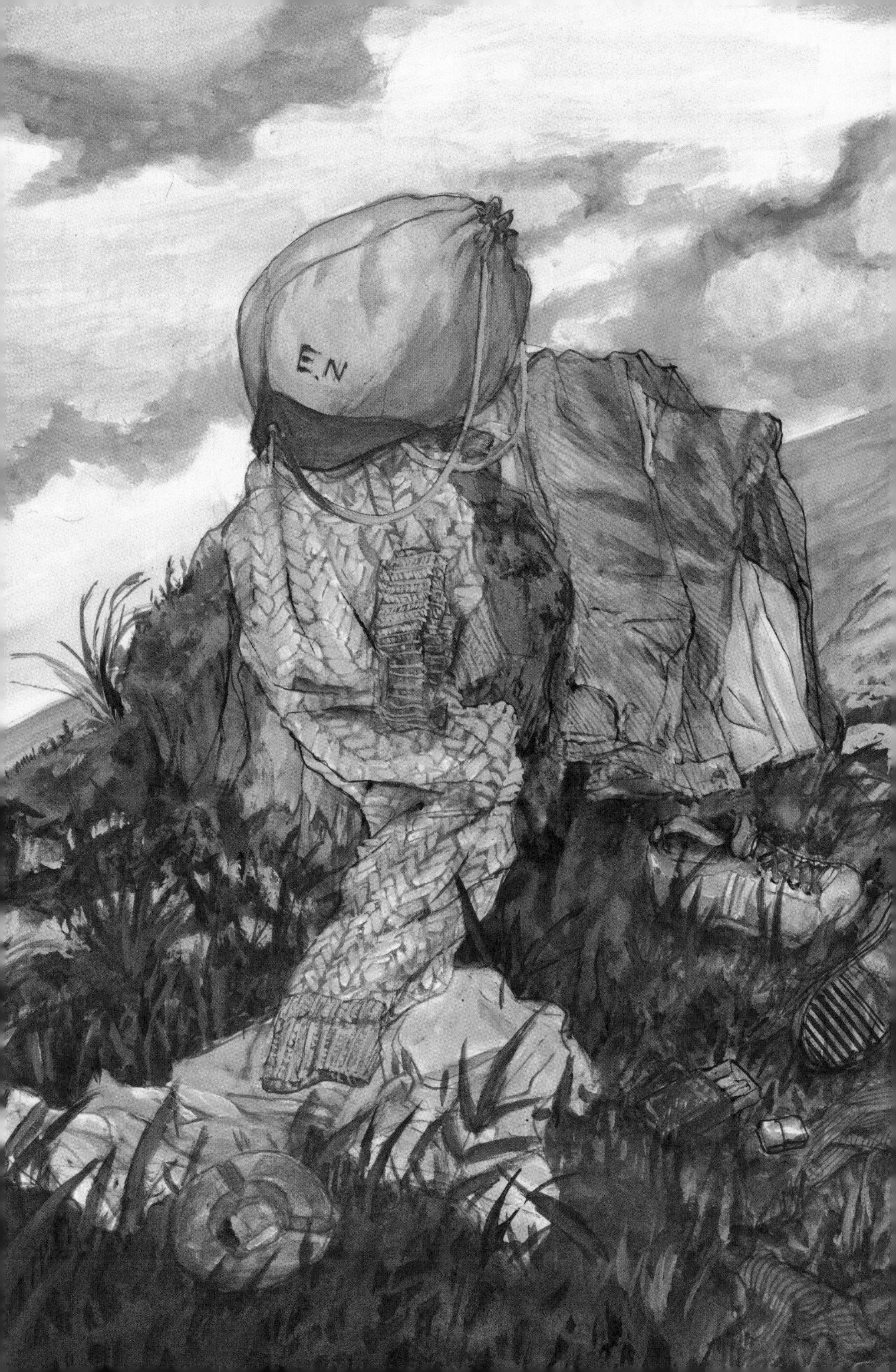
E.N

C O N T E N T S

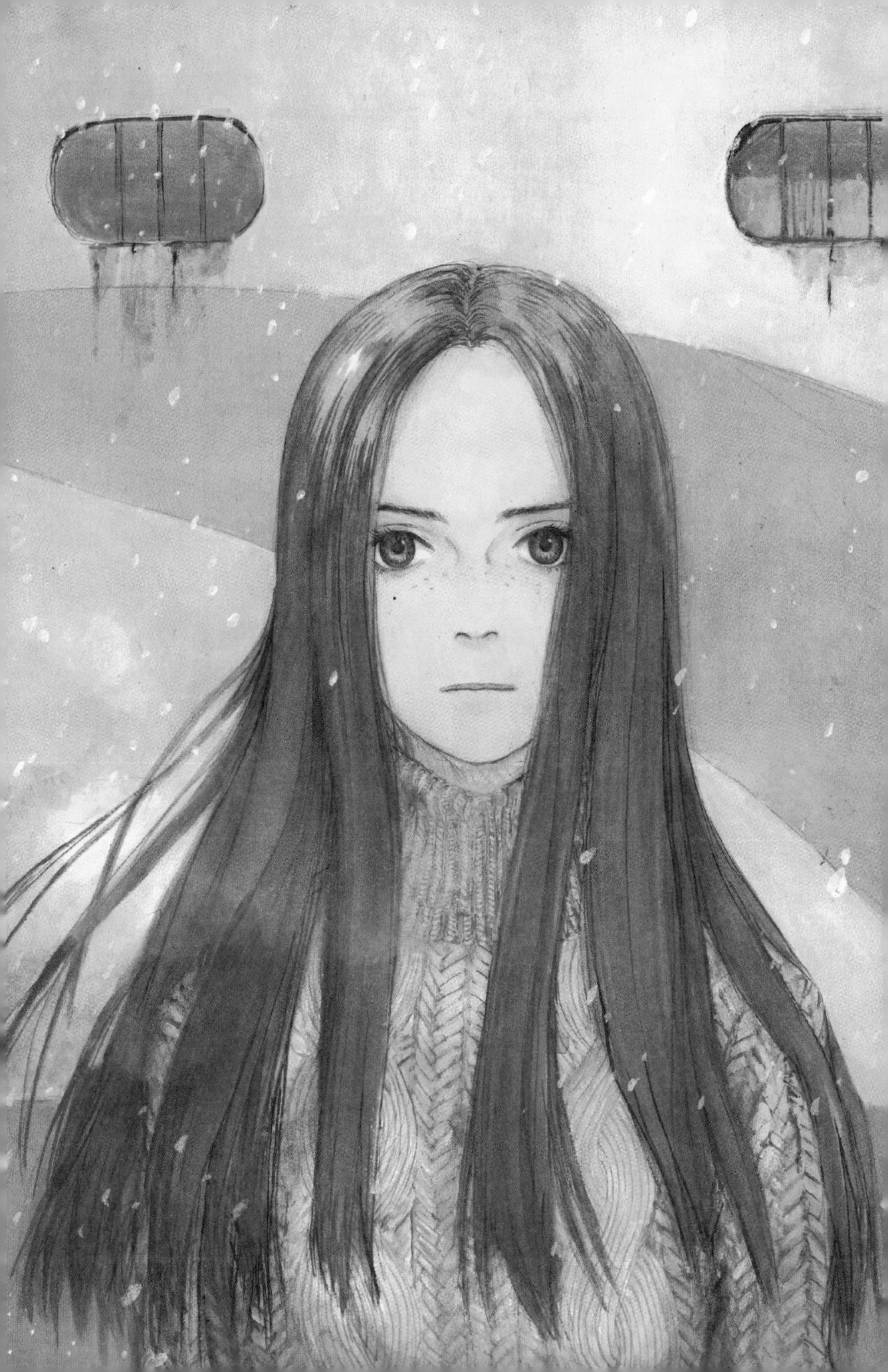

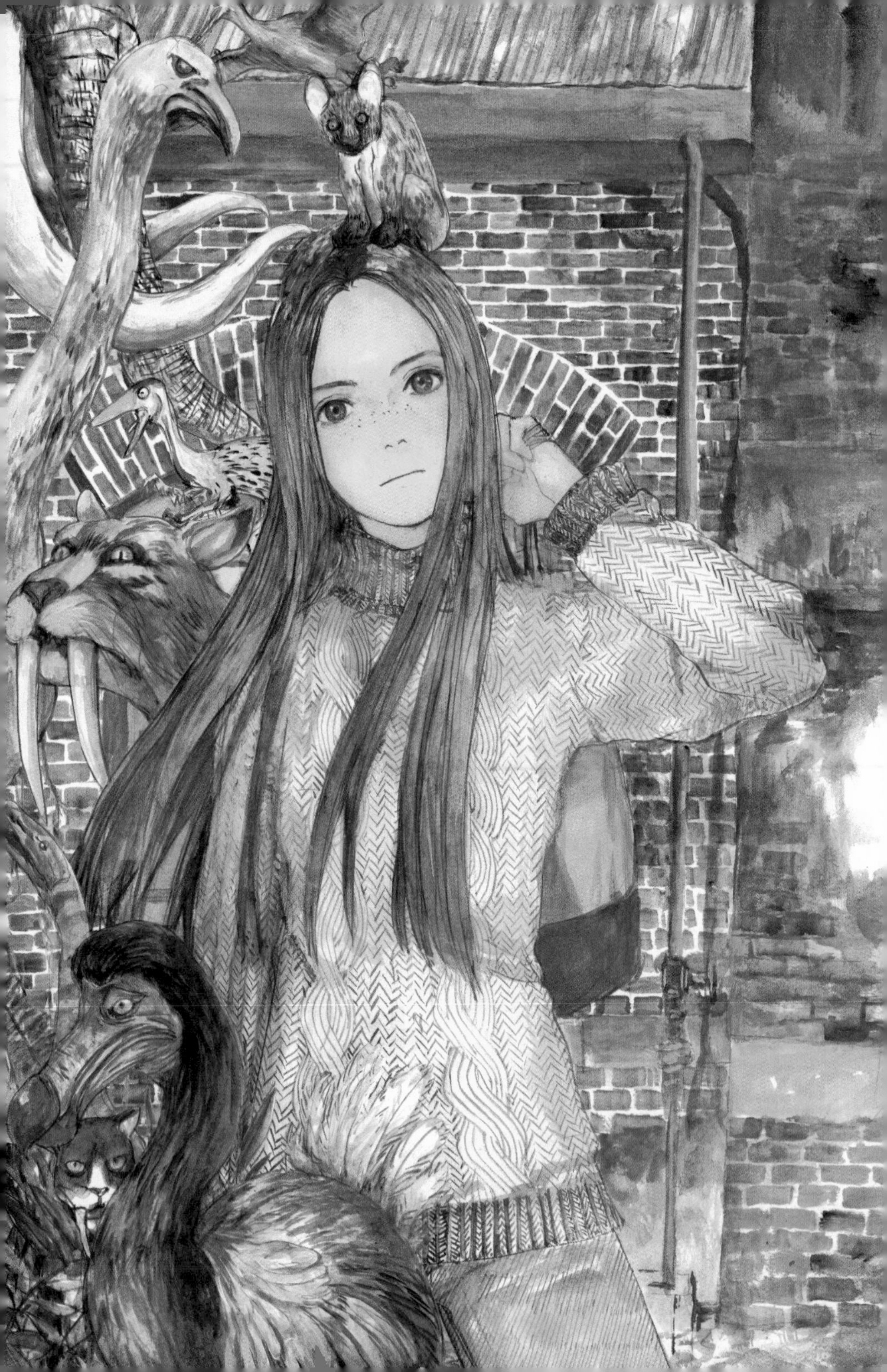

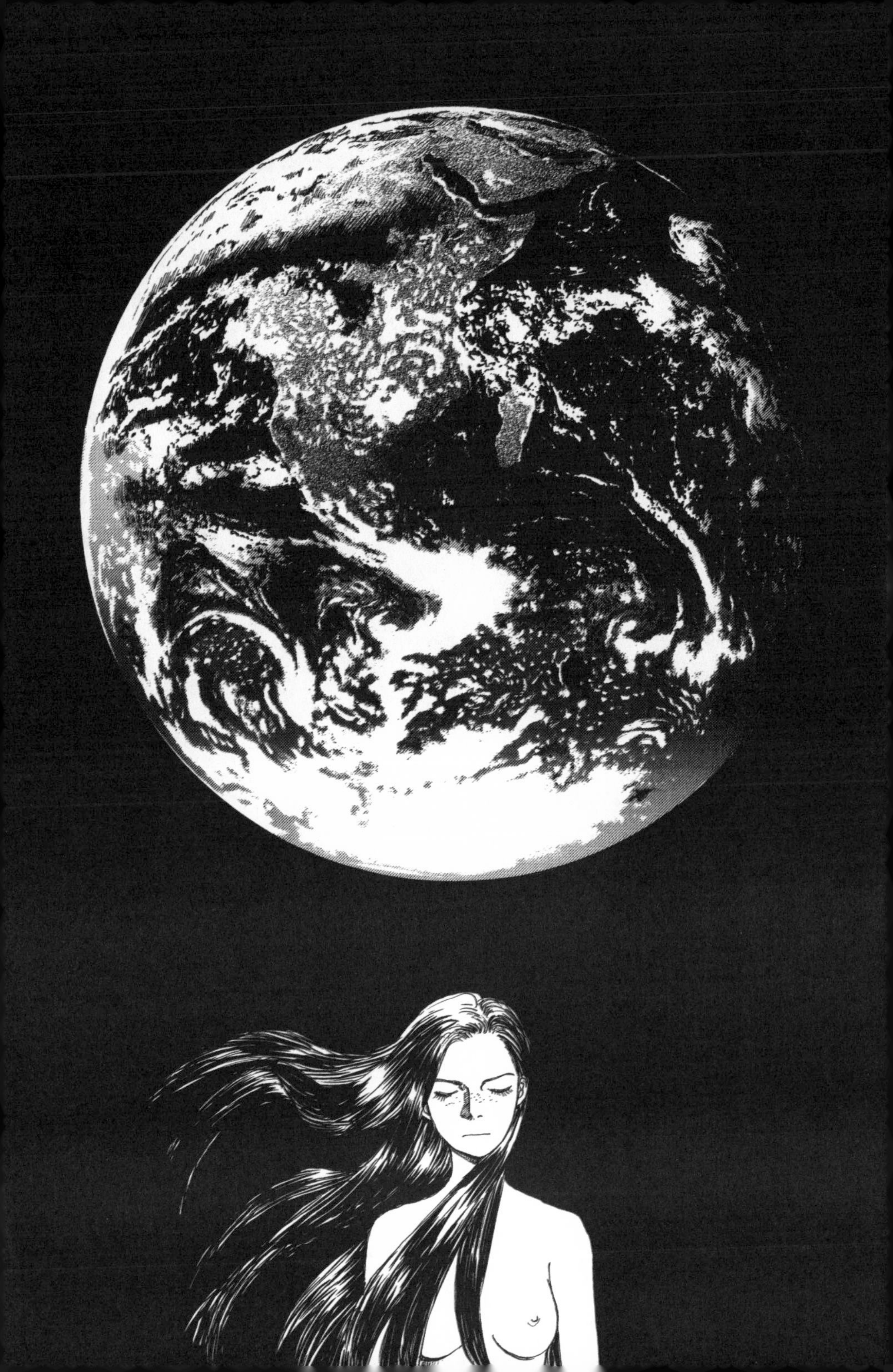

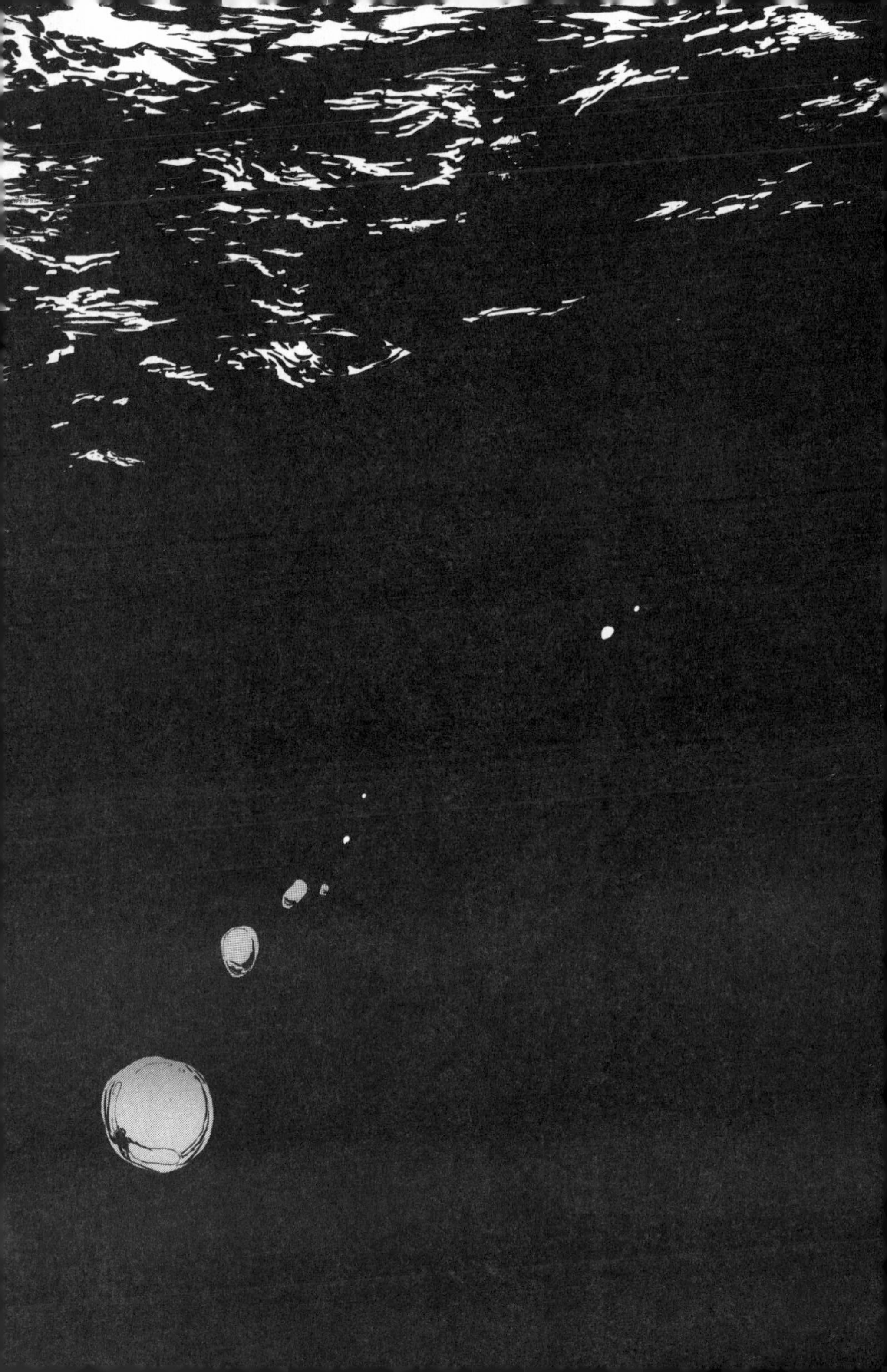

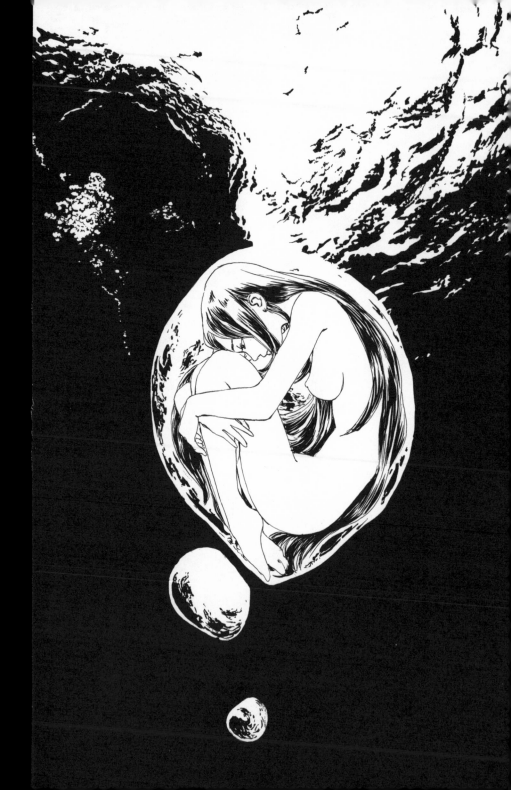

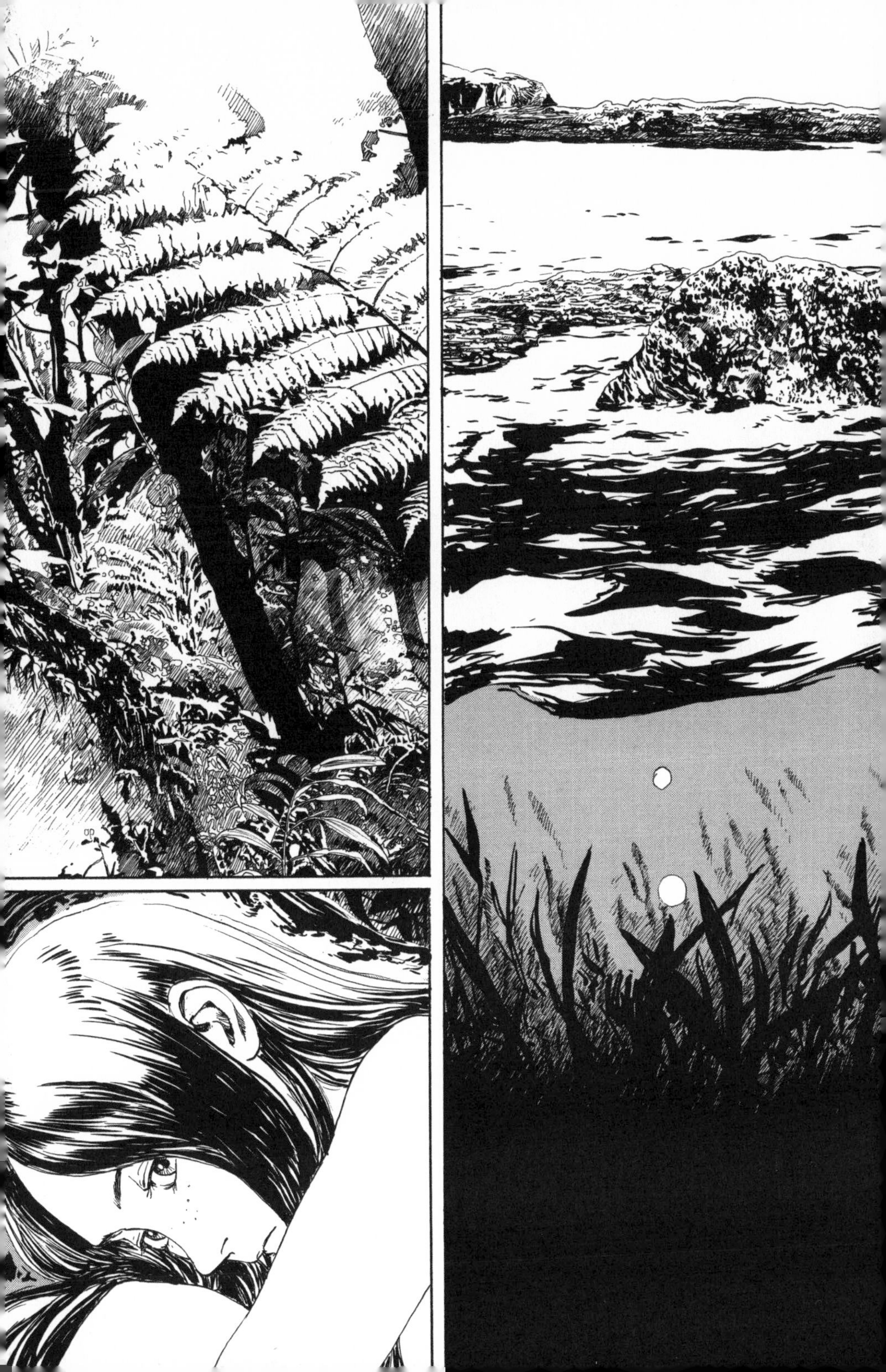

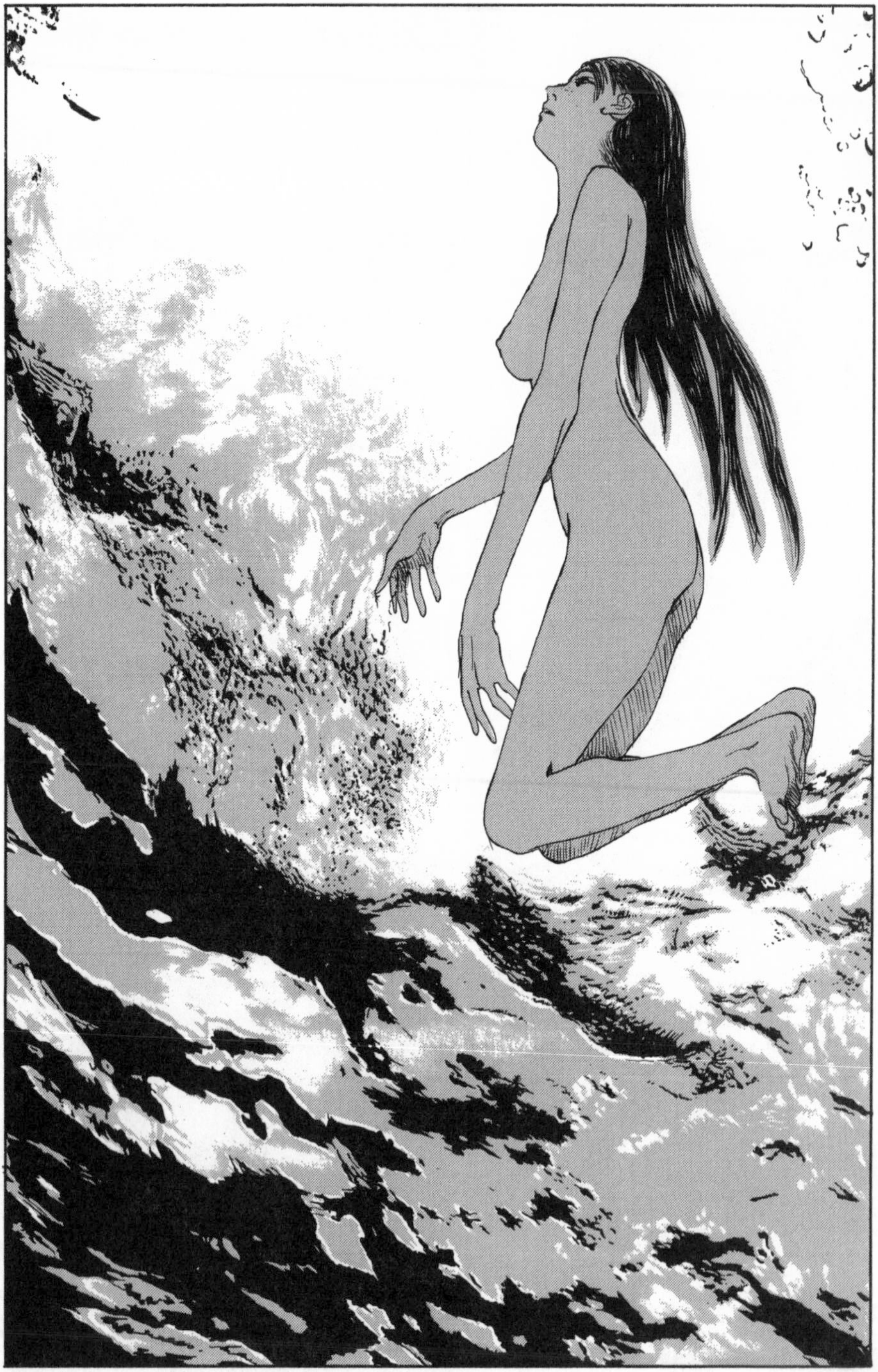

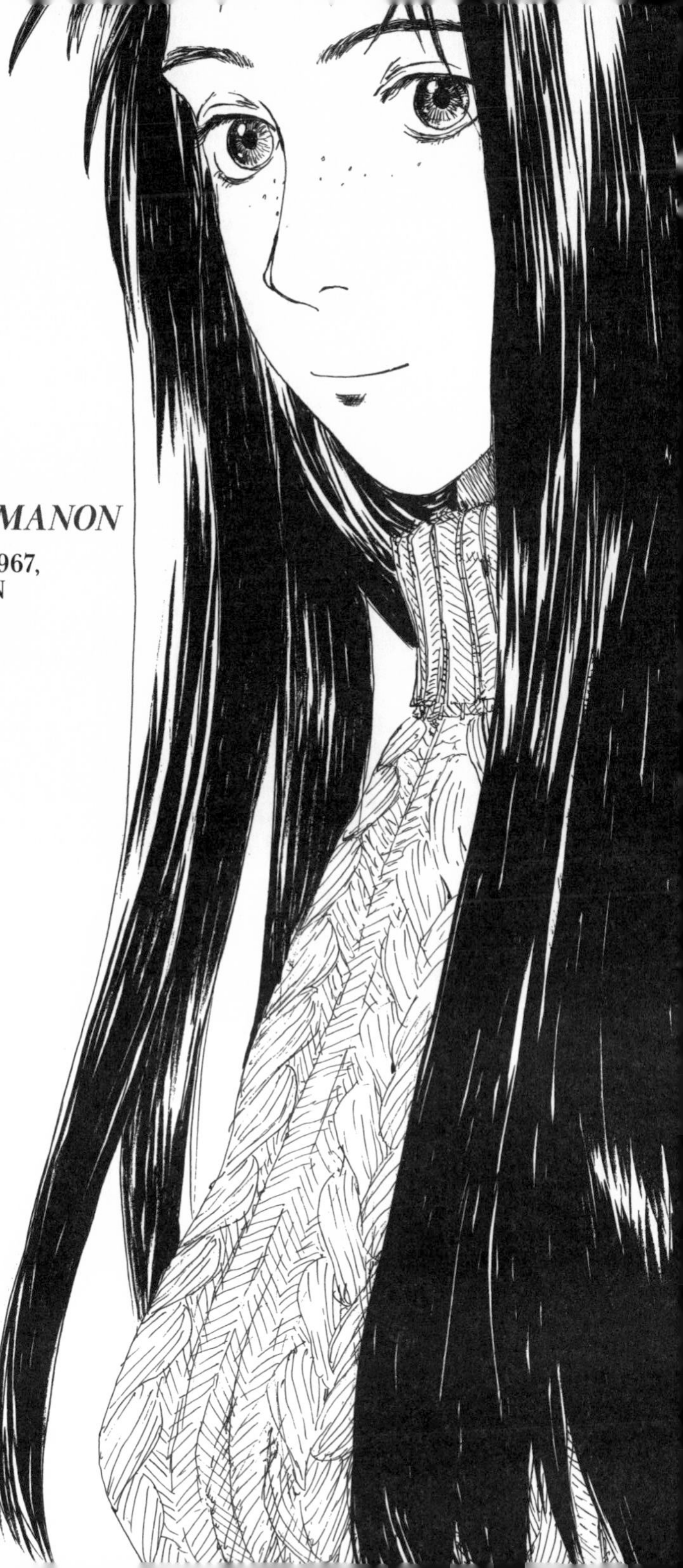

MEMORIES OF EMANON

FEBRUARY 24, 1967, AFTERNOON

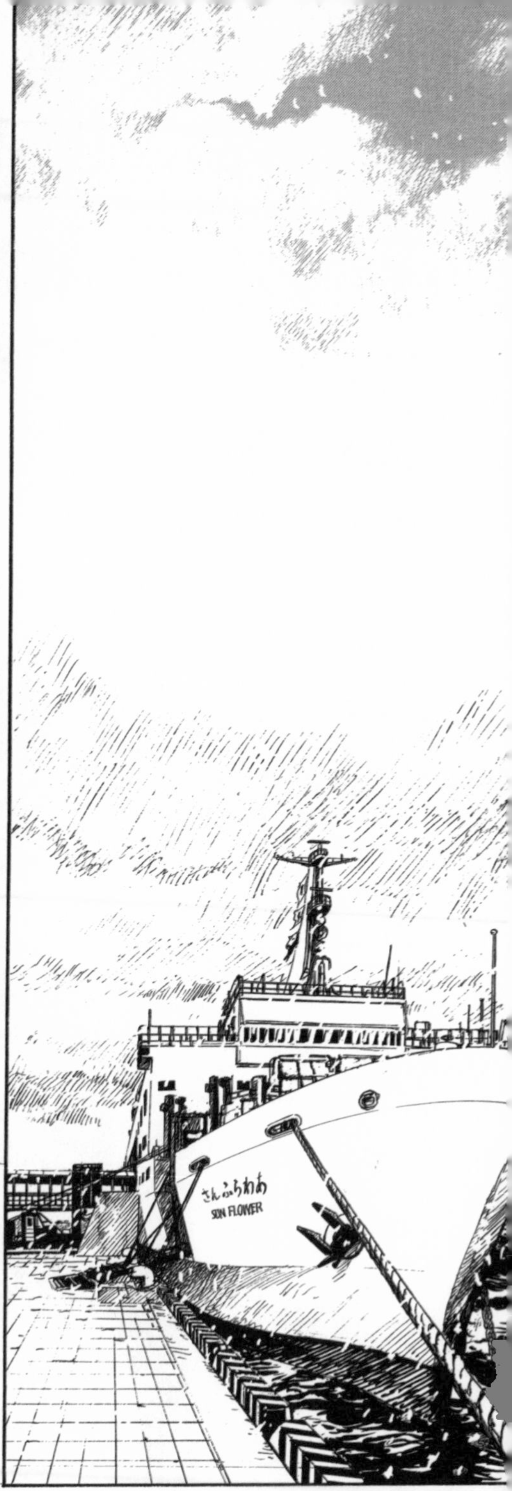
さんふらわあ
SUN FLOWER

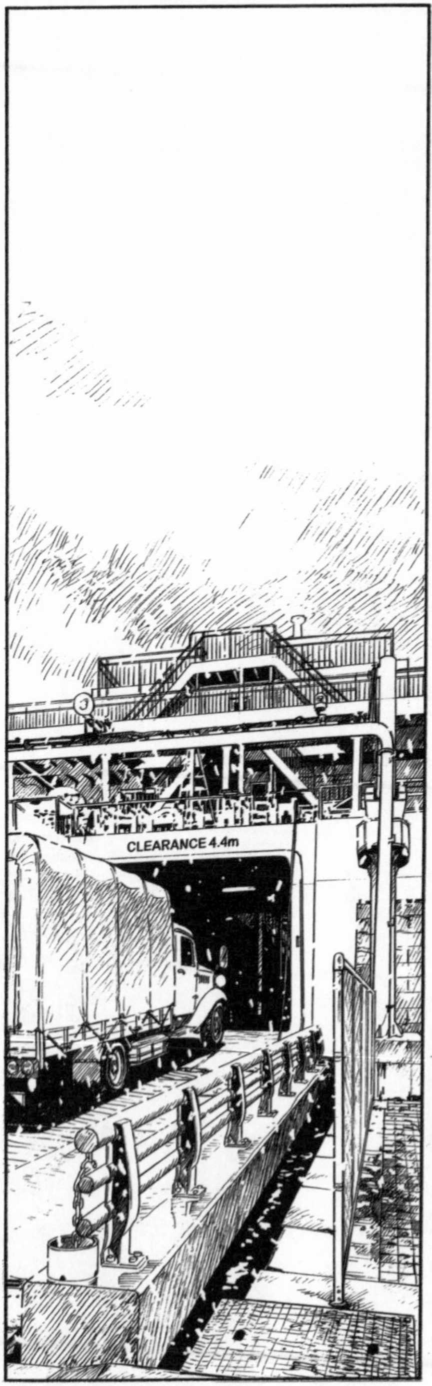
CLEARANCE 4.4m

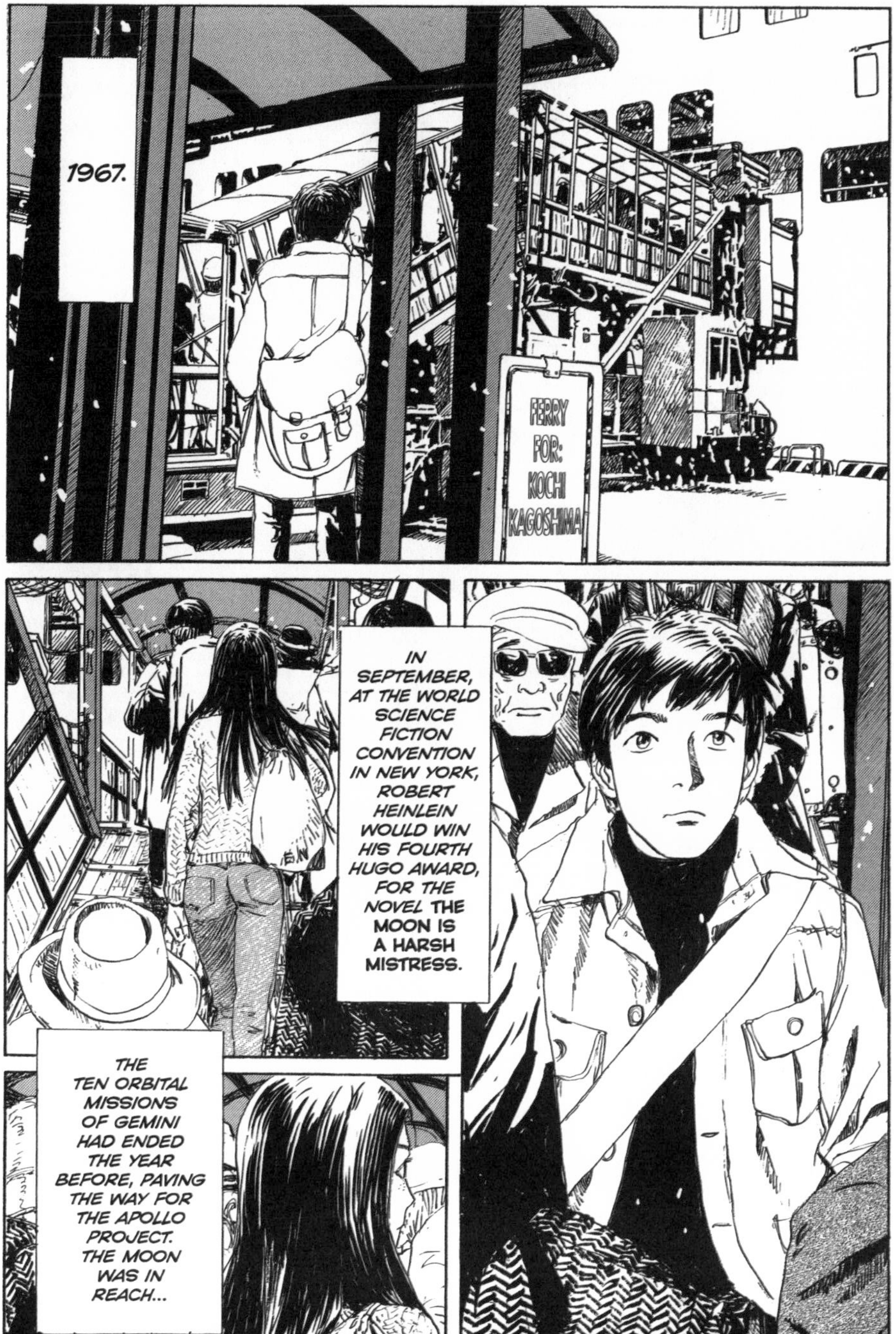
1967.
FERRY FOR: KOCHI KAGOSHIMA
IN SEPTEMBER, AT THE WORLD SCIENCE FICTION CONVENTION IN NEW YORK, ROBERT HEINLEIN WOULD WIN HIS FOURTH HUGO AWARD, FOR THE NOVEL THE MOON IS A HARSH MISTRESS.
THE TEN ORBITAL MISSIONS OF GEMINI HAD ENDED THE YEAR BEFORE, PAVING THE WAY FOR THE APOLLO PROJECT. THE MOON WAS IN REACH...

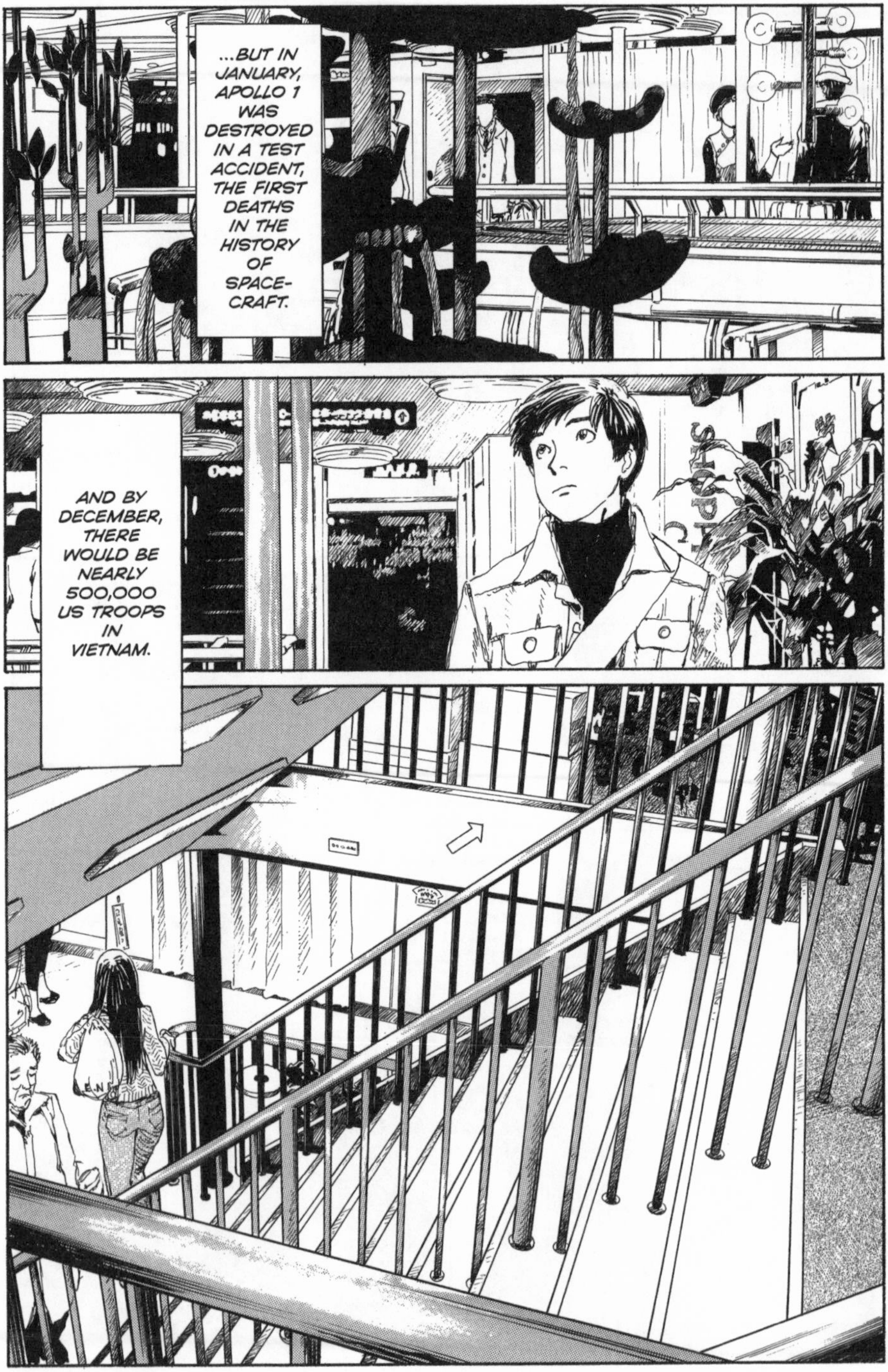
...BUT IN JANUARY, APOLLO 1 WAS DESTROYED IN A TEST ACCIDENT, THE FIRST DEATHS IN THE HISTORY OF SPACE-CRAFT.
AND BY DECEMBER, THERE WOULD BE NEARLY 500,000 US TROOPS IN VIETNAM.

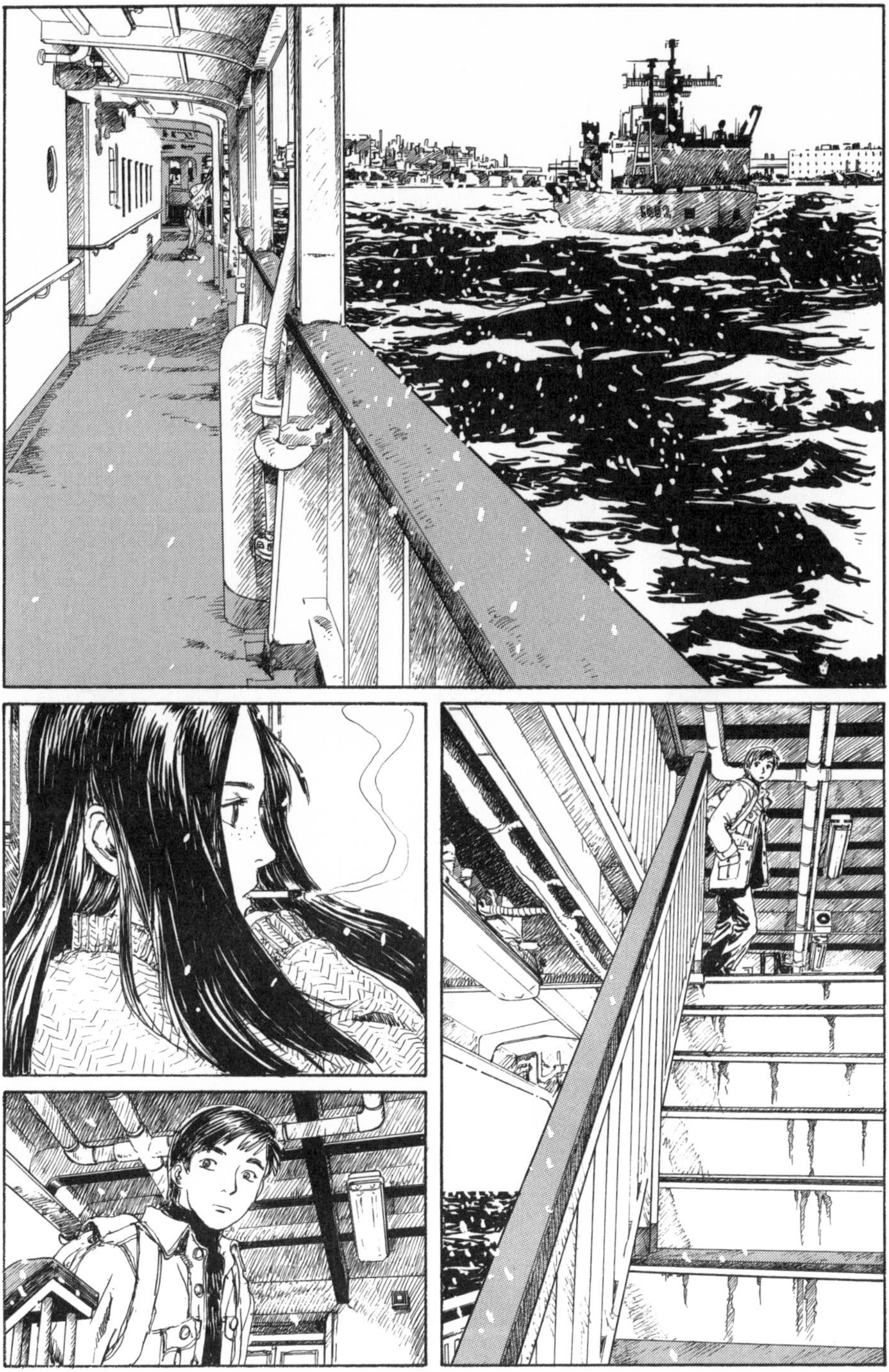

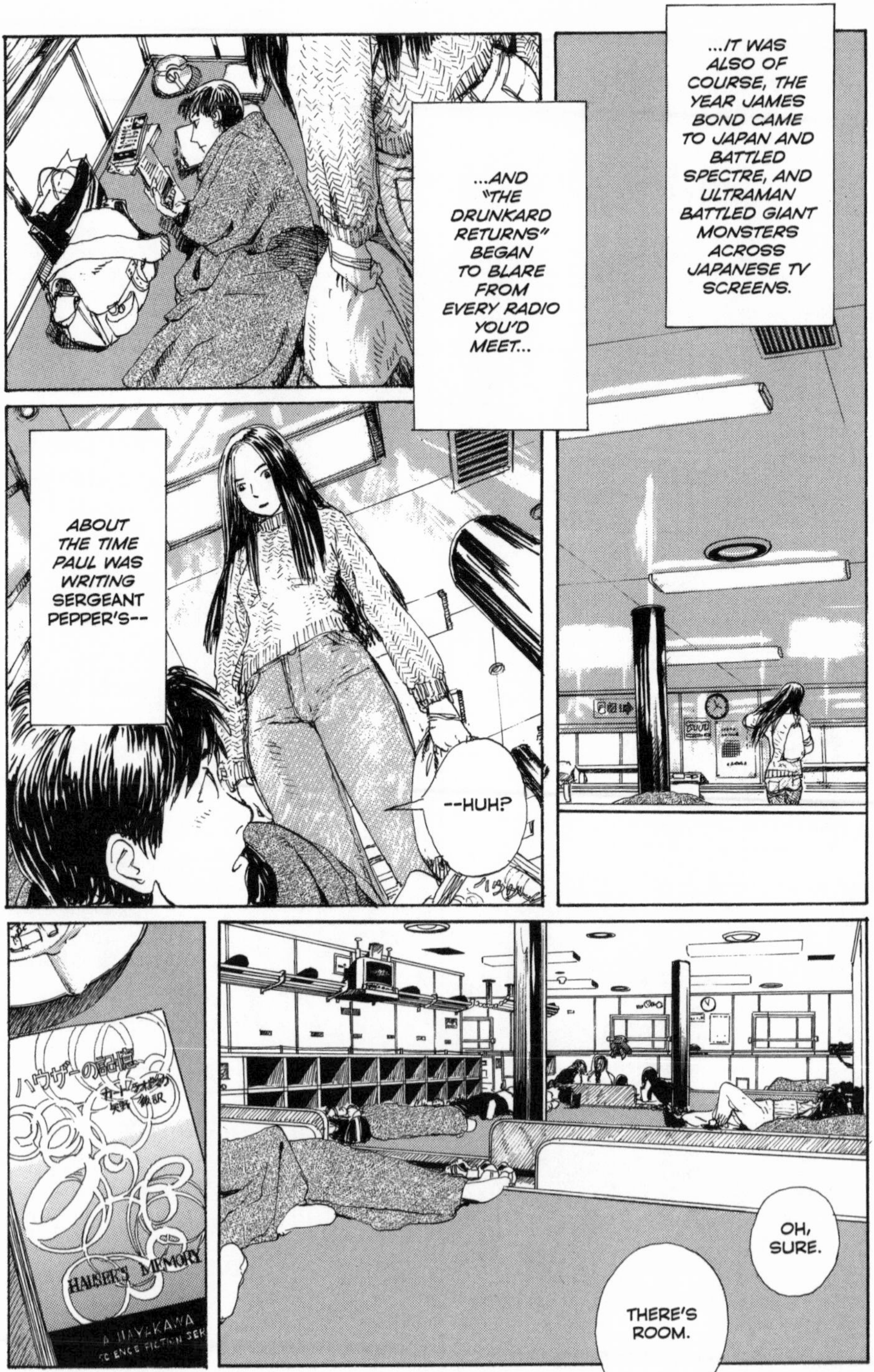
...IT WAS ALSO OF COURSE, THE YEAR JAMES BOND CAME TO JAPAN AND BATTLED SPECTRE, AND ULTRAMAN BATTLED GIANT MONSTERS ACROSS JAPANESE TV SCREENS.
...AND "THE DRUNKARD RETURNS" BEGAN TO BLARE FROM EVERY RADIO YOU'D MEET...
ABOUT THE TIME PAUL WAS WRITING SERGEANT PEPPER'S--
--HUH?
OH, SURE.
THERE'S ROOM.
ハウザーの記憶
HAUSER'S MEMORY
A HAYAKAWA

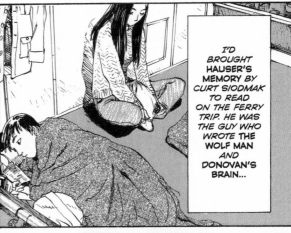

I'D BROUGHT HAUSER'S MEMORY *BY CURT SIODMAK* TO READ ON THE FERRY TRIP. *HE WAS THE GUY WHO WROTE* THE WOLF MAN *AND* DONOVAN'S BRAIN...

...GIRLS SHOULDN'T SMOKE.

THERE WAS THIS HIPPIE CHICK.

...

...WHY
NOT?

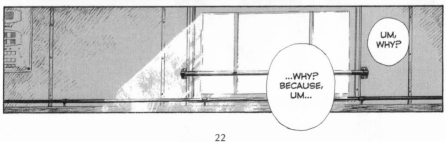

UM,
WHY?

...WHY?
BECAUSE,
UM...

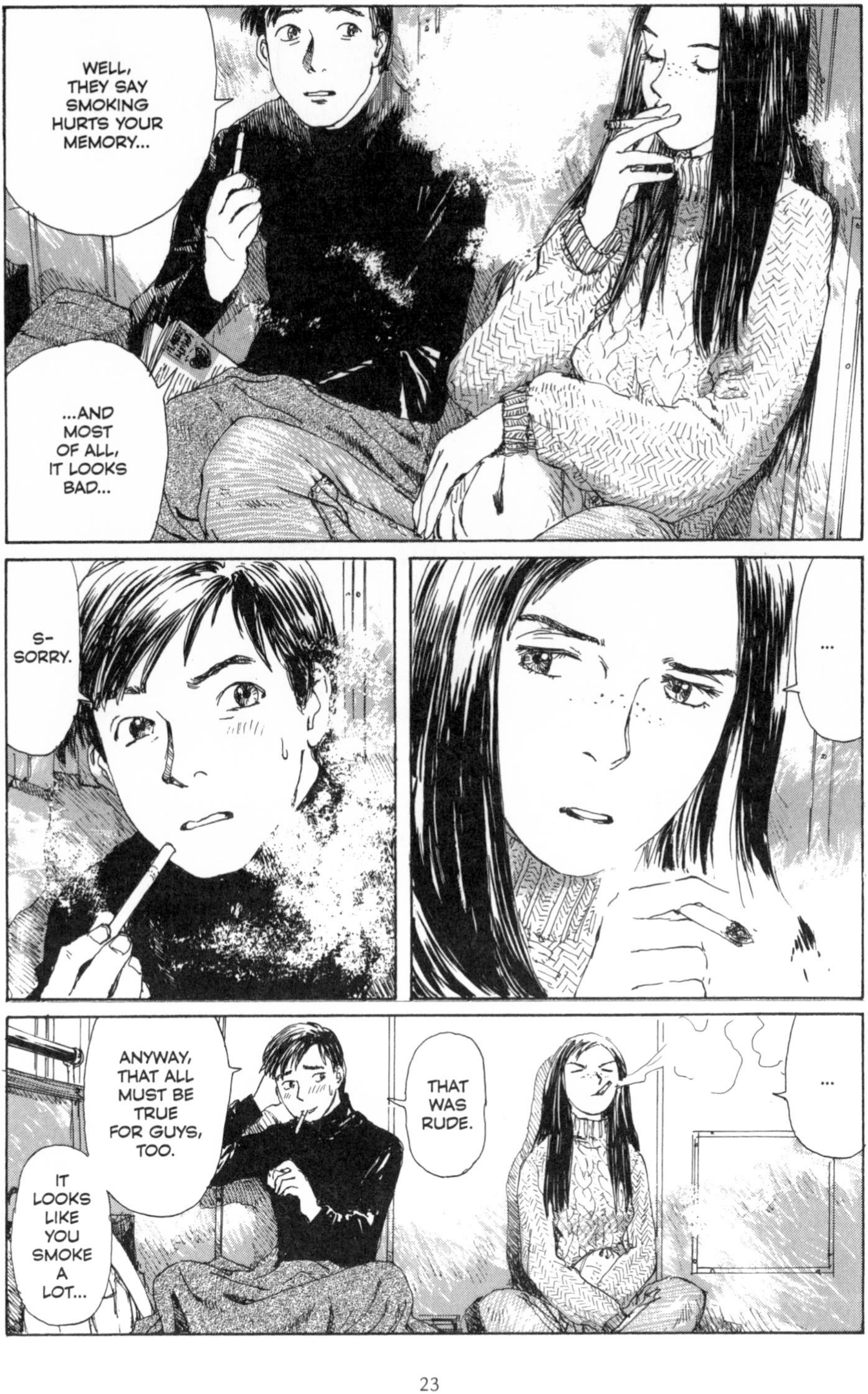
WELL, THEY SAY SMOKING HURTS YOUR MEMORY...
...AND MOST OF ALL, IT LOOKS BAD...
...
S-SORRY.
...
THAT WAS RUDE.
ANYWAY, THAT ALL MUST BE TRUE FOR GUYS, TOO.
IT LOOKS LIKE YOU SMOKE A LOT...

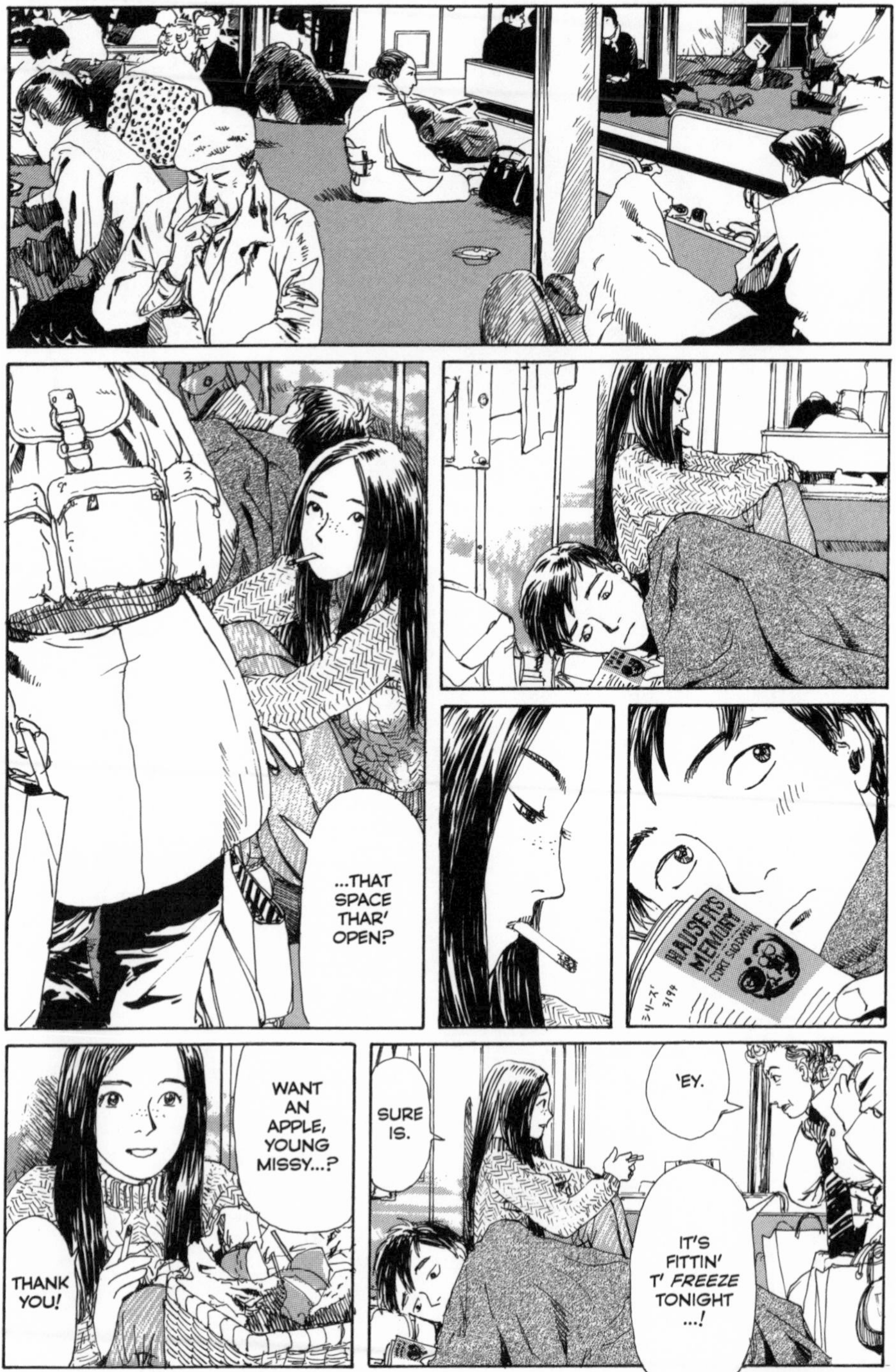

HAUSER'S MEMORY
...THAT SPACE THAR' OPEN?
'EY.
IT'S FITTIN' T' *FREEZE* TONIGHT ...!
SURE IS.
WANT AN APPLE, YOUNG MISSY...?
THANK YOU!

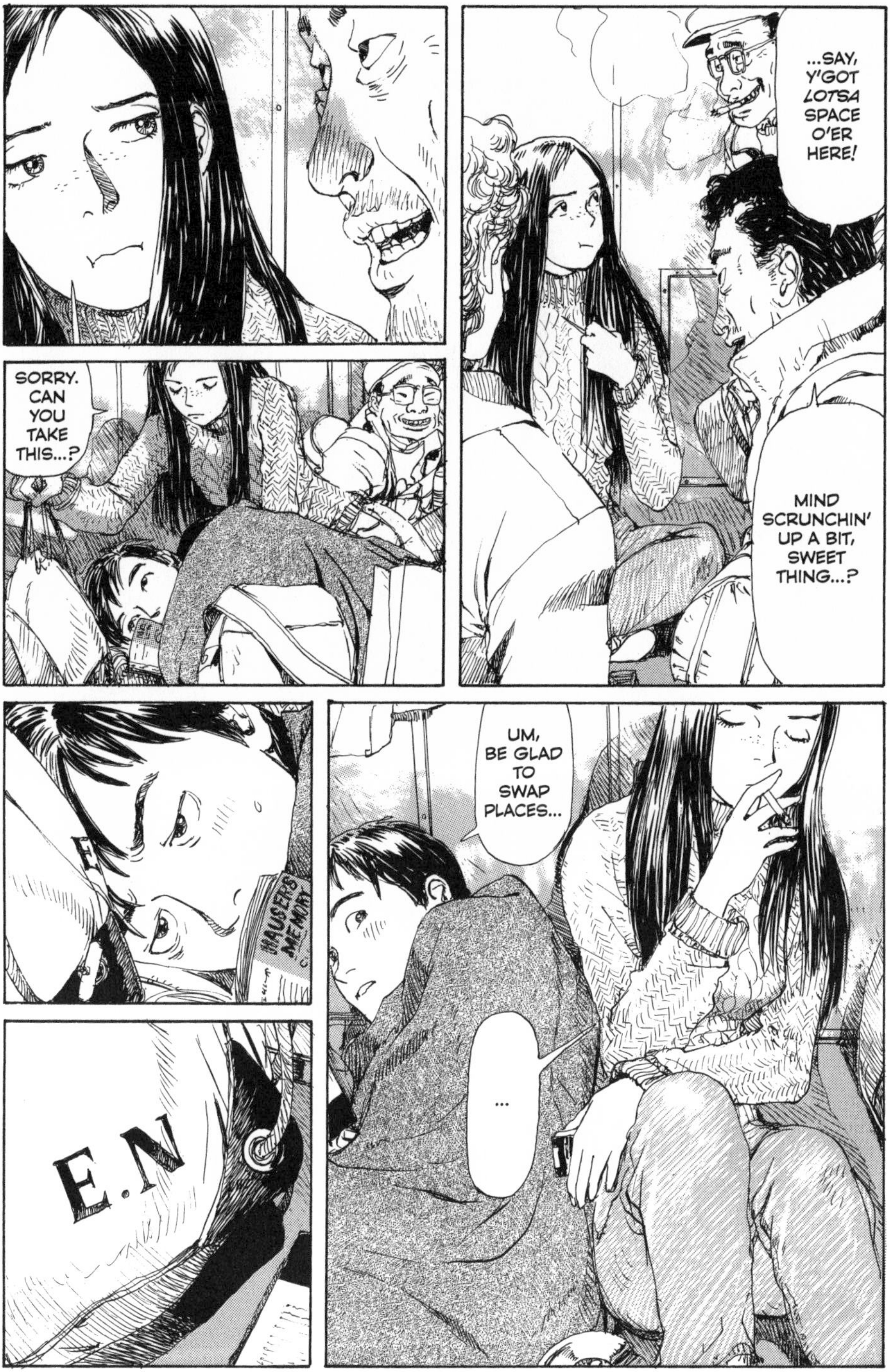
...SAY, Y'GOT *LOTSA* SPACE O'ER HERE!
MIND SCRUNCHIN' UP A BIT, SWEET THING...?
SORRY. CAN YOU TAKE THIS...?
UM, BE GLAD TO SWAP PLACES...
...
HAUSER'S MEMORY
E.N

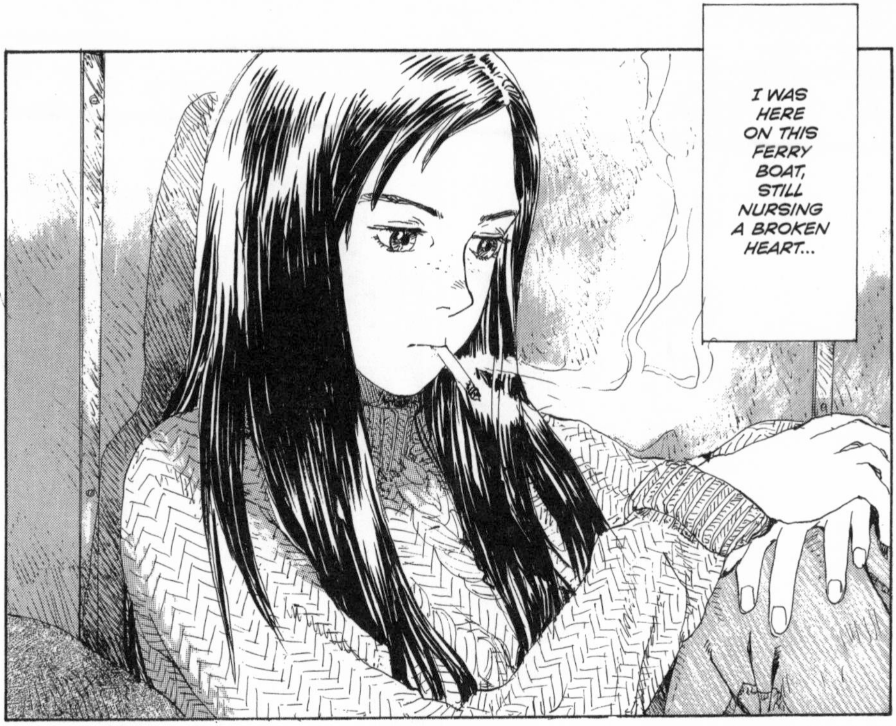
I WAS HERE ON THIS FERRY BOAT, STILL NURSING A BROKEN HEART...

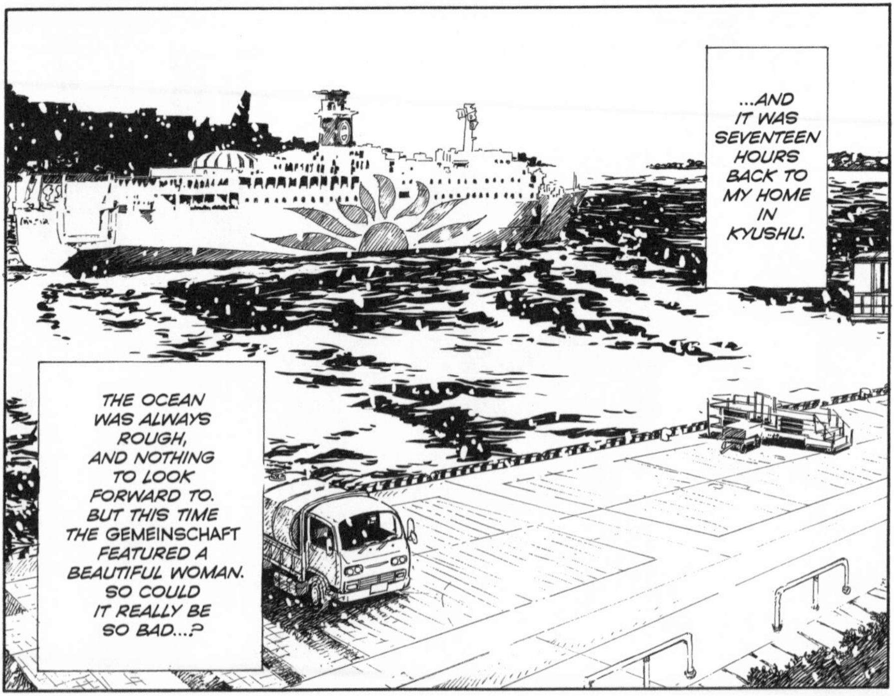
...AND IT WAS SEVENTEEN HOURS BACK TO MY HOME IN KYUSHU.
THE OCEAN WAS ALWAYS ROUGH, AND NOTHING TO LOOK FORWARD TO. BUT THIS TIME THE GEMEINSCHAFT FEATURED A BEAUTIFUL WOMAN. SO COULD IT REALLY BE SO BAD...?

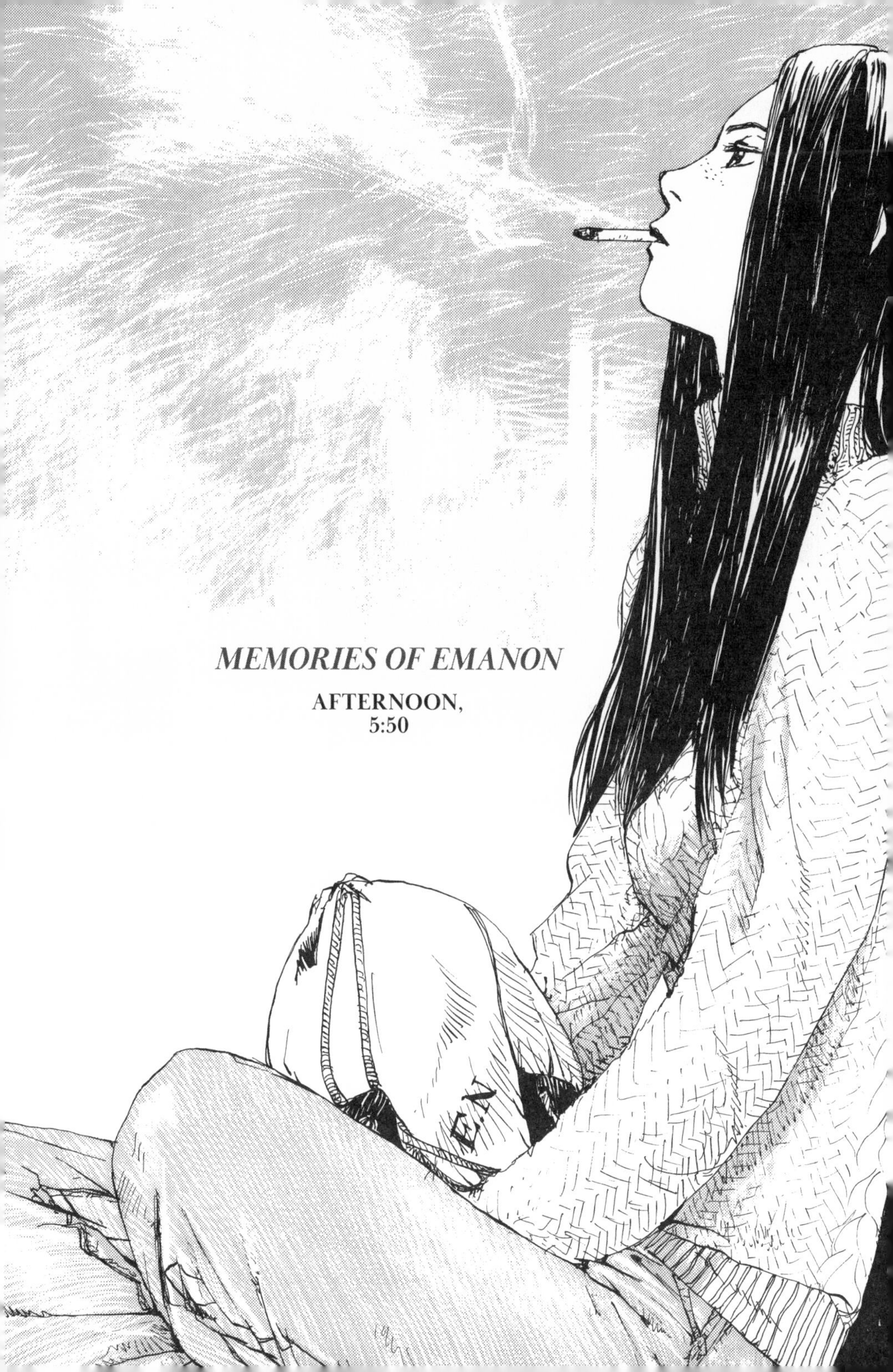
E.N.

MEMORIES OF EMANON

AFTERNOON, 5:50

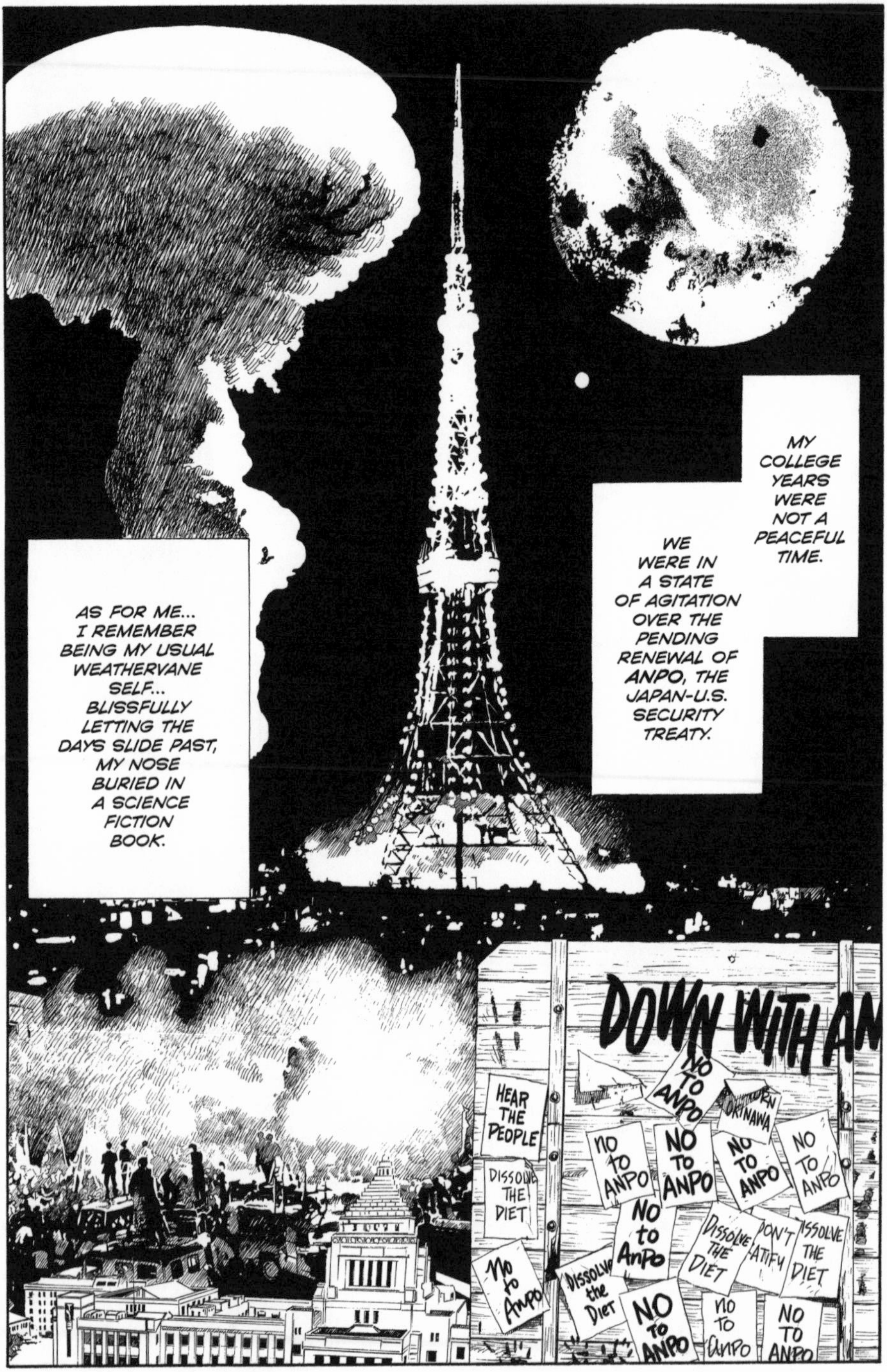
MY COLLEGE YEARS WERE NOT A PEACEFUL TIME.
WE WERE IN A STATE OF AGITATION OVER THE PENDING RENEWAL OF ANPO, THE JAPAN-U.S. SECURITY TREATY.
AS FOR ME... I REMEMBER BEING MY USUAL WEATHERVANE SELF... BLISSFULLY LETTING THE DAYS SLIDE PAST, MY NOSE BURIED IN A SCIENCE FICTION BOOK.
DOWN WITH AN
NO TO ANPO
OKINAWA
NO TO ANPO
NO TO ANPO
NO TO ANPO
NO TO ANPO
HEAR THE PEOPLE
DISSOLVE THE DIET
NO to AnPo
DISSOLVE THE DIET
DISSOLVE THE DIET
No to Anpo
DISSOLVE the DIET
NO to ANPO
no to Anpo
NO TO ANPO

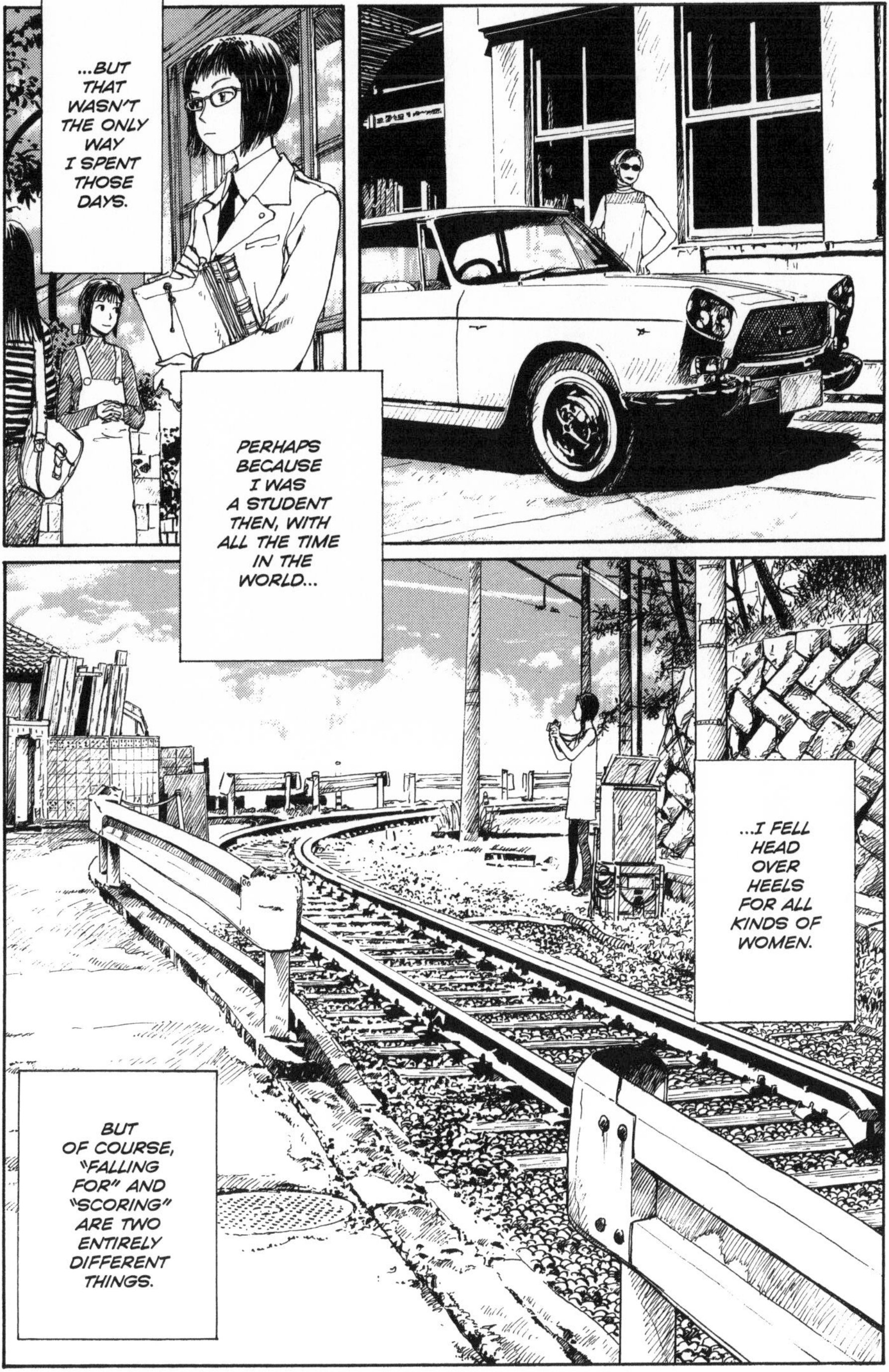
...BUT THAT WASN'T THE ONLY WAY I SPENT THOSE DAYS.
PERHAPS BECAUSE I WAS A STUDENT THEN, WITH ALL THE TIME IN THE WORLD...
...I FELL HEAD OVER HEELS FOR ALL KINDS OF WOMEN.
BUT OF COURSE, "FALLING FOR" AND "SCORING" ARE TWO ENTIRELY DIFFERENT THINGS.

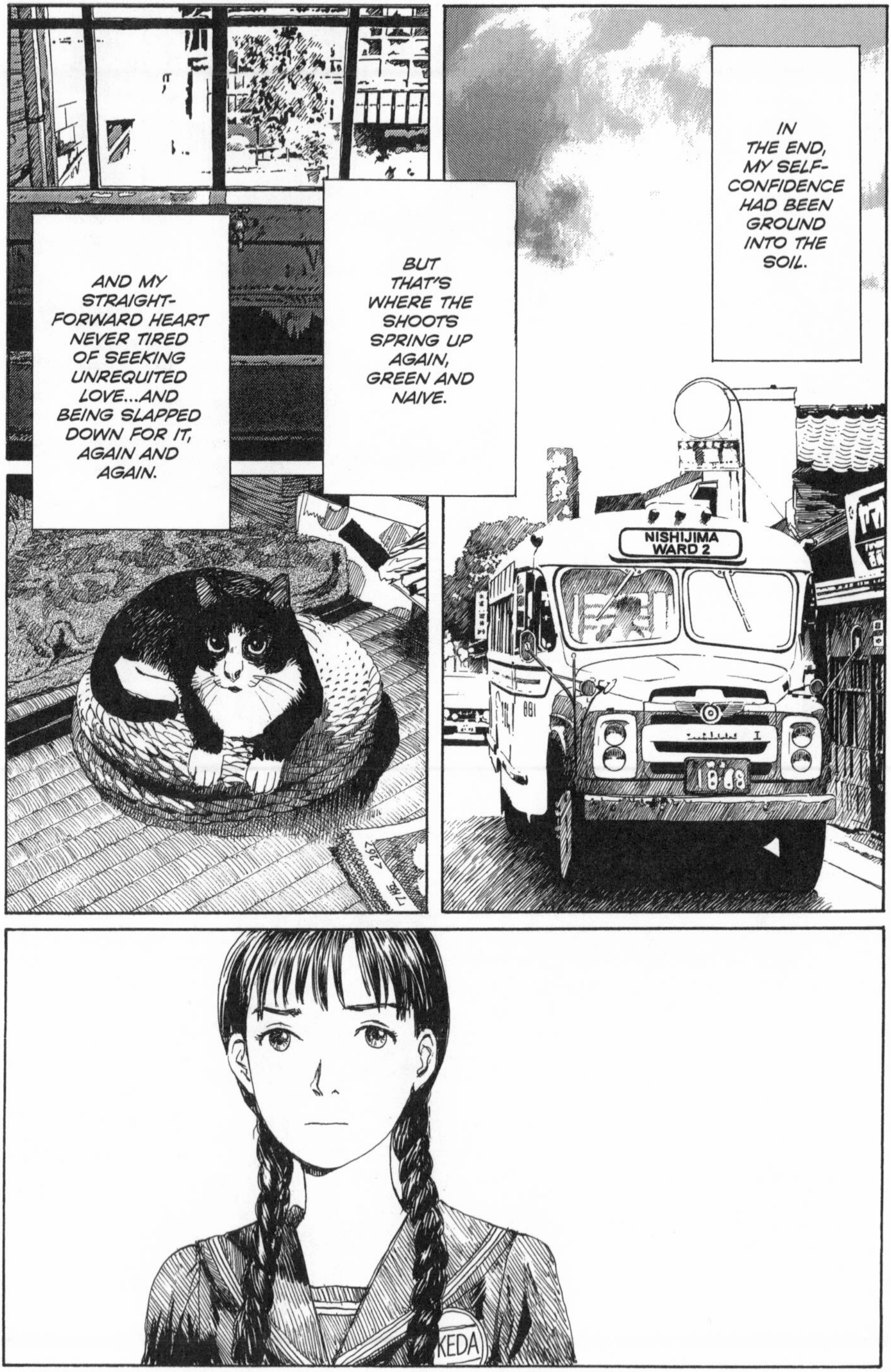
IN THE END, MY SELF-CONFIDENCE HAD BEEN GROUND INTO THE SOIL.
NISHIJIMA WARD 2
BUT THAT'S WHERE THE SHOOTS SPRING UP AGAIN, GREEN AND NAIVE.
AND MY STRAIGHT-FORWARD HEART NEVER TIRED OF SEEKING UNREQUITED LOVE...AND BEING SLAPPED DOWN FOR IT, AGAIN AND AGAIN.
KEDA

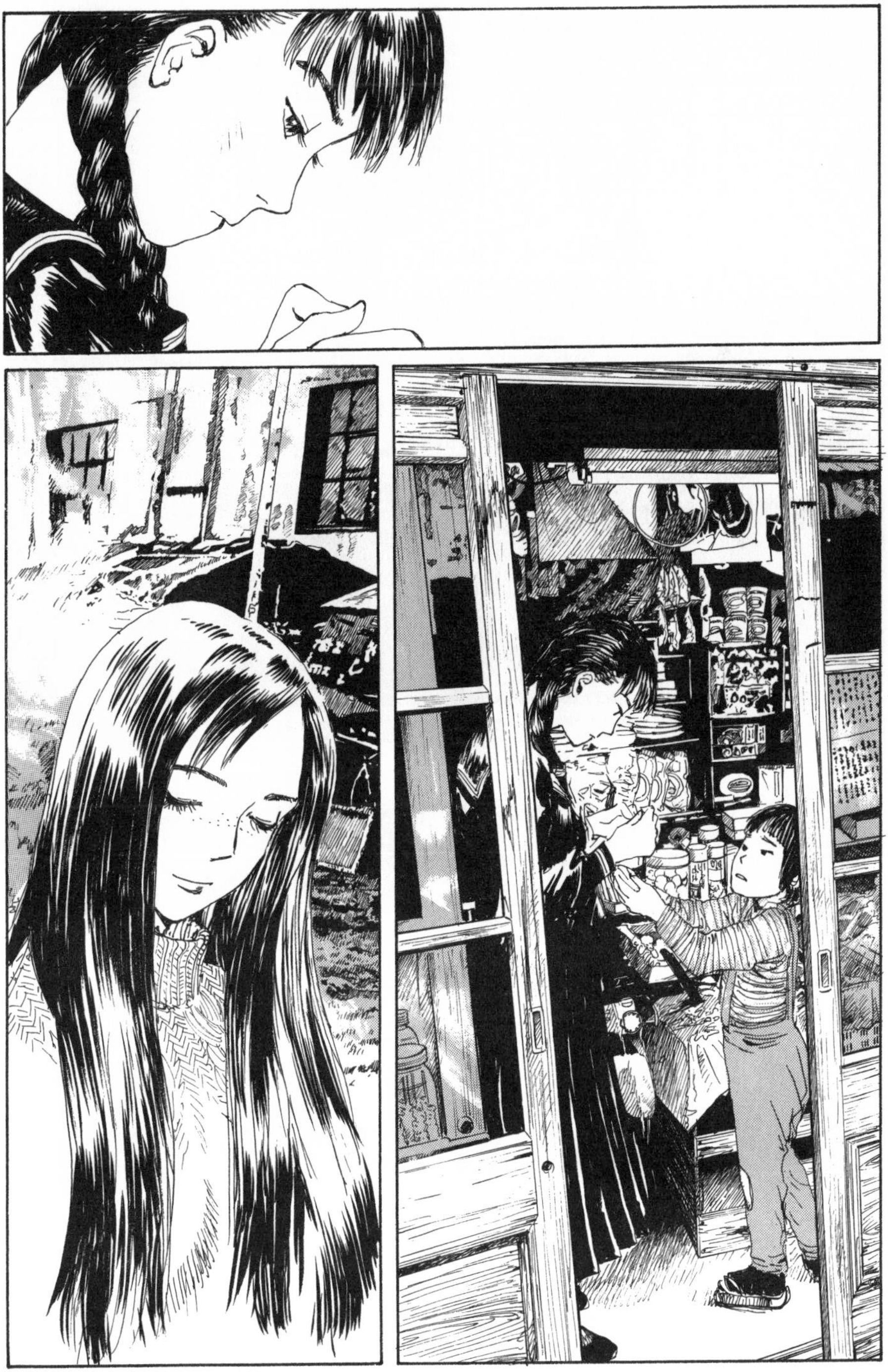

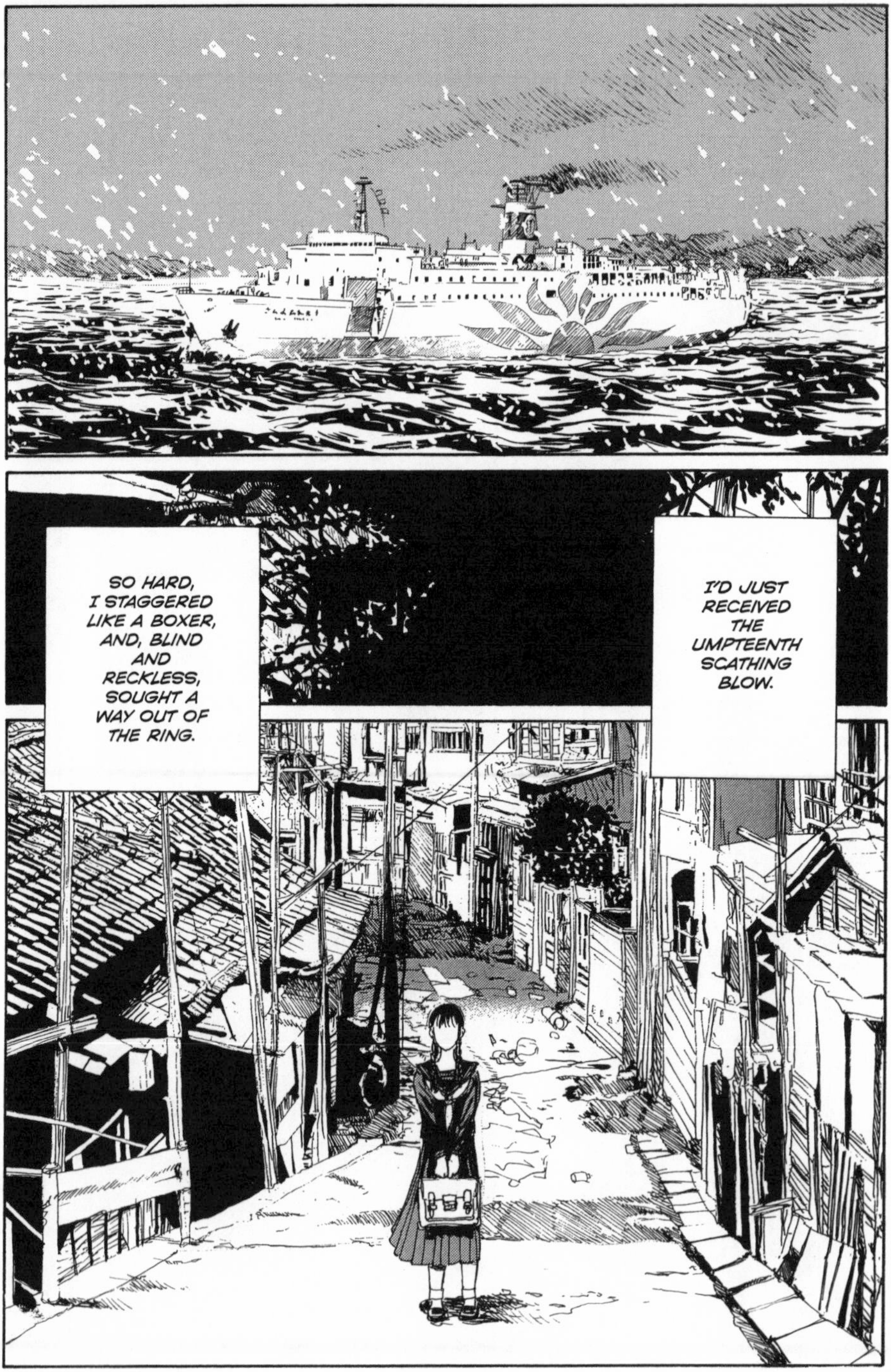
I'D JUST RECEIVED THE UMPTEENTH SCATHING BLOW.
SO HARD, I STAGGERED LIKE A BOXER, AND, BLIND AND RECKLESS, SOUGHT A WAY OUT OF THE RING.

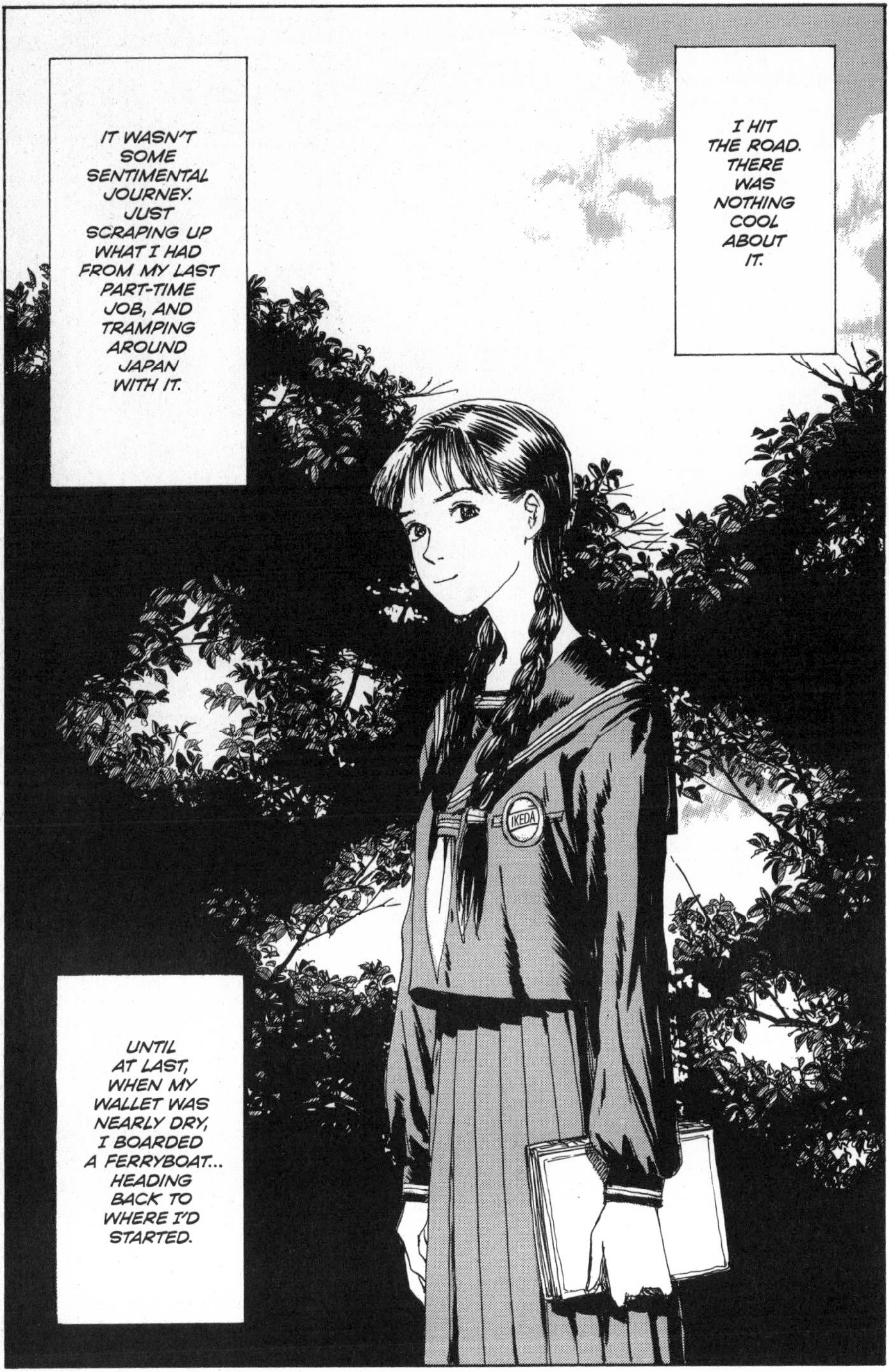
I HIT THE ROAD. THERE WAS NOTHING COOL ABOUT IT.
IT WASN'T SOME SENTIMENTAL JOURNEY. JUST SCRAPING UP WHAT I HAD FROM MY LAST PART-TIME JOB, AND TRAMPING AROUND JAPAN WITH IT.
UNTIL AT LAST, WHEN MY WALLET WAS NEARLY DRY, I BOARDED A FERRYBOAT... HEADING BACK TO WHERE I'D STARTED.
IKEDA

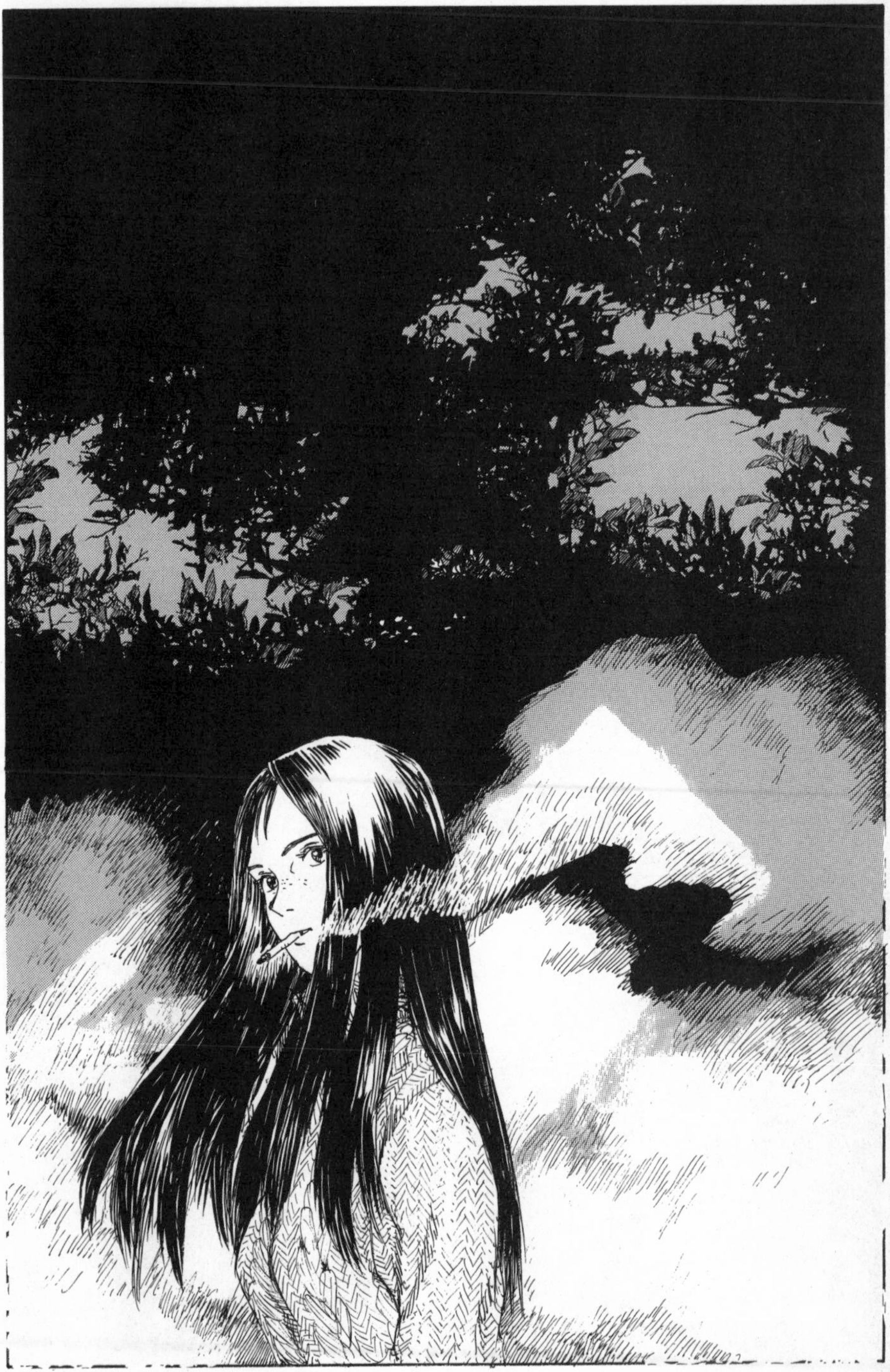

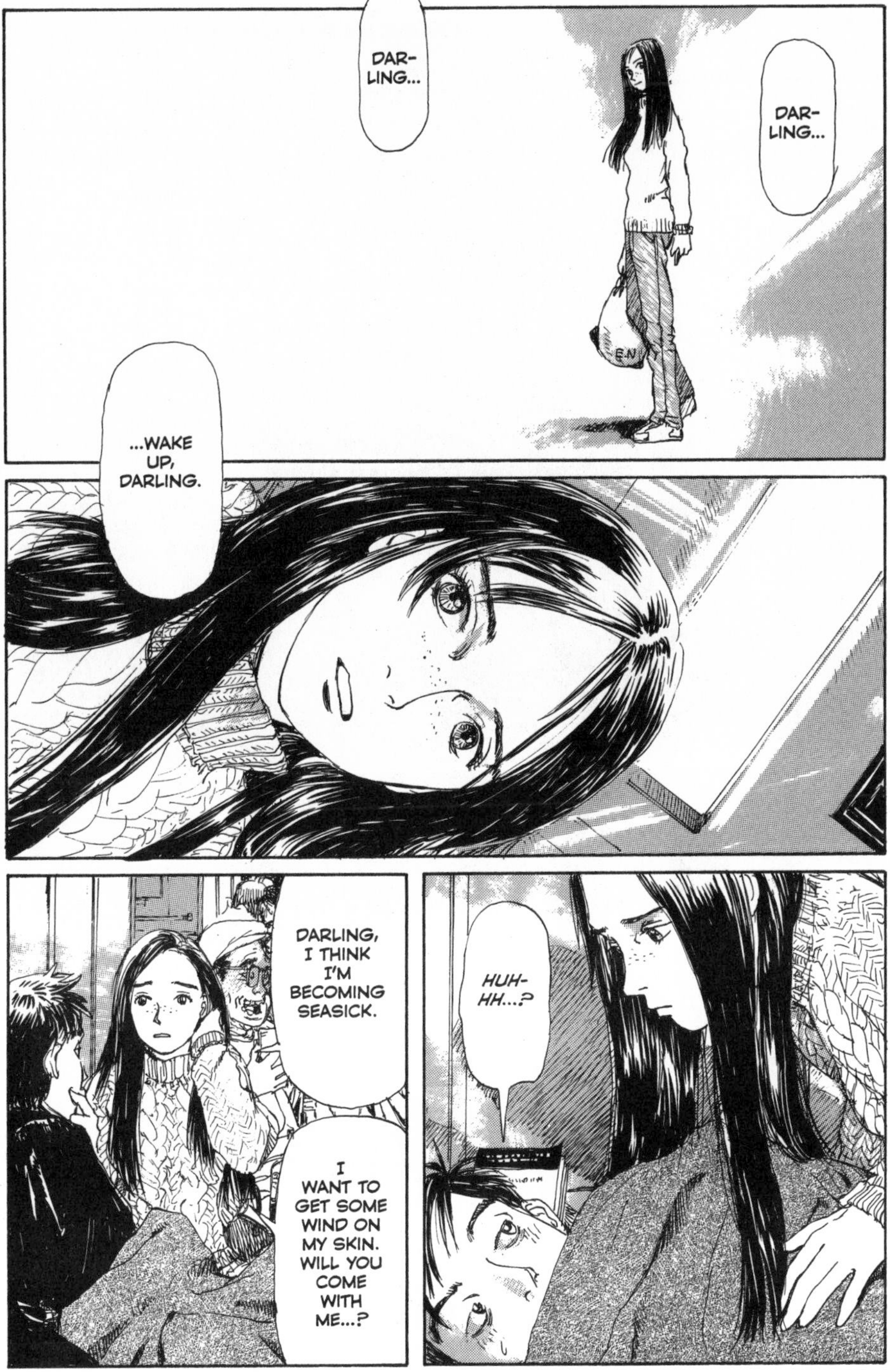
DAR-LING...
DAR-LING...
...WAKE UP, DARLING.
HUH-HH...?
DARLING, I THINK I'M BECOMING SEASICK.
I WANT TO GET SOME WIND ON MY SKIN. WILL YOU COME WITH ME...?

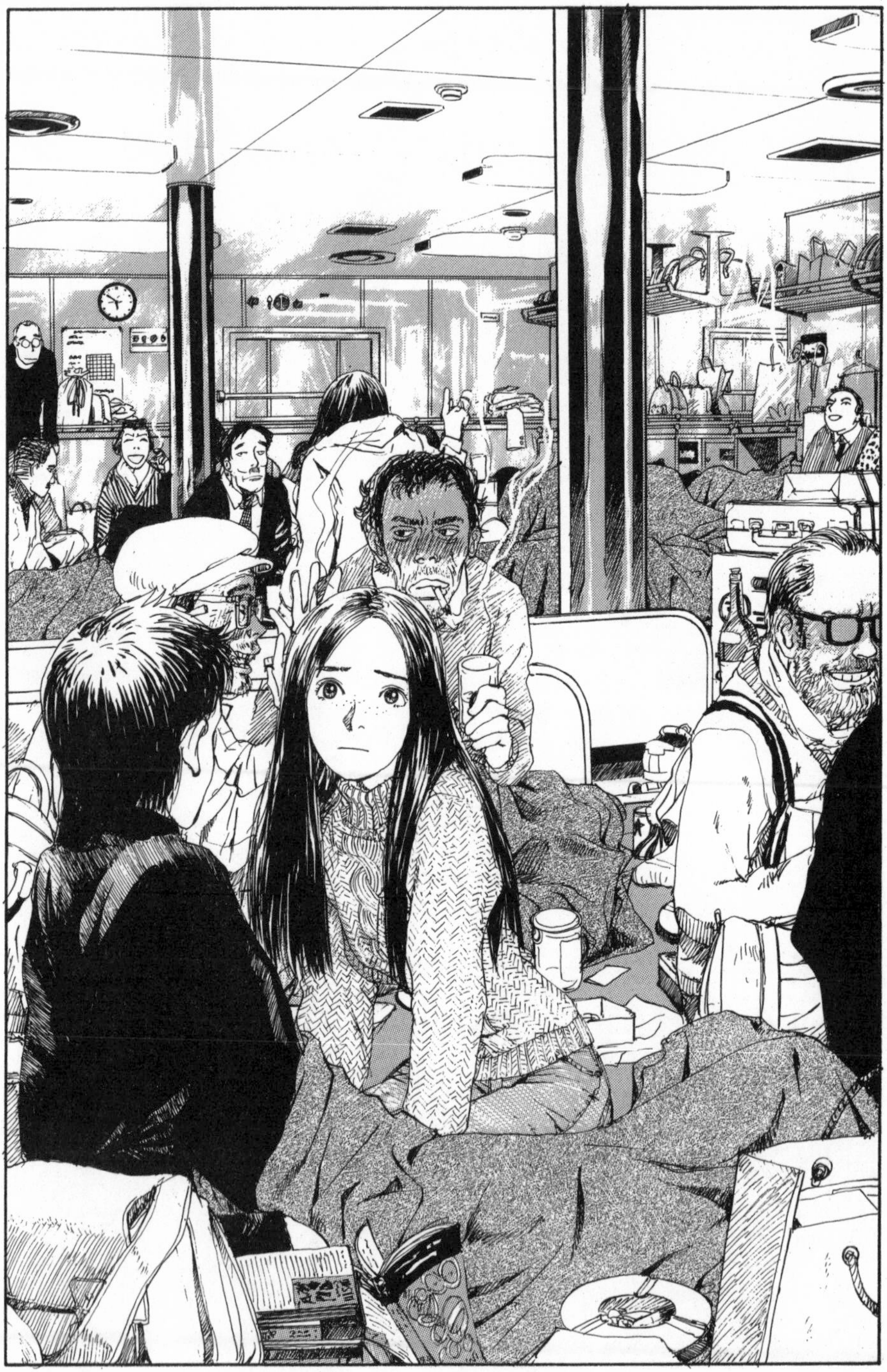

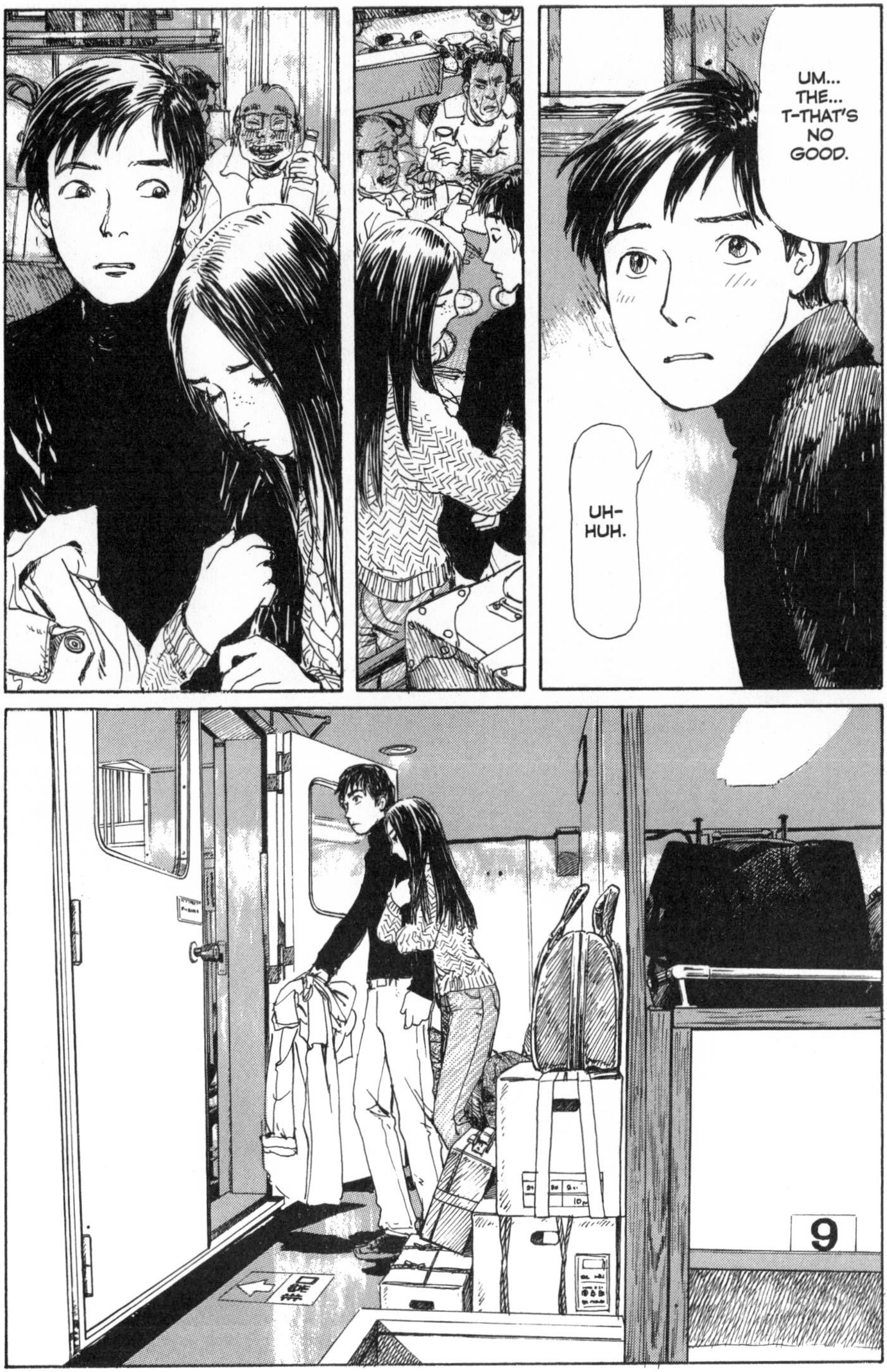
UM... THE... T-THAT'S NO GOOD.
UH-HUH.
9

HEE,
HEE,
HEE...

...THAT
WAS BAD
OF ME...
I'M SORRY.
I BET
YOU WERE
SURPRISED.

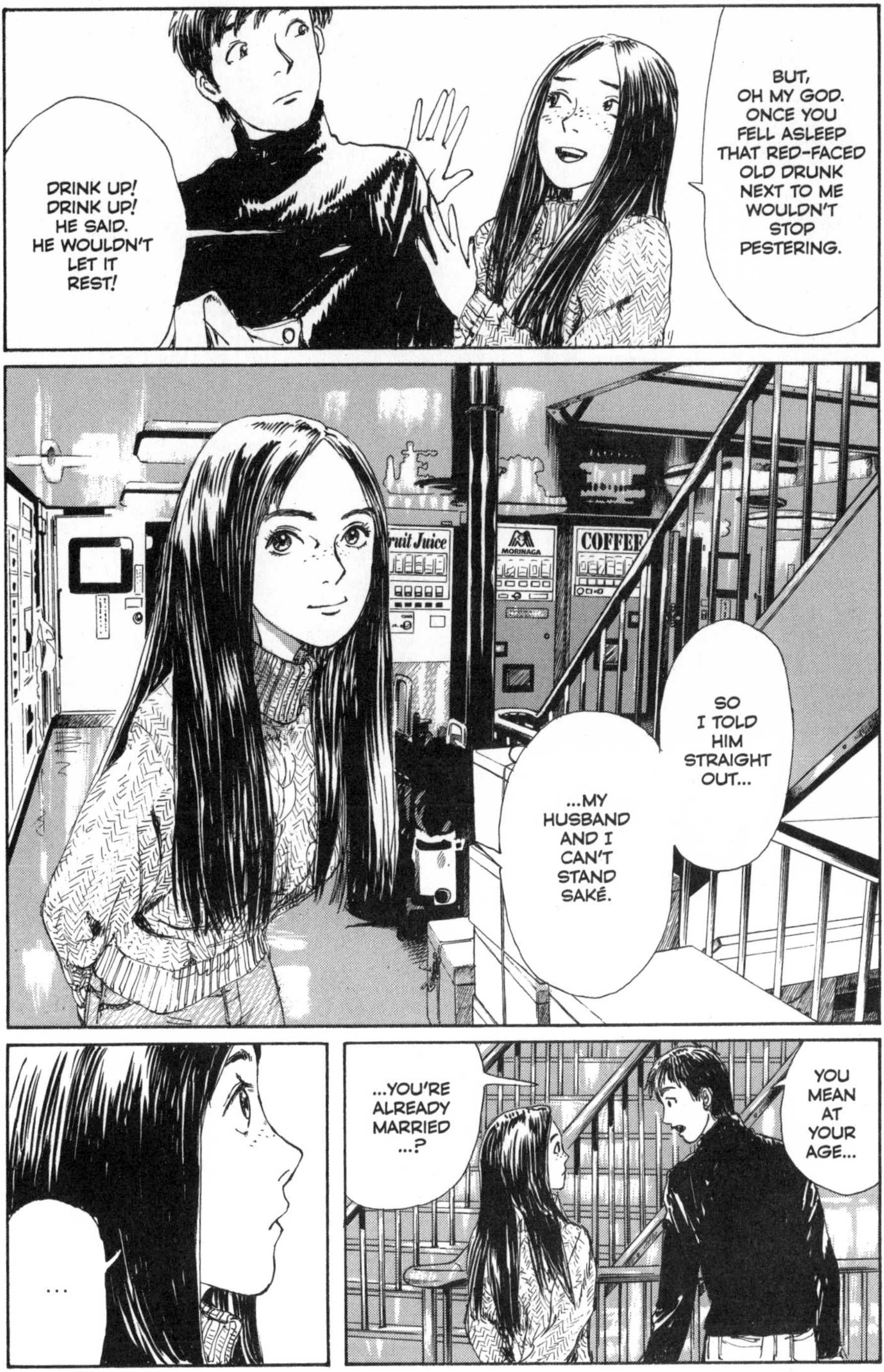
BUT, OH MY GOD. ONCE YOU FELL ASLEEP THAT RED-FACED OLD DRUNK NEXT TO ME WOULDN'T STOP PESTERING.
DRINK UP! DRINK UP! HE SAID. HE WOULDN'T LET IT REST!
COFFEE
MORINAGA
SO I TOLD HIM STRAIGHT OUT...
...MY HUSBAND AND I CAN'T STAND SAKÉ.
YOU MEAN AT YOUR AGE...
...YOU'RE ALREADY MARRIED ...?
...

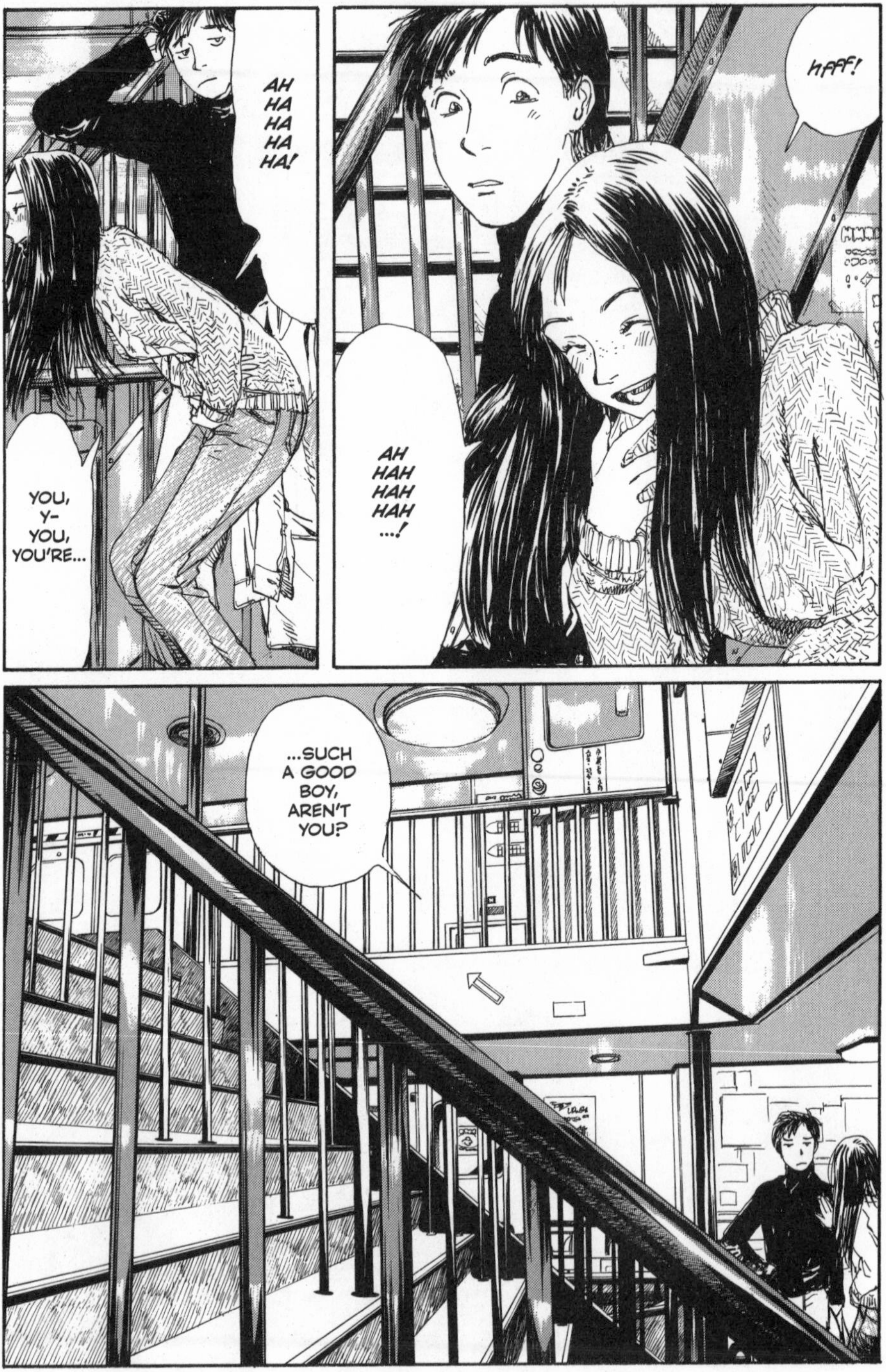
hfff!
AH HAH HAH HAH ...!
AH HA HA HA HA!
YOU, Y- YOU, YOU'RE...
...SUCH A GOOD BOY, AREN'T YOU?

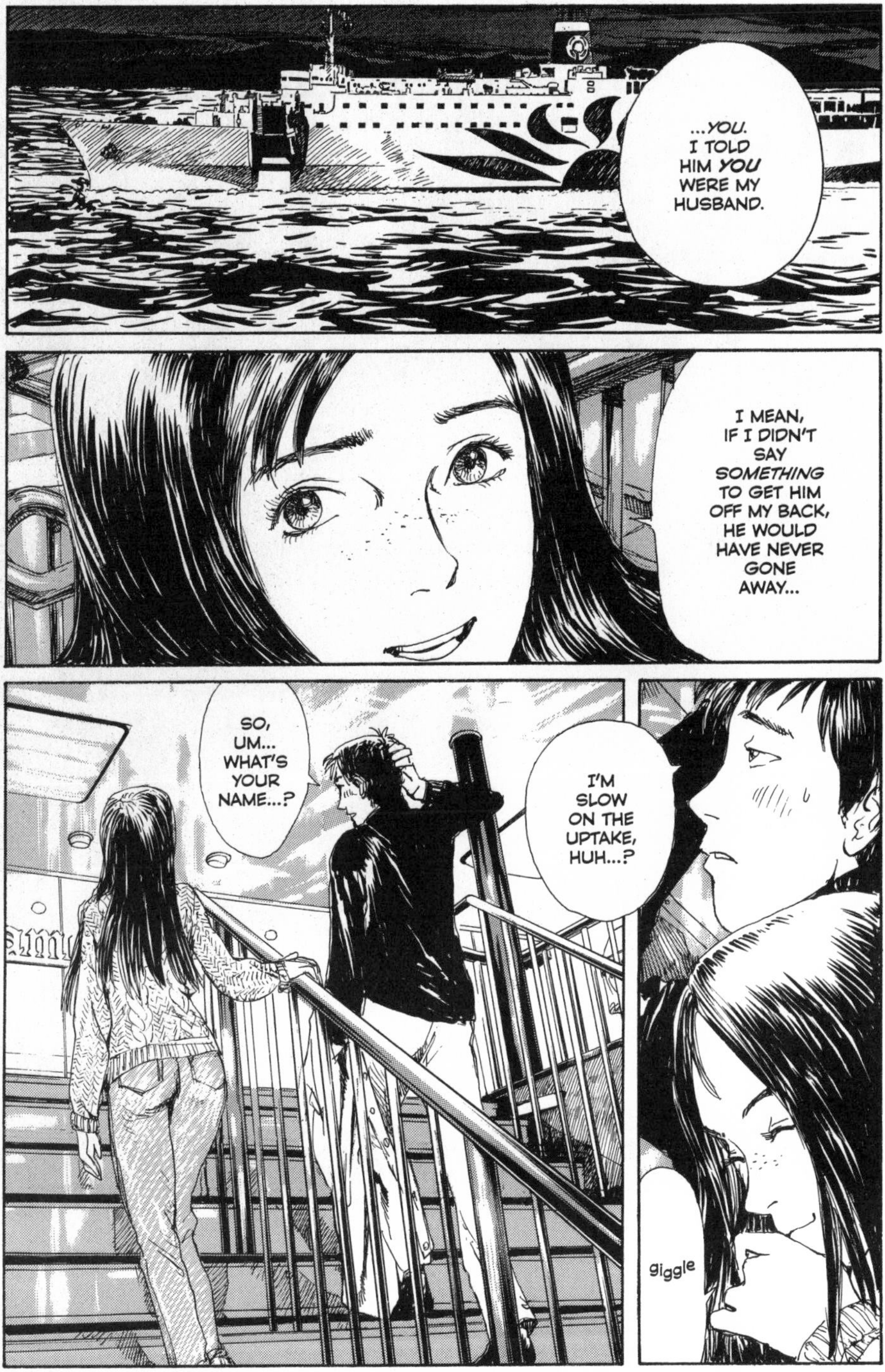
...YOU. I TOLD HIM YOU WERE MY HUSBAND.
I MEAN, IF I DIDN'T SAY SOMETHING TO GET HIM OFF MY BACK, HE WOULD HAVE NEVER GONE AWAY...
I'M SLOW ON THE UPTAKE, HUH...?
giggle
SO, UM... WHAT'S YOUR NAME...?

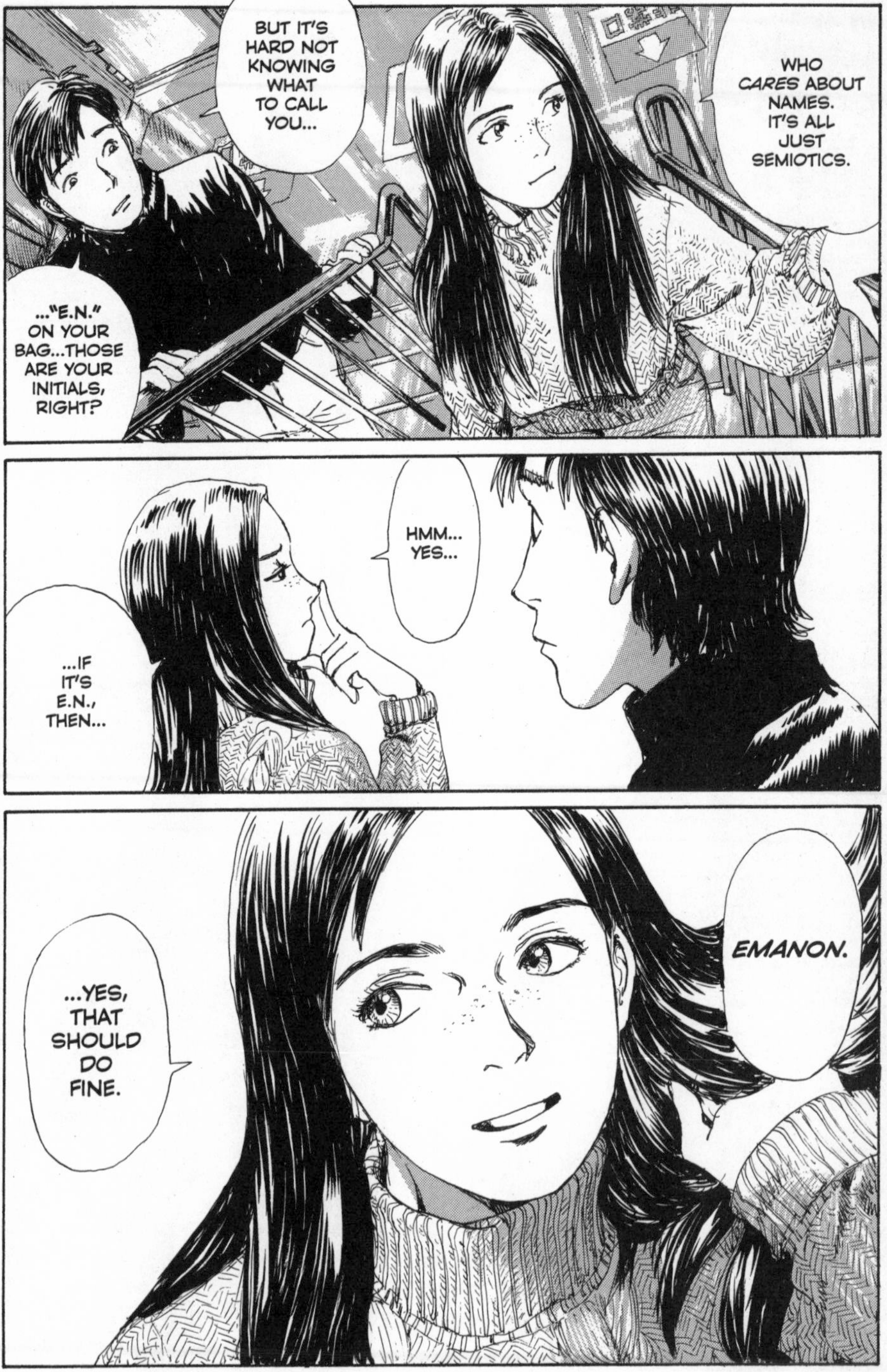
WHO *CARES* ABOUT NAMES. IT'S ALL JUST SEMIOTICS.
BUT IT'S HARD NOT KNOWING WHAT TO CALL YOU...
..."E.N." ON YOUR BAG...THOSE ARE YOUR INITIALS, RIGHT?
HMM... YES...
...IF IT'S E.N., THEN...
EMANON.
...YES, THAT SHOULD DO FINE.

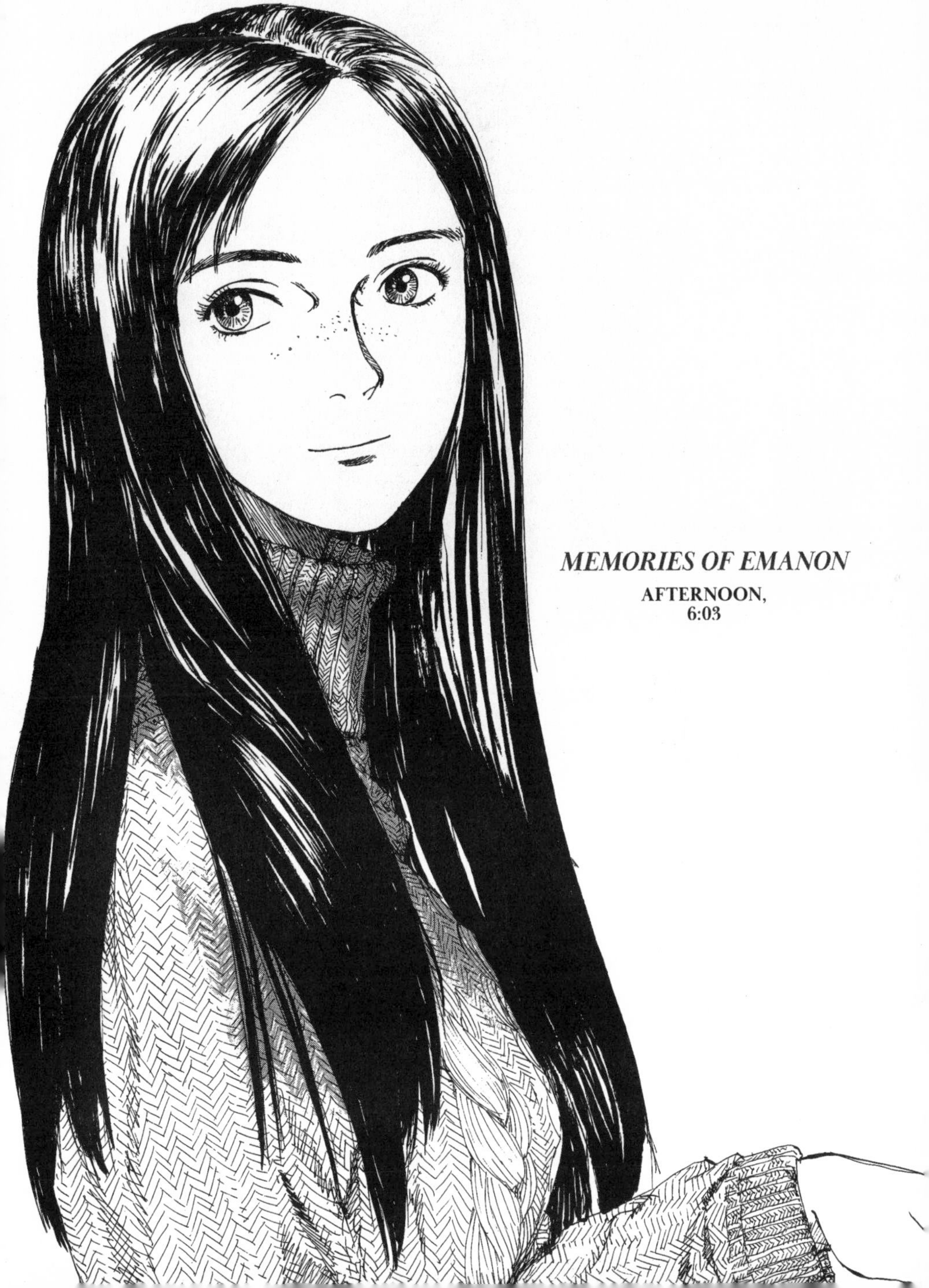

MEMORIES OF EMANON

AFTERNOON,
6:03

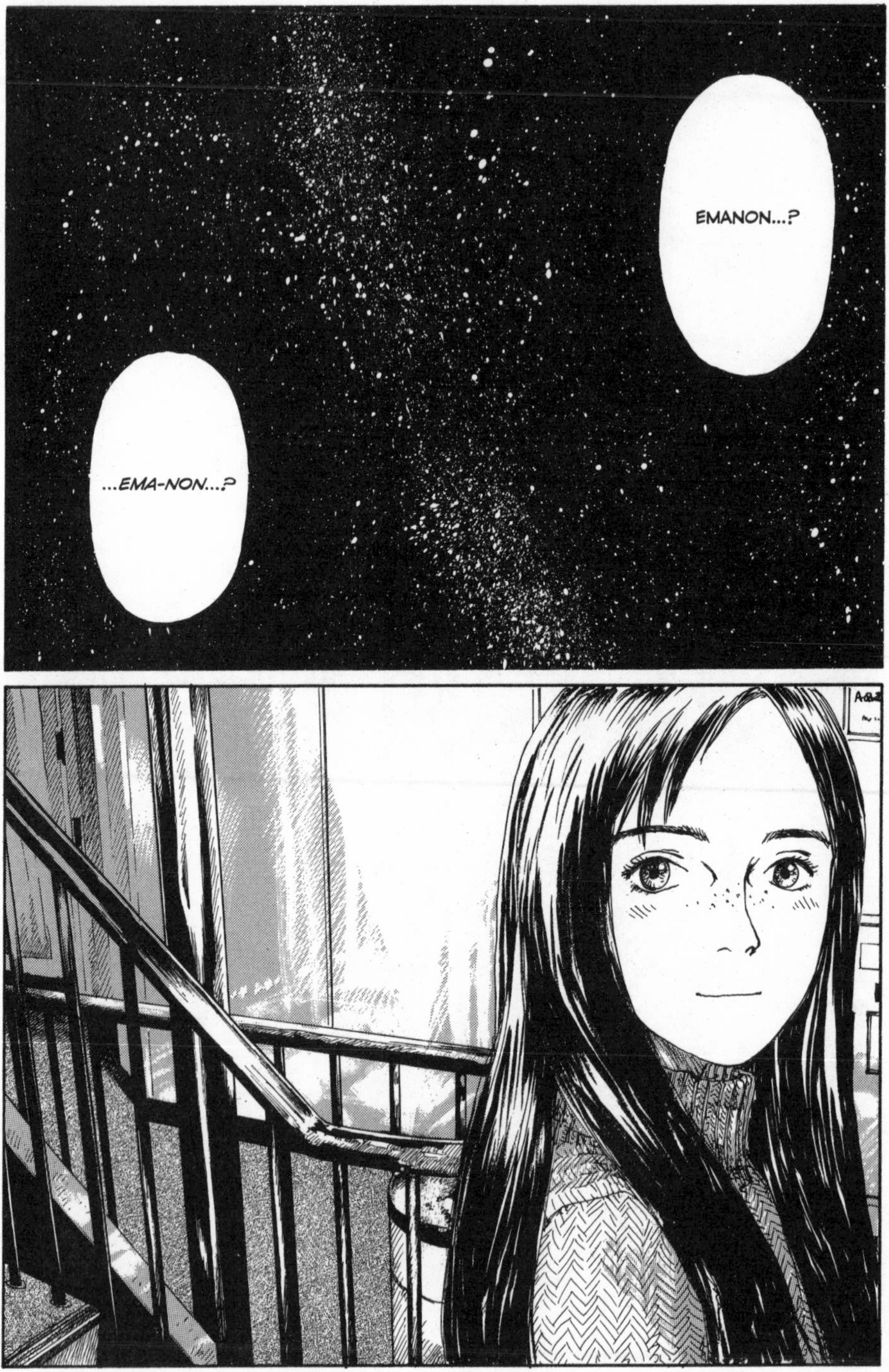
EMANON...?
...EMA-NON...?

"NO NAME." SPELL IT BACKWARDS.

EMANON.

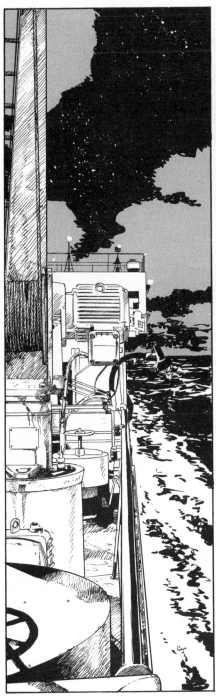

...

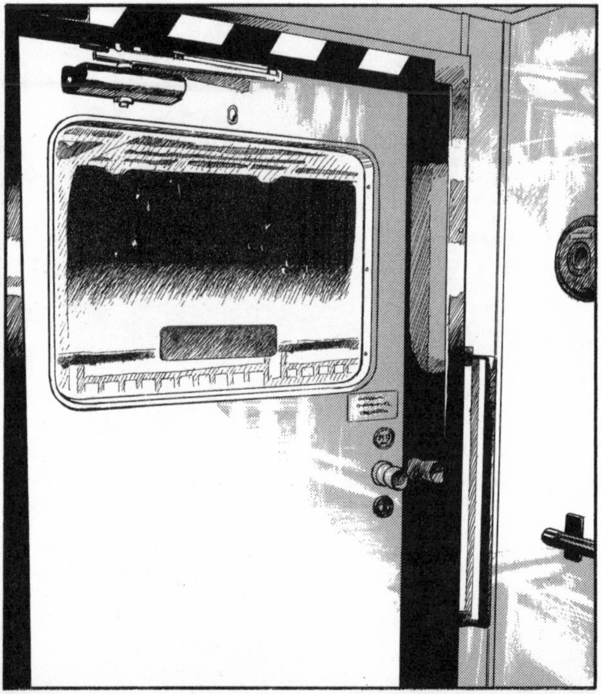
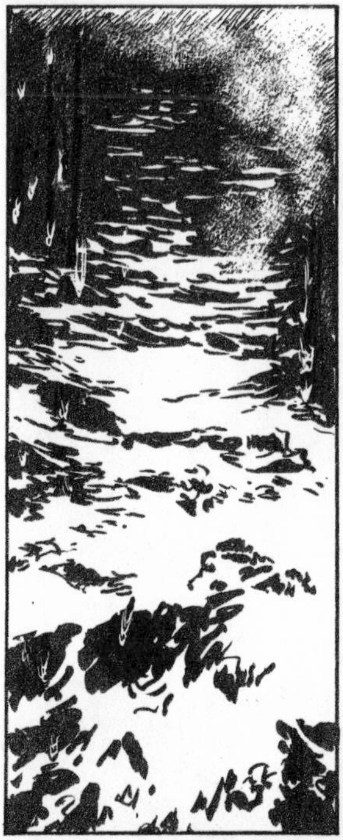
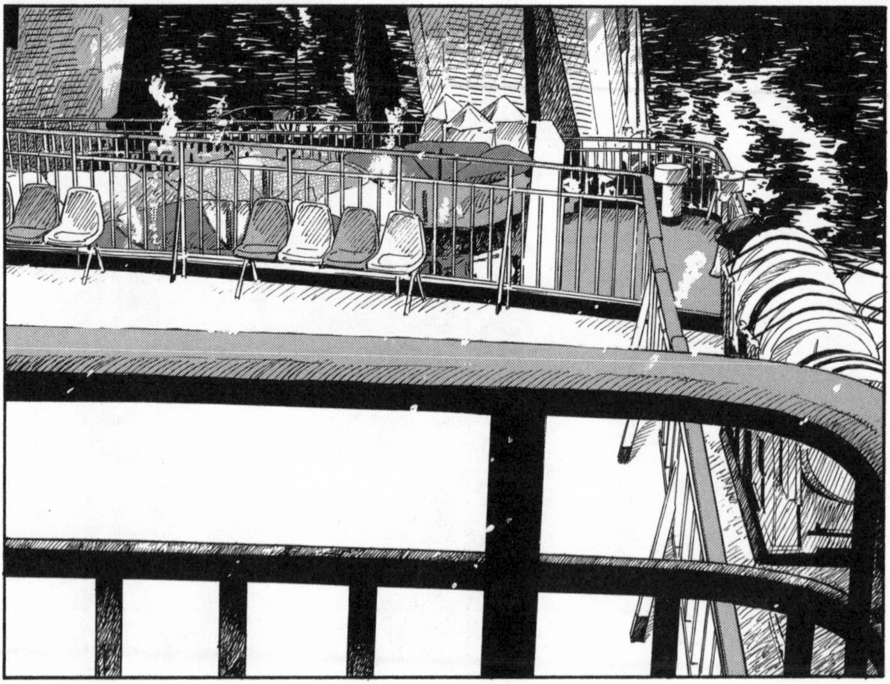

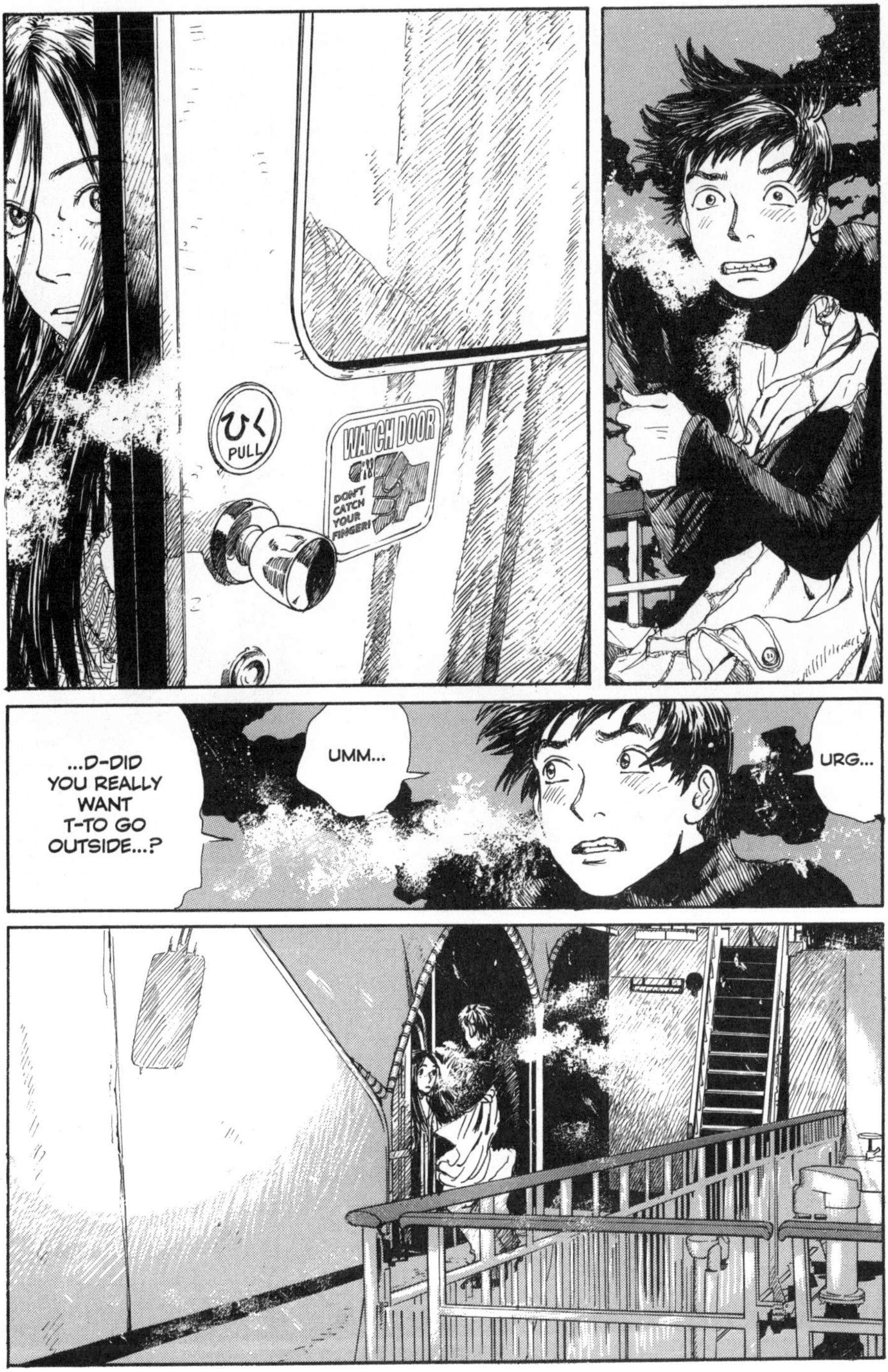
ひく
PULL
WATCH DOOR
DON'T CATCH YOUR FINGER!
URG...
UMM...
...D-DID YOU REALLY WANT T-TO GO OUTSIDE...?

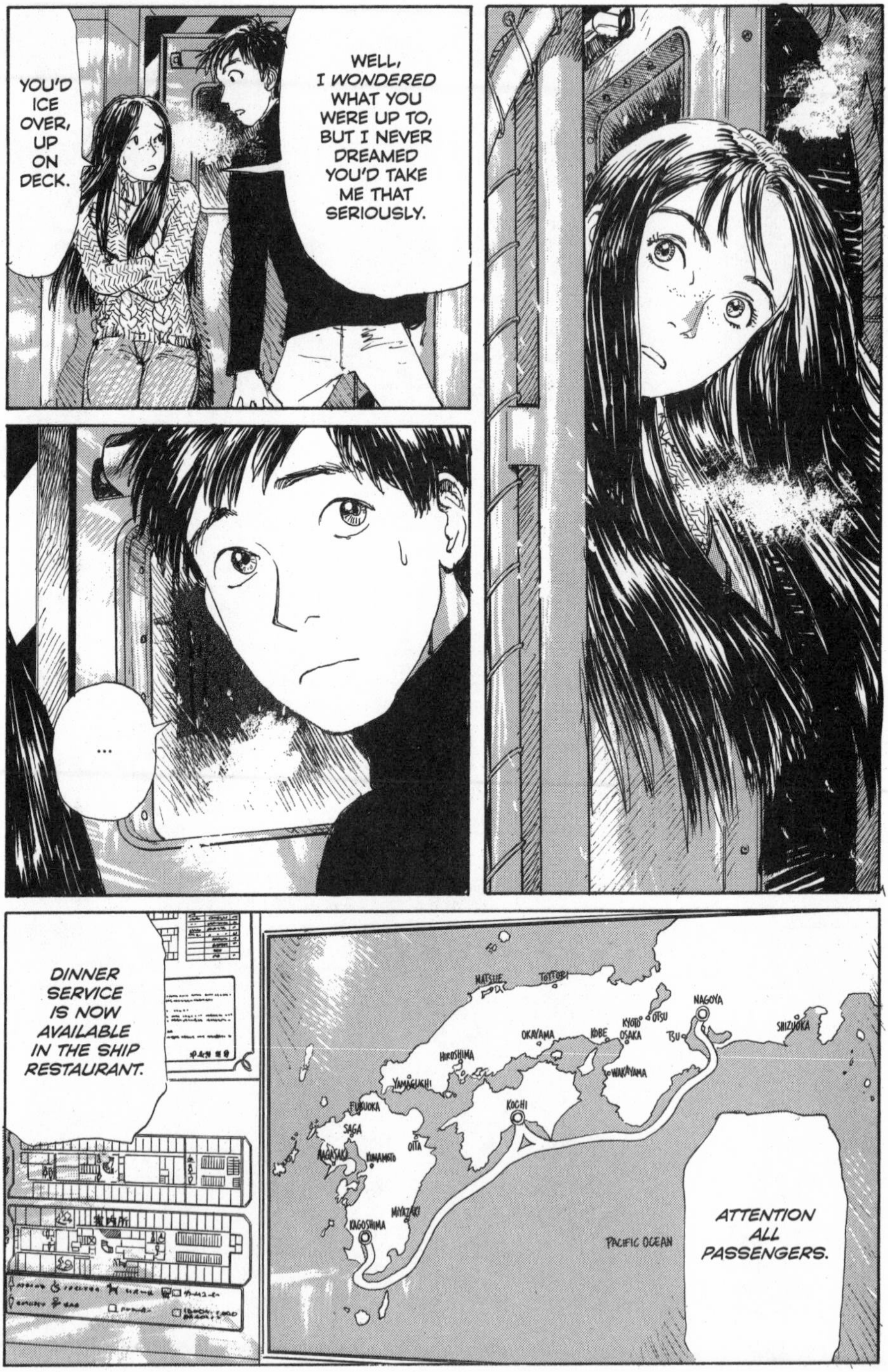
WELL, I *WONDERED* WHAT YOU WERE UP TO, BUT I NEVER DREAMED YOU'D TAKE ME THAT SERIOUSLY.
YOU'D ICE OVER, UP ON DECK.
...
ATTENTION ALL PASSENGERS.
DINNER SERVICE IS NOW AVAILABLE IN THE SHIP RESTAURANT.
MATSUE
TOTTORI
NAGOYA
KYOTO
OTSU
OKAYAMA
KOBE
OSAKA
TSU
SHIZUOKA
HIROSHIMA
WAKAYAMA
YAMAGUCHI
FUKUOKA
KOCHI
SAGA
NAGASAKI
KUMAMOTO
OITA
MIYAZAKI
KAGOSHIMA
PACIFIC OCEAN

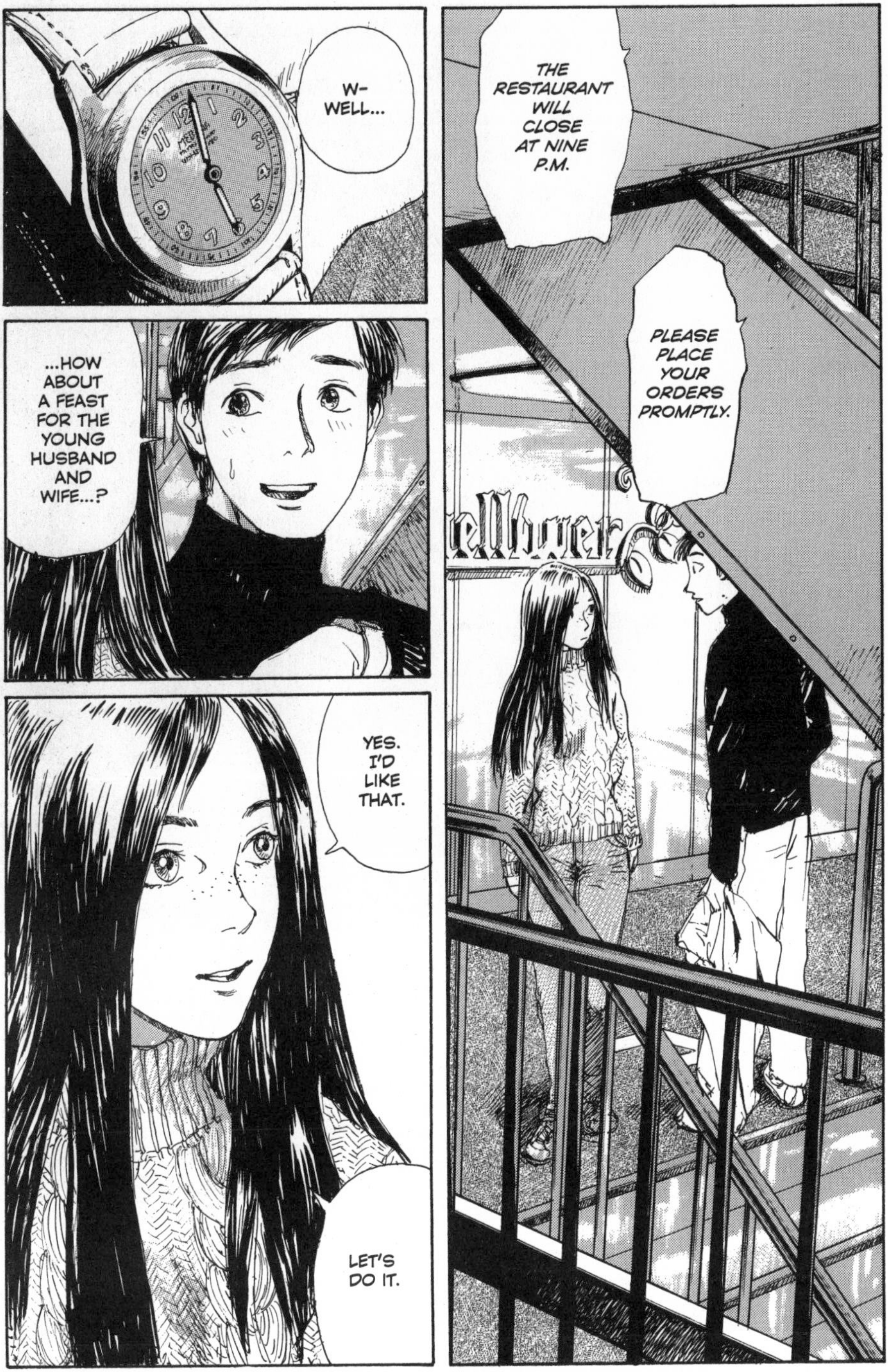
THE RESTAURANT WILL CLOSE AT NINE P.M.
PLEASE PLACE YOUR ORDERS PROMPTLY.
W-WELL...
...HOW ABOUT A FEAST FOR THE YOUNG HUSBAND AND WIFE...?
YES. I'D LIKE THAT.
LET'S DO IT.

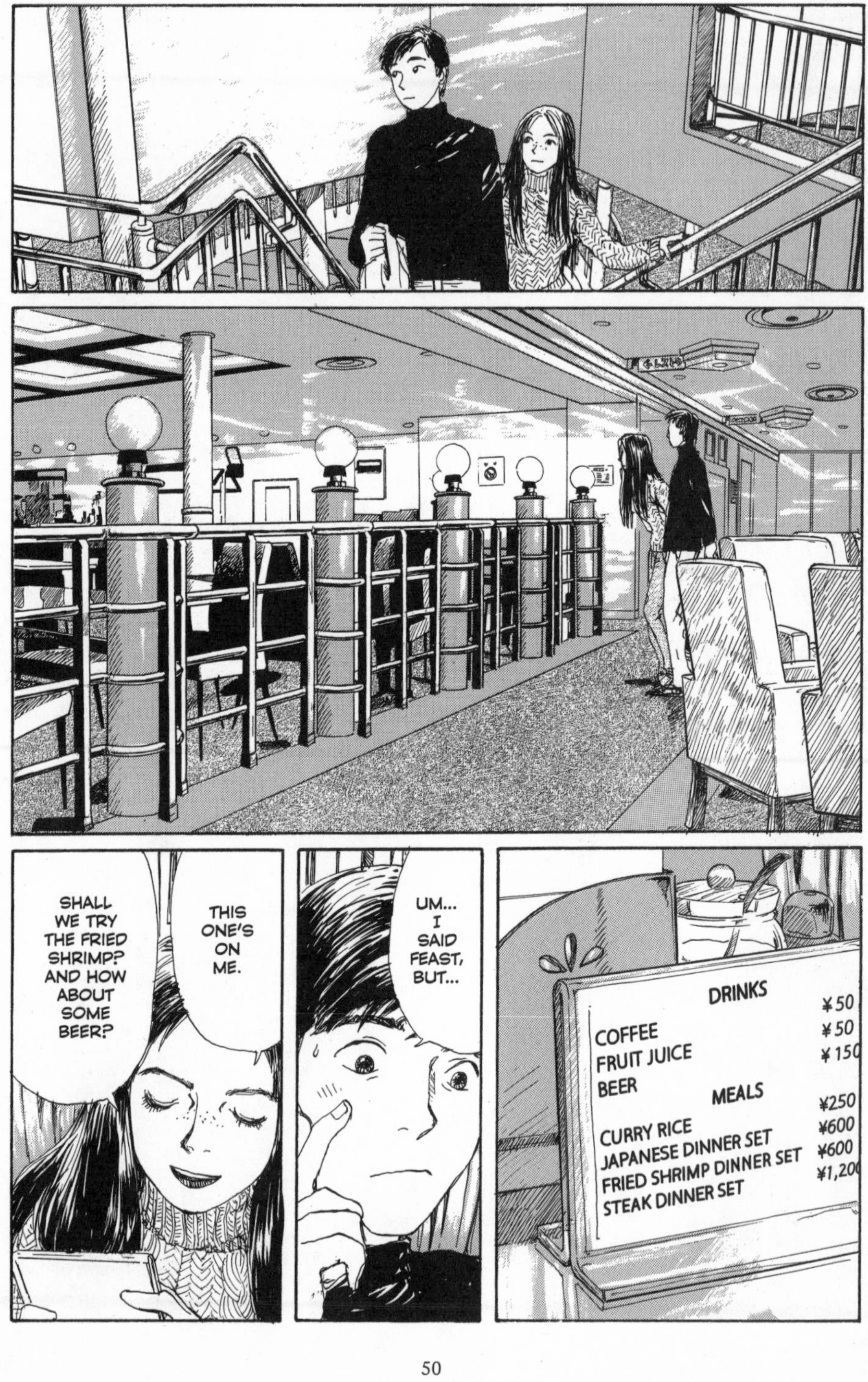
DRINKS
¥50
COFFEE
¥50
FRUIT JUICE
¥150
BEER
MEALS
¥250
CURRY RICE
¥600
JAPANESE DINNER SET
¥600
FRIED SHRIMP DINNER SET
¥1,20
STEAK DINNER SET
UM... I SAID FEAST, BUT...
SHALL WE TRY THE FRIED SHRIMP? AND HOW ABOUT SOME BEER?
THIS ONE'S ON ME.

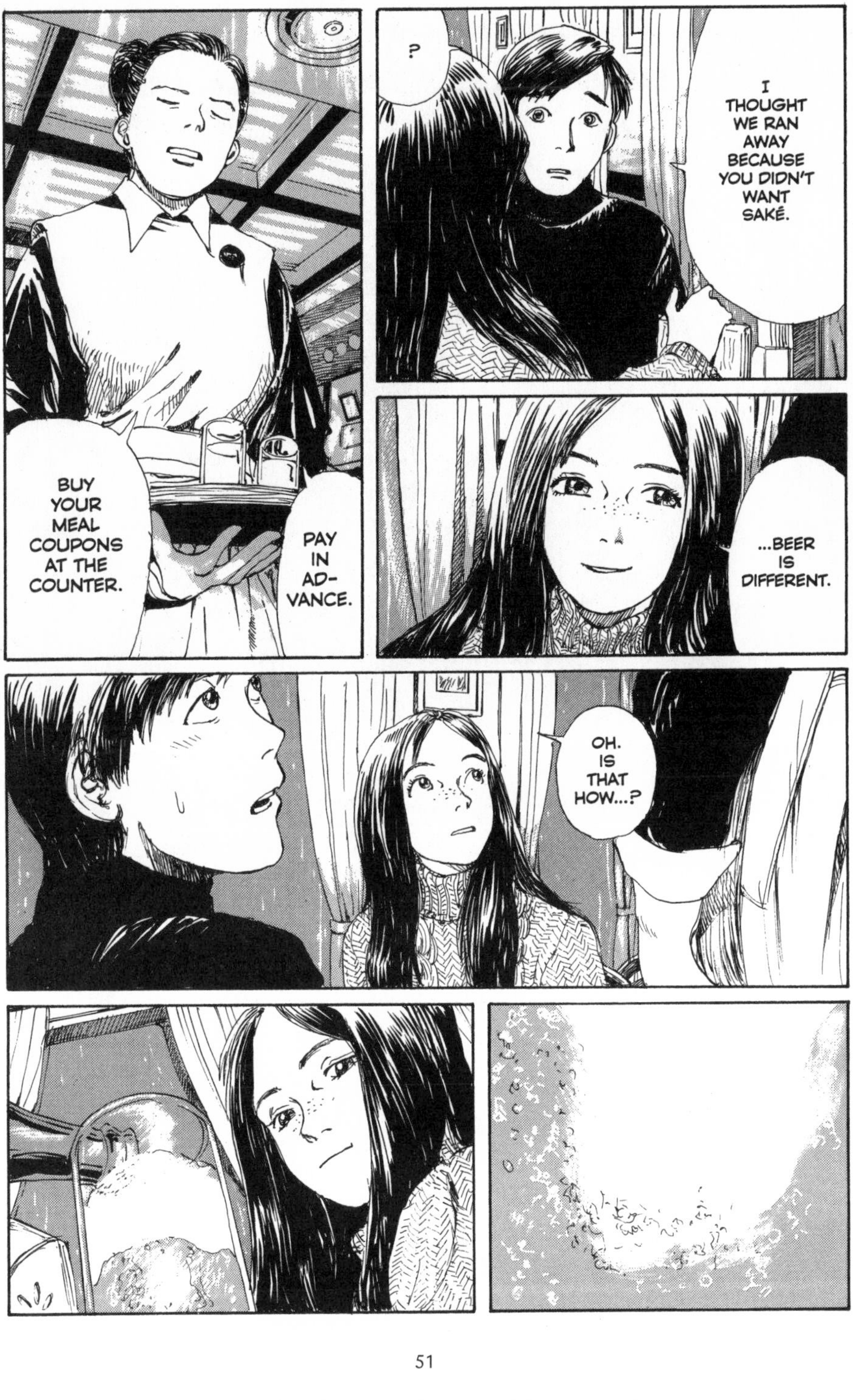
?
I THOUGHT WE RAN AWAY BECAUSE YOU DIDN'T WANT SAKÉ.
...BEER IS DIFFERENT.
PAY IN AD-VANCE.
BUY YOUR MEAL COUPONS AT THE COUNTER.
OH. IS THAT HOW...?

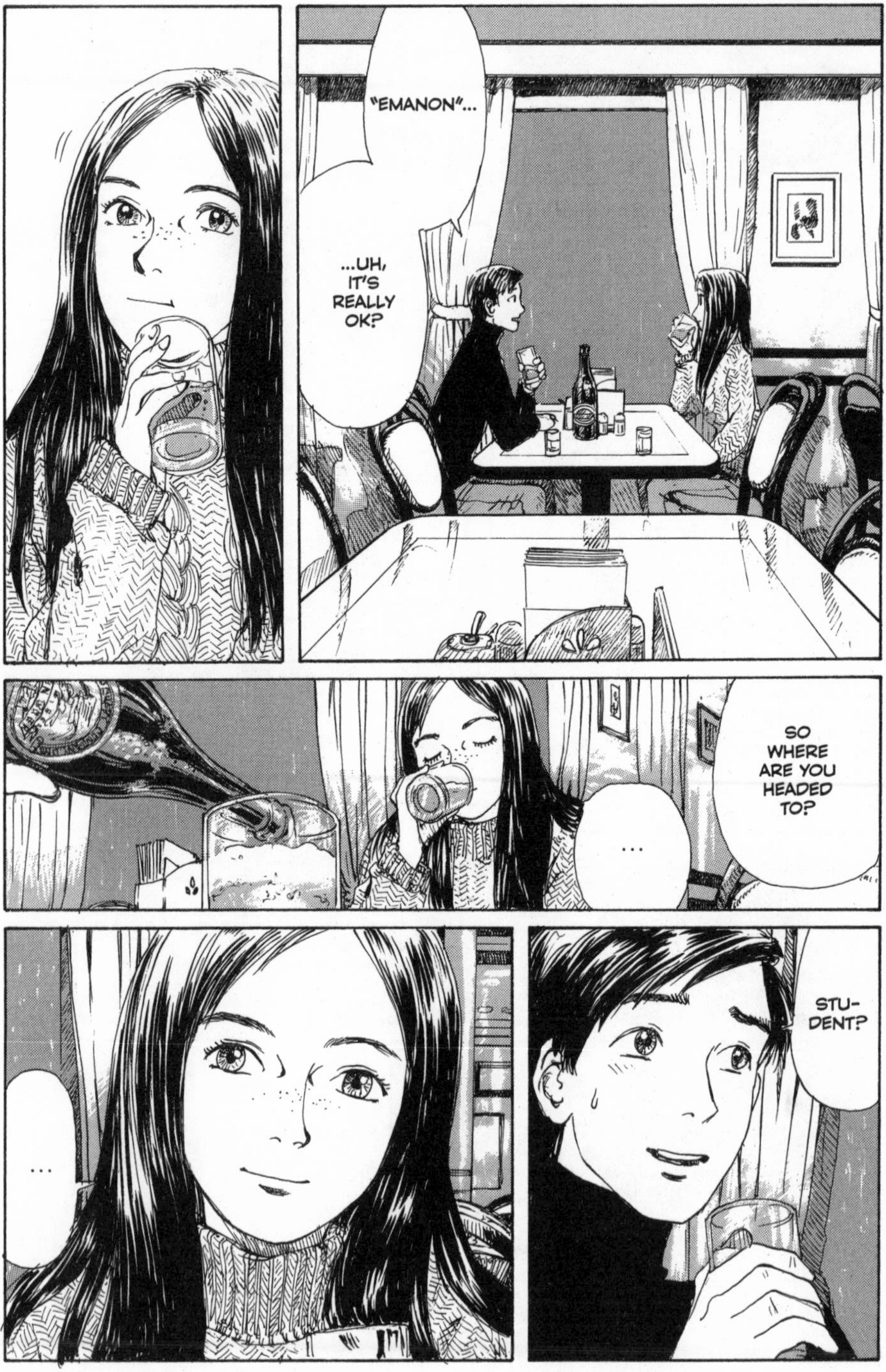
"EMANON"...
...UH, IT'S REALLY OK?
SO WHERE ARE YOU HEADED TO?
...
STU-DENT?
...

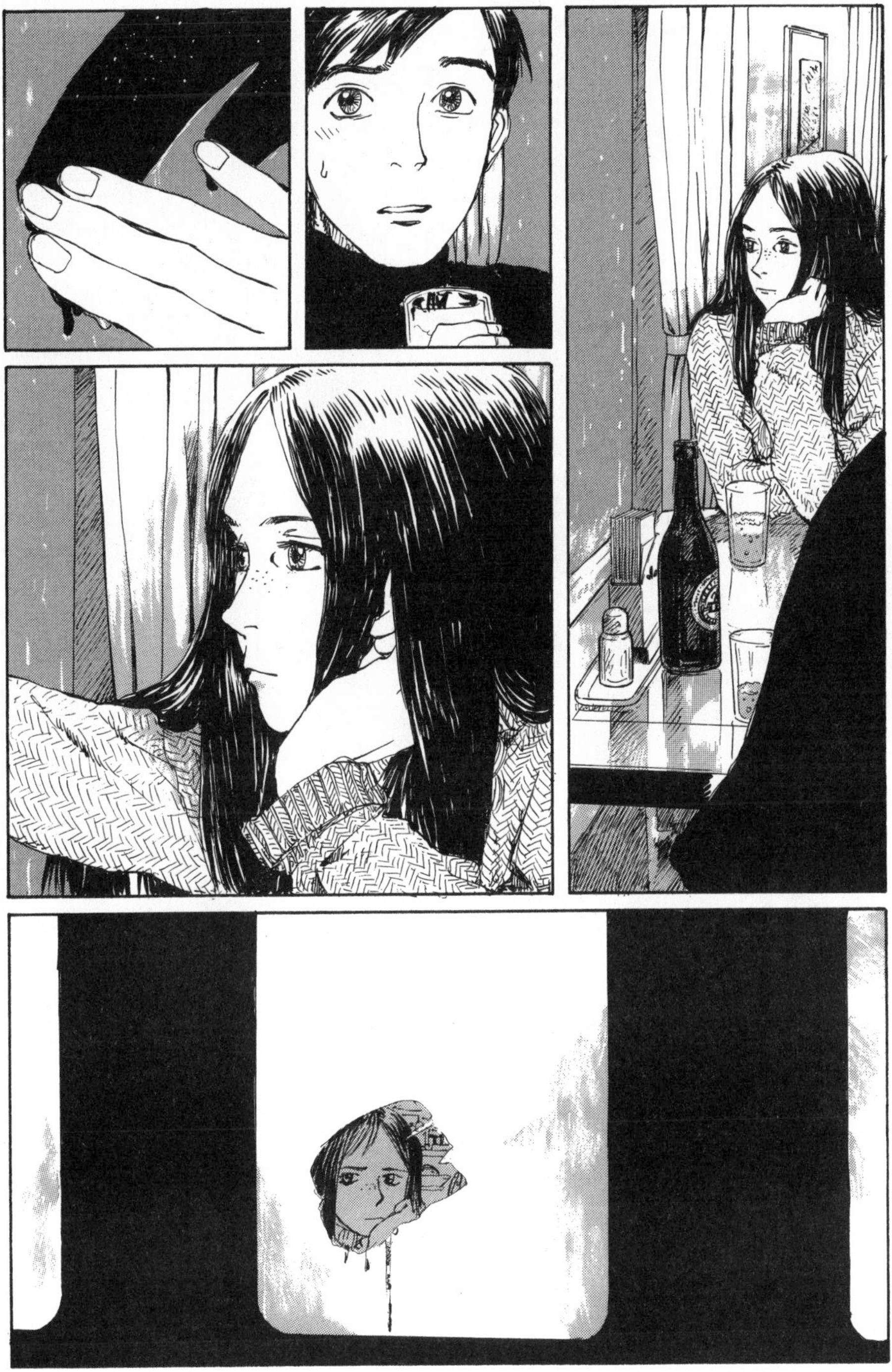

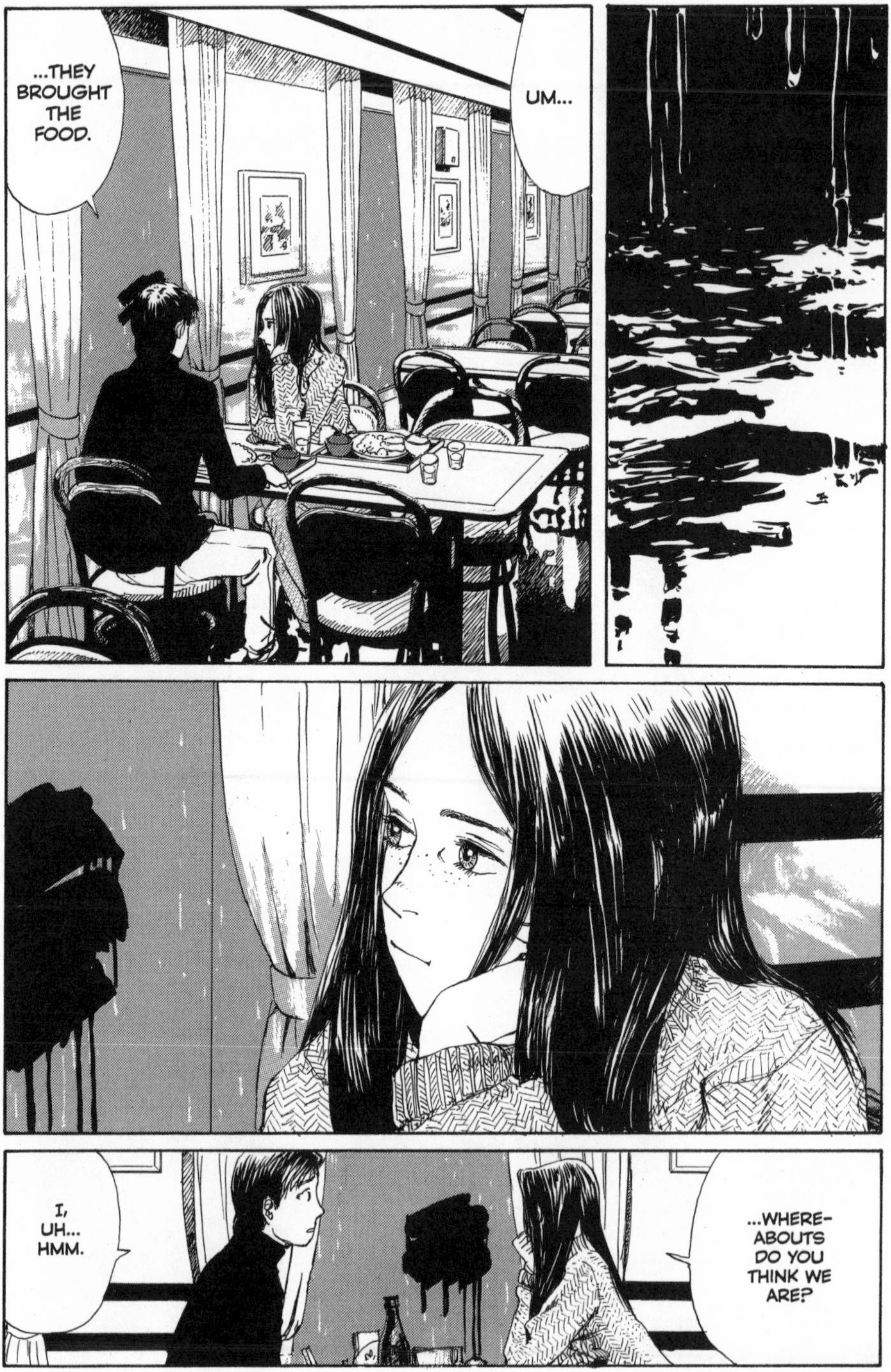
UM...
...THEY BROUGHT THE FOOD.
...WHERE-ABOUTS DO YOU THINK WE ARE?
I, UH... HMM.

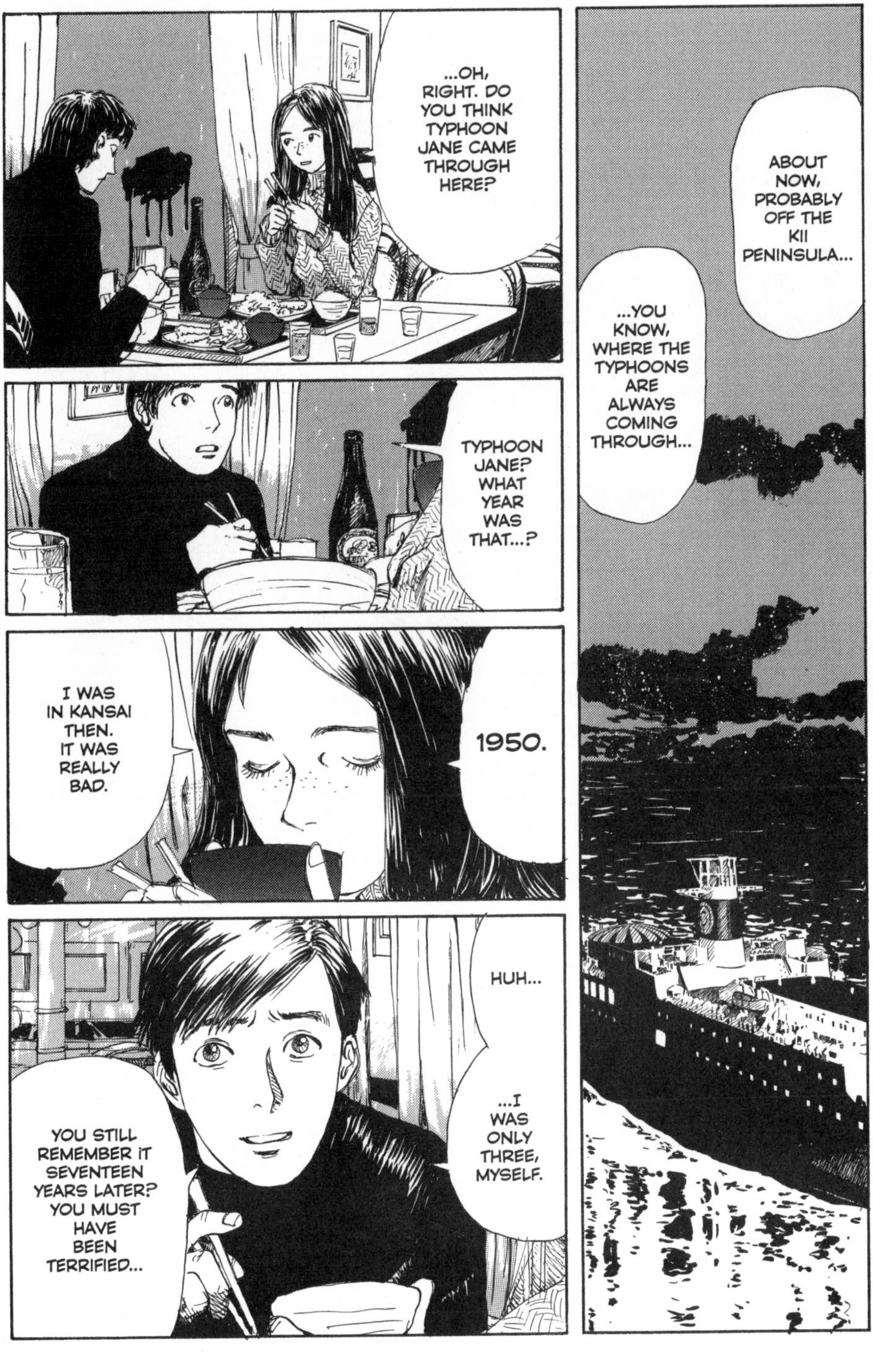
ABOUT NOW, PROBABLY OFF THE KII PENINSULA...
...YOU KNOW, WHERE THE TYPHOONS ARE ALWAYS COMING THROUGH...
...OH, RIGHT. DO YOU THINK TYPHOON JANE CAME THROUGH HERE?
TYPHOON JANE? WHAT YEAR WAS THAT...?
1950.
I WAS IN KANSAI THEN. IT WAS REALLY BAD.
HUH...
...I WAS ONLY THREE, MYSELF.
YOU STILL REMEMBER IT SEVENTEEN YEARS LATER? YOU MUST HAVE BEEN TERRIFIED...

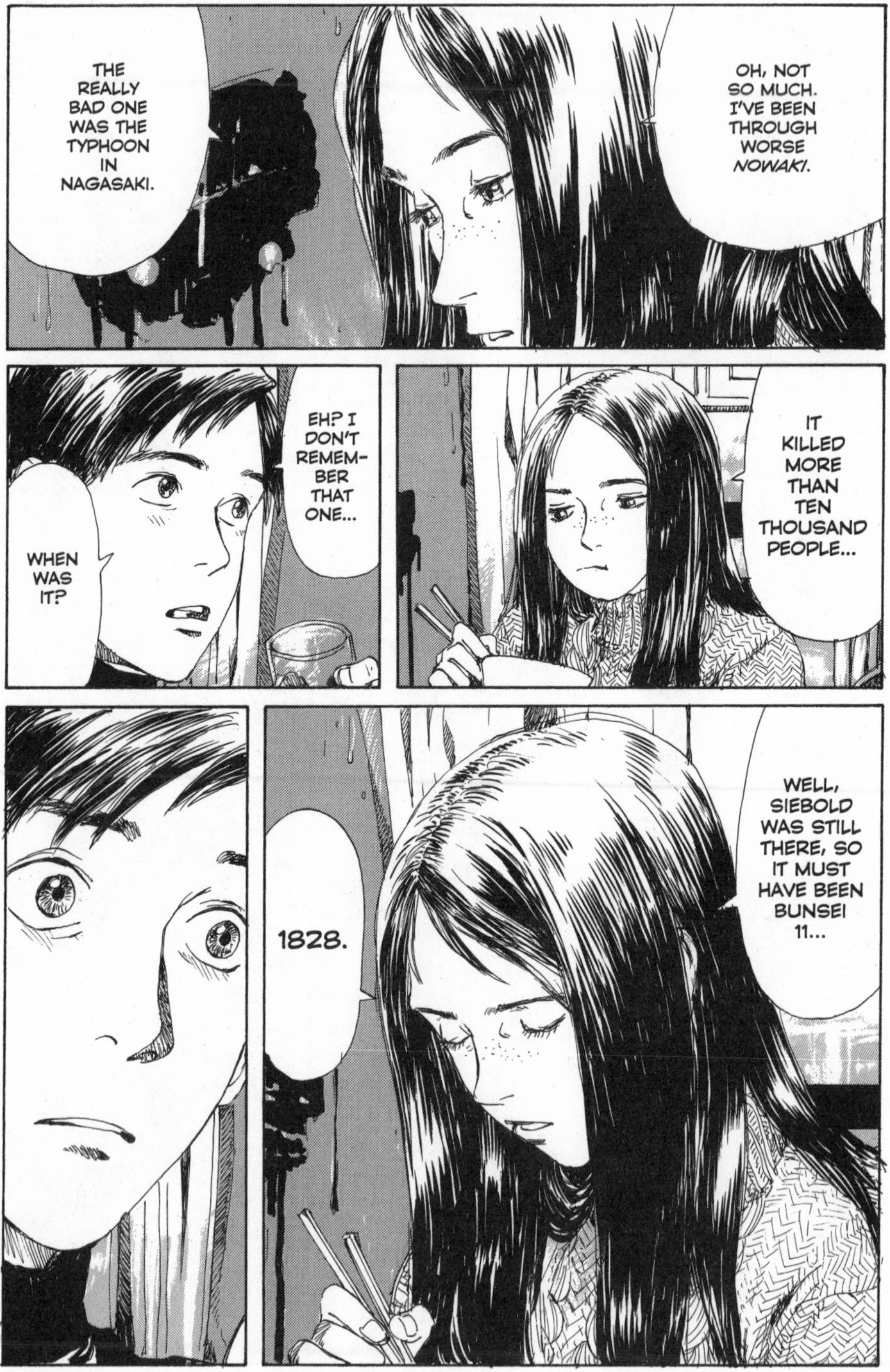
OH, NOT SO MUCH. I'VE BEEN THROUGH WORSE *NOWAKI*.
THE REALLY BAD ONE WAS THE TYPHOON IN NAGASAKI.
IT KILLED MORE THAN TEN THOUSAND PEOPLE...
EH? I DON'T REMEMBER THAT ONE...
WHEN WAS IT?
WELL, SIEBOLD WAS STILL THERE, SO IT MUST HAVE BEEN BUNSEI 11...
1828.

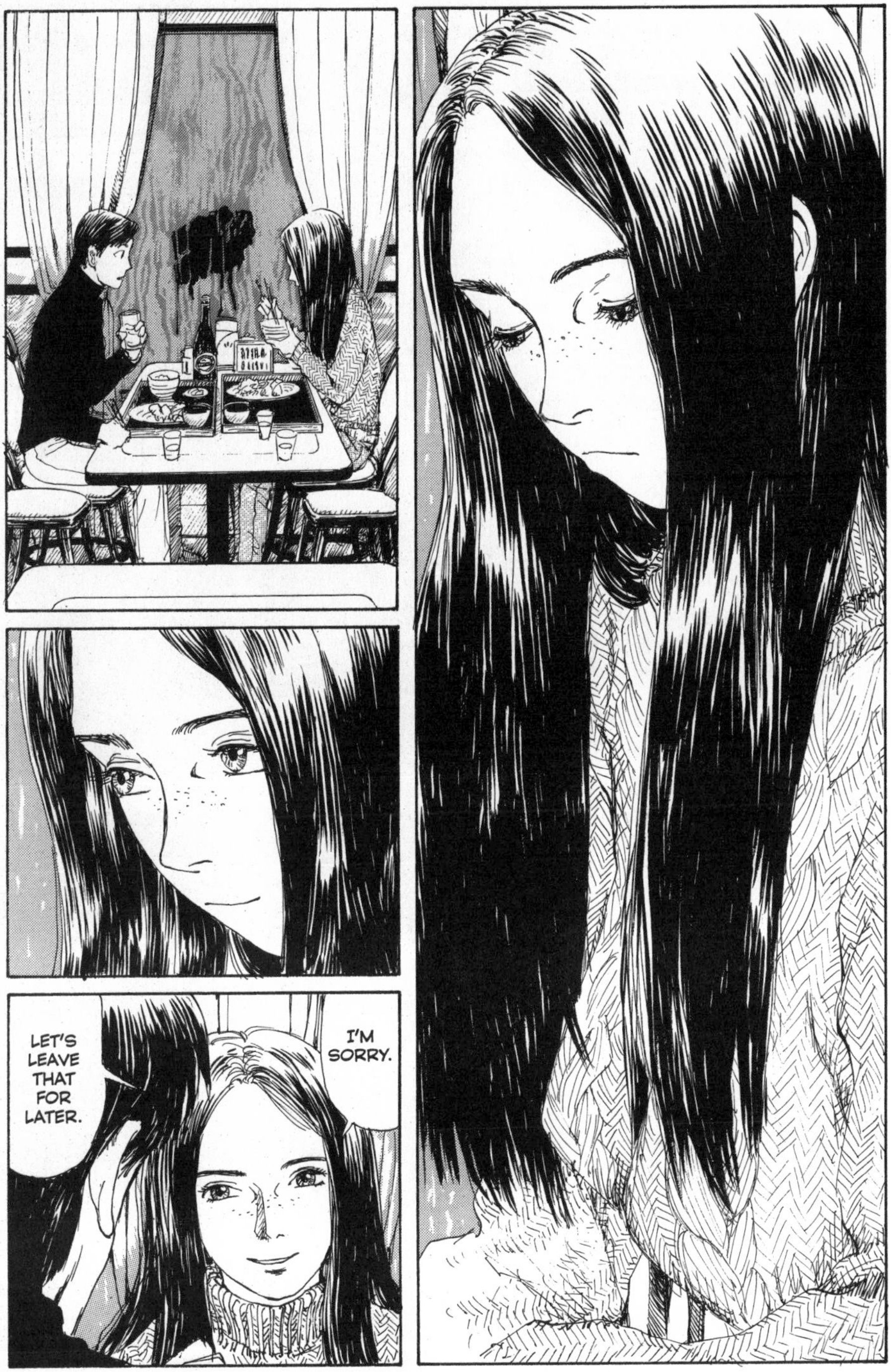
I'M SORRY.
LET'S LEAVE THAT FOR LATER.

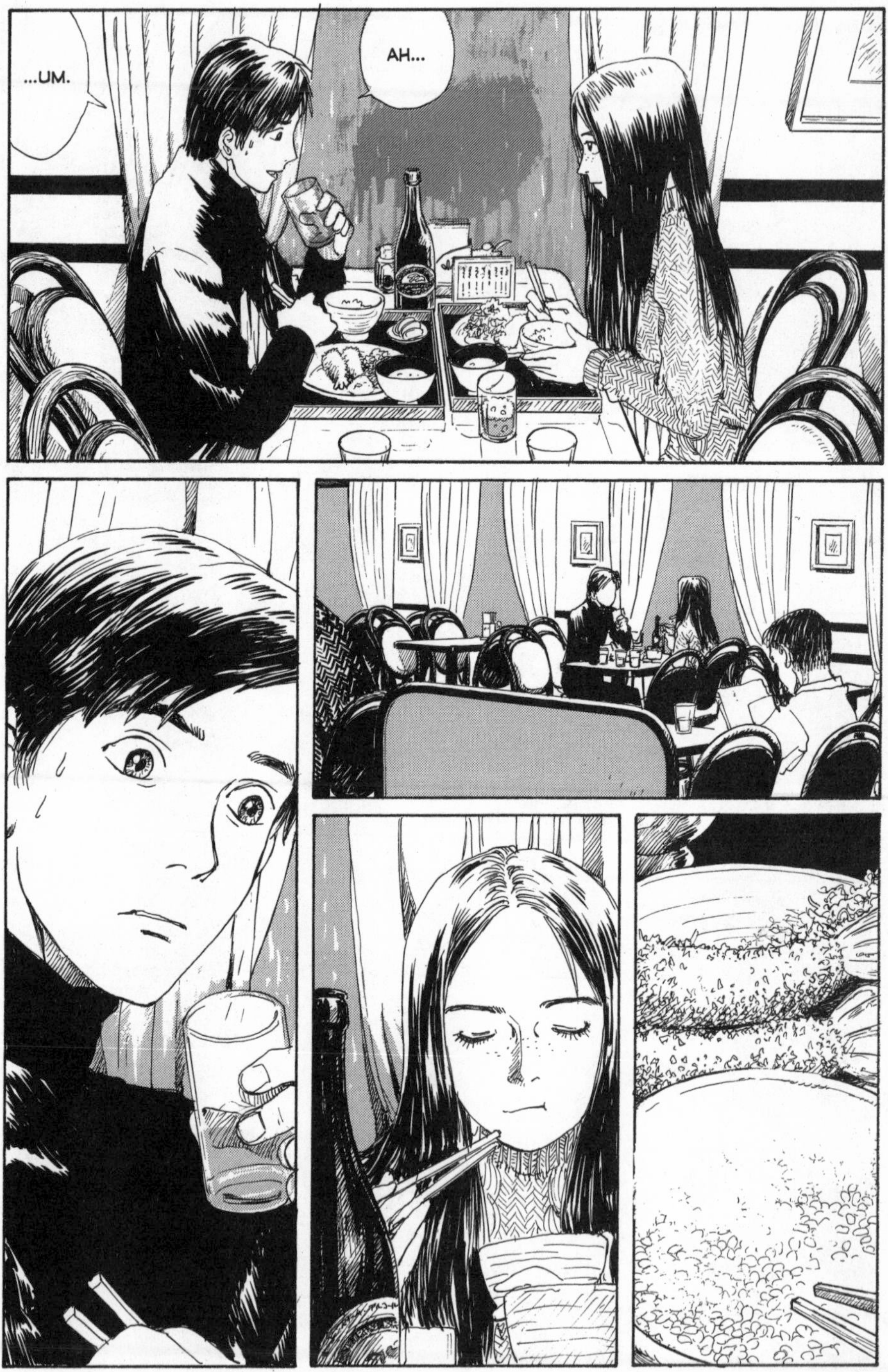
AH...
...UM.

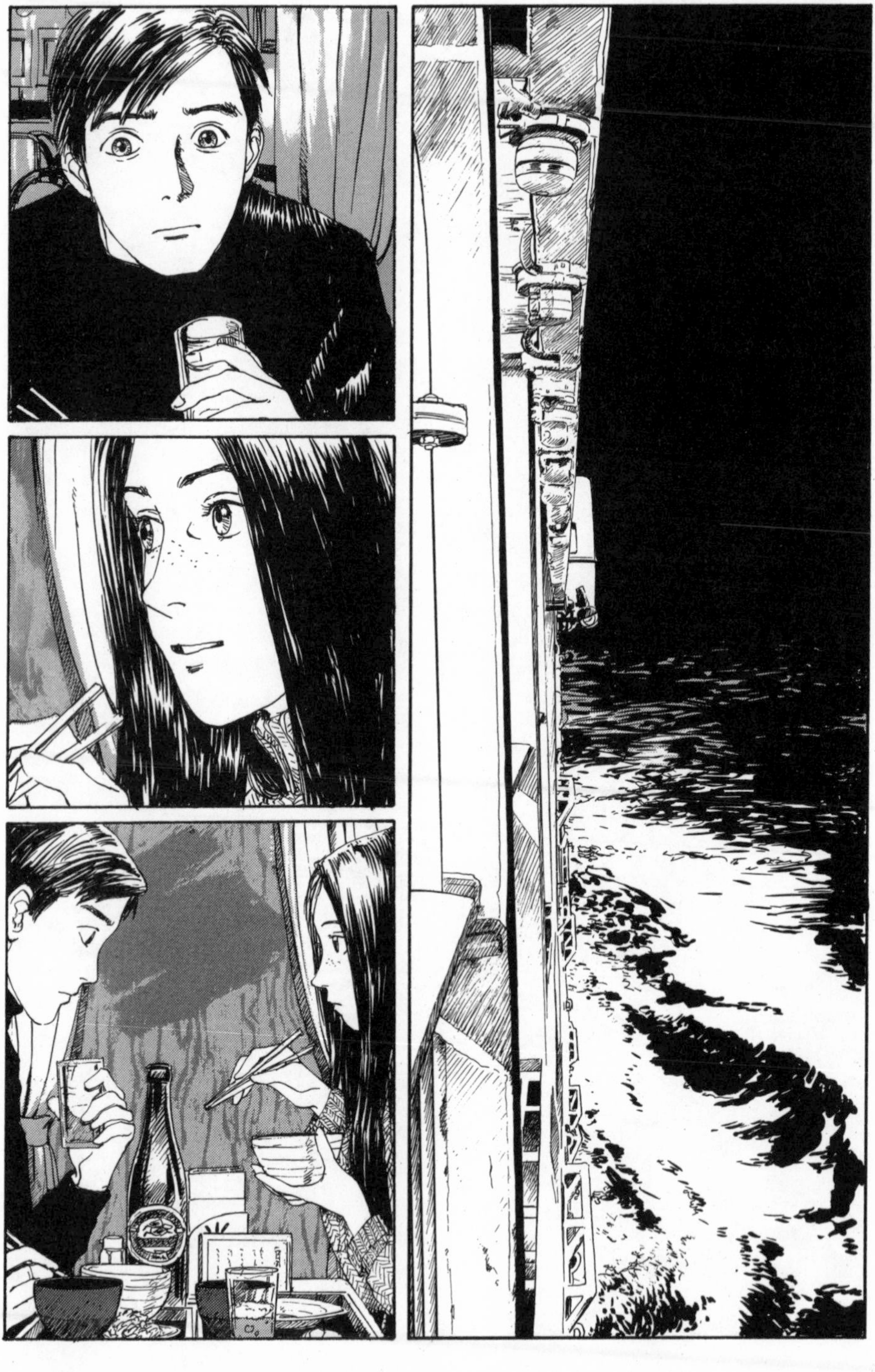

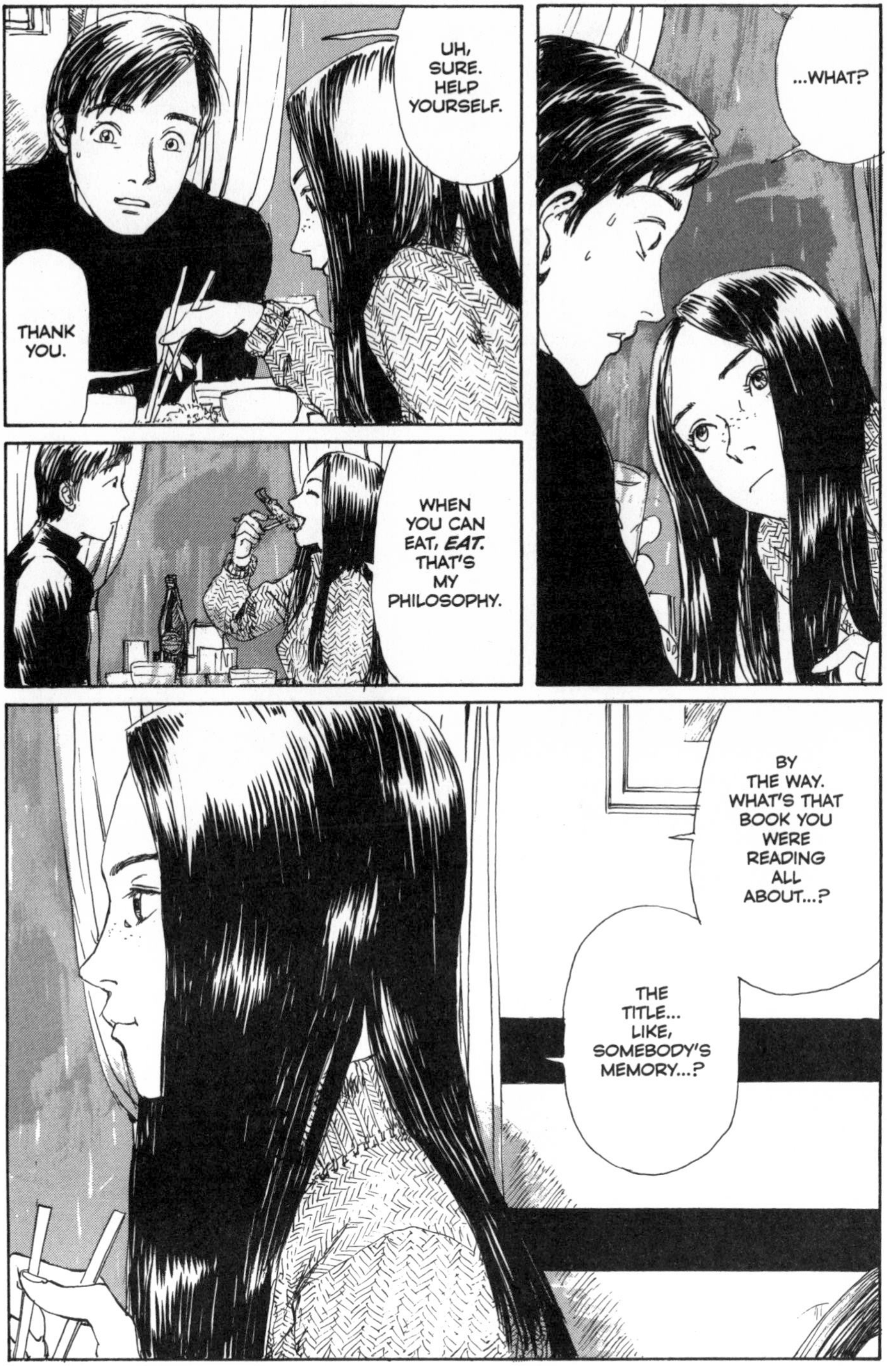
...WHAT?
UH, SURE. HELP YOURSELF.
THANK YOU.
WHEN YOU CAN EAT, *EAT.* THAT'S MY PHILOSOPHY.
BY THE WAY. WHAT'S THAT BOOK YOU WERE READING ALL ABOUT...?
THE TITLE... LIKE, SOMEBODY'S MEMORY...?

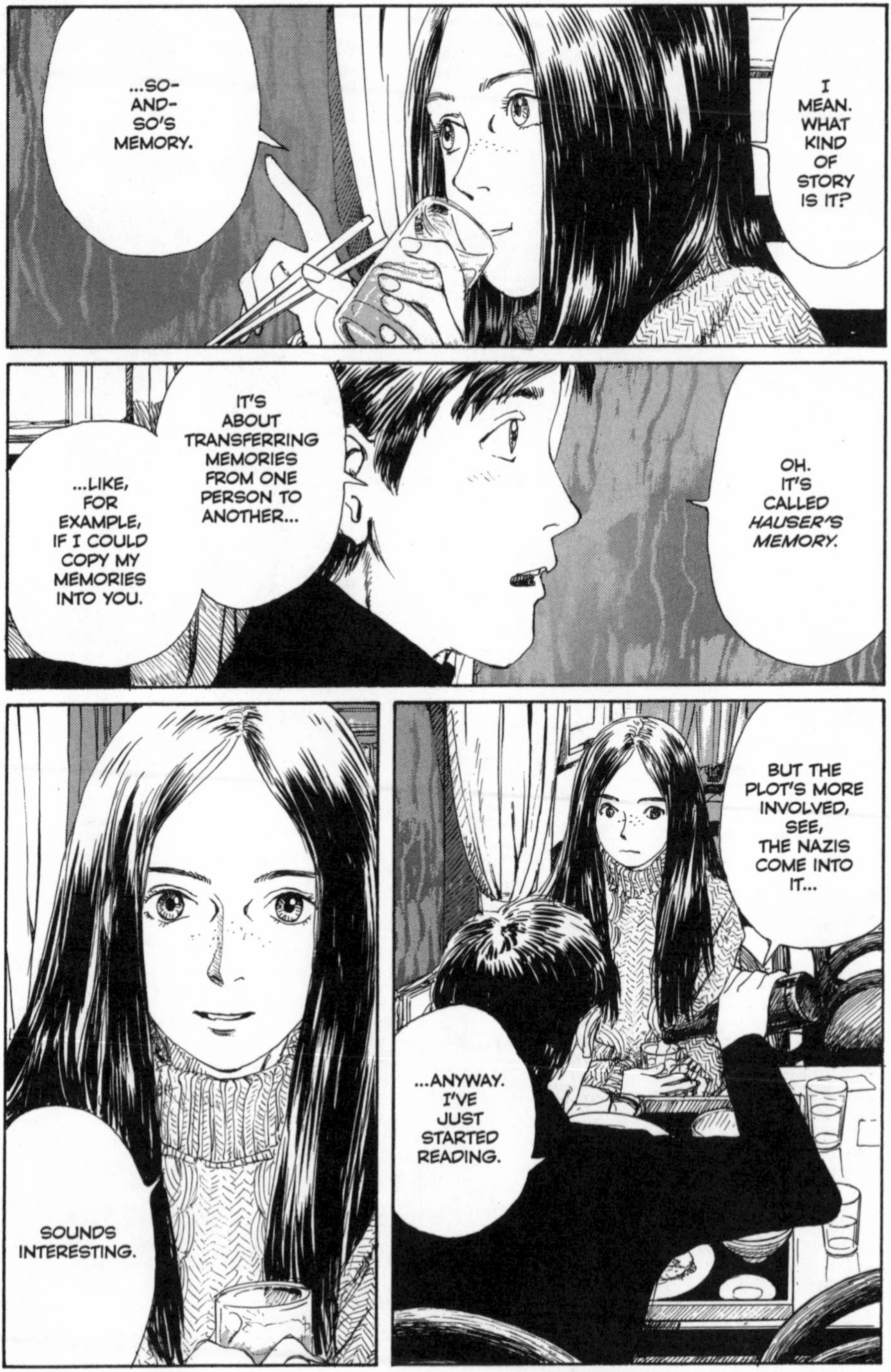
I MEAN. WHAT KIND OF STORY IS IT?
...SO-AND-SO'S MEMORY.
OH. IT'S CALLED *HAUSER'S MEMORY.*
IT'S ABOUT TRANSFERRING MEMORIES FROM ONE PERSON TO ANOTHER...
...LIKE, FOR EXAMPLE, IF I COULD COPY MY MEMORIES INTO YOU.
BUT THE PLOT'S MORE INVOLVED, SEE, THE NAZIS COME INTO IT...
...ANYWAY. I'VE JUST STARTED READING.
SOUNDS INTERESTING.

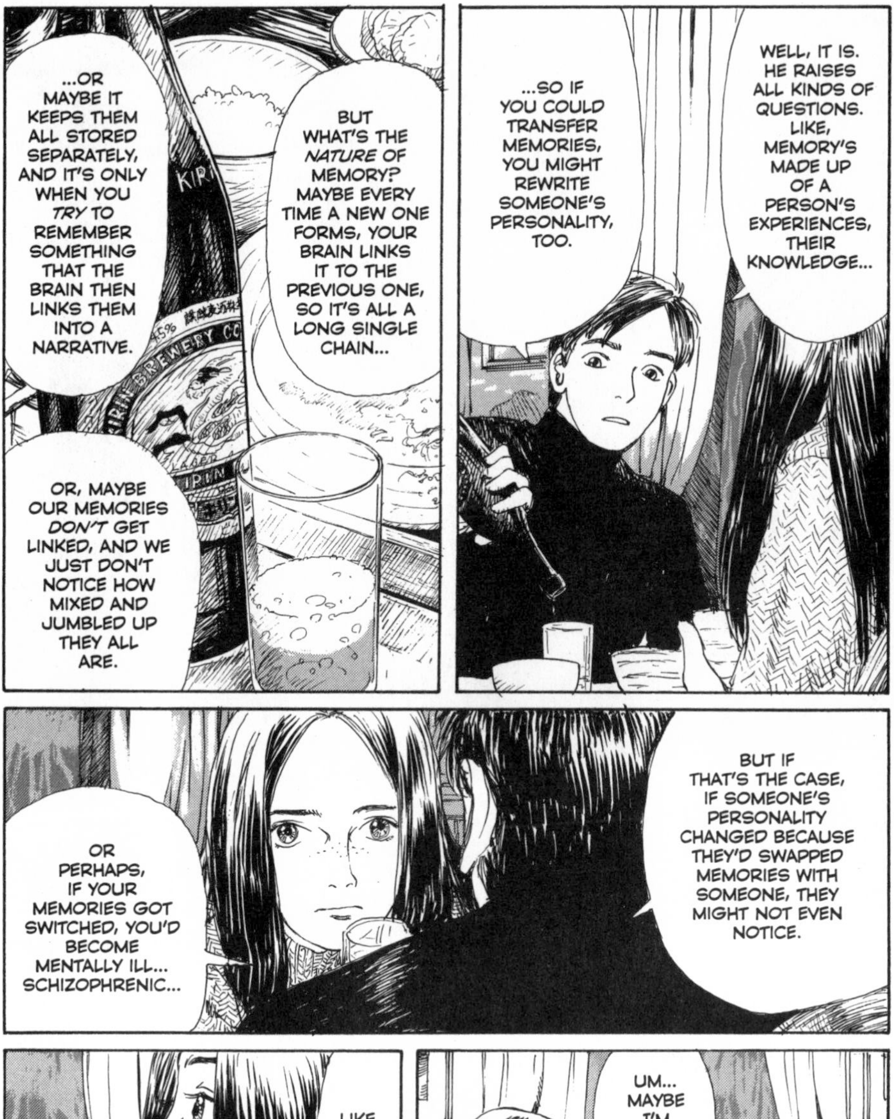
WELL, IT IS. HE RAISES ALL KINDS OF QUESTIONS. LIKE, MEMORY'S MADE UP OF A PERSON'S EXPERIENCES, THEIR KNOWLEDGE...
...SO IF YOU COULD TRANSFER MEMORIES, YOU MIGHT REWRITE SOMEONE'S PERSONALITY, TOO.
BUT WHAT'S THE *NATURE* OF MEMORY? MAYBE EVERY TIME A NEW ONE FORMS, YOUR BRAIN LINKS IT TO THE PREVIOUS ONE, SO IT'S ALL A LONG SINGLE CHAIN...
...OR MAYBE IT KEEPS THEM ALL STORED SEPARATELY, AND IT'S ONLY WHEN YOU *TRY* TO REMEMBER SOMETHING THAT THE BRAIN THEN LINKS THEM INTO A NARRATIVE.
OR, MAYBE OUR MEMORIES *DON'T* GET LINKED, AND WE JUST DON'T NOTICE HOW MIXED AND JUMBLED UP THEY ALL ARE.
BUT IF THAT'S THE CASE, IF SOMEONE'S PERSONALITY CHANGED BECAUSE THEY'D SWAPPED MEMORIES WITH SOMEONE, THEY MIGHT NOT EVEN NOTICE.
OR PERHAPS, IF YOUR MEMORIES GOT SWITCHED, YOU'D BECOME MENTALLY ILL... SCHIZOPHRENIC...
UM... MAYBE I'M BORING YOU.
LIKE I SAID...
...IT'S INTEREST-ING.

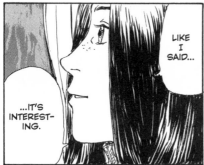

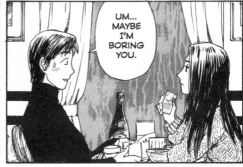

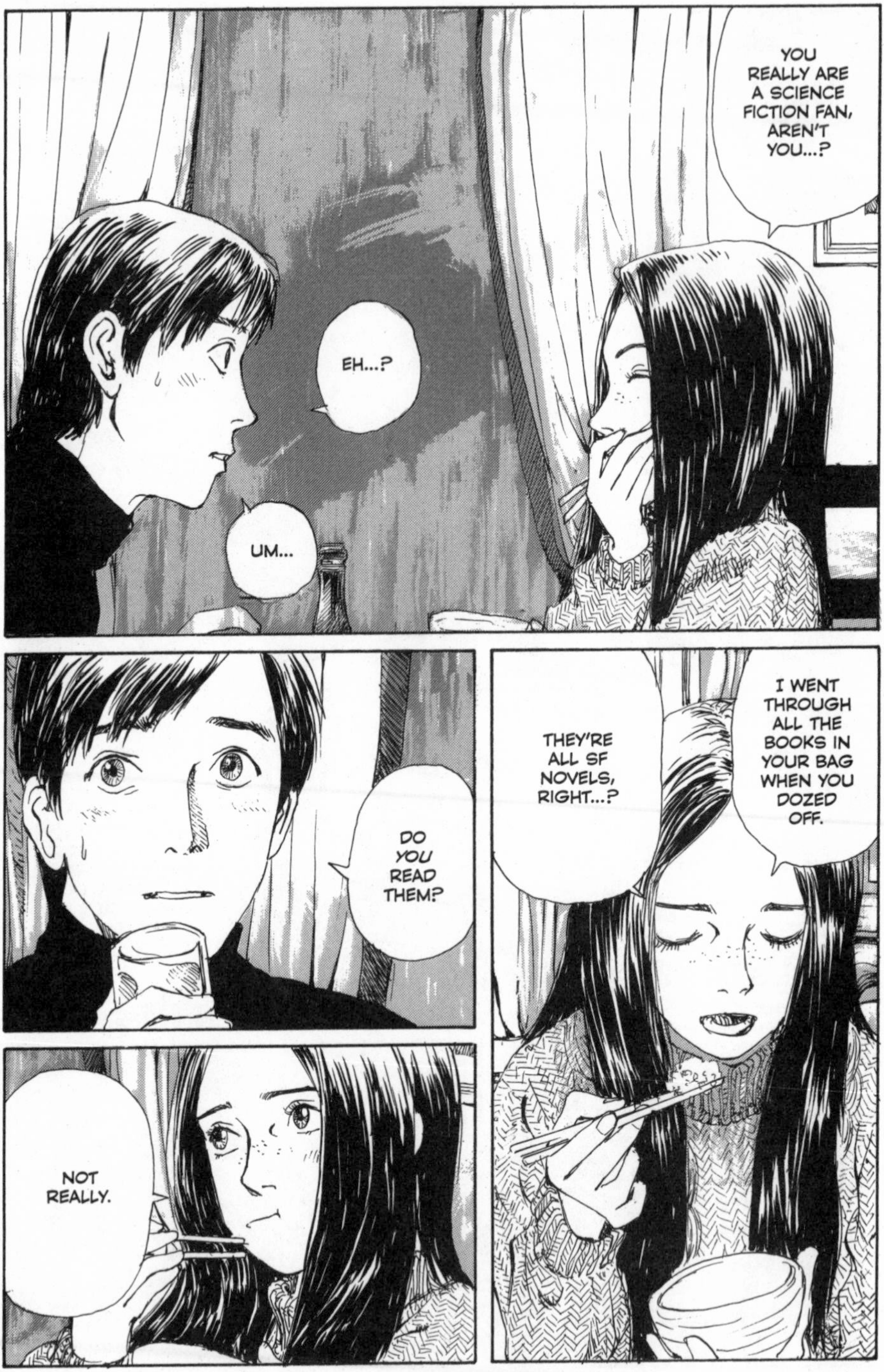
YOU REALLY ARE A SCIENCE FICTION FAN, AREN'T YOU...?
EH...?
UM...
I WENT THROUGH ALL THE BOOKS IN YOUR BAG WHEN YOU DOZED OFF.
THEY'RE ALL SF NOVELS, RIGHT...?
DO *YOU* READ THEM?
NOT REALLY.

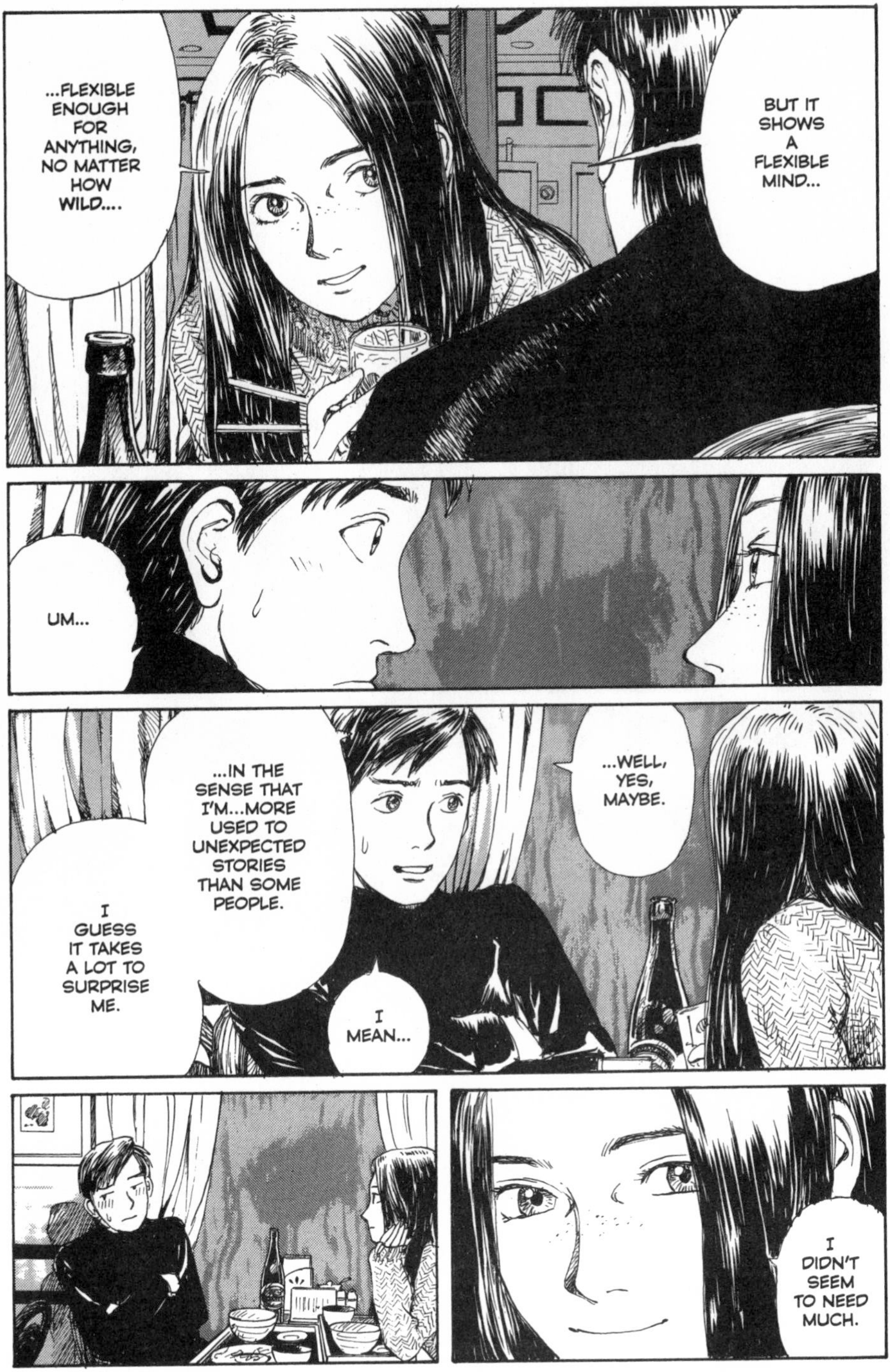

BUT IT SHOWS A FLEXIBLE MIND...
...FLEXIBLE ENOUGH FOR ANYTHING, NO MATTER HOW WILD....
UM...
...WELL, YES, MAYBE.
...IN THE SENSE THAT I'M...MORE USED TO UNEXPECTED STORIES THAN SOME PEOPLE.
I MEAN...
I GUESS IT TAKES A LOT TO SURPRISE ME.
I DIDN'T SEEM TO NEED MUCH.

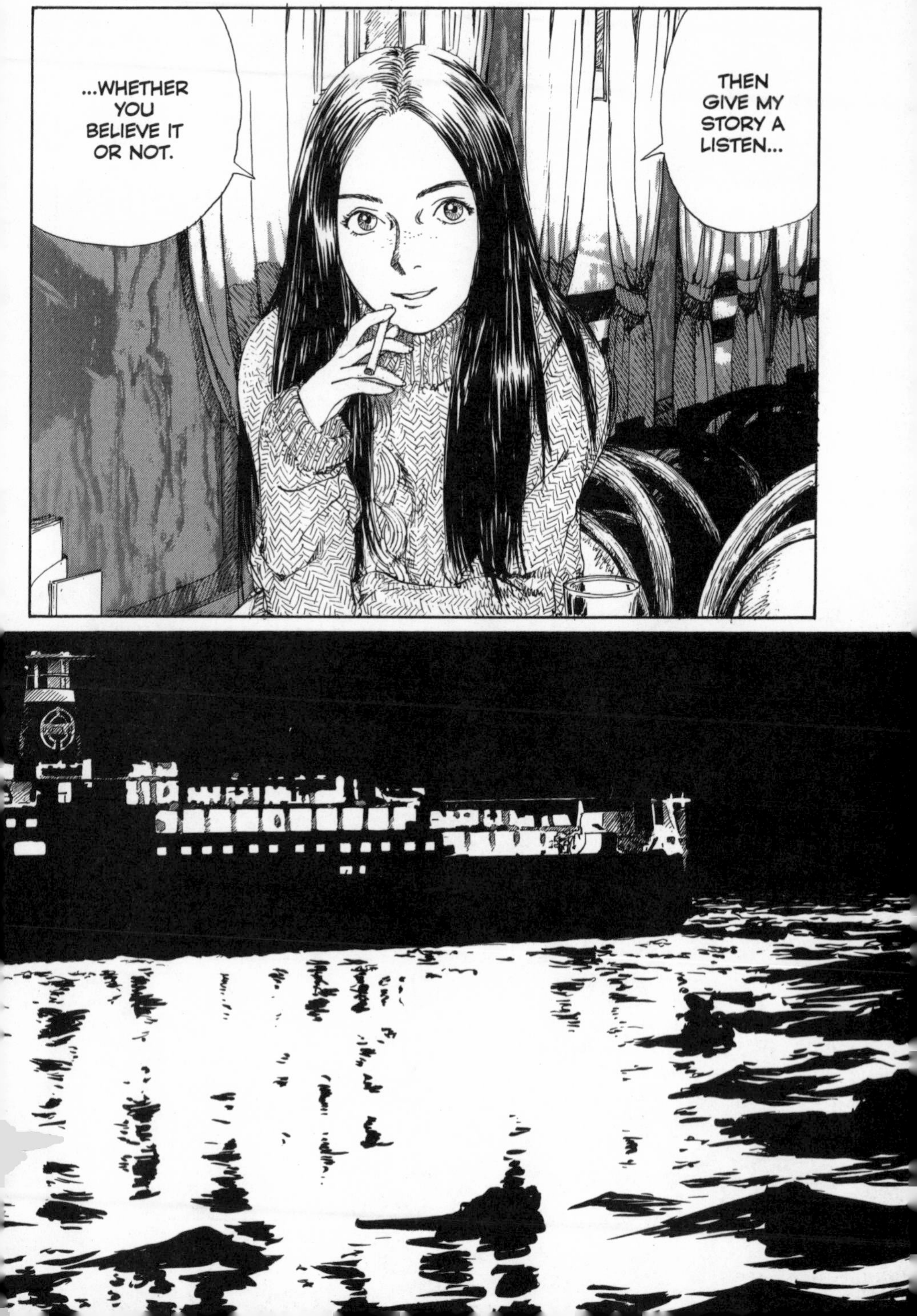
THEN GIVE MY STORY A LISTEN...
...WHETHER YOU BELIEVE IT OR NOT.

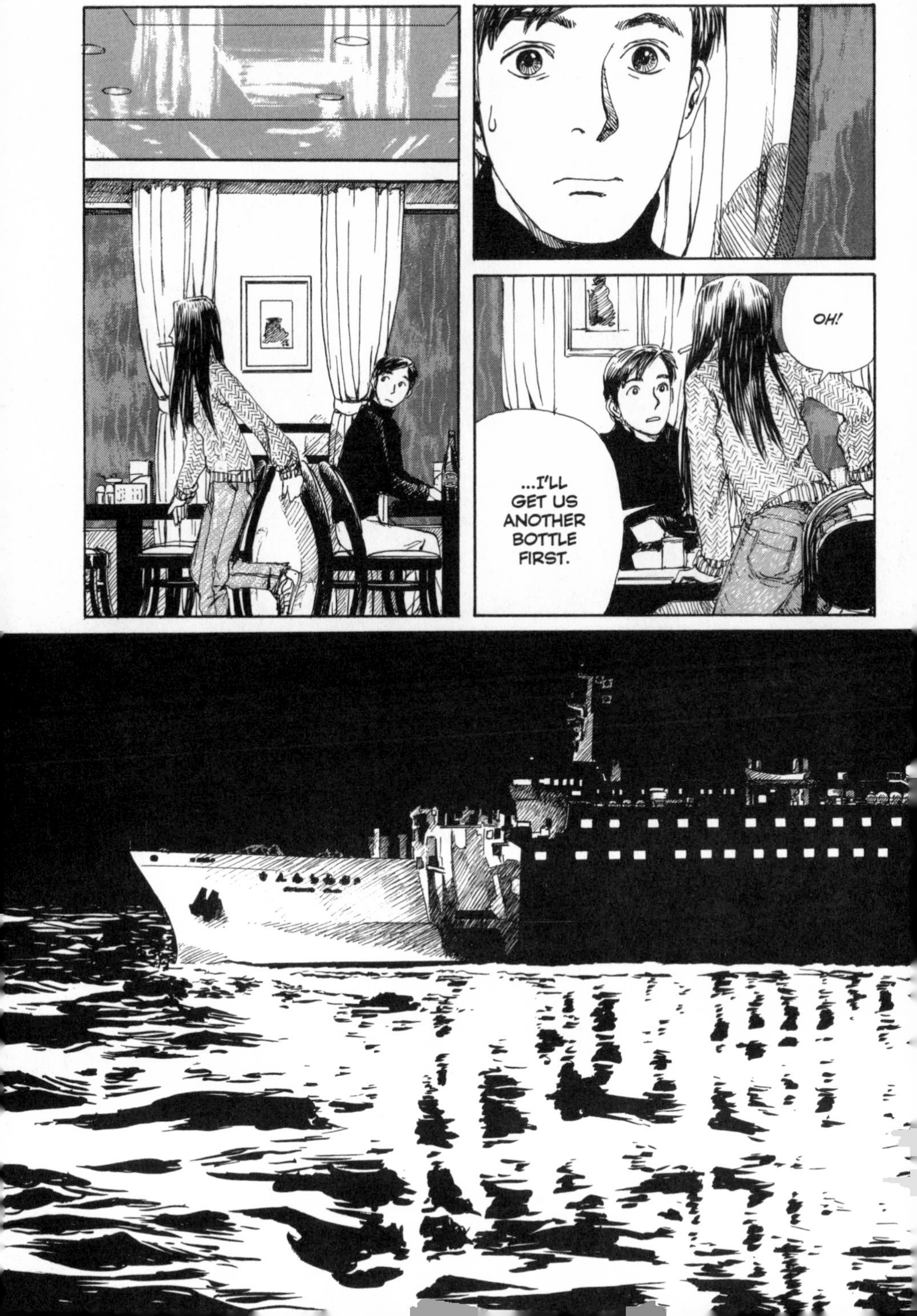
OH!
...I'LL GET US ANOTHER BOTTLE FIRST.

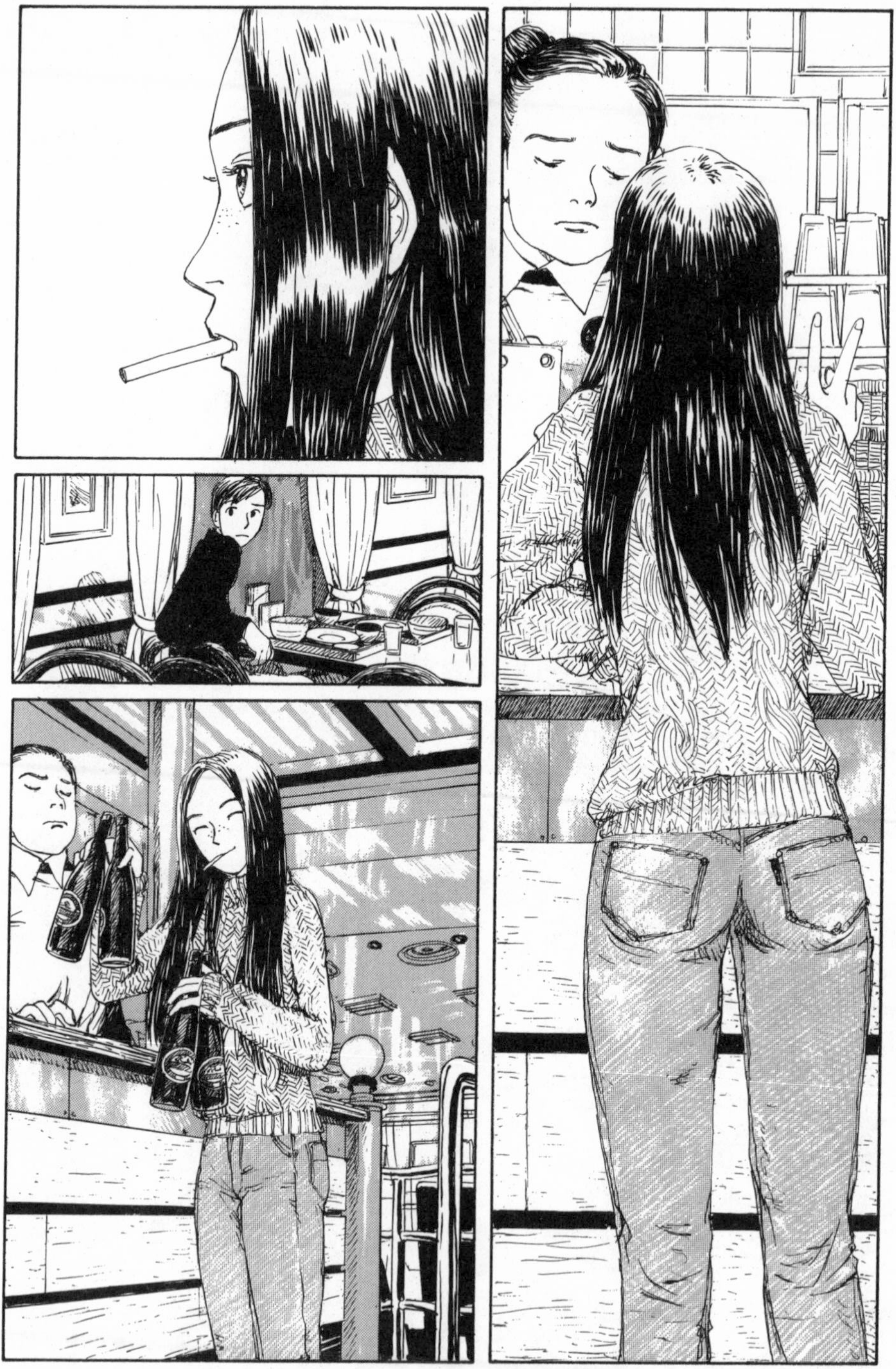

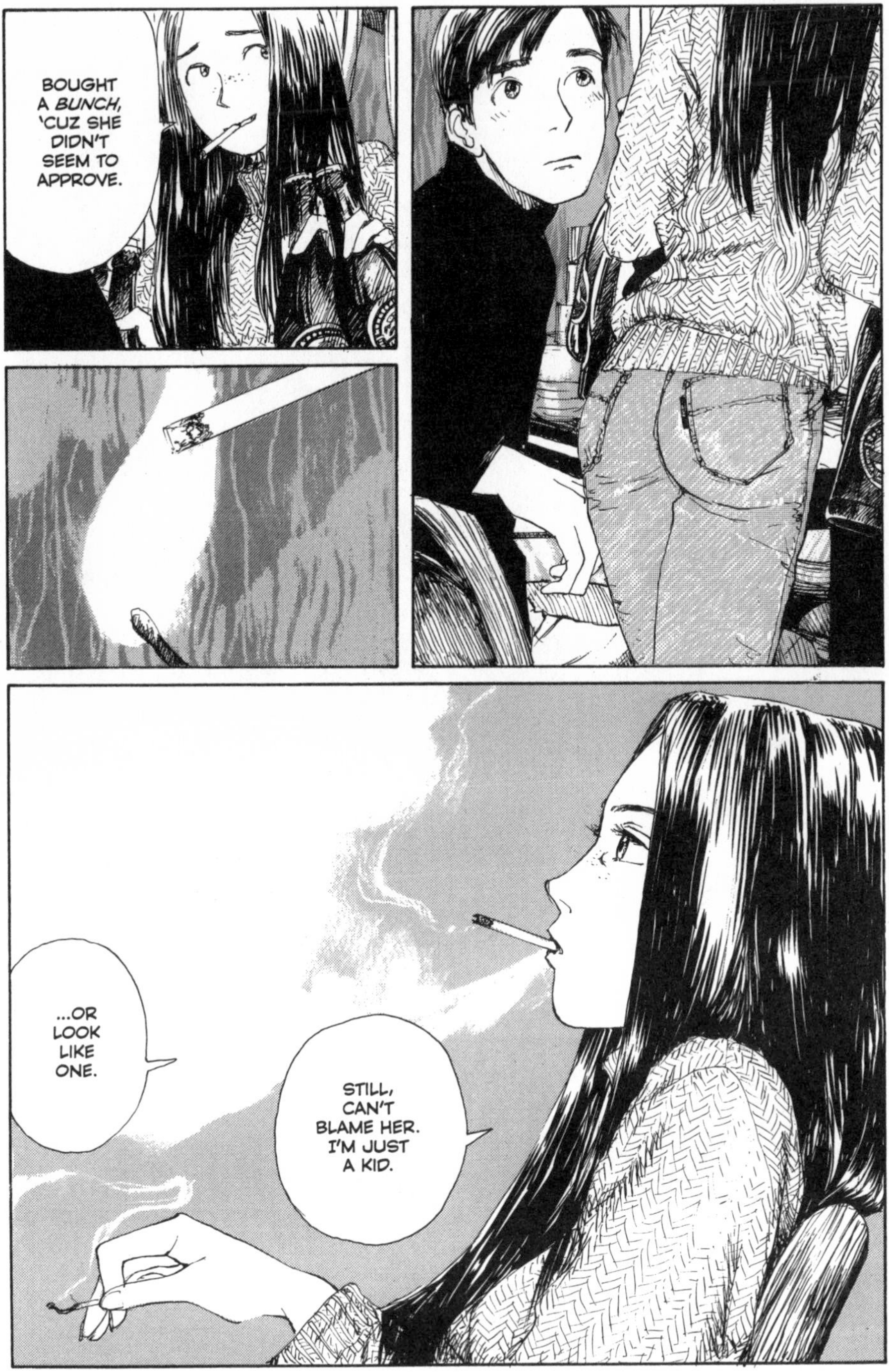
BOUGHT A *BUNCH,* 'CUZ SHE DIDN'T SEEM TO APPROVE.
STILL, CAN'T BLAME HER. I'M JUST A KID.
...OR LOOK LIKE ONE.

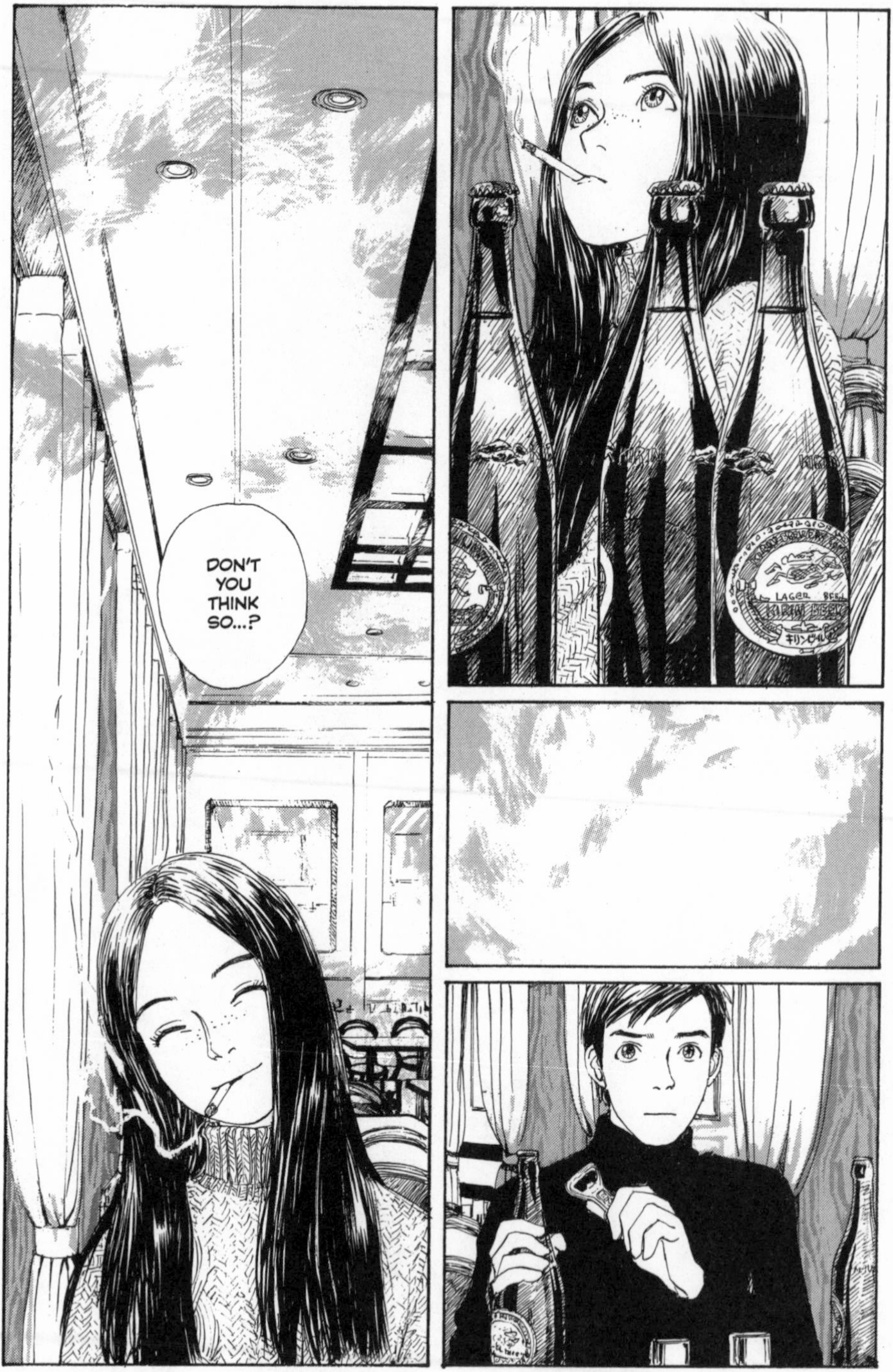
DON'T YOU THINK SO...?
LAGER BEER
KIRIN BEER

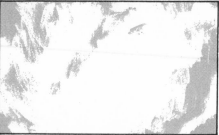

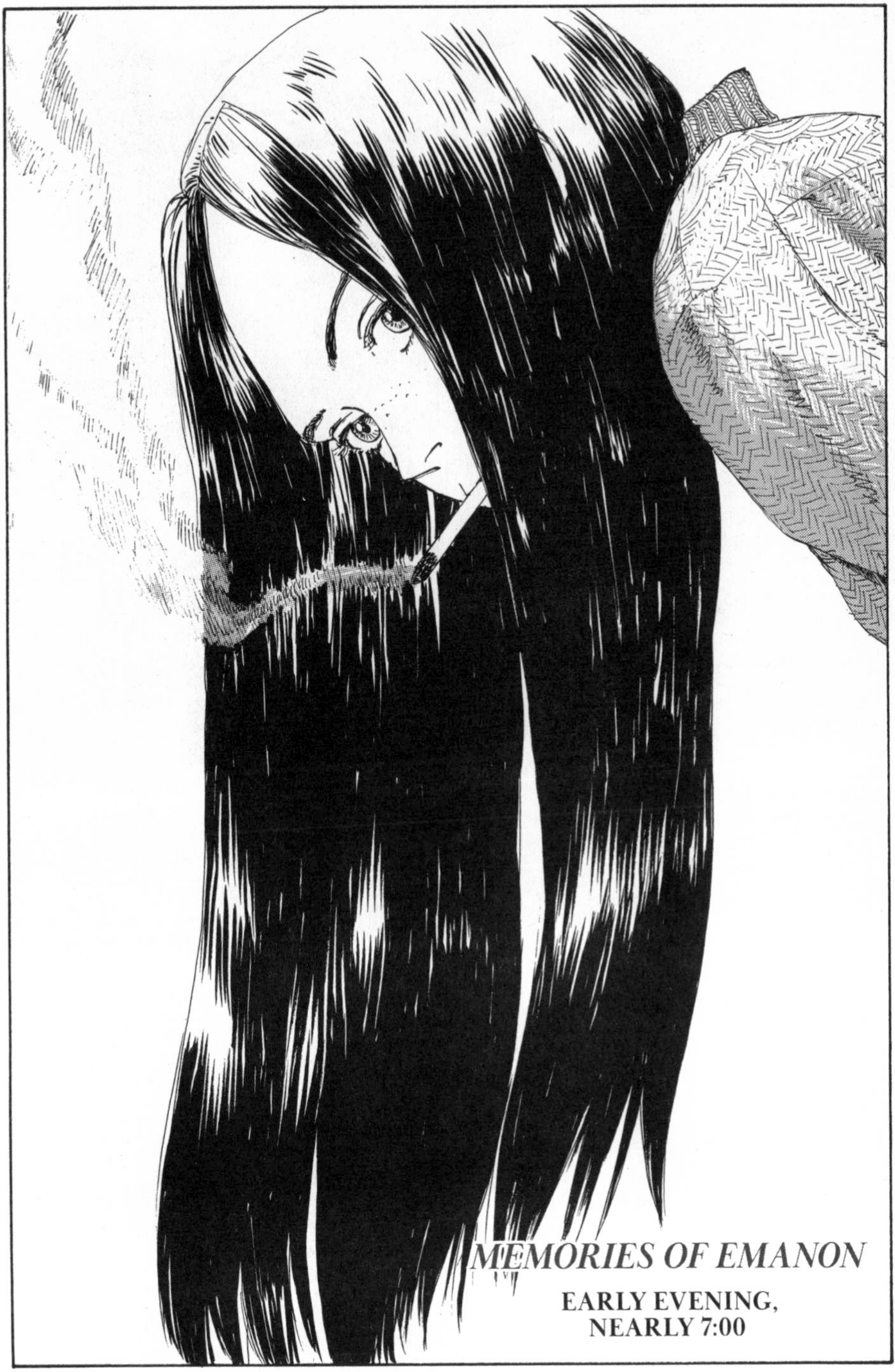
MEMORIES OF EMANON
EARLY EVENING,
NEARLY 7:00

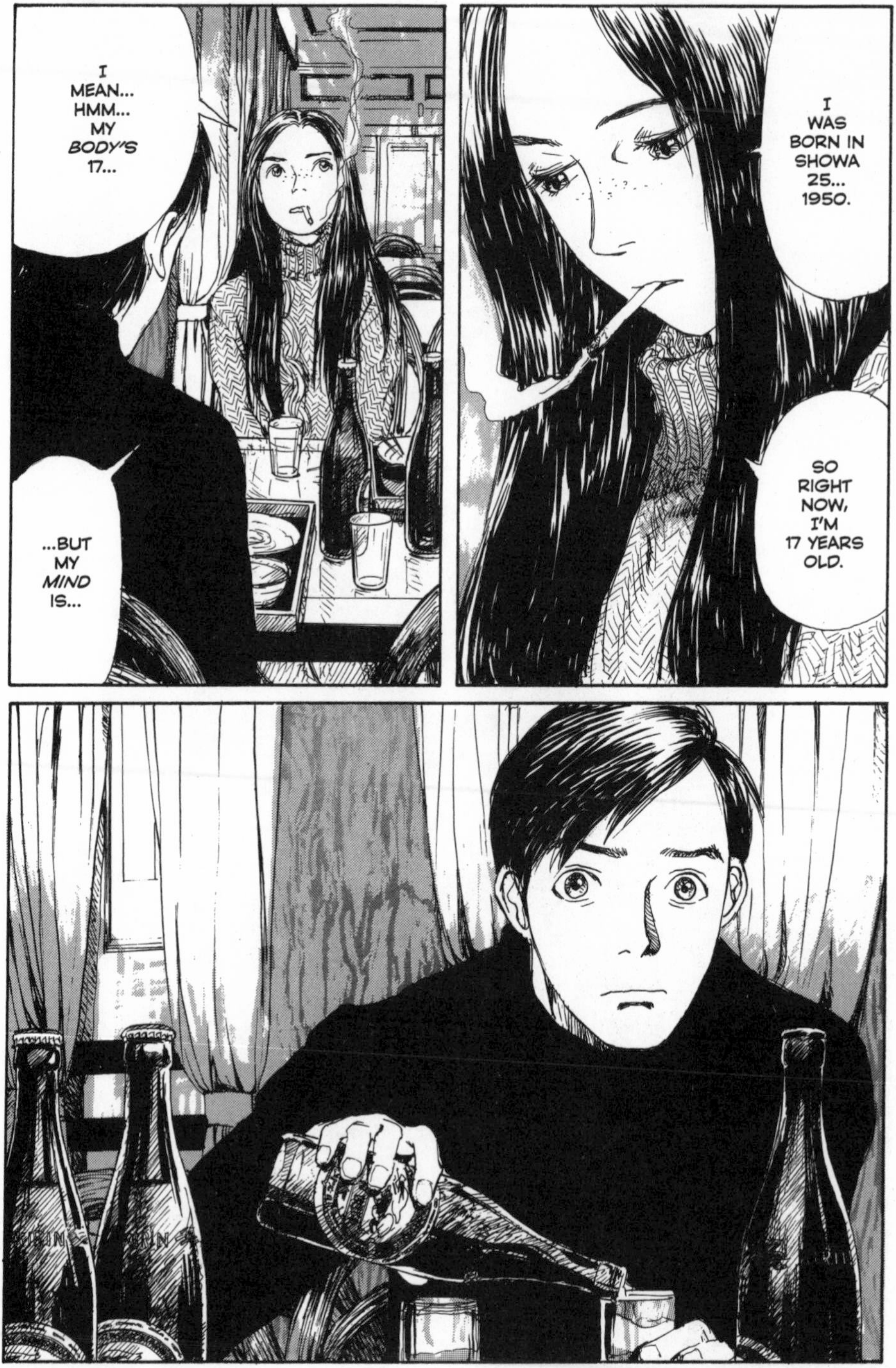
I WAS BORN IN SHOWA 25... 1950.
SO RIGHT NOW, I'M 17 YEARS OLD.
I MEAN... HMM... MY *BODY'S* 17...
...BUT MY *MIND* IS...

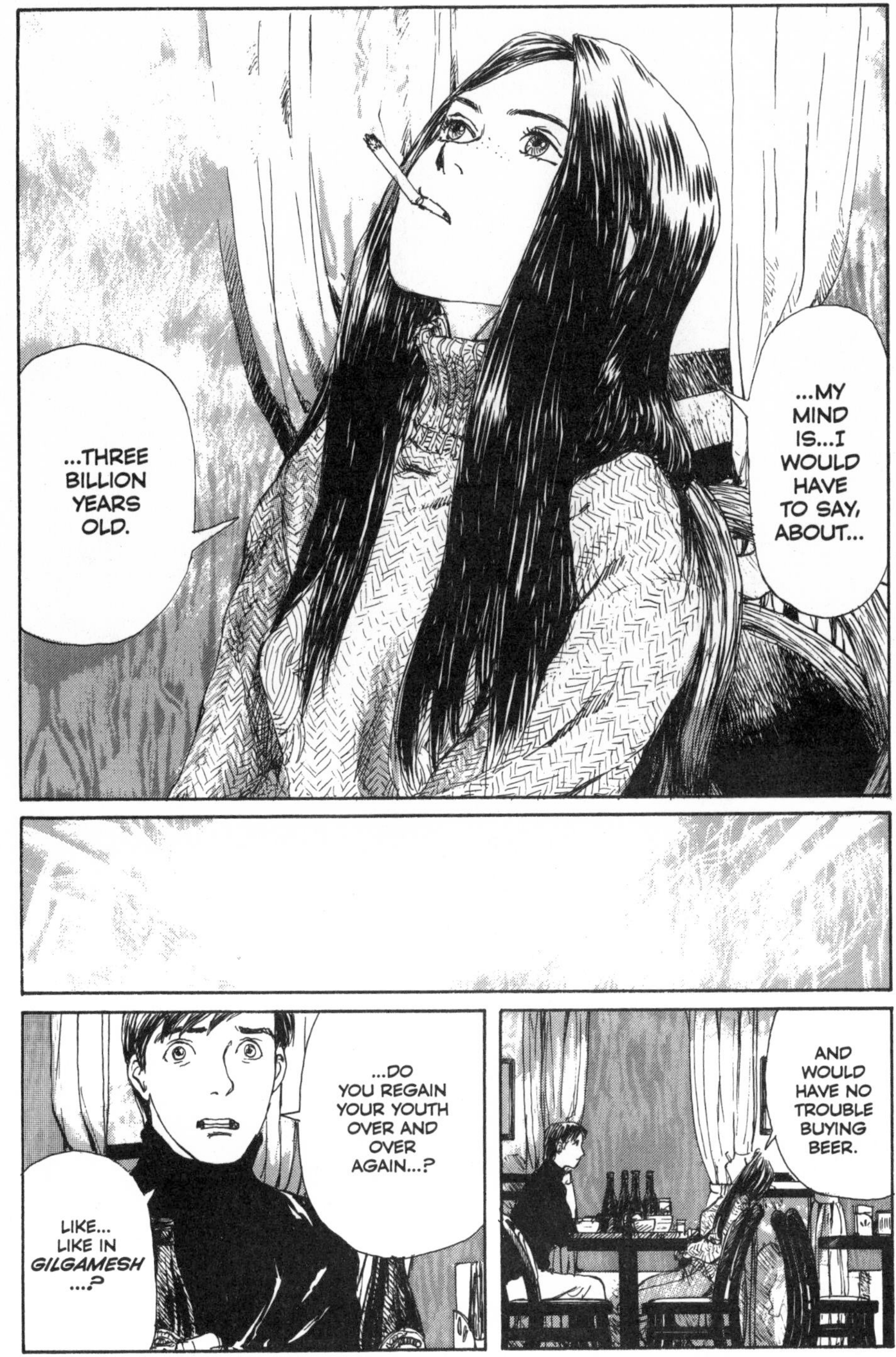
...MY MIND IS...I WOULD HAVE TO SAY, ABOUT...
...THREE BILLION YEARS OLD.
AND WOULD HAVE NO TROUBLE BUYING BEER.
...DO YOU REGAIN YOUR YOUTH OVER AND OVER AGAIN...?
LIKE... LIKE IN *GILGAMESH* ...?

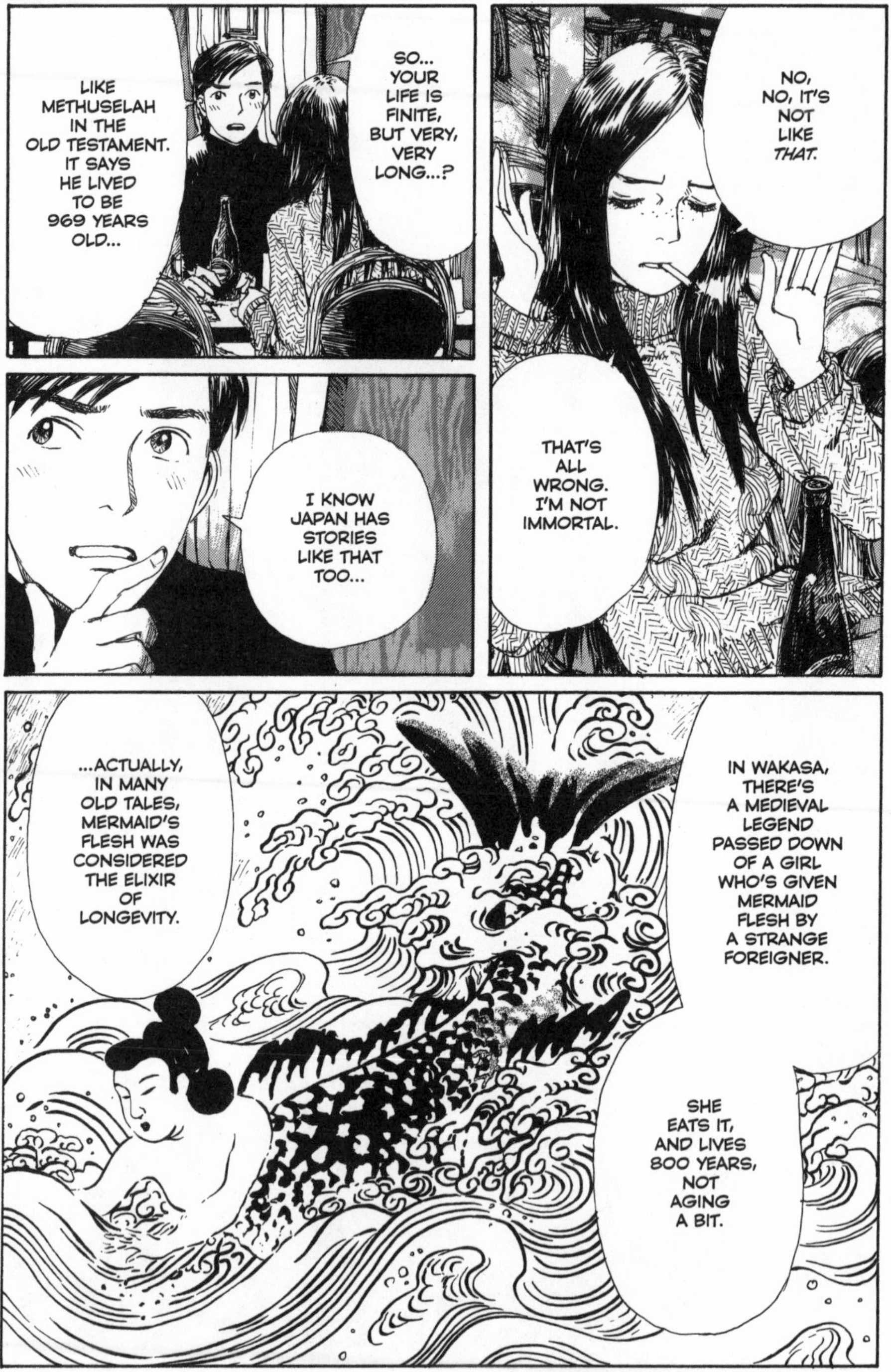
NO, NO, IT'S NOT LIKE *THAT*.
THAT'S ALL WRONG. I'M NOT IMMORTAL.
SO... YOUR LIFE IS FINITE, BUT VERY, VERY LONG...?
LIKE METHUSELAH IN THE OLD TESTAMENT. IT SAYS HE LIVED TO BE 969 YEARS OLD...
I KNOW JAPAN HAS STORIES LIKE THAT TOO...
IN WAKASA, THERE'S A MEDIEVAL LEGEND PASSED DOWN OF A GIRL WHO'S GIVEN MERMAID FLESH BY A STRANGE FOREIGNER.
...ACTUALLY, IN MANY OLD TALES, MERMAID'S FLESH WAS CONSIDERED THE ELIXIR OF LONGEVITY.
SHE EATS IT, AND LIVES 800 YEARS, NOT AGING A BIT.

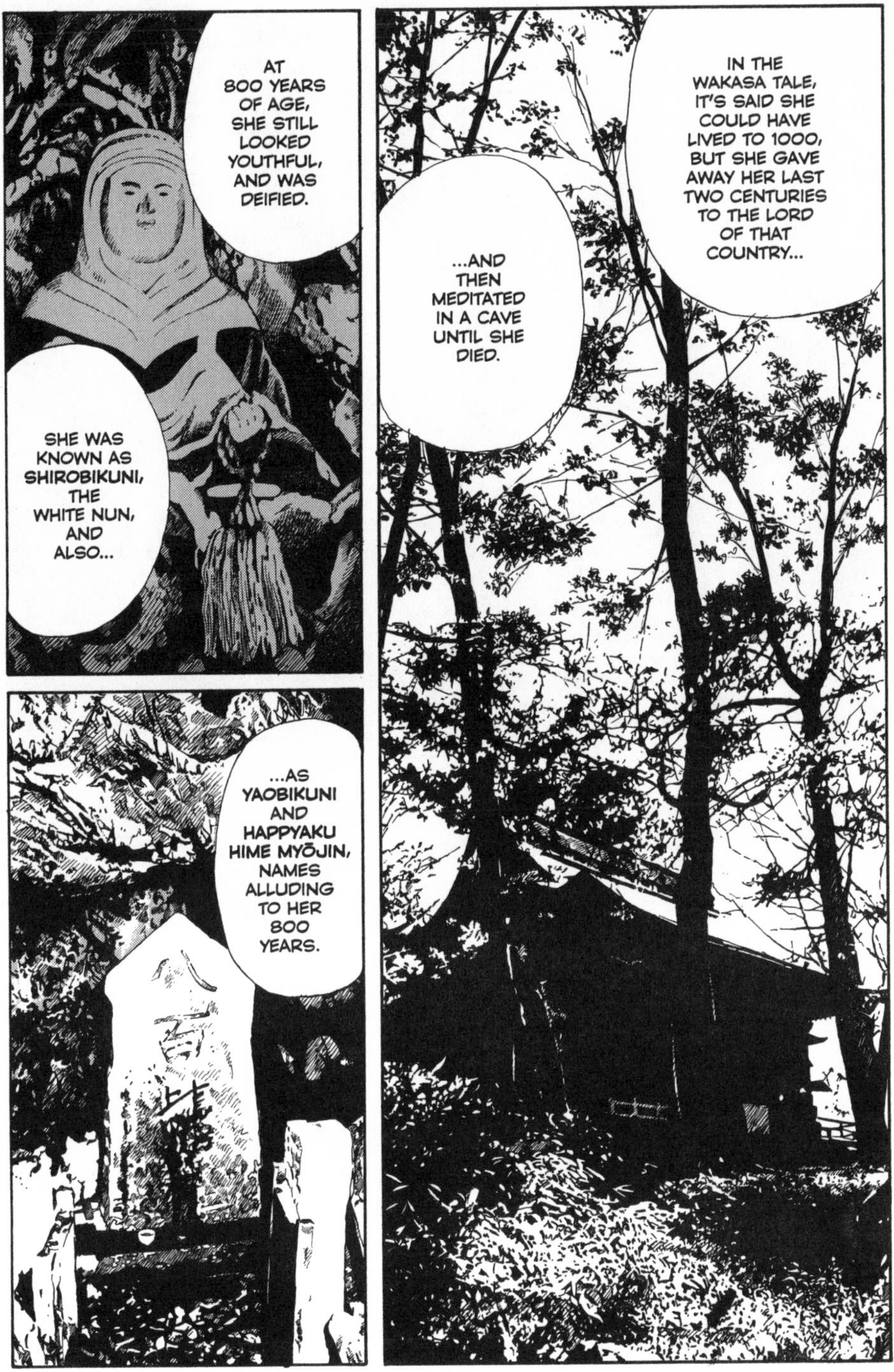
IN THE WAKASA TALE, IT'S SAID SHE COULD HAVE LIVED TO 1000, BUT SHE GAVE AWAY HER LAST TWO CENTURIES TO THE LORD OF THAT COUNTRY...
...AND THEN MEDITATED IN A CAVE UNTIL SHE DIED.
AT 800 YEARS OF AGE, SHE STILL LOOKED YOUTHFUL, AND WAS DEIFIED.
SHE WAS KNOWN AS SHIROBIKUNI, THE WHITE NUN, AND ALSO...
...AS YAOBIKUNI AND HAPPYAKU HIME MYŌJIN, NAMES ALLUDING TO HER 800 YEARS.

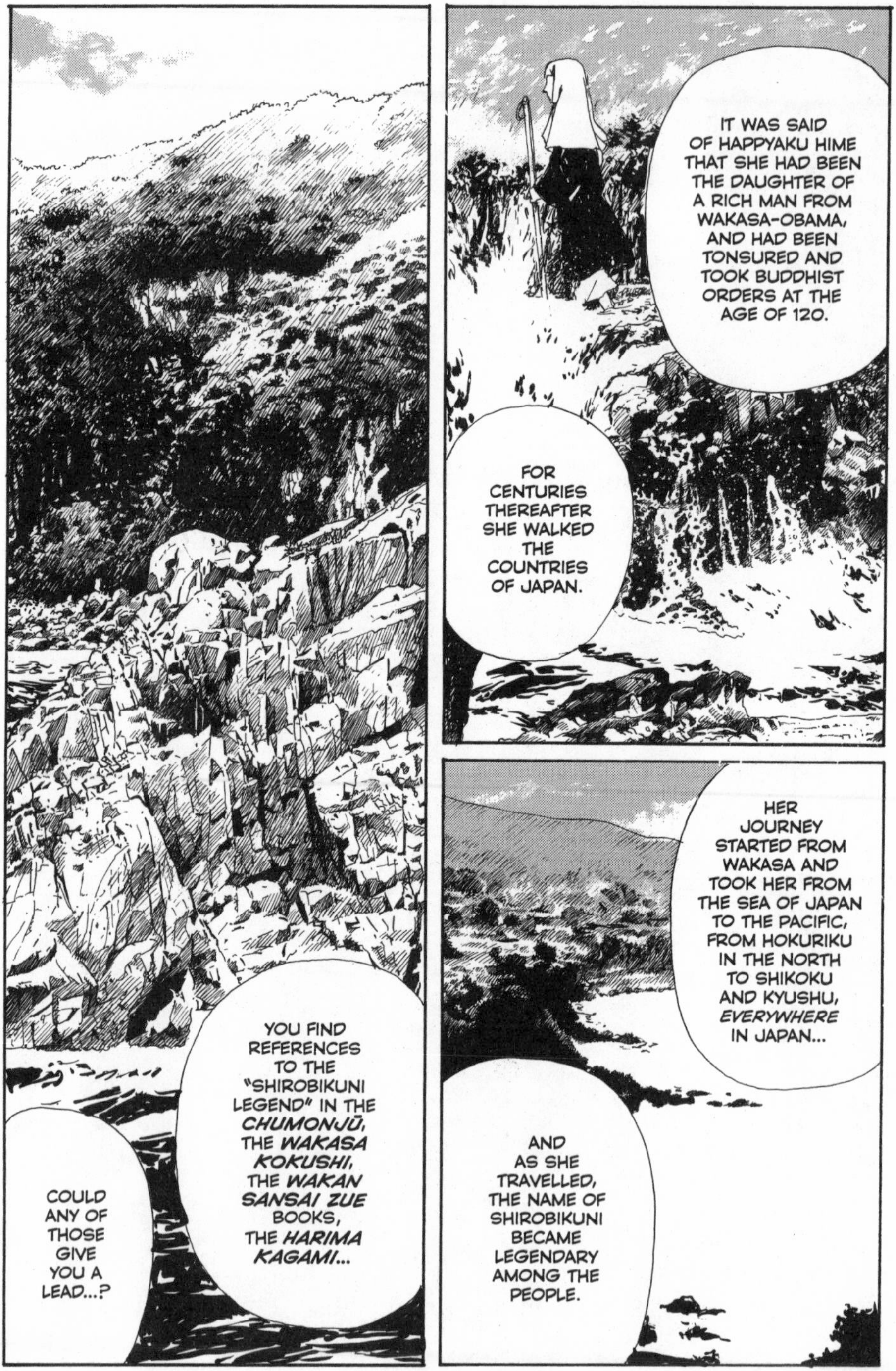
IT WAS SAID OF HAPPYAKU HIME THAT SHE HAD BEEN THE DAUGHTER OF A RICH MAN FROM WAKASA-OBAMA, AND HAD BEEN TONSURED AND TOOK BUDDHIST ORDERS AT THE AGE OF 120.
FOR CENTURIES THEREAFTER SHE WALKED THE COUNTRIES OF JAPAN.
HER JOURNEY STARTED FROM WAKASA AND TOOK HER FROM THE SEA OF JAPAN TO THE PACIFIC, FROM HOKURIKU IN THE NORTH TO SHIKOKU AND KYUSHU, *EVERYWHERE* IN JAPAN...
AND AS SHE TRAVELLED, THE NAME OF SHIROBIKUNI BECAME LEGENDARY AMONG THE PEOPLE.
YOU FIND REFERENCES TO THE "SHIROBIKUNI LEGEND" IN THE *CHUMONJŪ*, THE *WAKASA KOKUSHI*, THE *WAKAN SANSAI ZUE* BOOKS, THE *HARIMA KAGAMI*...
COULD ANY OF THOSE GIVE YOU A LEAD...?

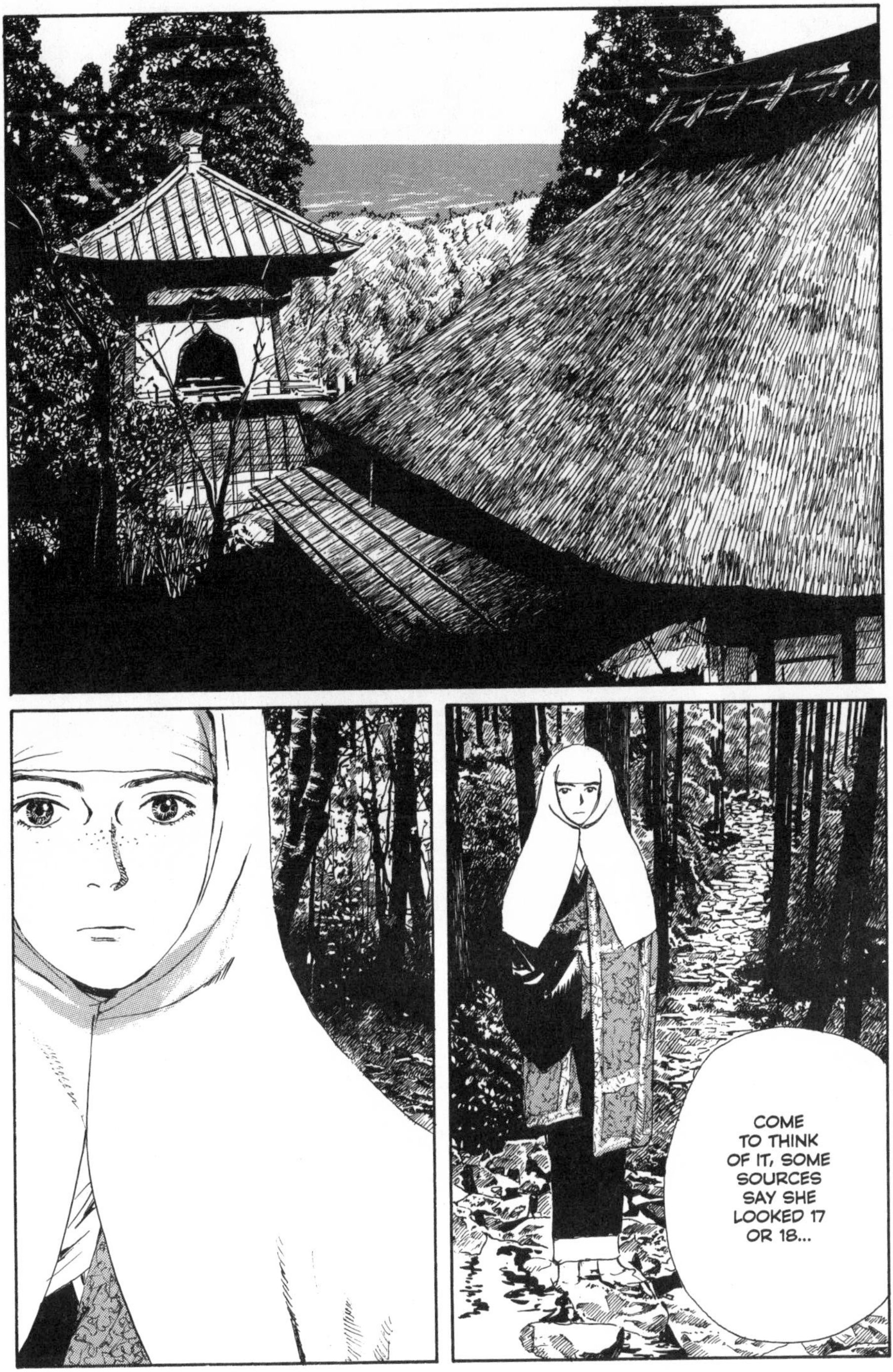
COME TO THINK OF IT, SOME SOURCES SAY SHE LOOKED 17 OR 18...

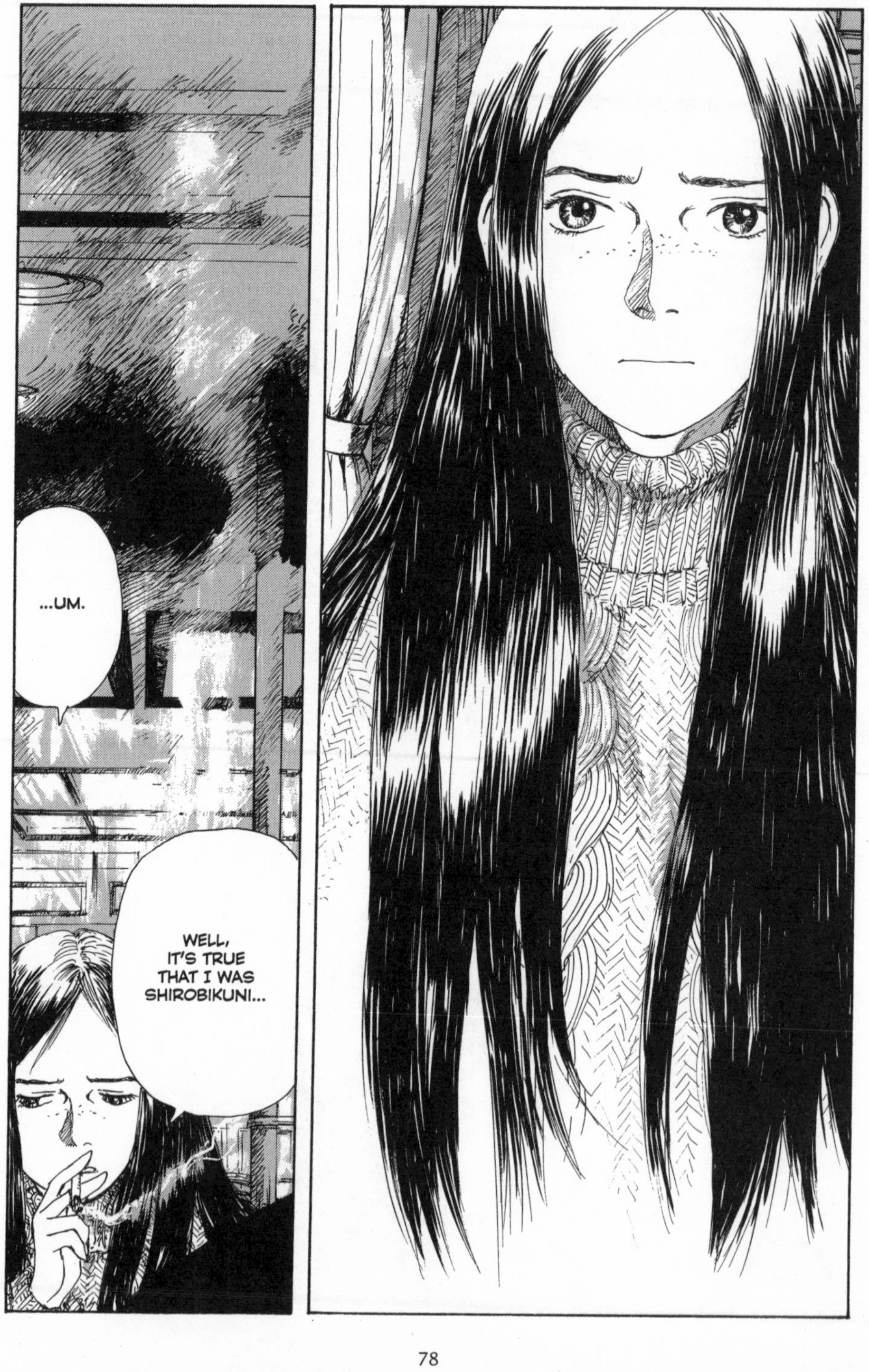
...UM.
WELL, IT'S TRUE THAT I WAS SHIROBIKUNI...

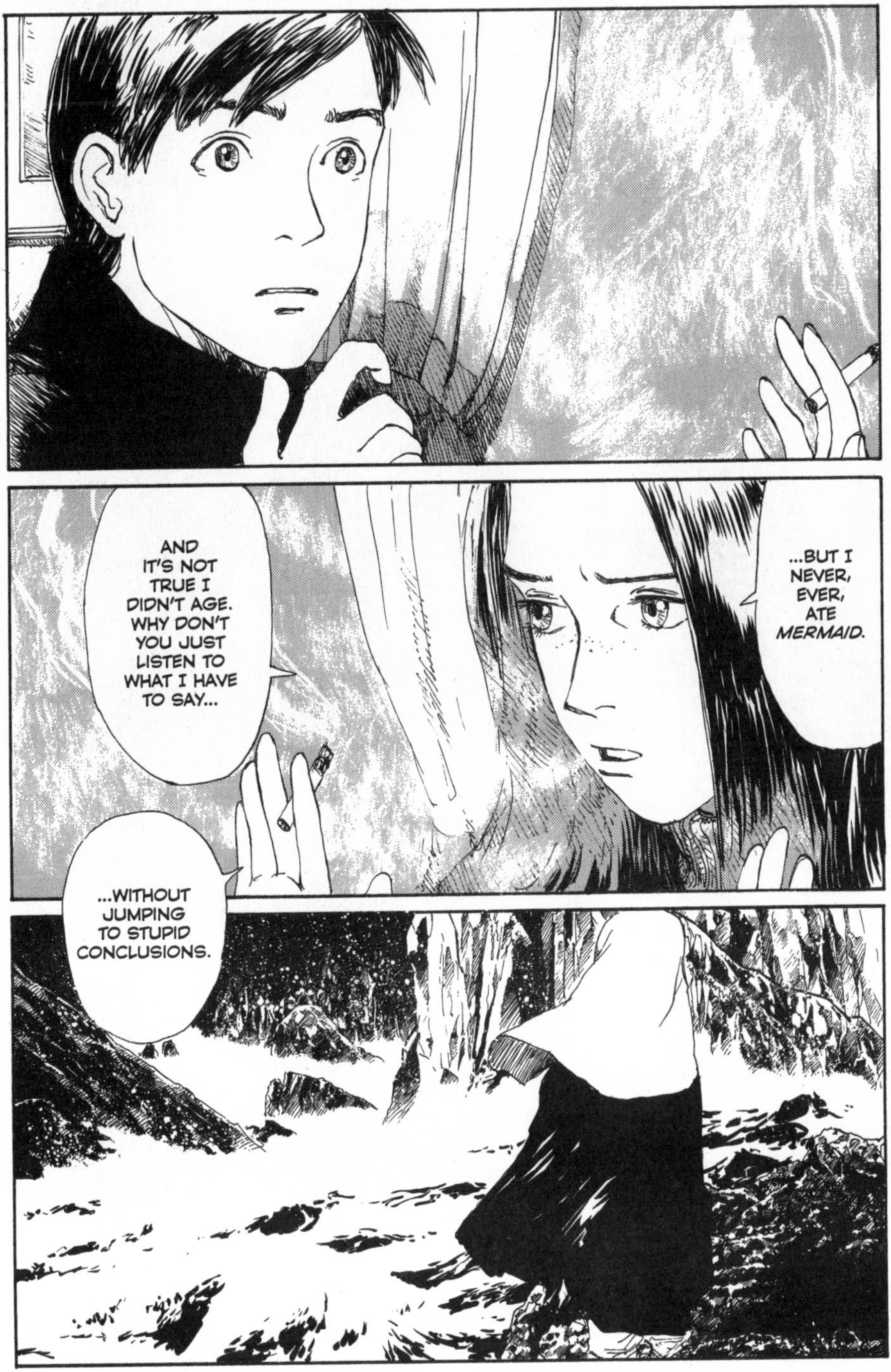
...BUT I NEVER, EVER, ATE *MERMAID*.
AND IT'S NOT TRUE I DIDN'T AGE. WHY DON'T YOU JUST LISTEN TO WHAT I HAVE TO SAY...
...WITHOUT JUMPING TO STUPID CONCLUSIONS.

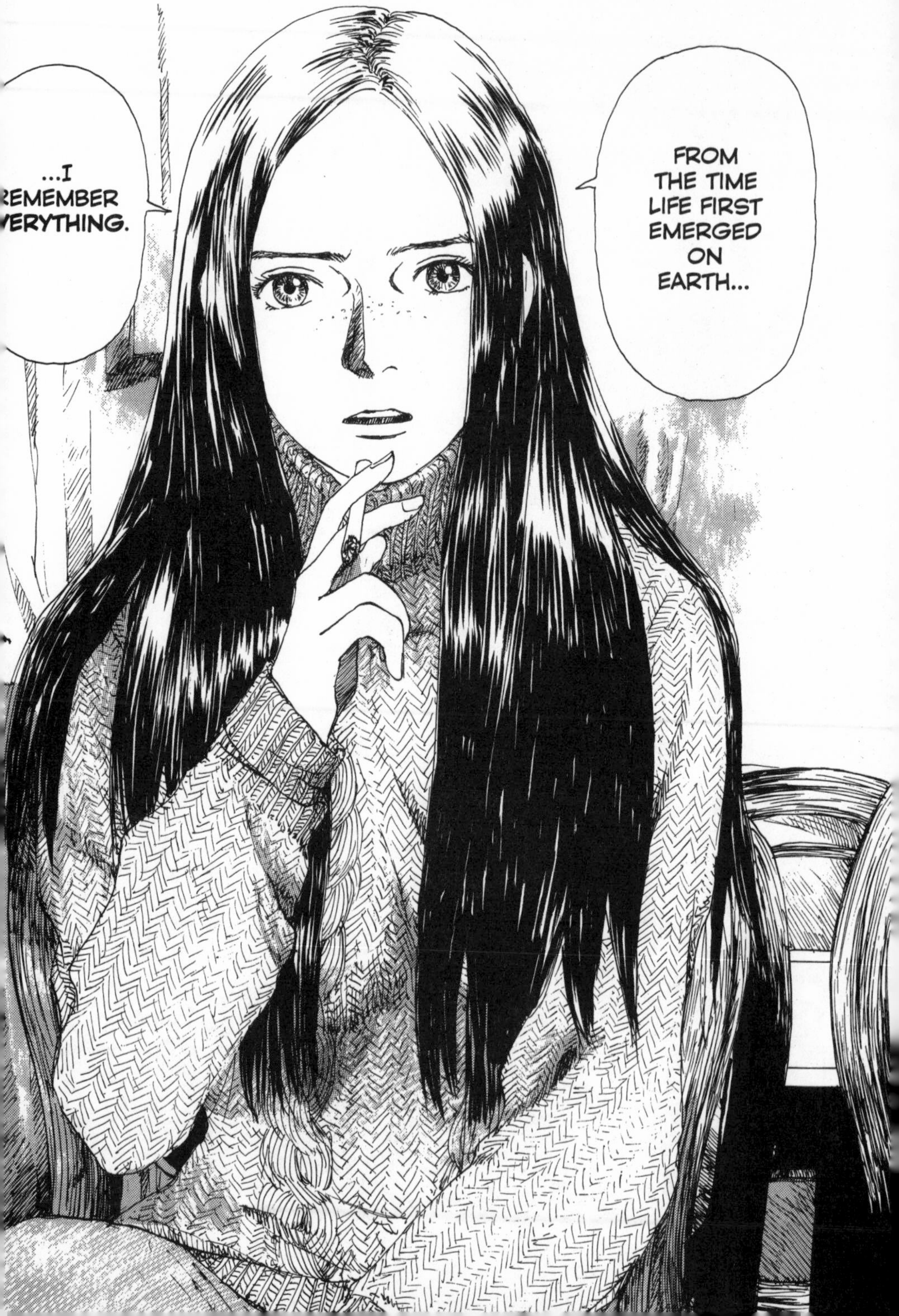
FROM THE TIME LIFE FIRST EMERGED ON EARTH...
...I REMEMBER VERYTHING.

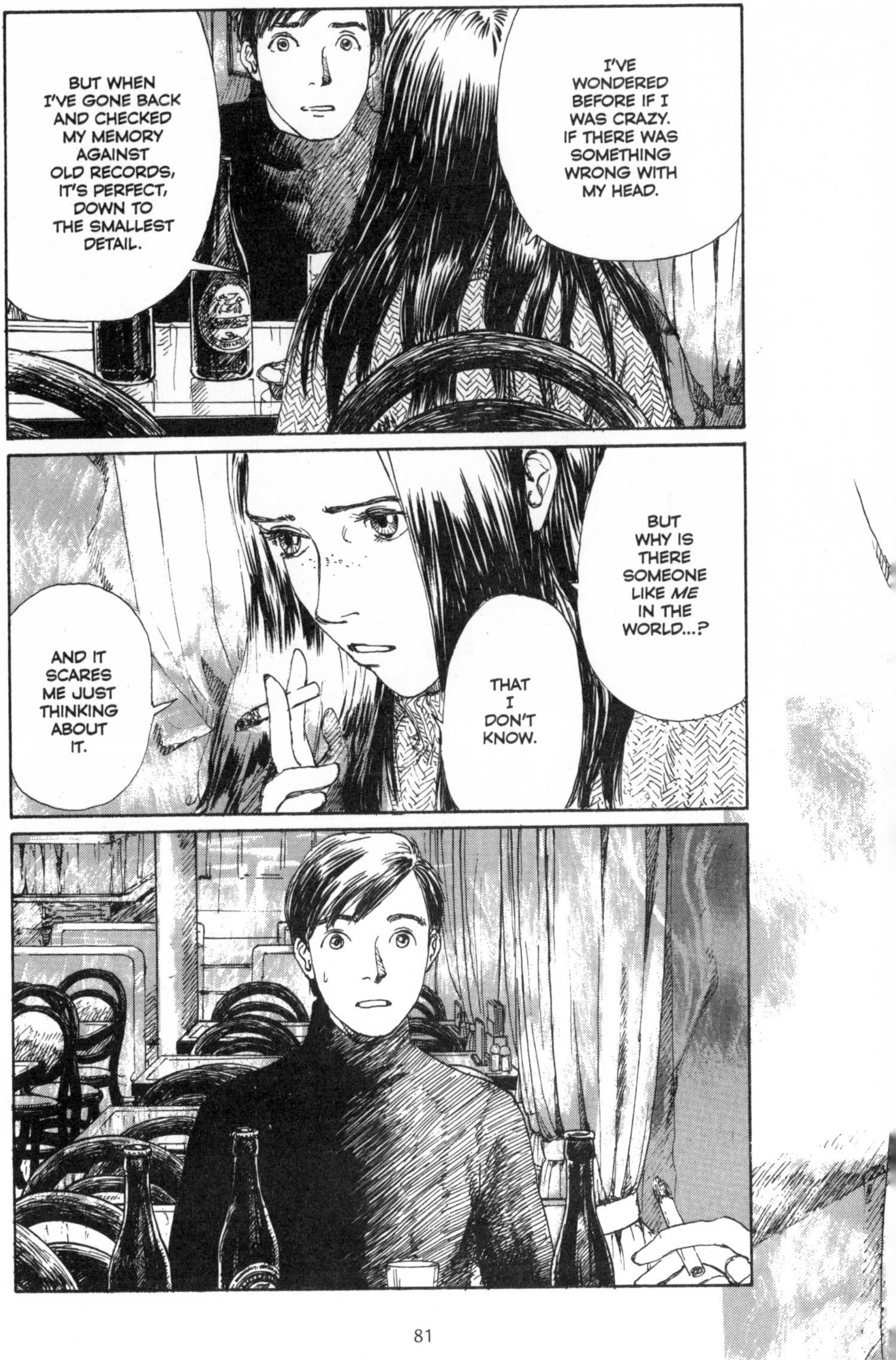
I'VE WONDERED BEFORE IF I WAS CRAZY. IF THERE WAS SOMETHING WRONG WITH MY HEAD.
BUT WHEN I'VE GONE BACK AND CHECKED MY MEMORY AGAINST OLD RECORDS, IT'S PERFECT, DOWN TO THE SMALLEST DETAIL.
BUT WHY IS THERE SOMEONE LIKE *ME* IN THE WORLD...?
THAT I DON'T KNOW.
AND IT SCARES ME JUST THINKING ABOUT IT.

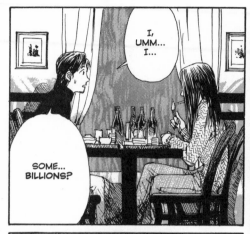

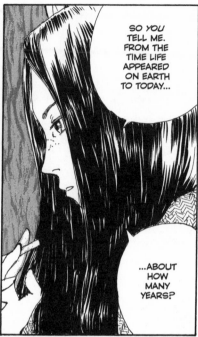

SO *YOU* TELL ME. FROM THE TIME LIFE APPEARED ON EARTH TO TODAY...
...ABOUT HOW MANY YEARS?
I, UMM... I...
SOME... BILLIONS?
RIGHT. BILLIONS. OVER THREE BILLION.
I HAD TO LOOK IT UP, TOO.

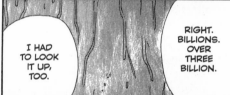

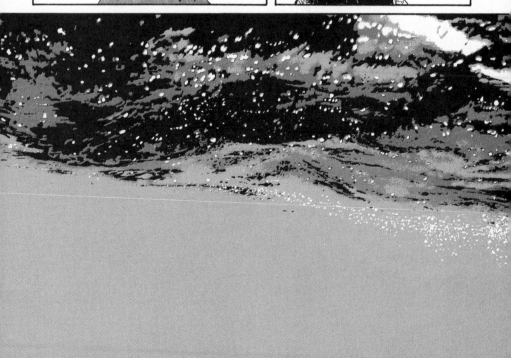

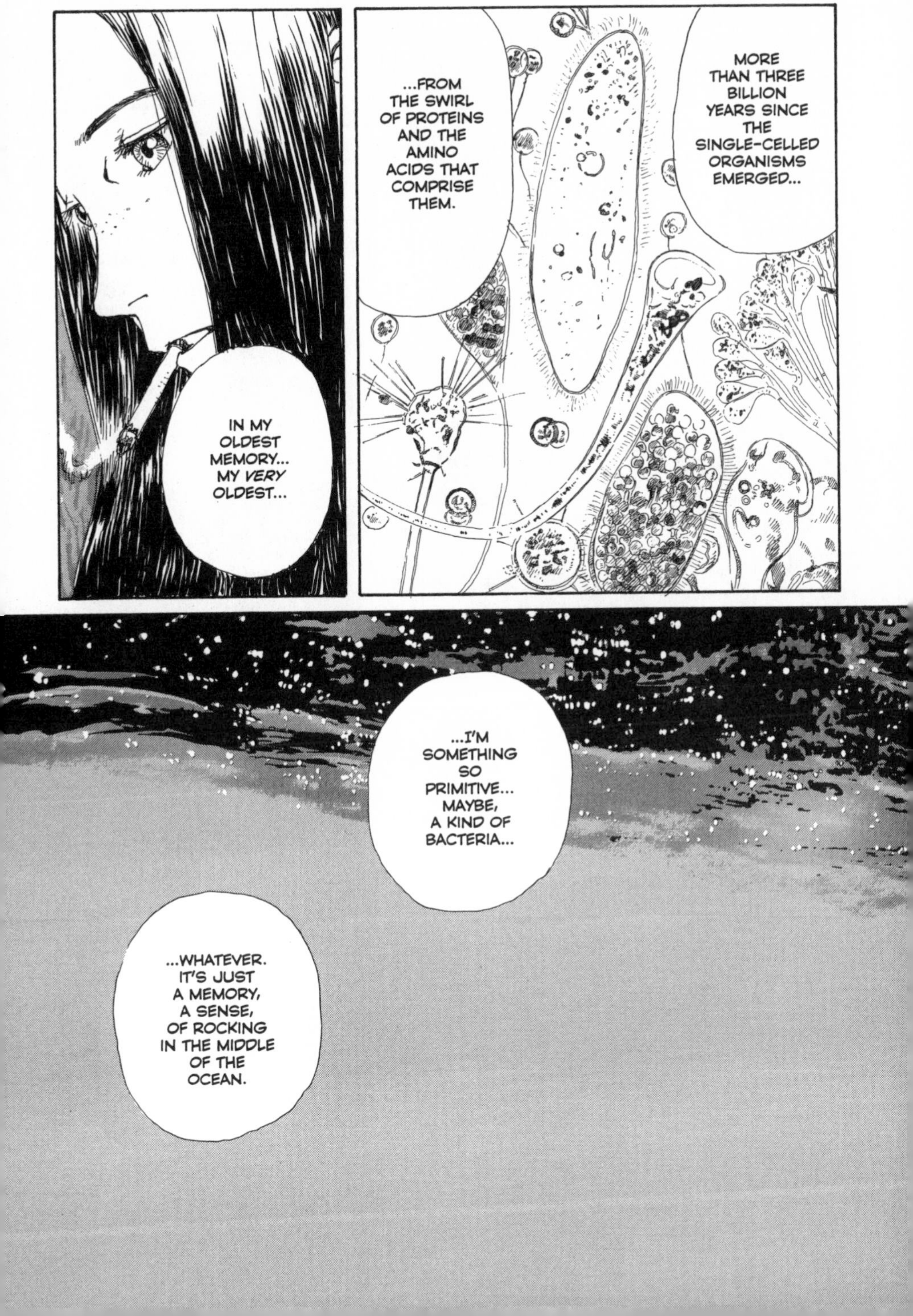
MORE THAN THREE BILLION YEARS SINCE THE SINGLE-CELLED ORGANISMS EMERGED...
...FROM THE SWIRL OF PROTEINS AND THE AMINO ACIDS THAT COMPRISE THEM.
IN MY OLDEST MEMORY... MY *VERY* OLDEST...
...I'M SOMETHING SO PRIMITIVE... MAYBE, A KIND OF BACTERIA...
...WHATEVER. IT'S JUST A MEMORY, A SENSE, OF ROCKING IN THE MIDDLE OF THE OCEAN.

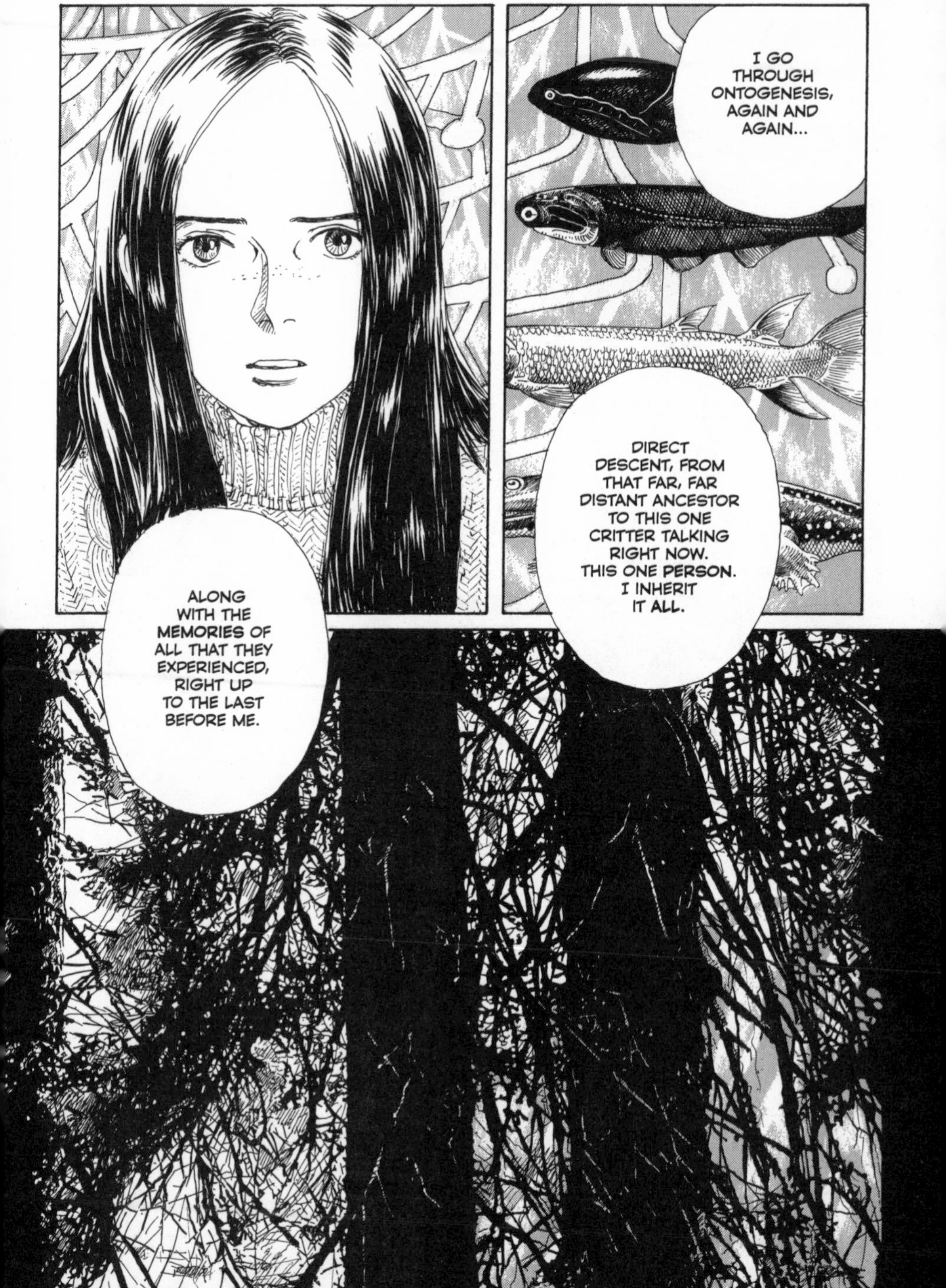
I GO THROUGH ONTOGENESIS, AGAIN AND AGAIN...
DIRECT DESCENT, FROM THAT FAR, FAR DISTANT ANCESTOR TO THIS ONE CRITTER TALKING RIGHT NOW. THIS ONE PERSON. I INHERIT IT ALL.
ALONG WITH THE MEMORIES OF ALL THAT THEY EXPERIENCED, RIGHT UP TO THE LAST BEFORE ME.

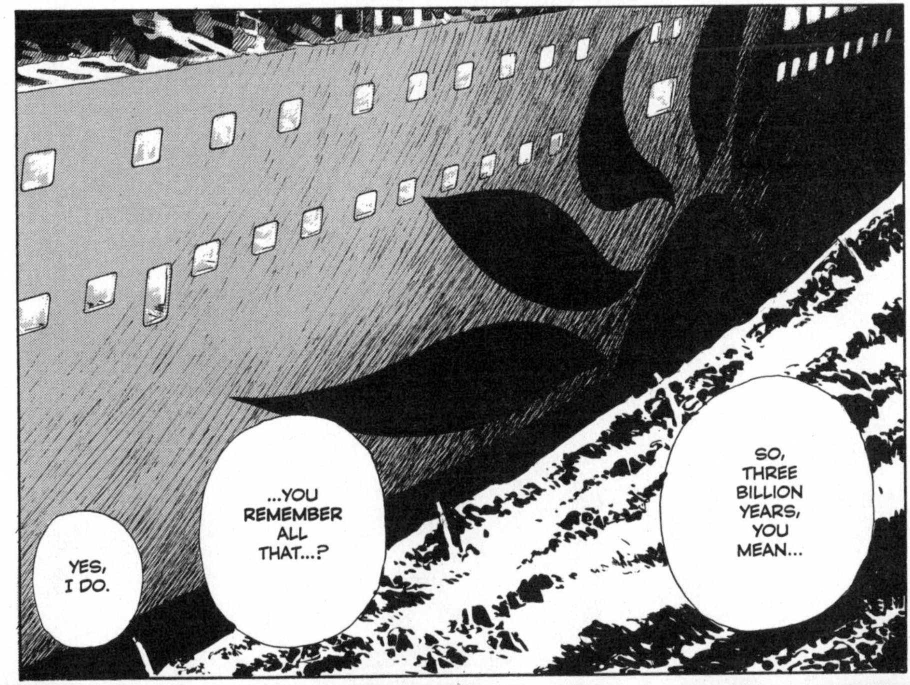
SO, THREE BILLION YEARS, YOU MEAN...
...YOU REMEMBER ALL THAT...?
YES, I DO.
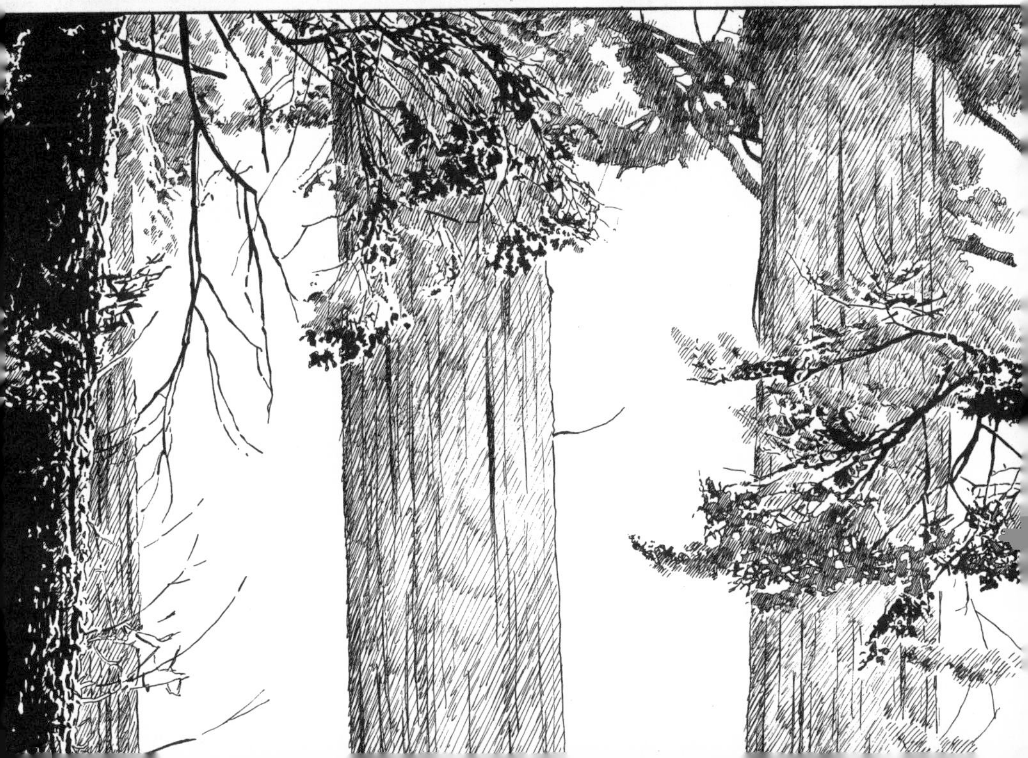

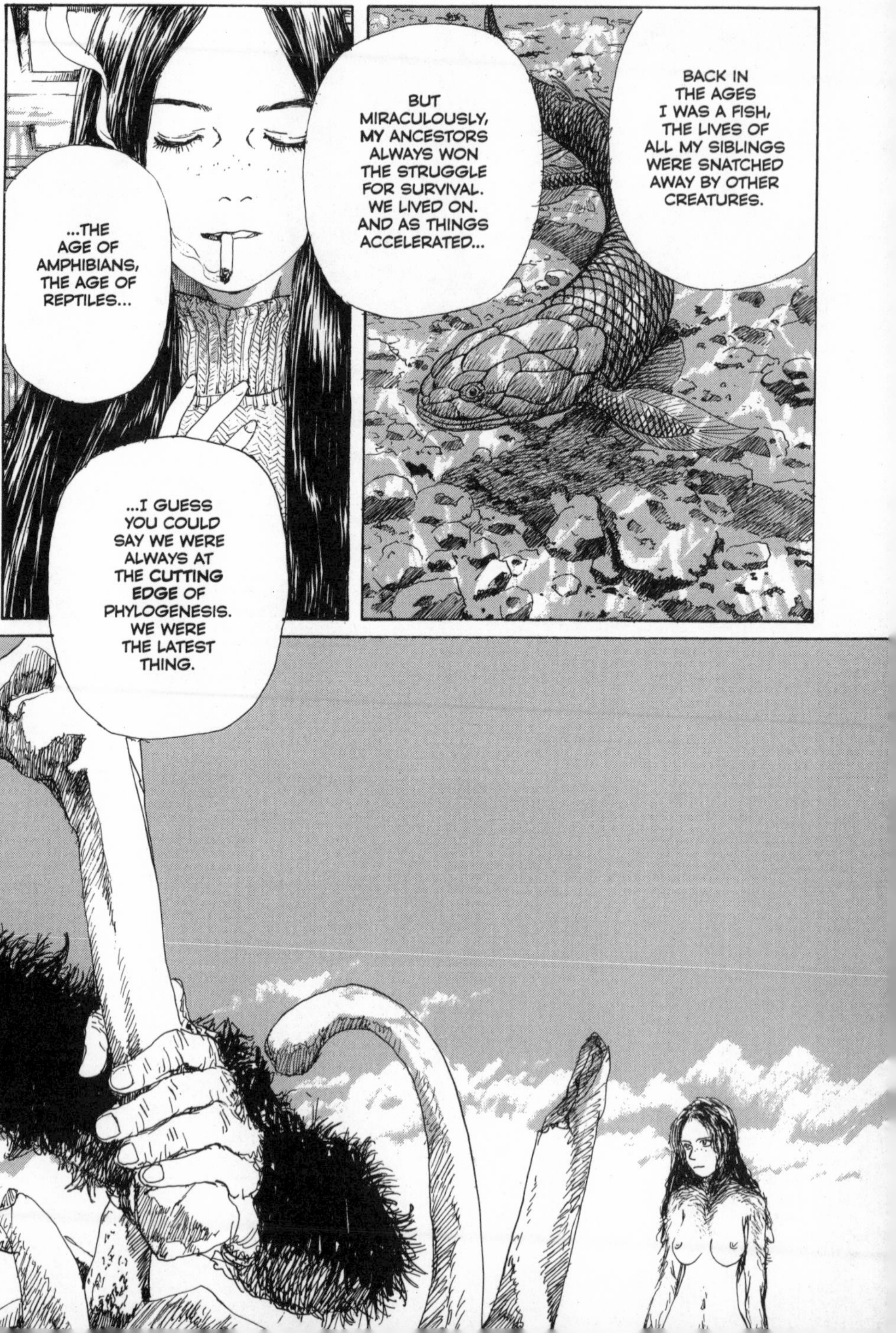
BACK IN THE AGES I WAS A FISH, THE LIVES OF ALL MY SIBLINGS WERE SNATCHED AWAY BY OTHER CREATURES.
BUT MIRACULOUSLY, MY ANCESTORS ALWAYS WON THE STRUGGLE FOR SURVIVAL. WE LIVED ON. AND AS THINGS ACCELERATED...
...THE AGE OF AMPHIBIANS, THE AGE OF REPTILES...
...I GUESS YOU COULD SAY WE WERE ALWAYS AT THE CUTTING EDGE OF PHYLOGENESIS. WE WERE THE LATEST THING.

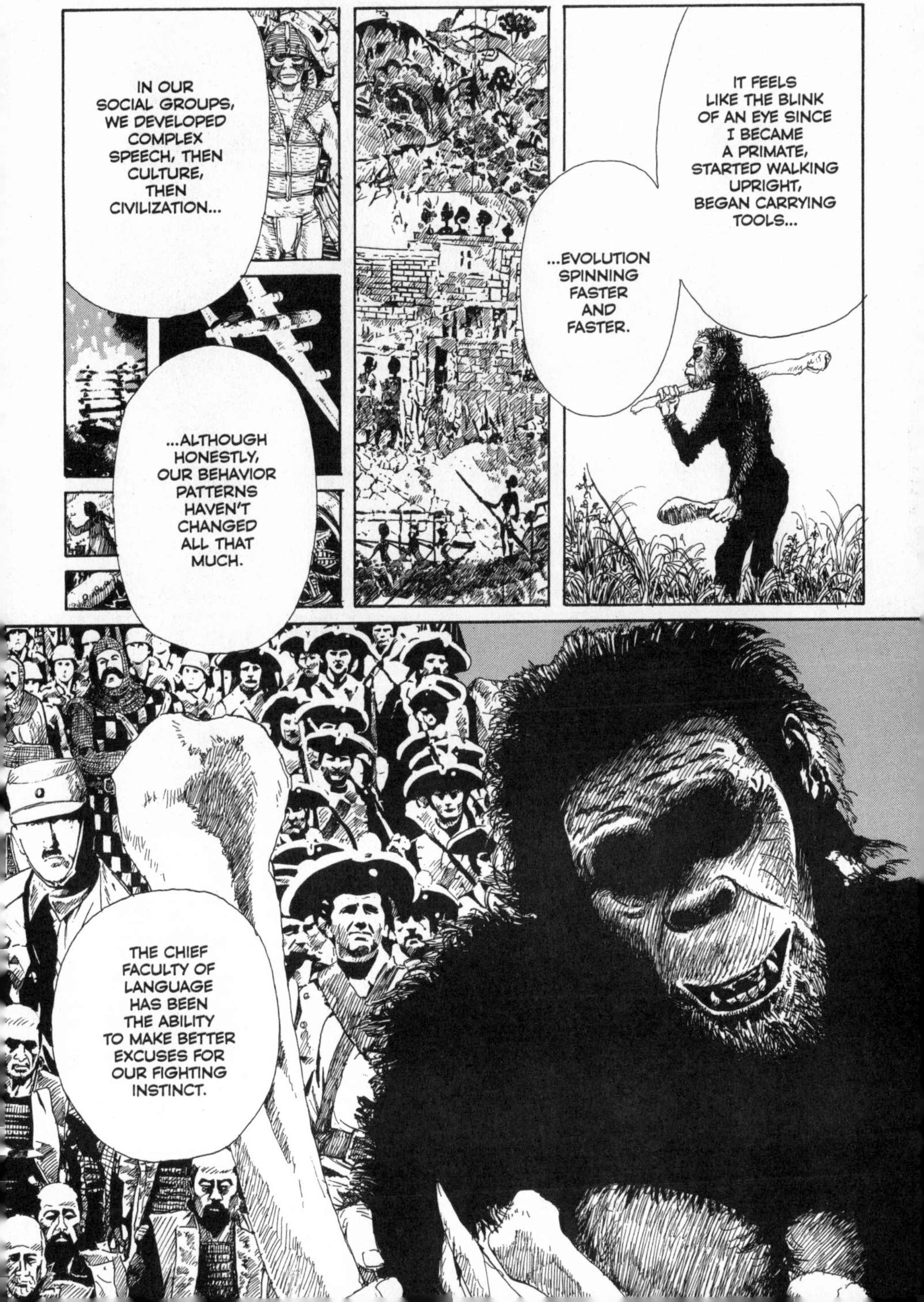
IT FEELS LIKE THE BLINK OF AN EYE SINCE I BECAME A PRIMATE, STARTED WALKING UPRIGHT, BEGAN CARRYING TOOLS...
...EVOLUTION SPINNING FASTER AND FASTER.
IN OUR SOCIAL GROUPS, WE DEVELOPED COMPLEX SPEECH, THEN CULTURE, THEN CIVILIZATION...
...ALTHOUGH HONESTLY, OUR BEHAVIOR PATTERNS HAVEN'T CHANGED ALL THAT MUCH.
THE CHIEF FACULTY OF LANGUAGE HAS BEEN THE ABILITY TO MAKE BETTER EXCUSES FOR OUR FIGHTING INSTINCT.

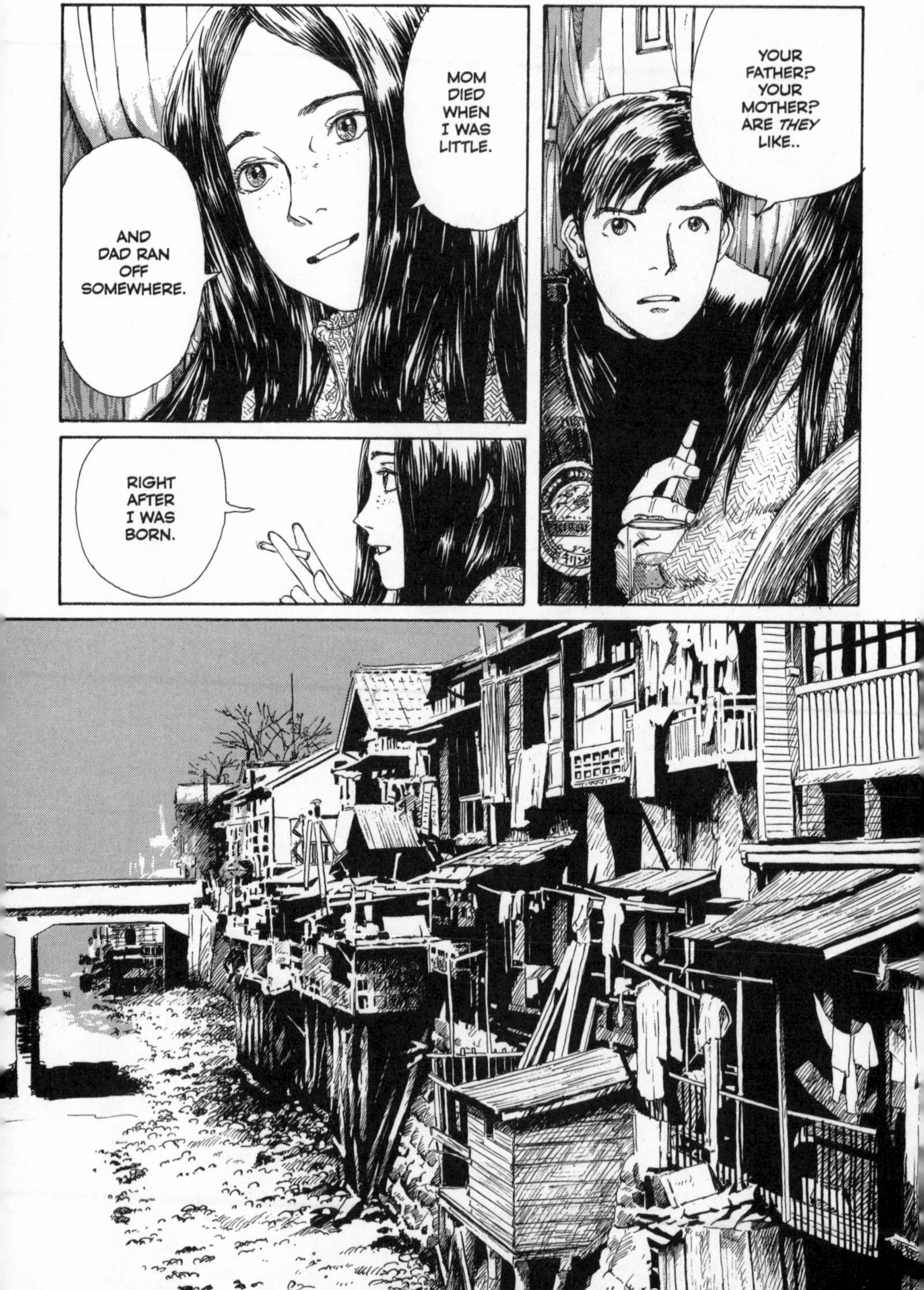
YOUR FATHER? YOUR MOTHER? ARE *THEY* LIKE..
MOM DIED WHEN I WAS LITTLE.
AND DAD RAN OFF SOMEWHERE.
RIGHT AFTER I WAS BORN.

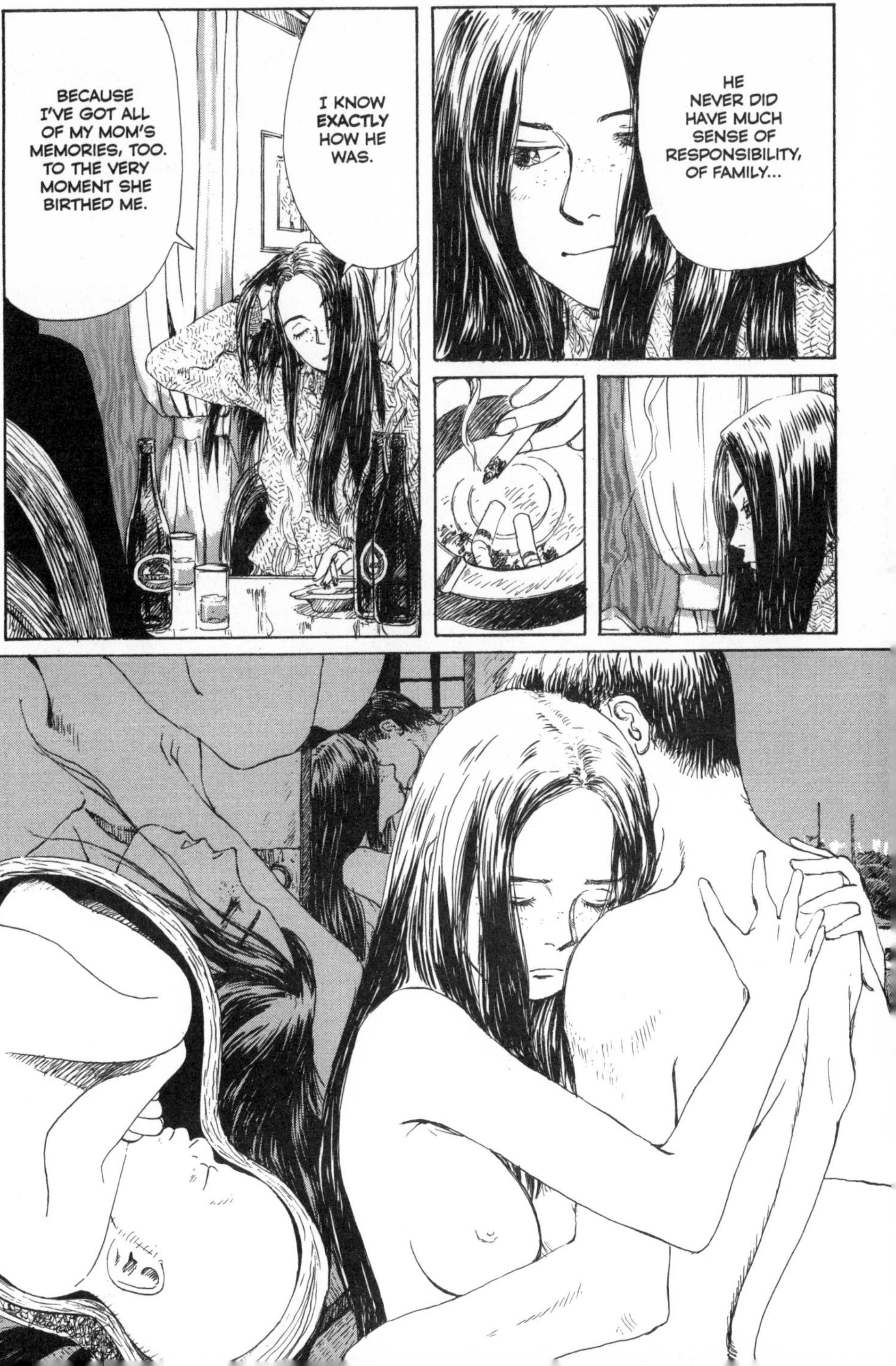
HE NEVER DID HAVE MUCH SENSE OF RESPONSIBILITY, OF FAMILY...
I KNOW EXACTLY HOW HE WAS.
BECAUSE I'VE GOT ALL OF MY MOM'S MEMORIES, TOO. TO THE VERY MOMENT SHE BIRTHED ME.

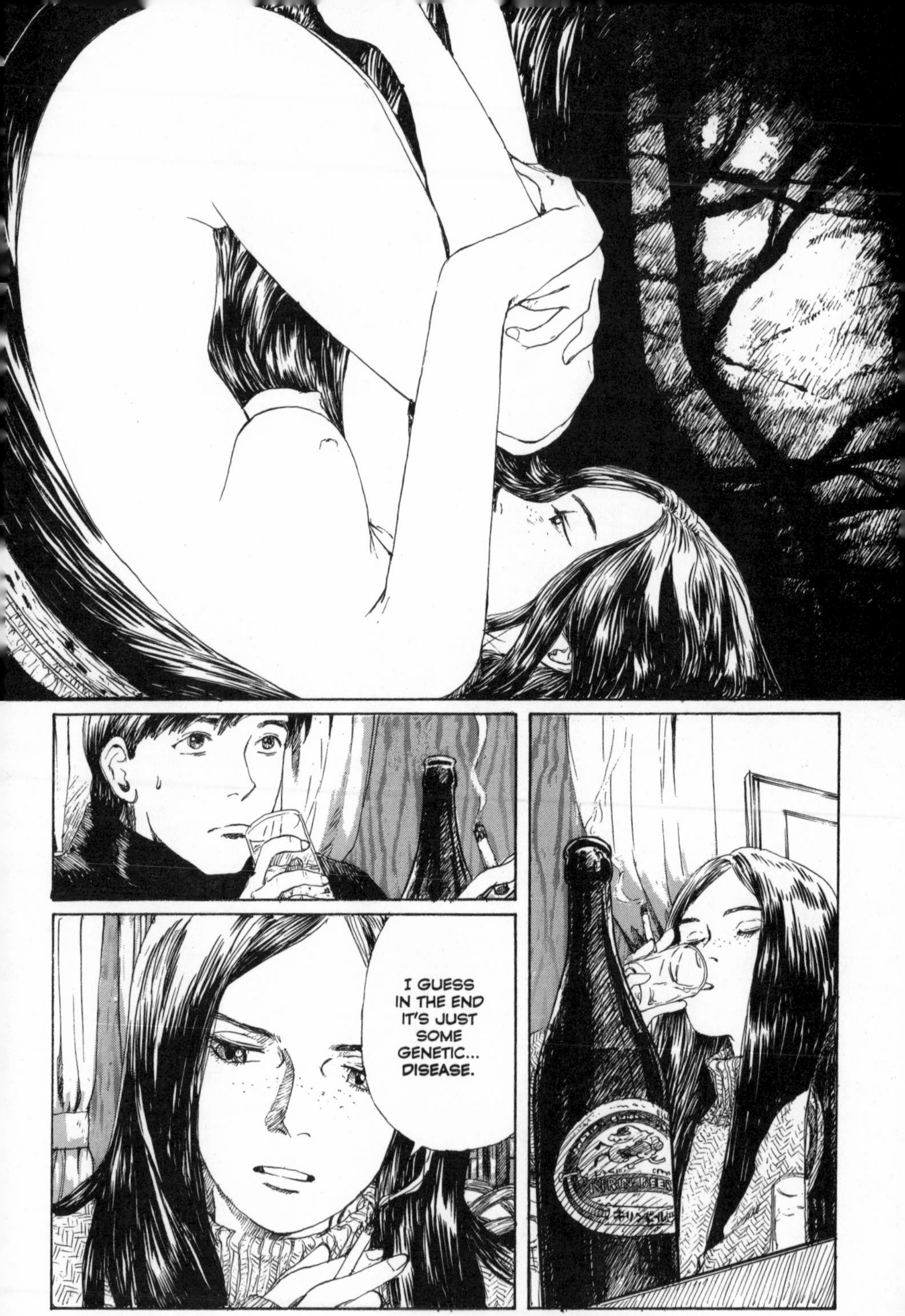
I GUESS IN THE END IT'S JUST SOME GENETIC... DISEASE.

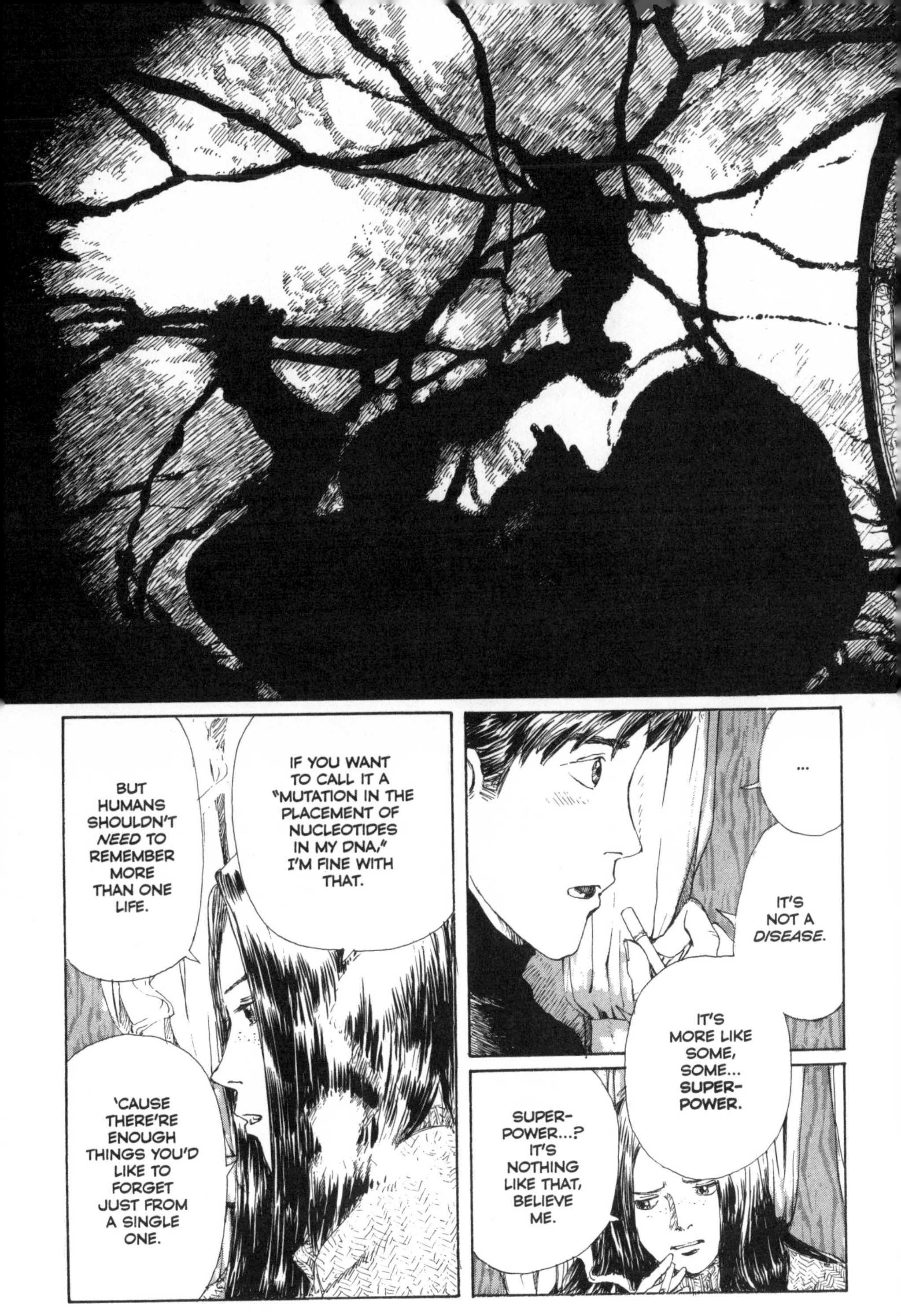
...
IT'S NOT A *DISEASE*.
IT'S MORE LIKE SOME, SOME... SUPER-POWER.
SUPER-POWER...? IT'S NOTHING LIKE THAT, BELIEVE ME.
IF YOU WANT TO CALL IT A "MUTATION IN THE PLACEMENT OF NUCLEOTIDES IN MY DNA," I'M FINE WITH THAT.
BUT HUMANS SHOULDN'T *NEED* TO REMEMBER MORE THAN ONE LIFE.
'CAUSE THERE'RE ENOUGH THINGS YOU'D LIKE TO FORGET JUST FROM A SINGLE ONE.

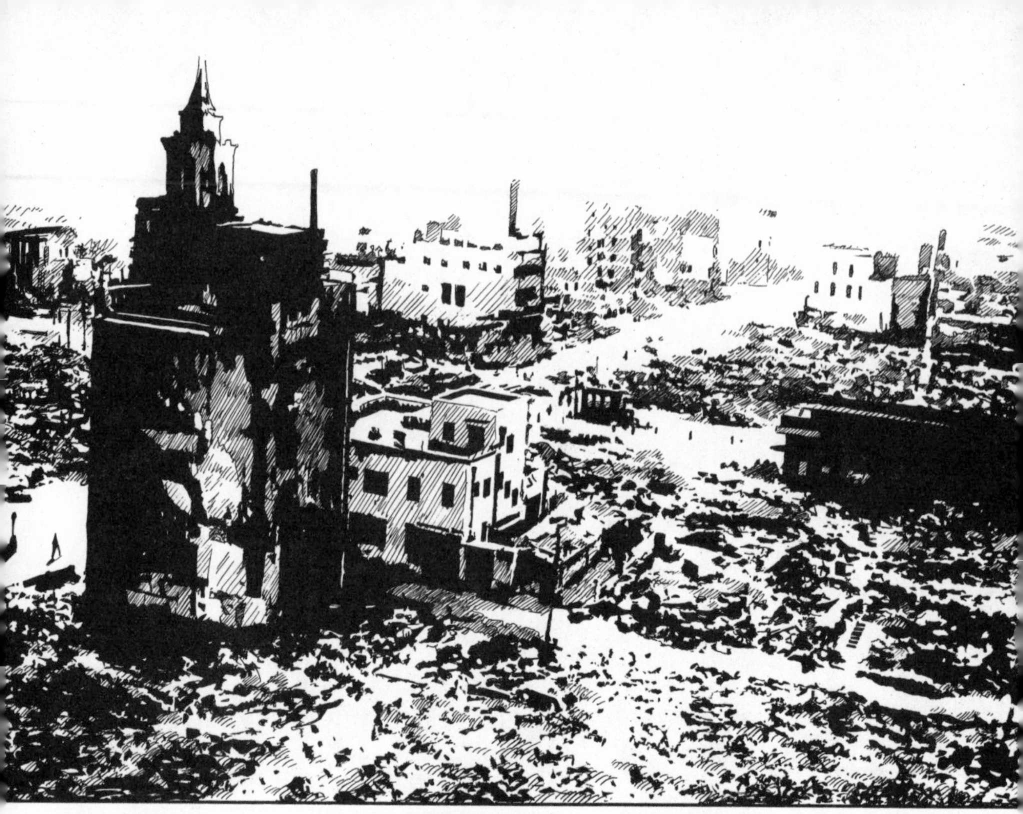

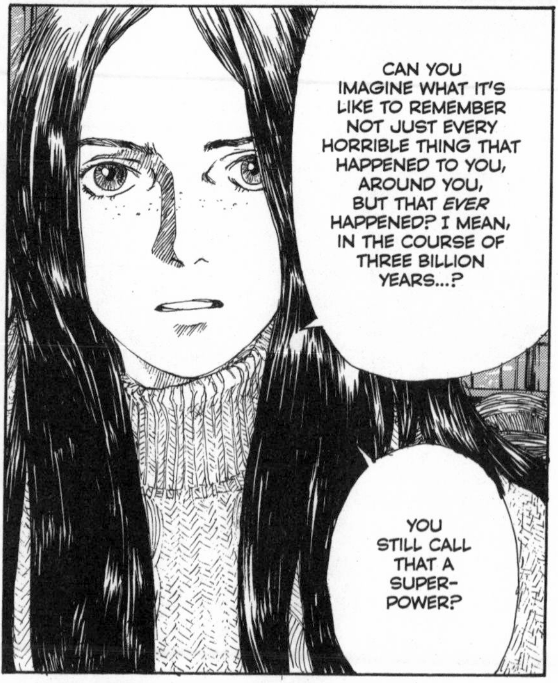
CAN YOU IMAGINE WHAT IT'S LIKE TO REMEMBER NOT JUST EVERY HORRIBLE THING THAT HAPPENED TO YOU, AROUND YOU, BUT THAT *EVER* HAPPENED? I MEAN, IN THE COURSE OF THREE BILLION YEARS...?
YOU STILL CALL THAT A SUPER-POWER?

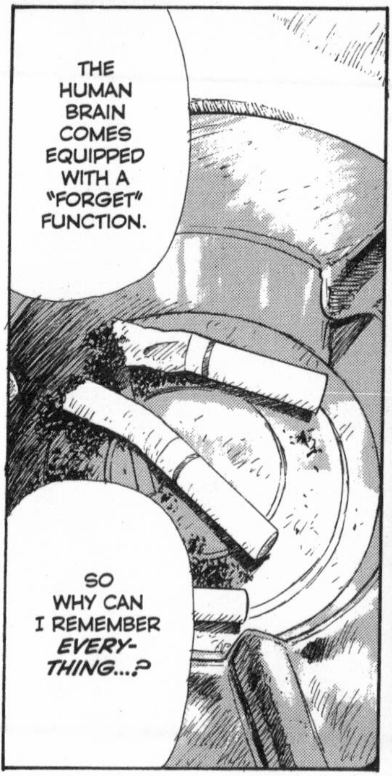
THE HUMAN BRAIN COMES EQUIPPED WITH A "FORGET" FUNCTION.
SO WHY CAN I REMEMBER ***EVERY-THING...?***

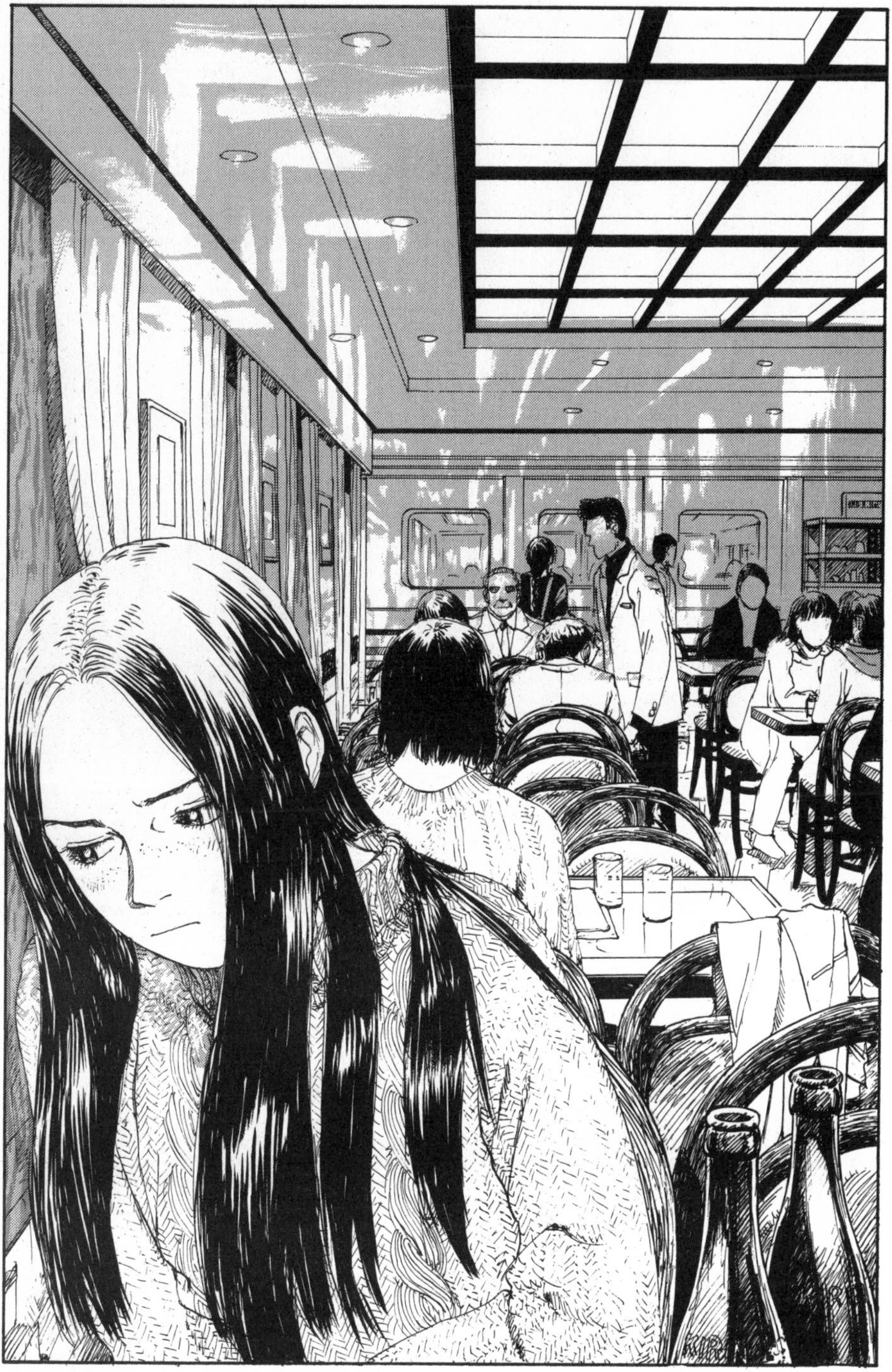

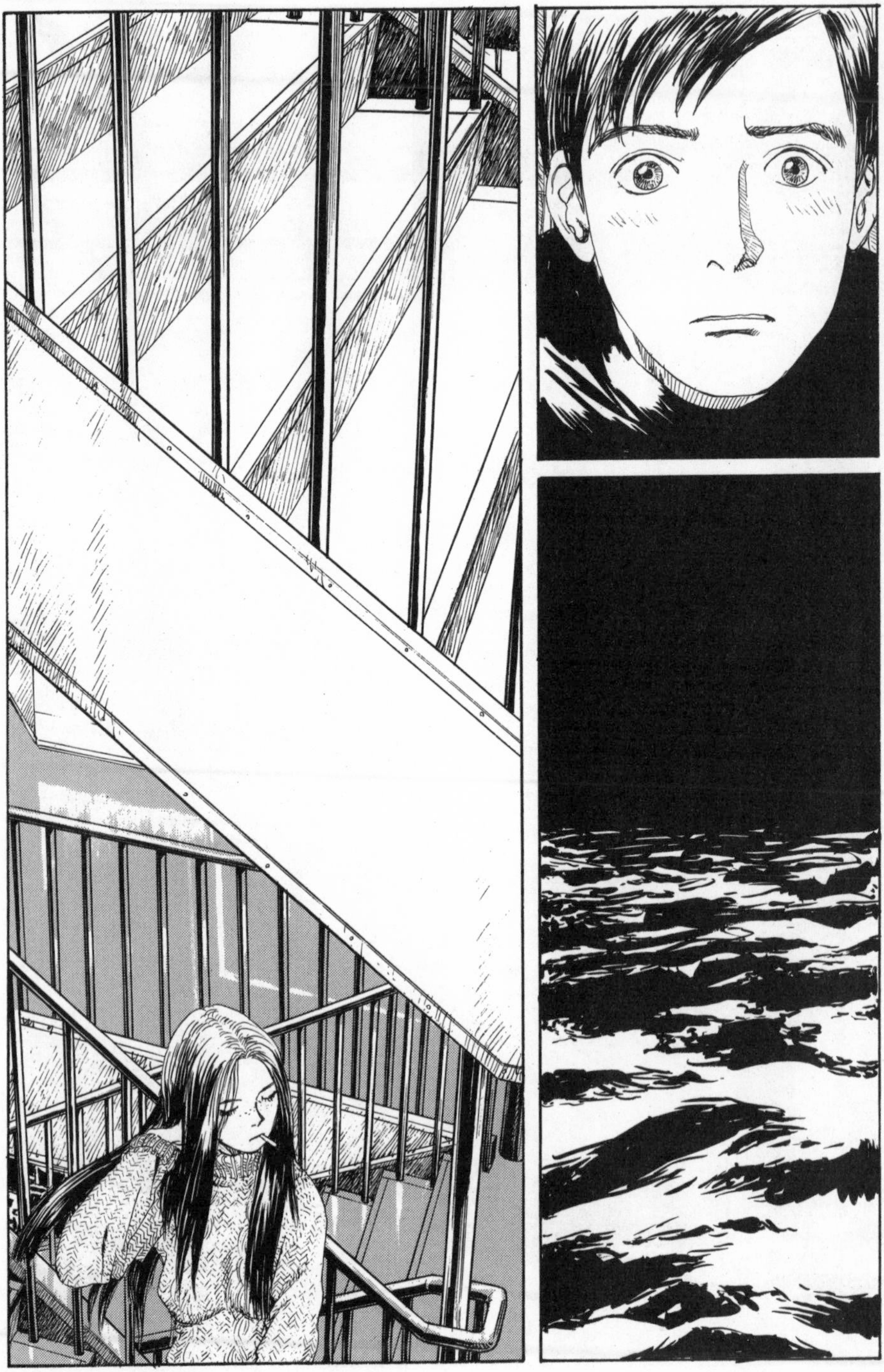

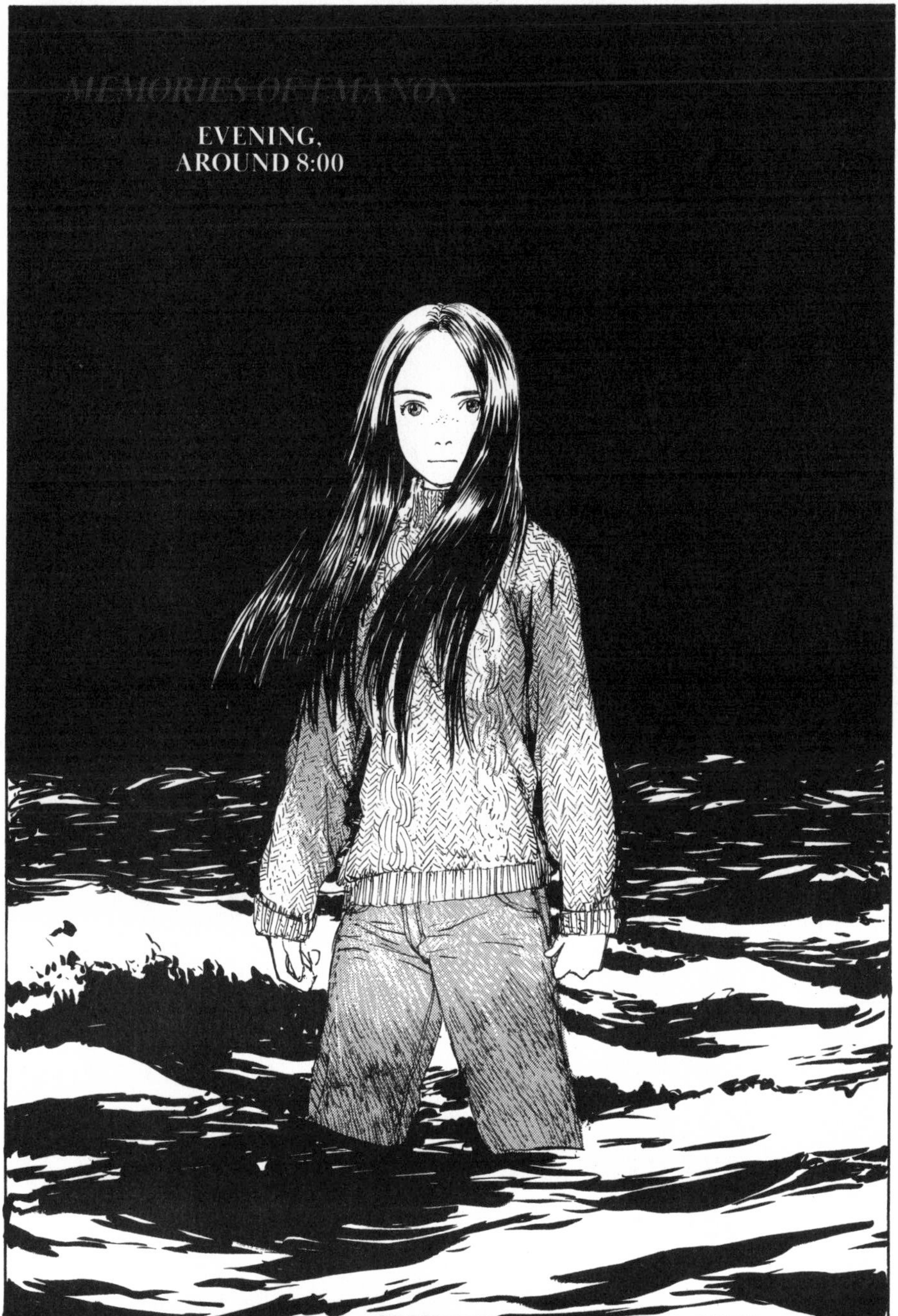
MEMORIES OF EMANON
EVENING, AROUND 8:00

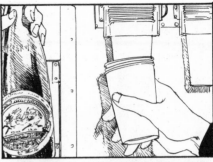

I
TOLD
YOU
BECAUSE...

...I
GUESS,
'CAUSE...

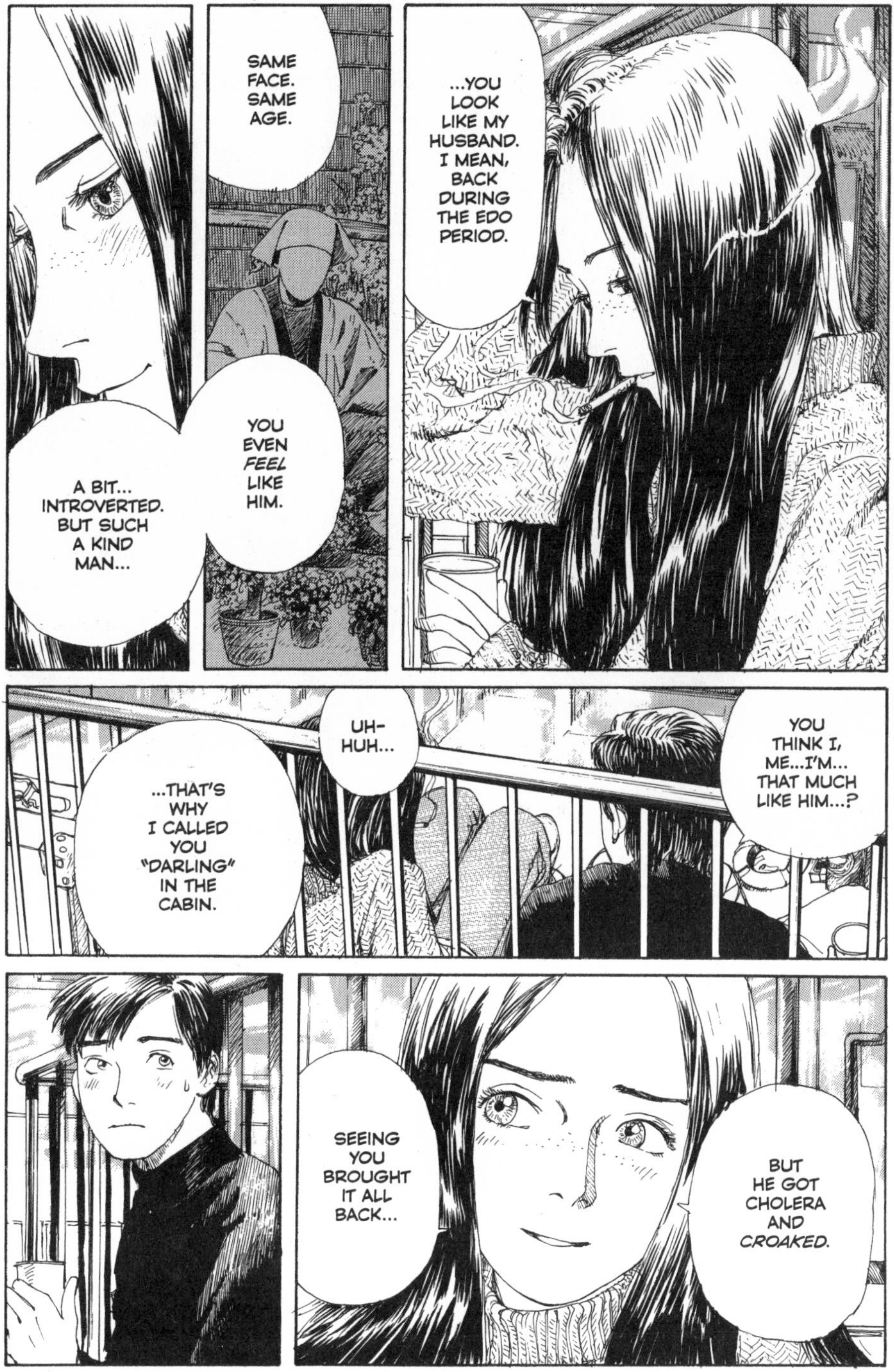
...YOU LOOK LIKE MY HUSBAND. I MEAN, BACK DURING THE EDO PERIOD.
SAME FACE. SAME AGE.
YOU EVEN *FEEL* LIKE HIM.
A BIT... INTROVERTED. BUT SUCH A KIND MAN...
YOU THINK I, ME...I'M... THAT MUCH LIKE HIM...?
UH-HUH...
...THAT'S WHY I CALLED YOU "DARLING" IN THE CABIN.
BUT HE GOT CHOLERA AND *CROAKED.*
SEEING YOU BROUGHT IT ALL BACK...

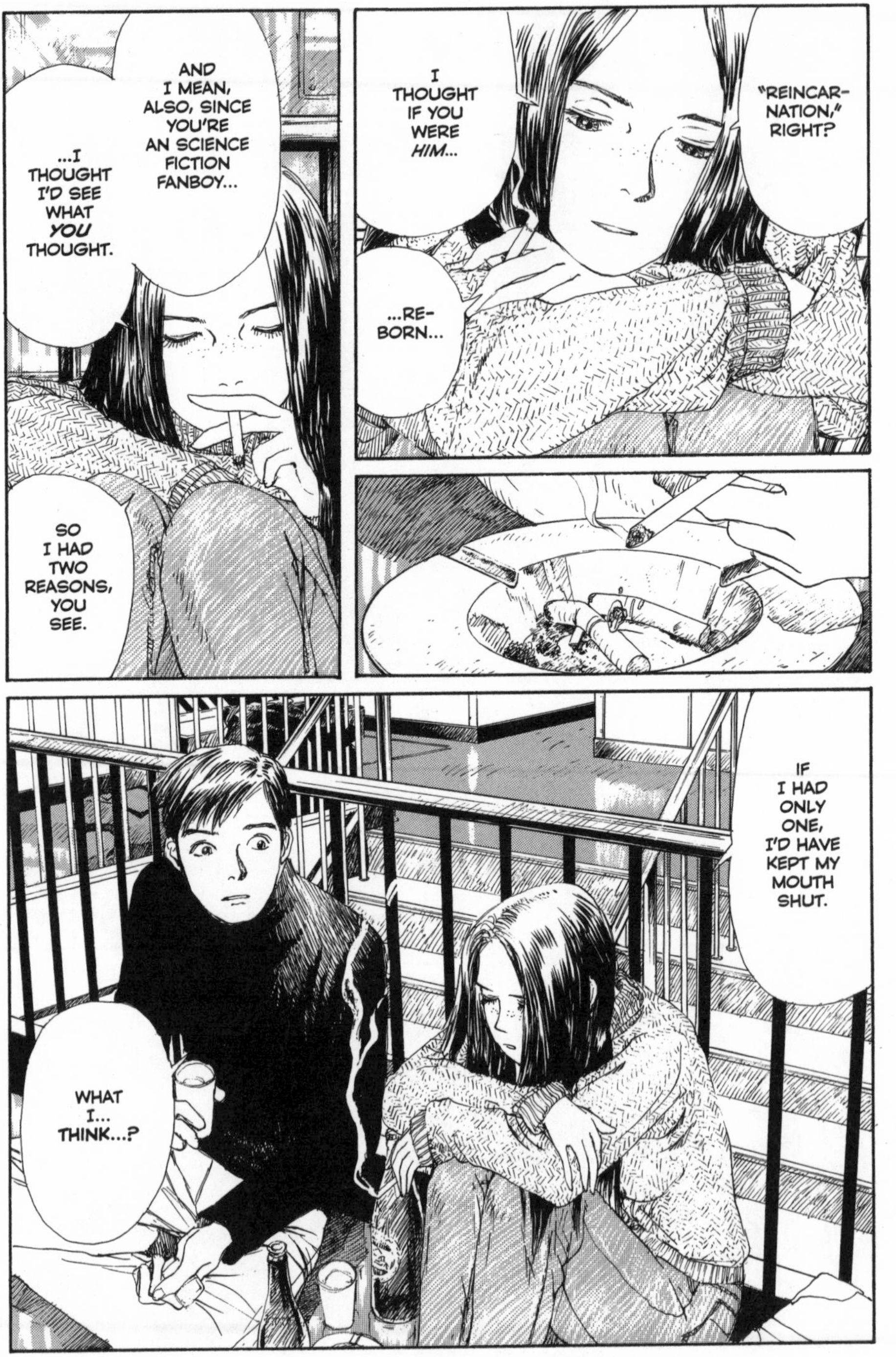
"REINCARNATION," RIGHT?
I THOUGHT IF YOU WERE *HIM*...
...REBORN...
AND I MEAN, ALSO, SINCE YOU'RE AN SCIENCE FICTION FANBOY...
...I THOUGHT I'D SEE WHAT *YOU* THOUGHT.
SO I HAD TWO REASONS, YOU SEE.
IF I HAD ONLY ONE, I'D HAVE KEPT MY MOUTH SHUT.
WHAT I... THINK...?

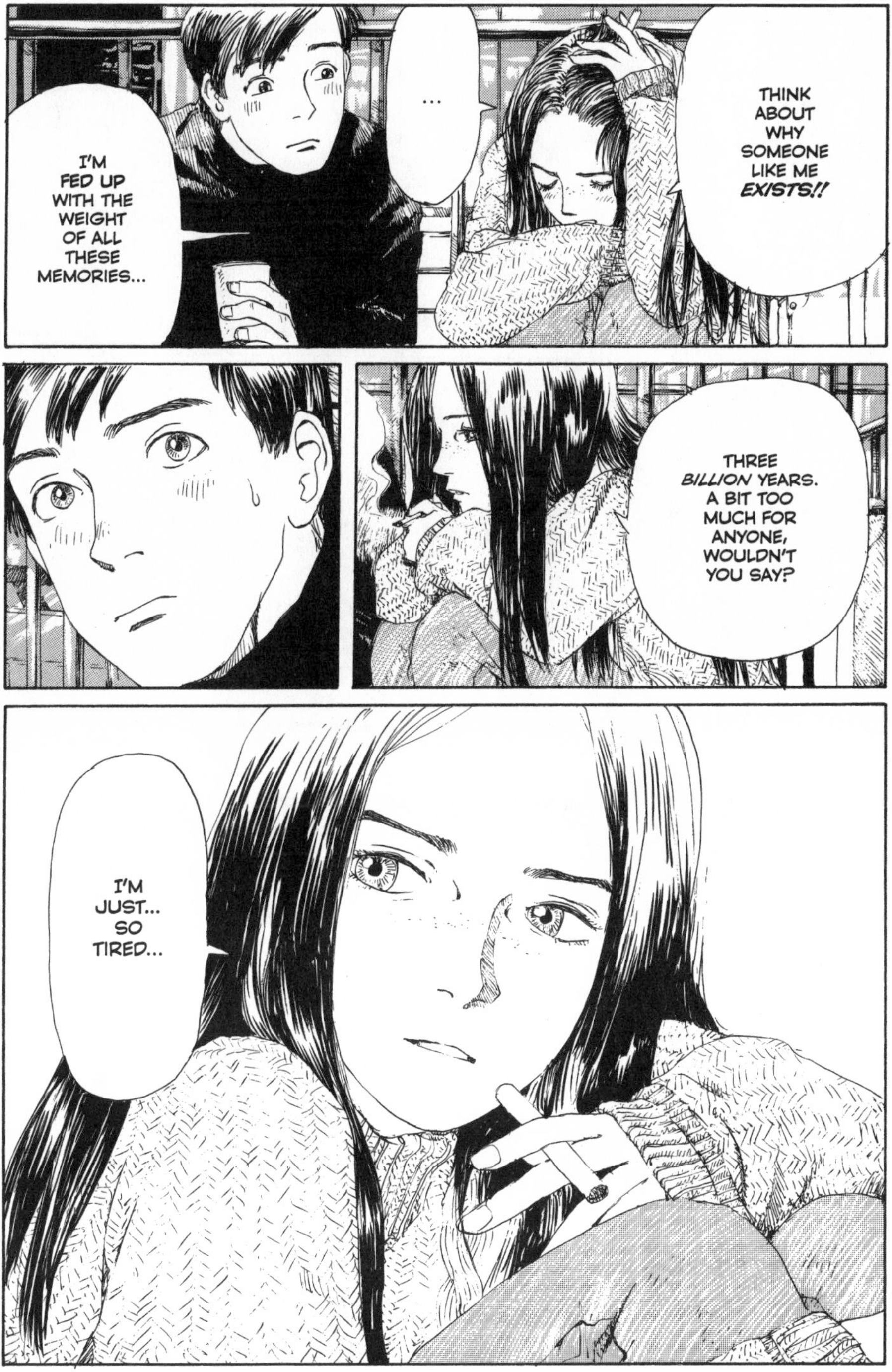
THINK ABOUT WHY SOMEONE LIKE ME *EXISTS!!*
...
I'M FED UP WITH THE WEIGHT OF ALL THESE MEMORIES...
THREE *BILLION* YEARS. A BIT TOO MUCH FOR ANYONE, WOULDN'T YOU SAY?
I'M JUST... SO TIRED...

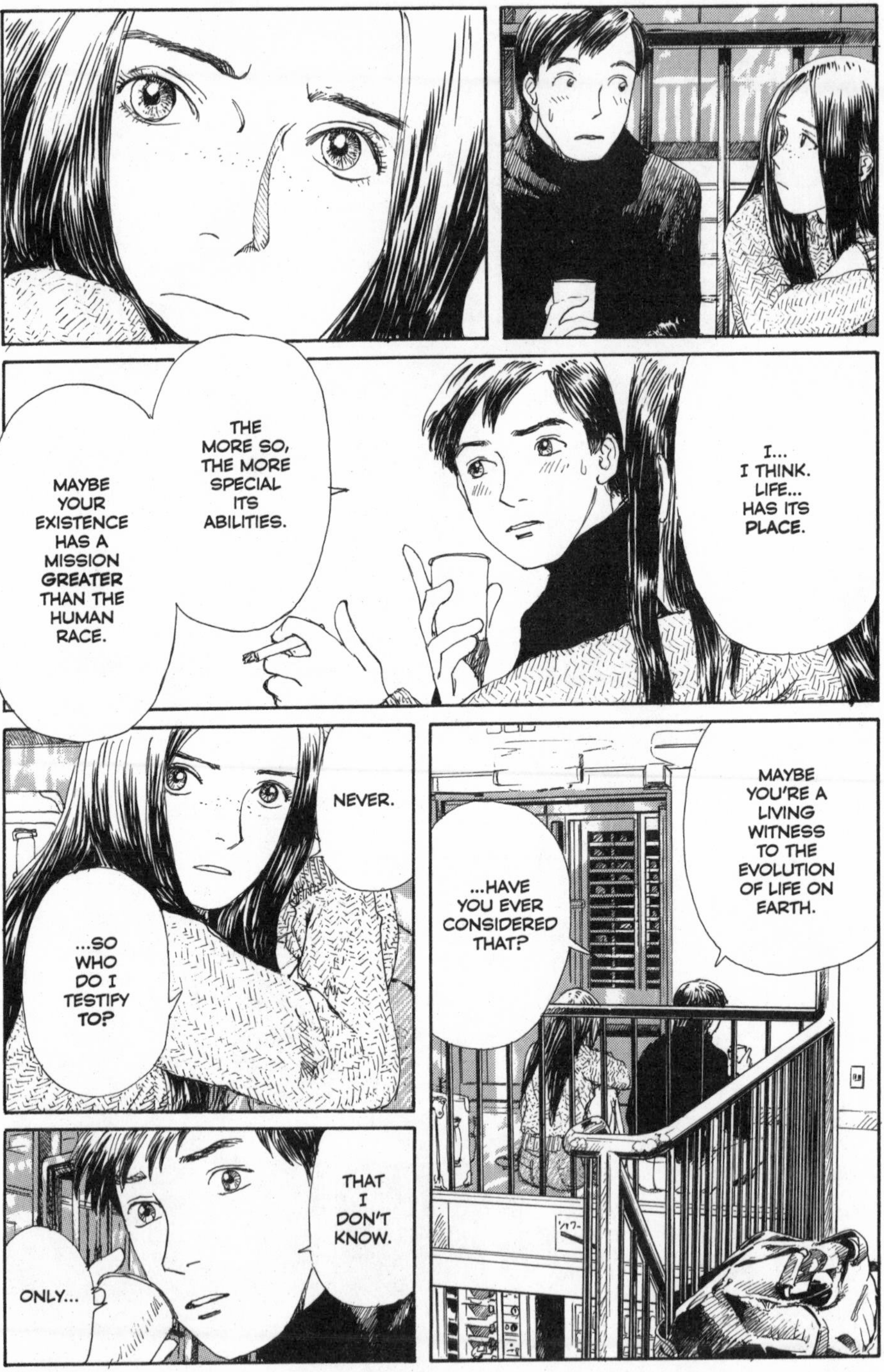
I... I THINK. LIFE... HAS ITS PLACE.
THE MORE SO, THE MORE SPECIAL ITS ABILITIES.
MAYBE YOUR EXISTENCE HAS A MISSION GREATER THAN THE HUMAN RACE.
MAYBE YOU'RE A LIVING WITNESS TO THE EVOLUTION OF LIFE ON EARTH.
...HAVE YOU EVER CONSIDERED THAT?
NEVER.
...SO WHO DO I TESTIFY TO?
THAT I DON'T KNOW.
ONLY...

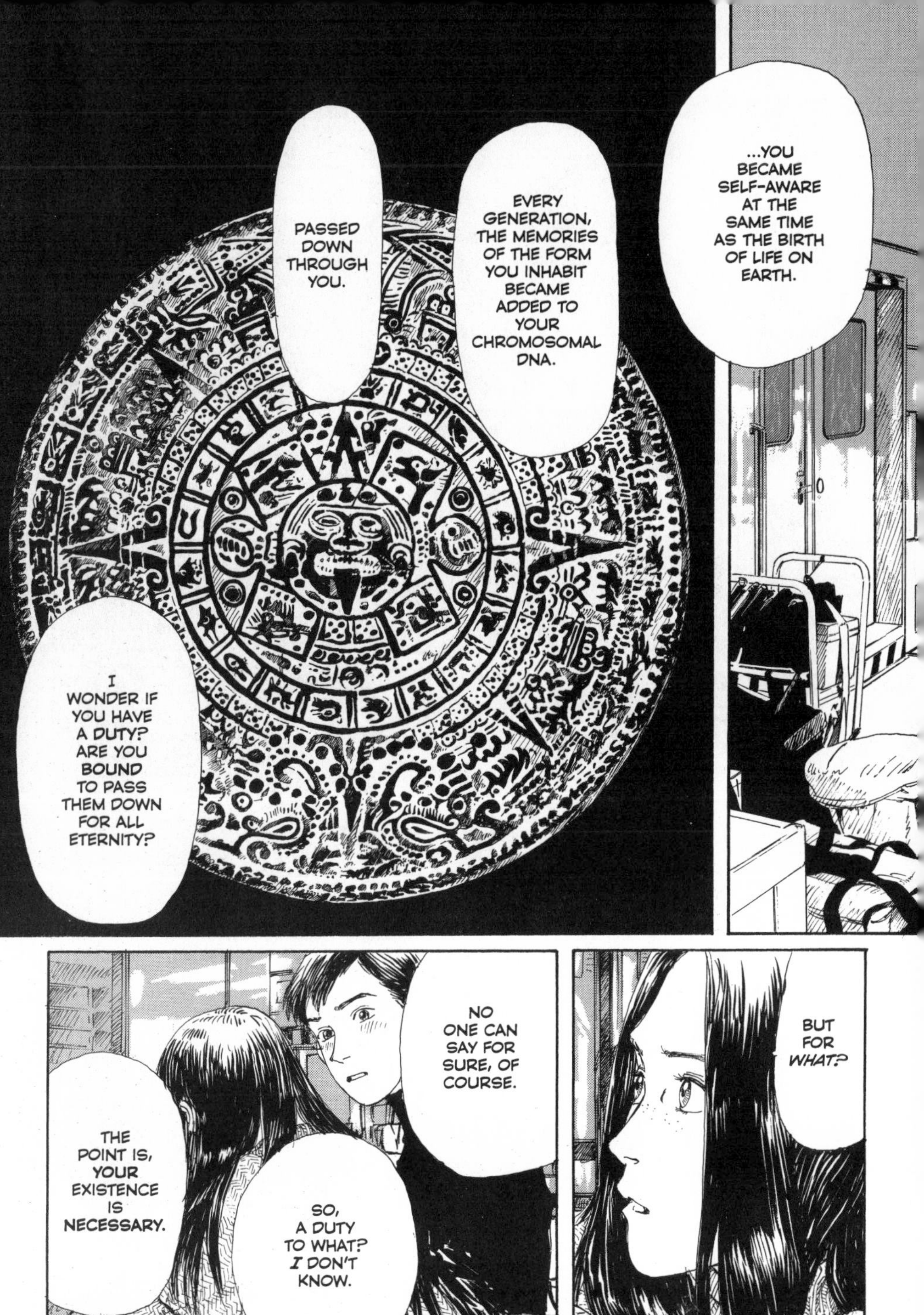
...YOU BECAME SELF-AWARE AT THE SAME TIME AS THE BIRTH OF LIFE ON EARTH.
EVERY GENERATION, THE MEMORIES OF THE FORM YOU INHABIT BECAME ADDED TO YOUR CHROMOSOMAL DNA.
PASSED DOWN THROUGH YOU.
I WONDER IF YOU HAVE A DUTY? ARE YOU BOUND TO PASS THEM DOWN FOR ALL ETERNITY?
BUT FOR *WHAT?*
NO ONE CAN SAY FOR SURE, OF COURSE.
SO, A DUTY TO WHAT? *I* DON'T KNOW.
THE POINT IS, YOUR EXISTENCE IS NECESSARY.

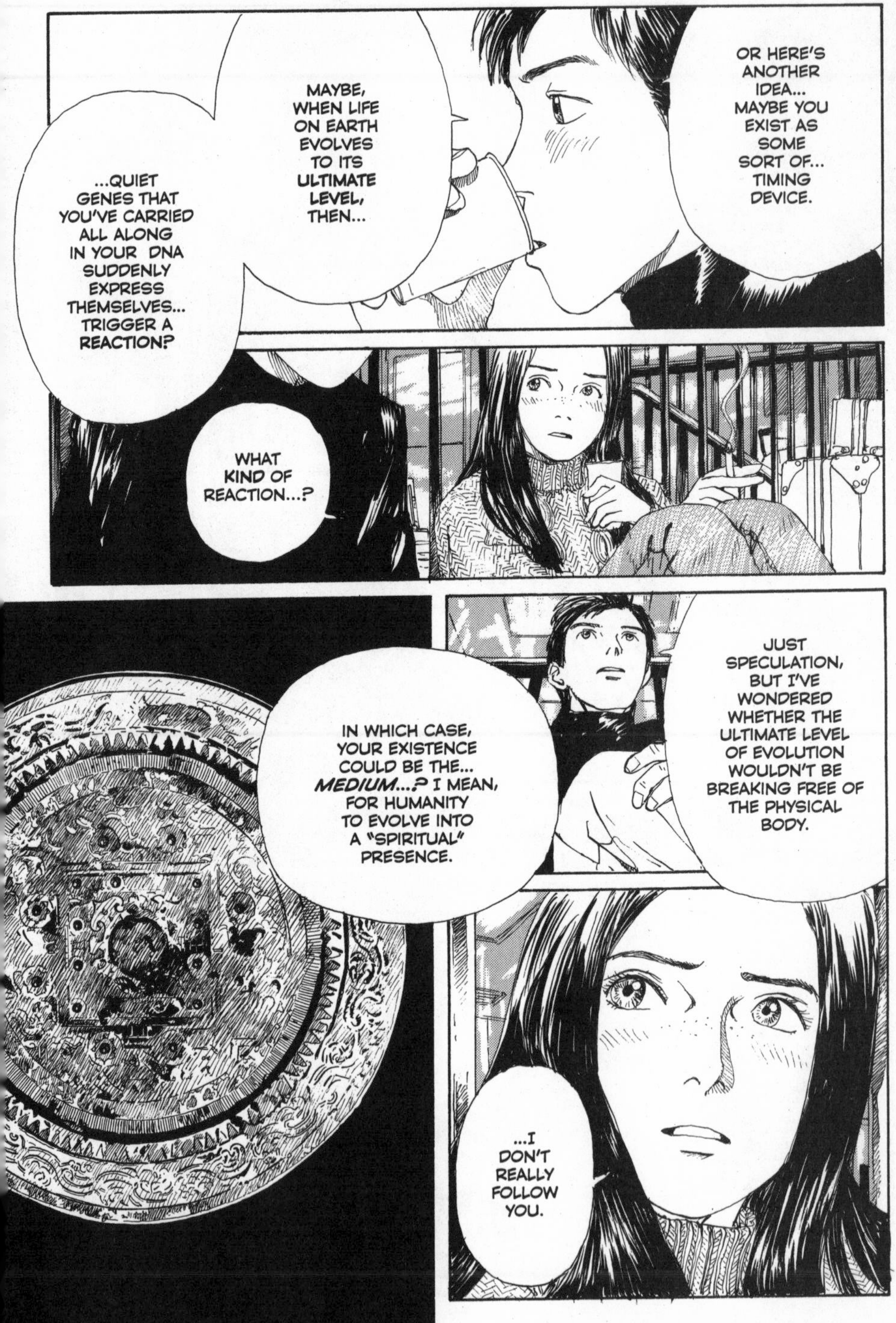
OR HERE'S ANOTHER IDEA... MAYBE YOU EXIST AS SOME SORT OF... TIMING DEVICE.
MAYBE, WHEN LIFE ON EARTH EVOLVES TO ITS ULTIMATE LEVEL, THEN...
...QUIET GENES THAT YOU'VE CARRIED ALL ALONG IN YOUR DNA SUDDENLY EXPRESS THEMSELVES... TRIGGER A REACTION?
WHAT KIND OF REACTION...?
JUST SPECULATION, BUT I'VE WONDERED WHETHER THE ULTIMATE LEVEL OF EVOLUTION WOULDN'T BE BREAKING FREE OF THE PHYSICAL BODY.
IN WHICH CASE, YOUR EXISTENCE COULD BE THE... *MEDIUM...?* I MEAN, FOR HUMANITY TO EVOLVE INTO A "SPIRITUAL" PRESENCE.
...I DON'T REALLY FOLLOW YOU.

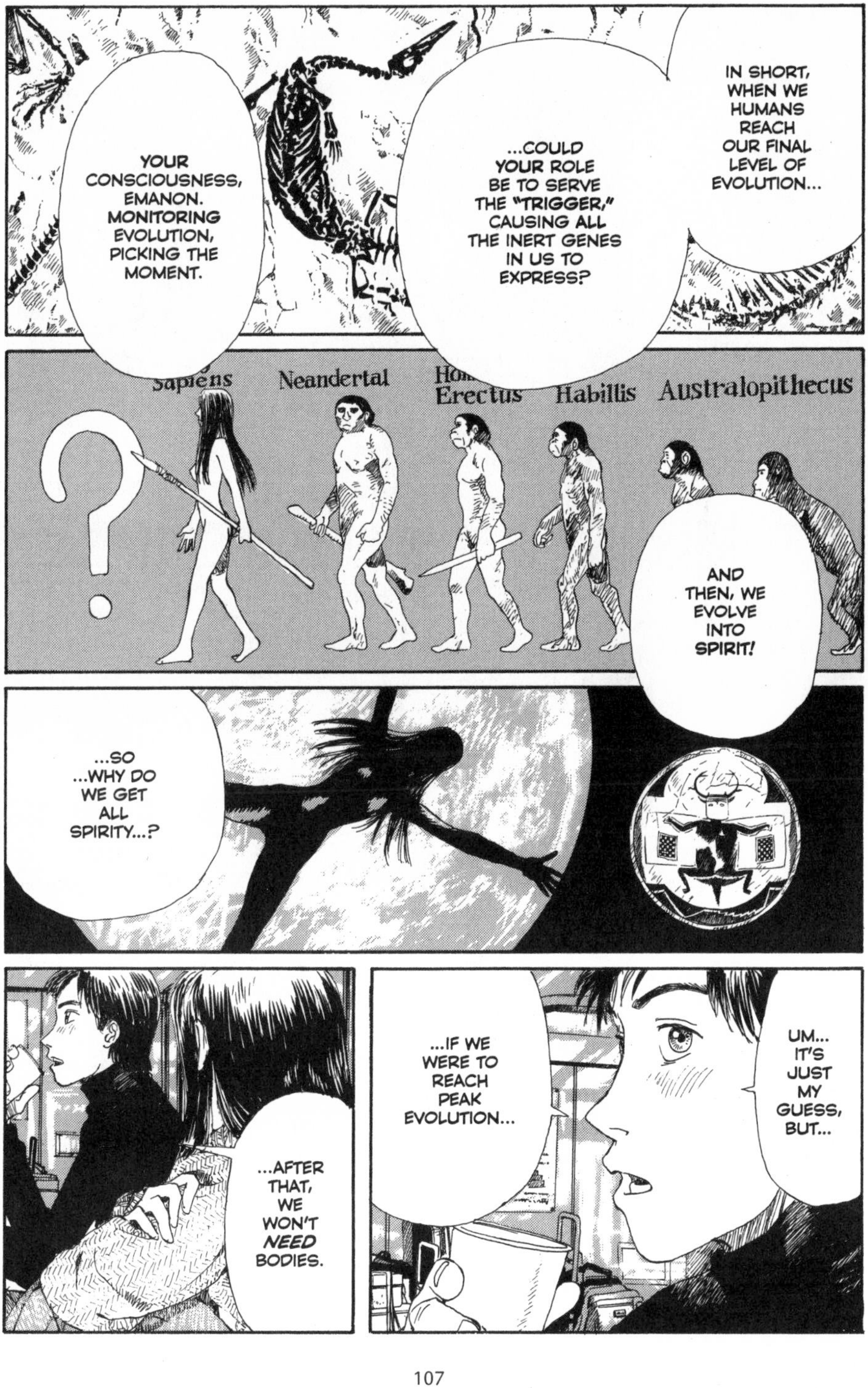
IN SHORT, WHEN WE HUMANS REACH OUR FINAL LEVEL OF EVOLUTION...
...COULD YOUR ROLE BE TO SERVE THE "TRIGGER," CAUSING ALL THE INERT GENES IN US TO EXPRESS?
YOUR CONSCIOUSNESS, EMANON. MONITORING EVOLUTION, PICKING THE MOMENT.
Australopithecus
Habillis
Erectus
Neandertal
Sapiens
AND THEN, WE EVOLVE INTO SPIRIT!
...SO ...WHY DO WE GET ALL SPIRITY...?
UM... IT'S JUST MY GUESS, BUT...
...IF WE WERE TO REACH PEAK EVOLUTION...
...AFTER THAT, WE WON'T *NEED* BODIES.

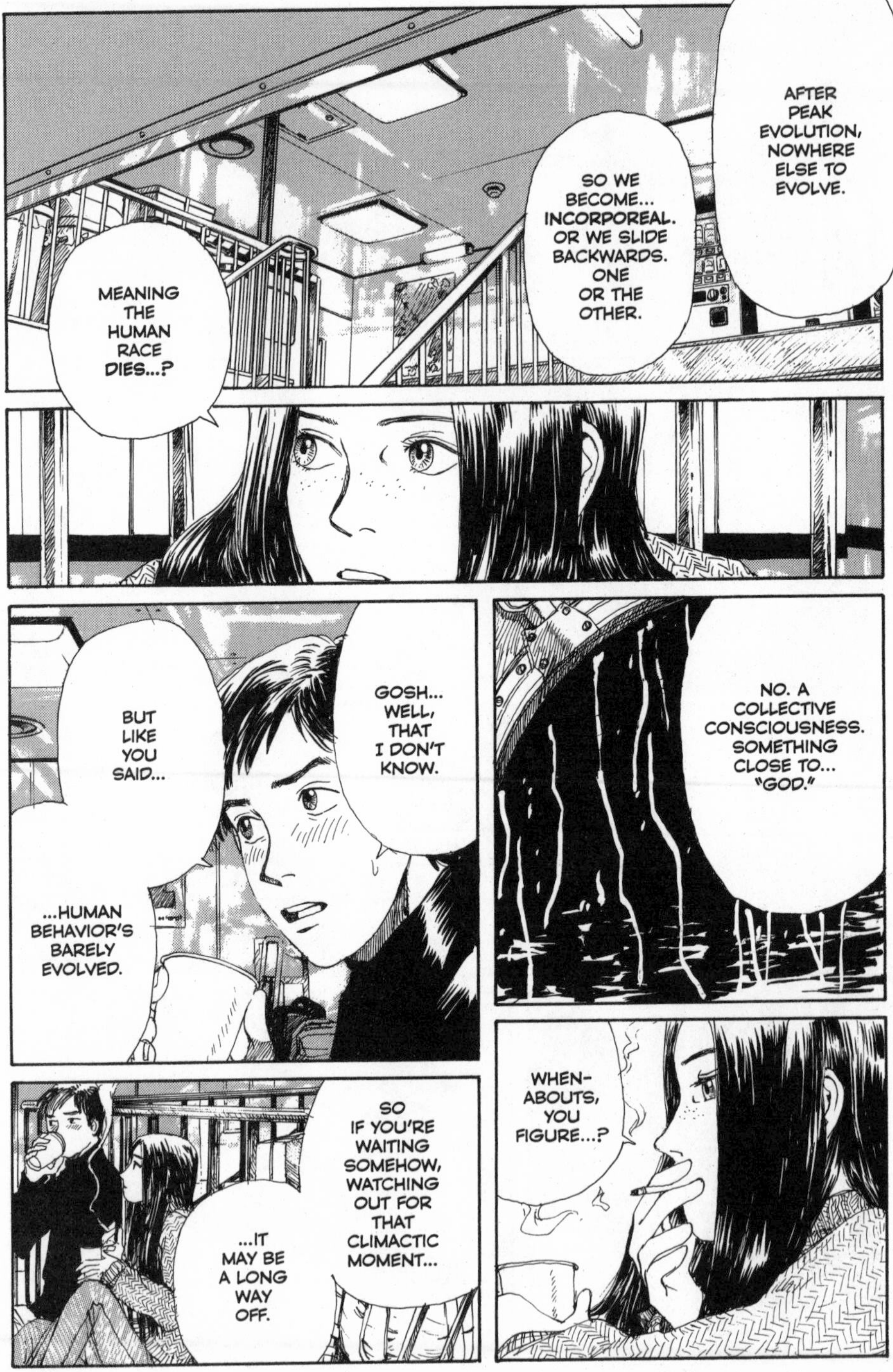
AFTER PEAK EVOLUTION, NOWHERE ELSE TO EVOLVE.
SO WE BECOME... INCORPOREAL. OR WE SLIDE BACKWARDS. ONE OR THE OTHER.
MEANING THE HUMAN RACE DIES...?
NO. A COLLECTIVE CONSCIOUSNESS. SOMETHING CLOSE TO... "GOD."
GOSH... WELL, THAT I DON'T KNOW.
BUT LIKE YOU SAID...
...HUMAN BEHAVIOR'S BARELY EVOLVED.
WHEN-ABOUTS, YOU FIGURE...?
SO IF YOU'RE WAITING SOMEHOW, WATCHING OUT FOR THAT CLIMACTIC MOMENT...
...IT MAY BE A LONG WAY OFF.

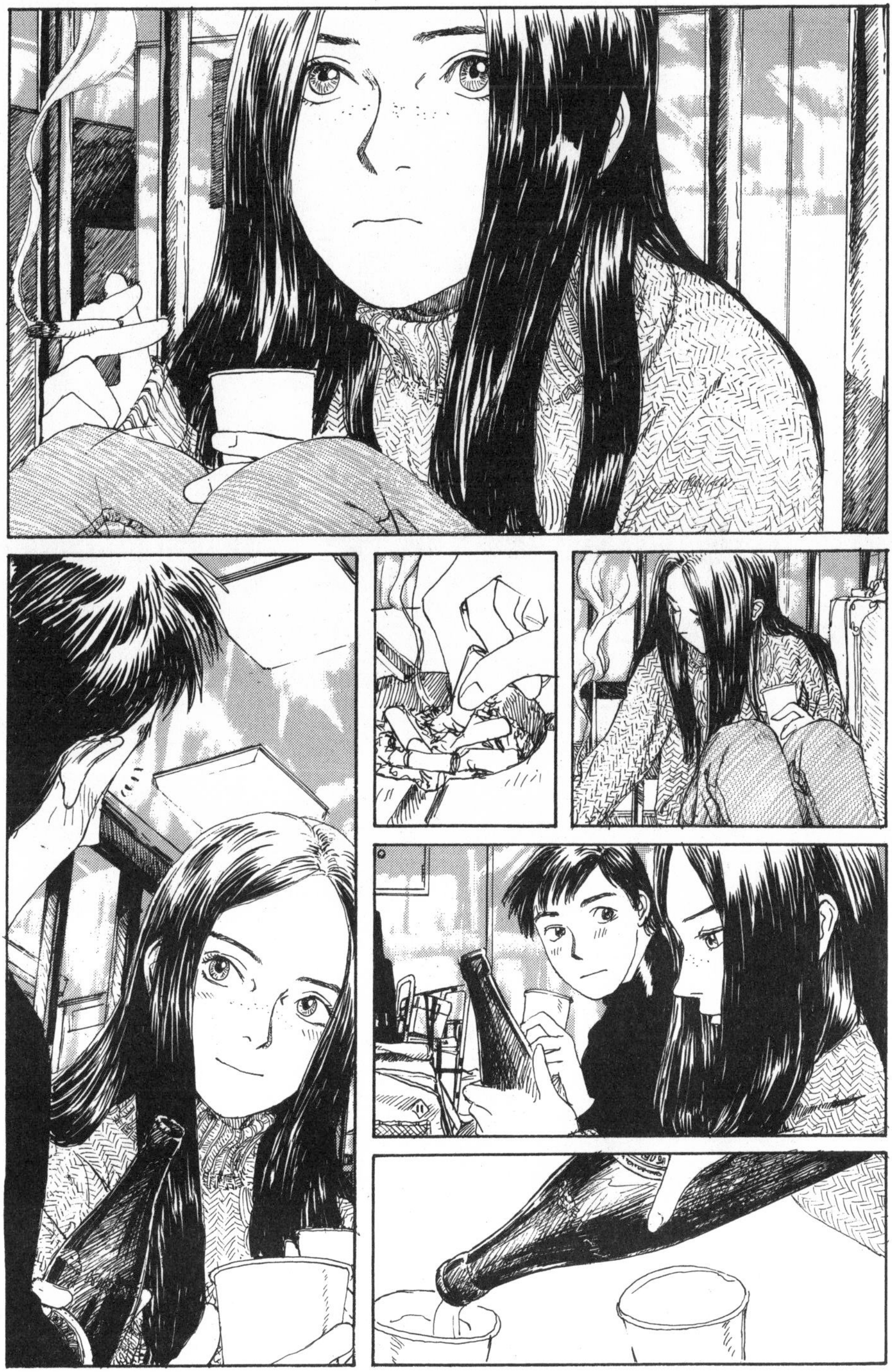

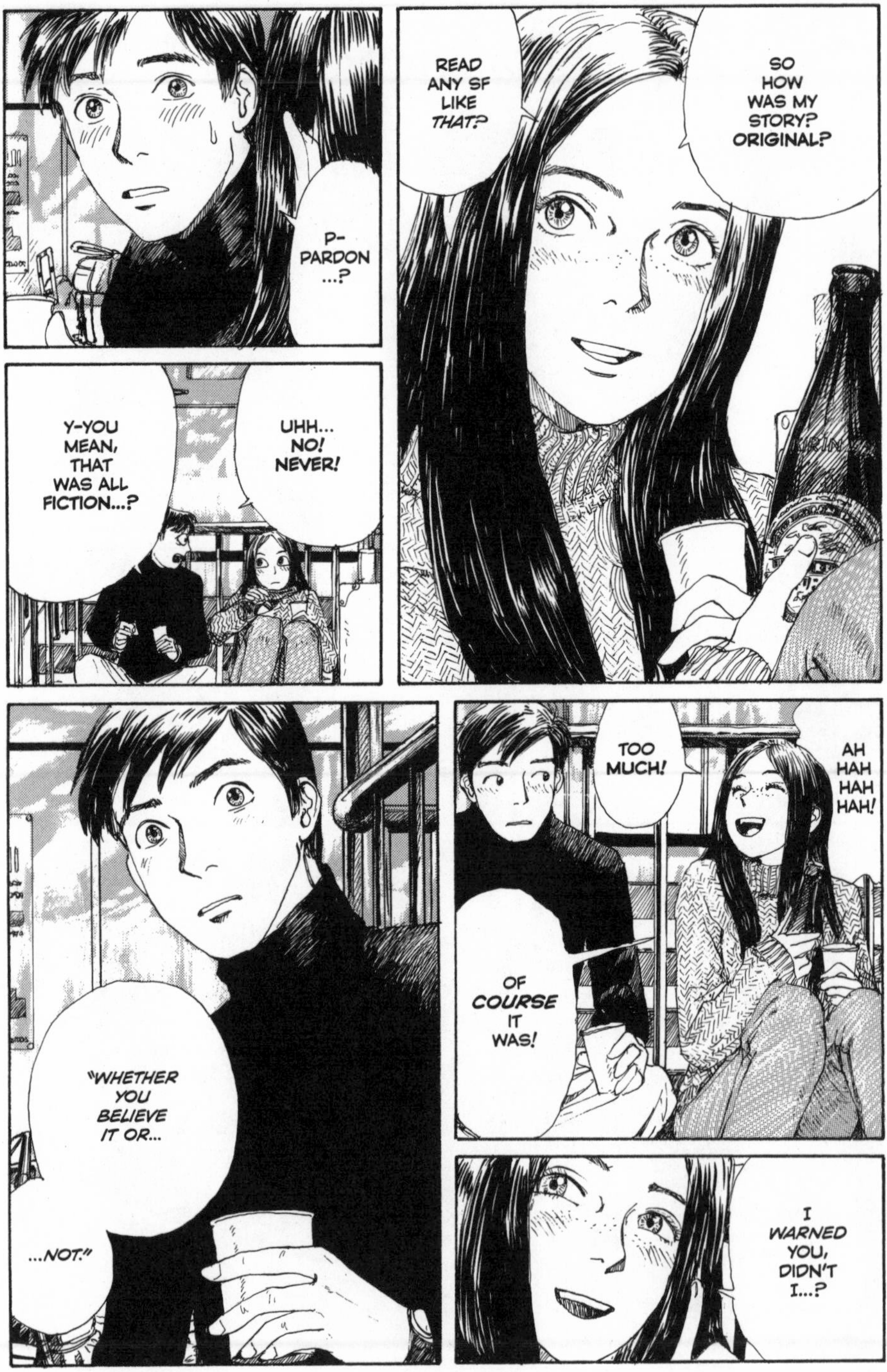
SO HOW WAS MY STORY? ORIGINAL?
READ ANY SF LIKE *THAT?*
P-PARDON ...?
UHH... NO! NEVER!
Y-YOU MEAN, THAT WAS ALL FICTION...?
AH HAH HAH HAH!
TOO MUCH!
OF *COURSE* IT WAS!
I *WARNED* YOU, DIDN'T I...?
"WHETHER YOU BELIEVE IT OR...
...NOT."

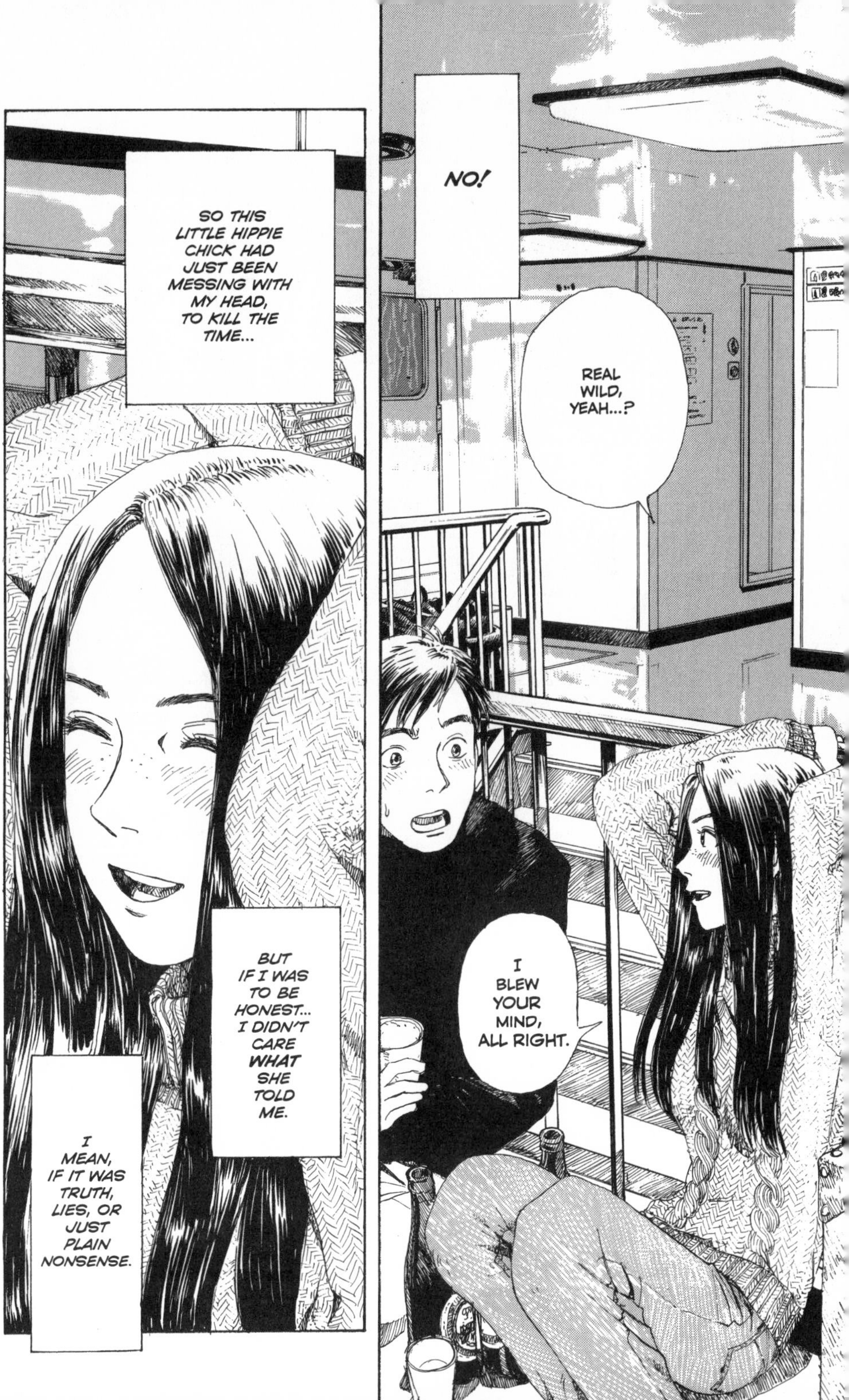
NO!
REAL WILD, YEAH...?
I BLEW YOUR MIND, ALL RIGHT.
SO THIS LITTLE HIPPIE CHICK HAD JUST BEEN MESSING WITH MY HEAD, TO KILL THE TIME...
BUT IF I WAS TO BE HONEST... I DIDN'T CARE WHAT SHE TOLD ME.
I MEAN, IF IT WAS TRUTH, LIES, OR JUST PLAIN NONSENSE.

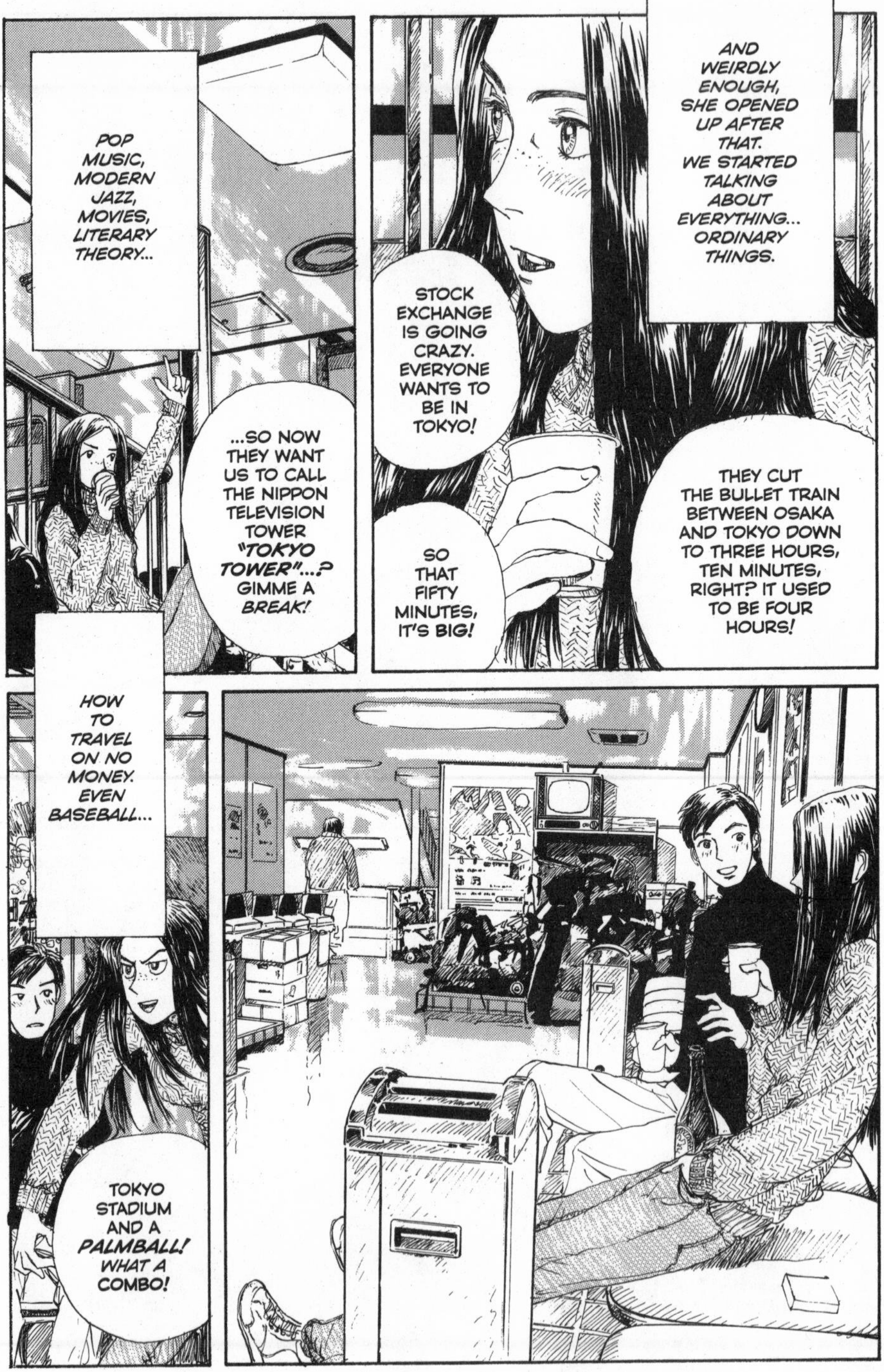
AND WEIRDLY ENOUGH, SHE OPENED UP AFTER THAT. WE STARTED TALKING ABOUT EVERYTHING... ORDINARY THINGS.
STOCK EXCHANGE IS GOING CRAZY. EVERYONE WANTS TO BE IN TOKYO!
THEY CUT THE BULLET TRAIN BETWEEN OSAKA AND TOKYO DOWN TO THREE HOURS, TEN MINUTES, RIGHT? IT USED TO BE FOUR HOURS!
SO THAT FIFTY MINUTES, IT'S BIG!
POP MUSIC, MODERN JAZZ, MOVIES, LITERARY THEORY...
...SO NOW THEY WANT US TO CALL THE NIPPON TELEVISION TOWER "TOKYO TOWER"...? GIMME A BREAK!
HOW TO TRAVEL ON NO MONEY. EVEN BASEBALL...
TOKYO STADIUM AND A PALMBALL! WHAT A COMBO!

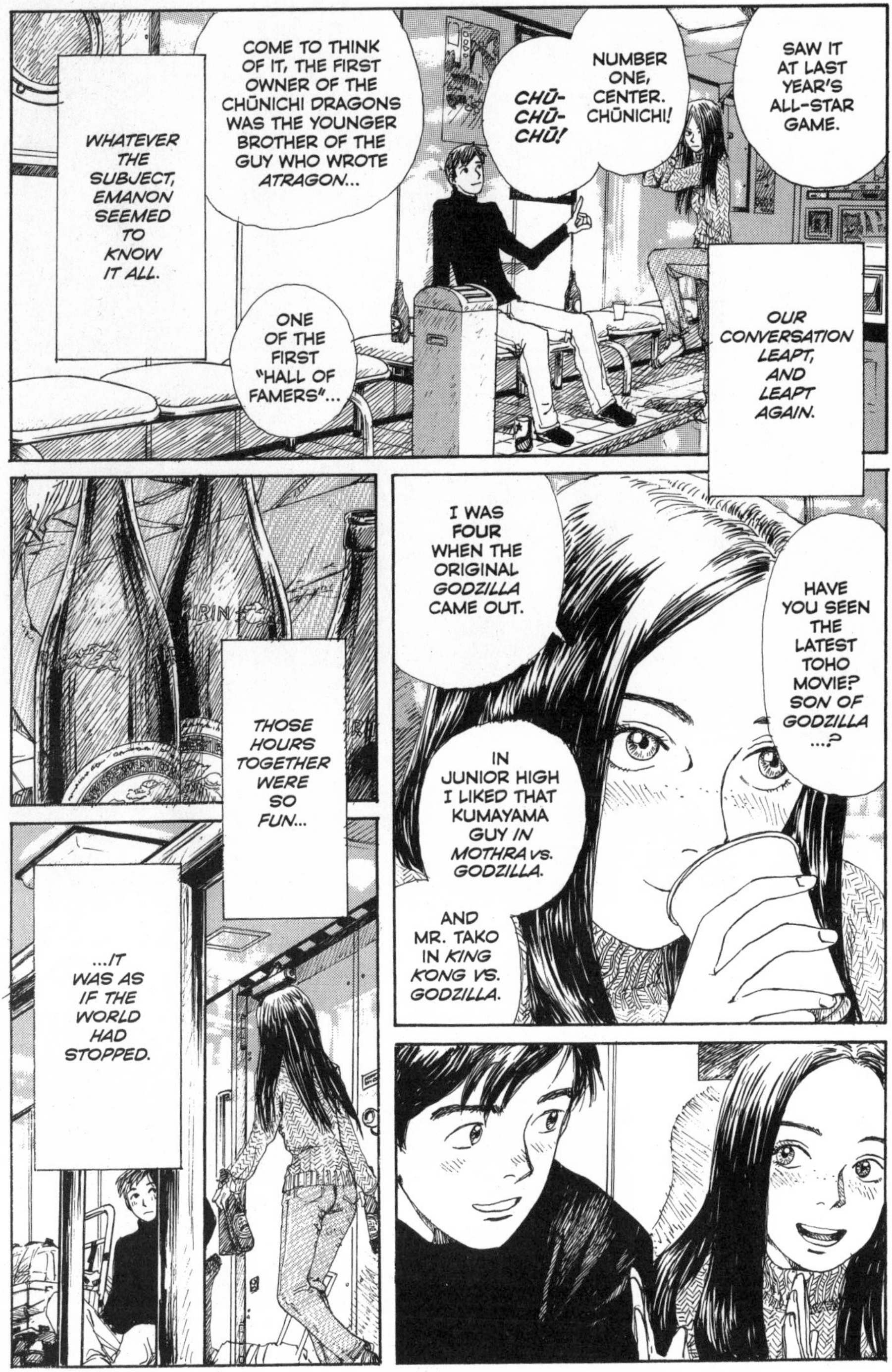
SAW IT AT LAST YEAR'S ALL-STAR GAME.
NUMBER ONE, CENTER. CHŪNICHI!
CHŪ-CHŪ-CHŪ!
COME TO THINK OF IT, THE FIRST OWNER OF THE CHŪNICHI DRAGONS WAS THE YOUNGER BROTHER OF THE GUY WHO WROTE ATRAGON...
WHATEVER THE SUBJECT, EMANON SEEMED TO KNOW IT ALL.
OUR CONVERSATION LEAPT, AND LEAPT AGAIN.
ONE OF THE FIRST "HALL OF FAMERS"...
HAVE YOU SEEN THE LATEST TOHO MOVIE? SON OF GODZILLA ...?
I WAS FOUR WHEN THE ORIGINAL GODZILLA CAME OUT.
IN JUNIOR HIGH I LIKED THAT KUMAYAMA GUY IN MOTHRA vs. GODZILLA.
AND MR. TAKO IN KING KONG VS. GODZILLA.
THOSE HOURS TOGETHER WERE SO FUN...
...IT WAS AS IF THE WORLD HAD STOPPED.

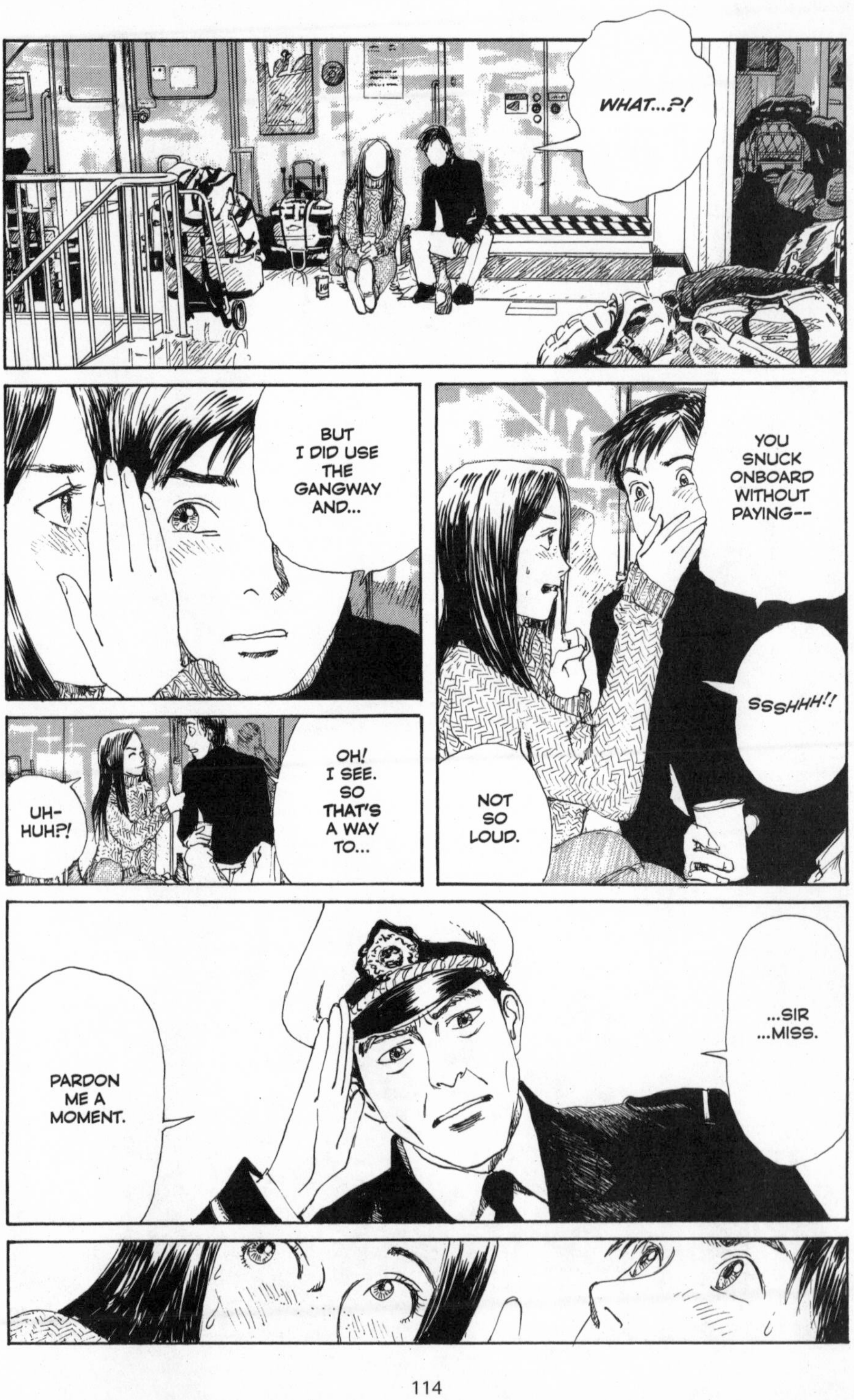
WHAT...?!
YOU SNUCK ONBOARD WITHOUT PAYING--
SSSHHH!!
NOT SO LOUD.
BUT I DID USE THE GANGWAY AND...
OH! I SEE. SO THAT'S A WAY TO...
UH-HUH?!
...SIR ...MISS.
PARDON ME A MOMENT.

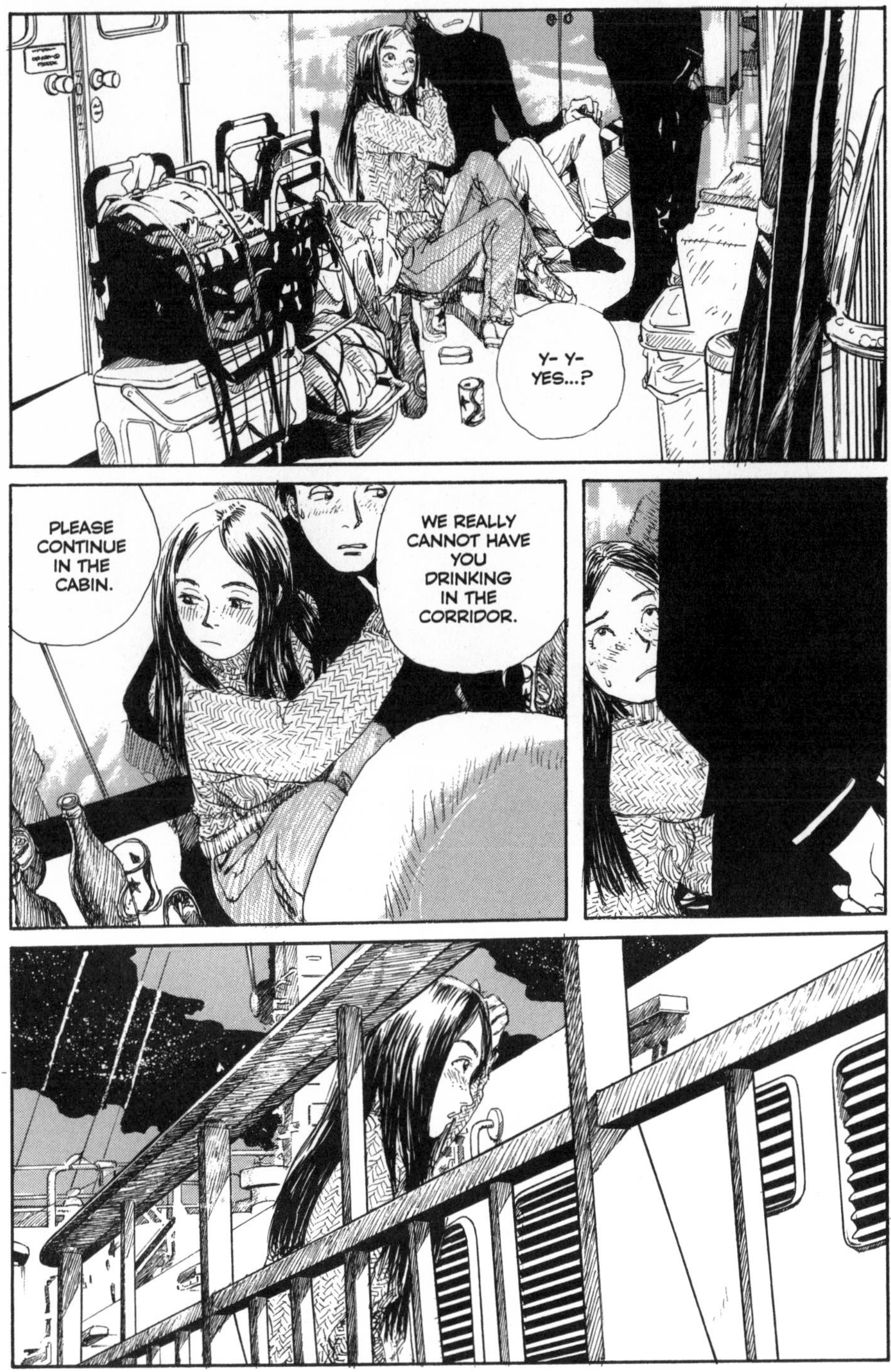
Y- Y- YES...?
WE REALLY CANNOT HAVE YOU DRINKING IN THE CORRIDOR.
PLEASE CONTINUE IN THE CABIN.

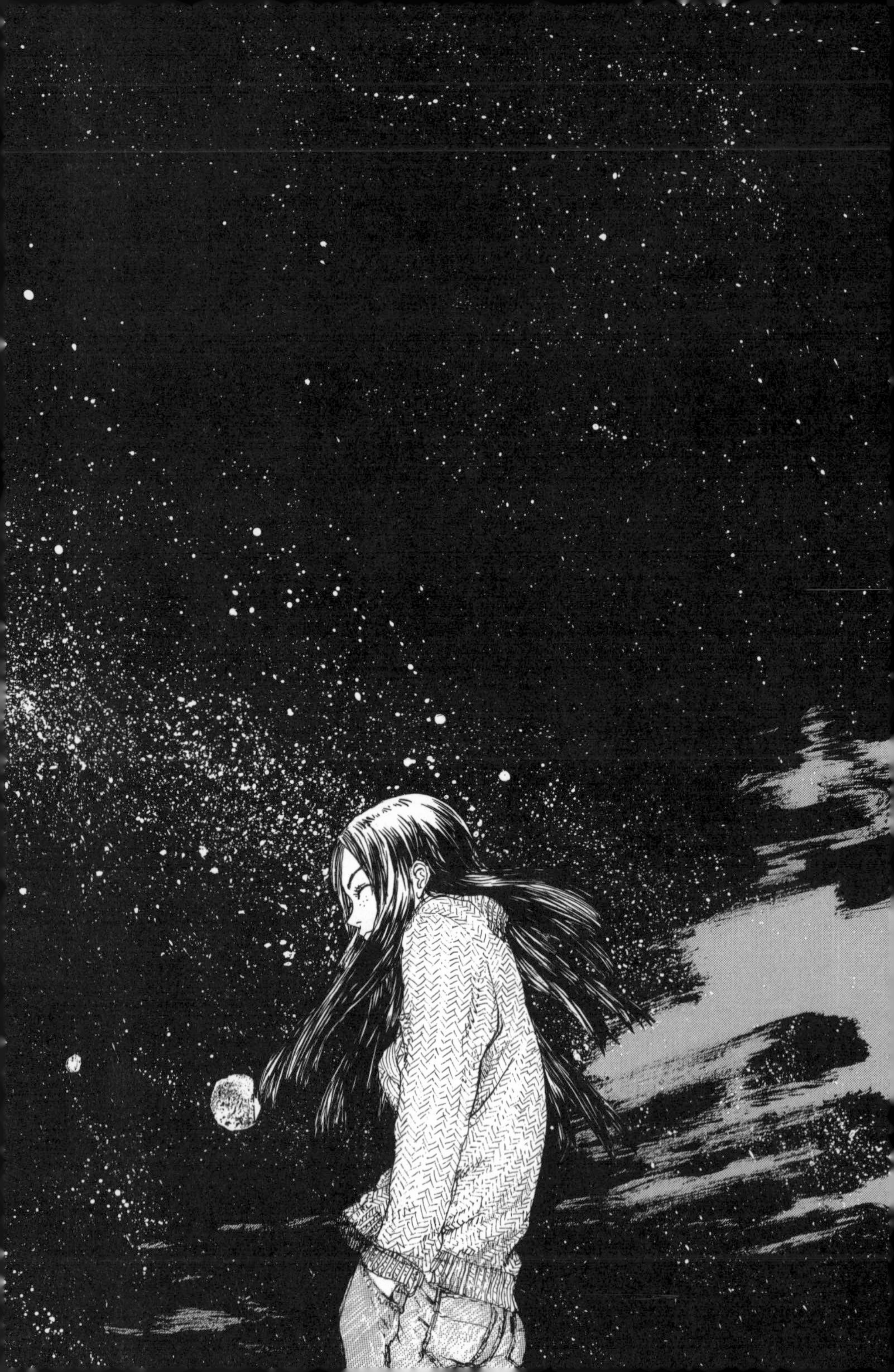

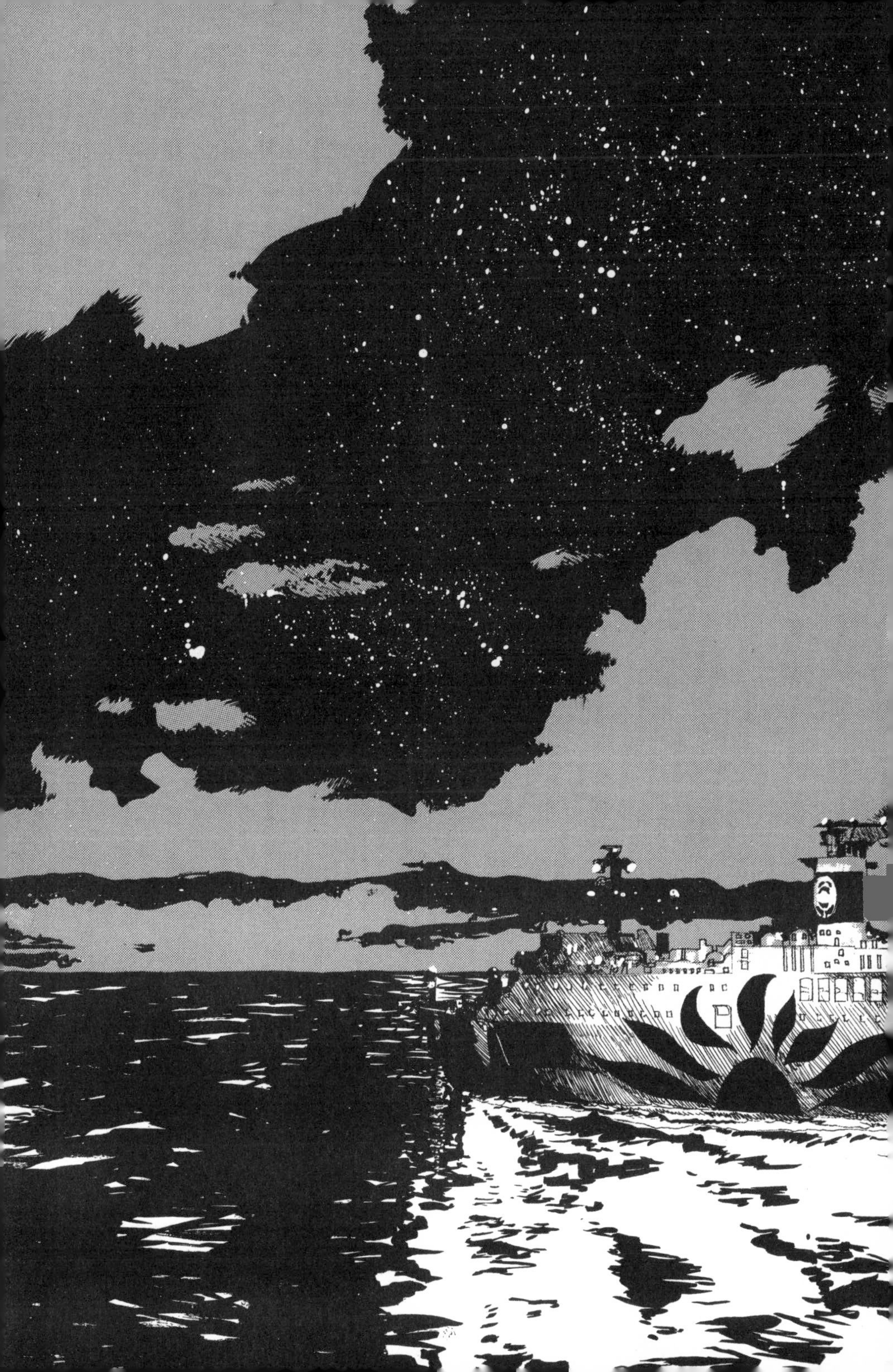

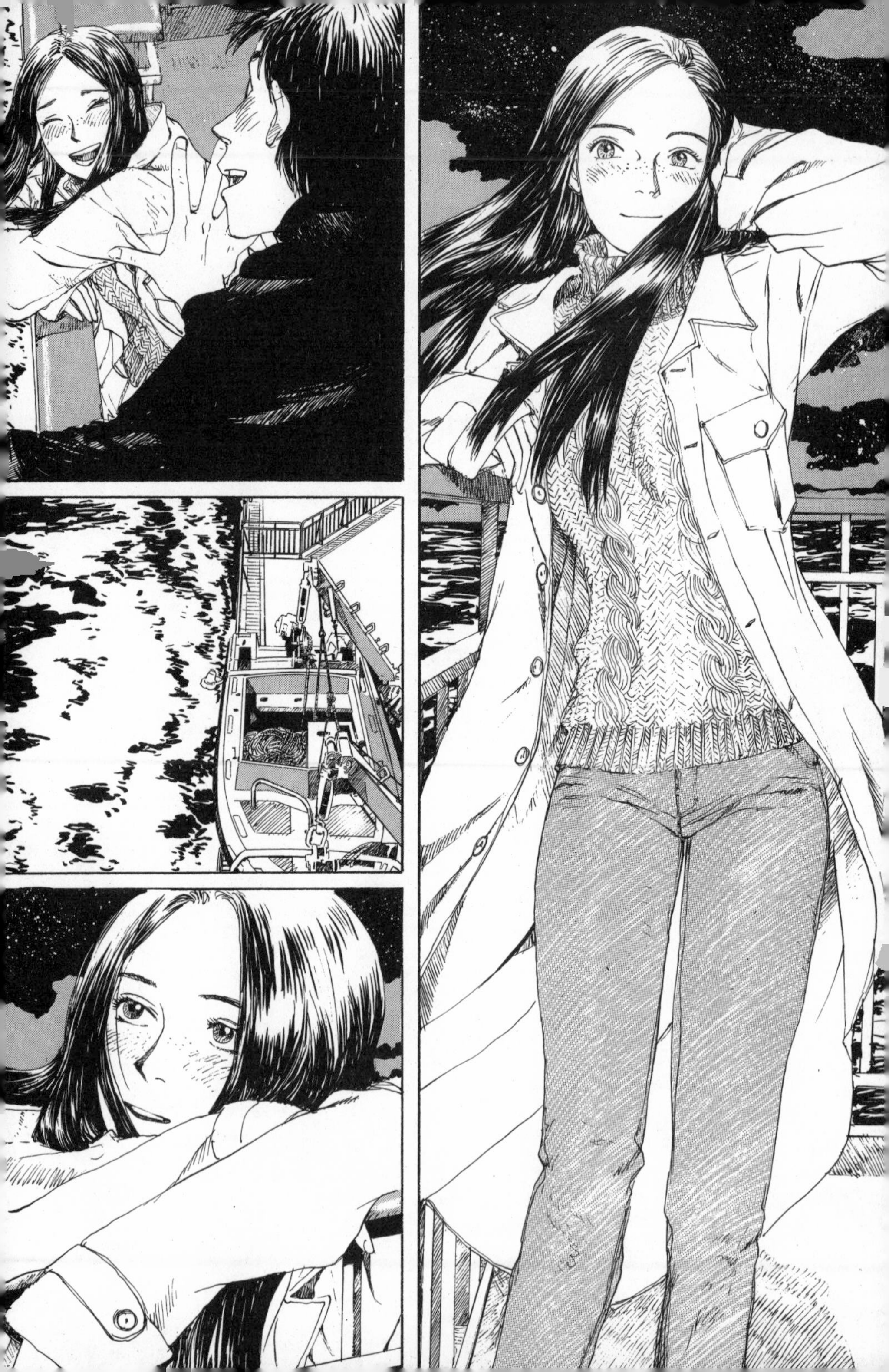

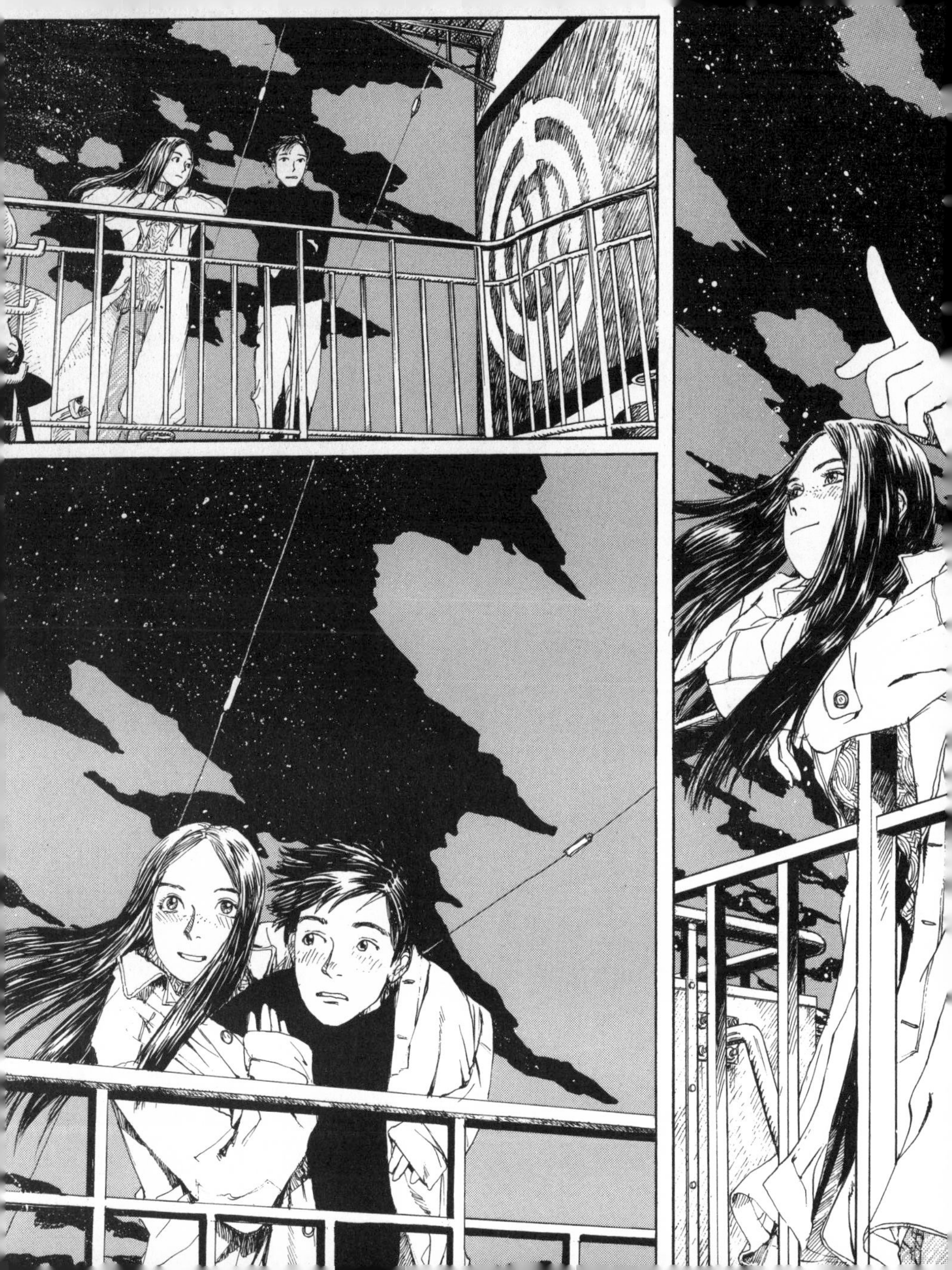

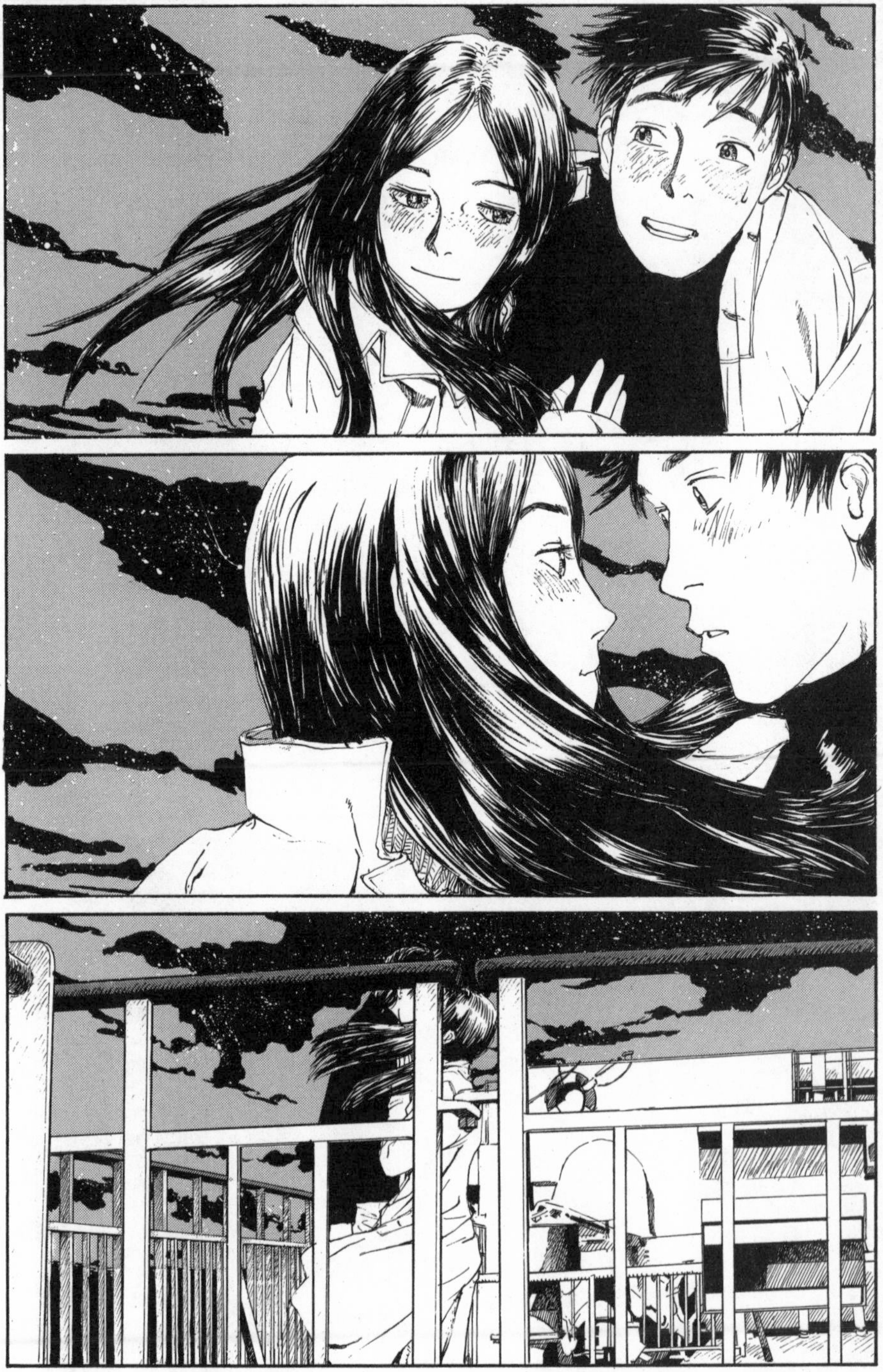

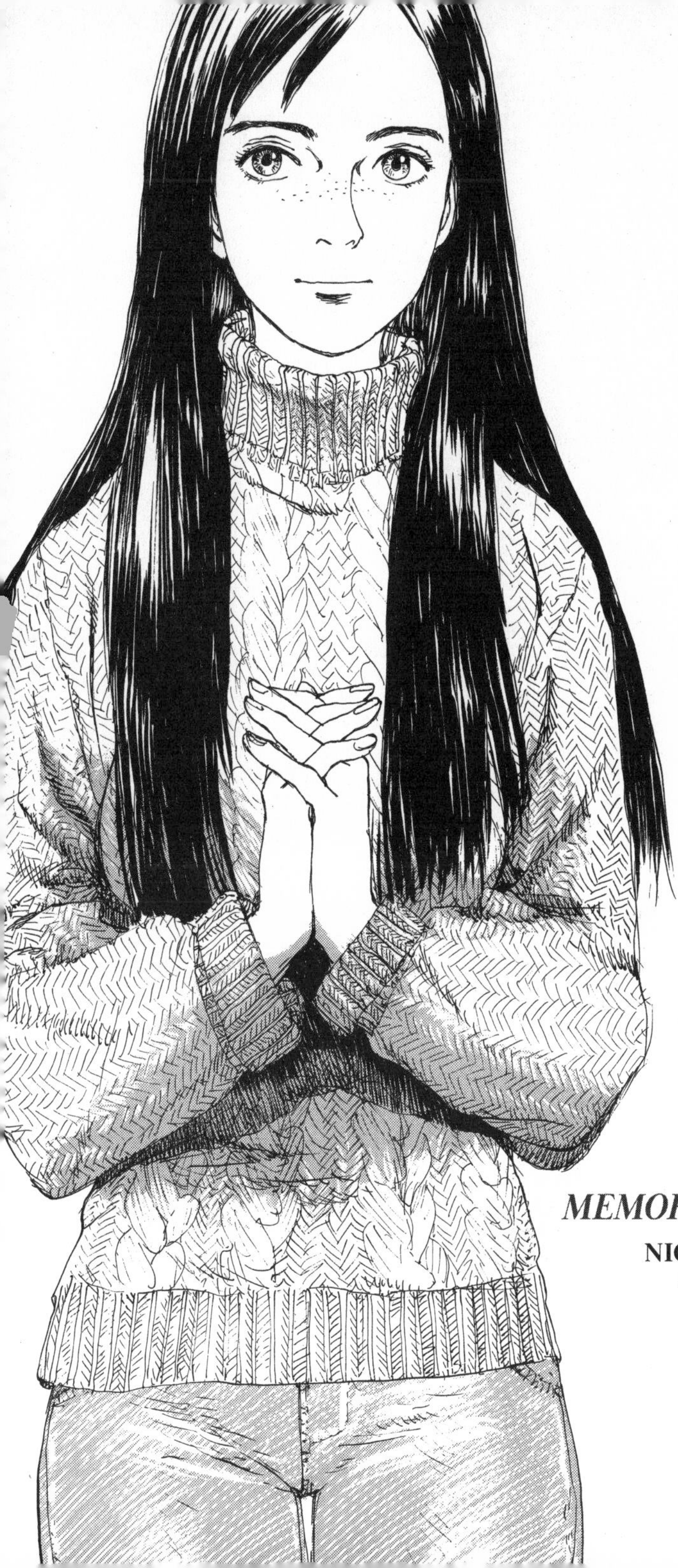

MEMORIES OF EMANON

**NIGHT, 9 OR 10:00,
AND THEN...**

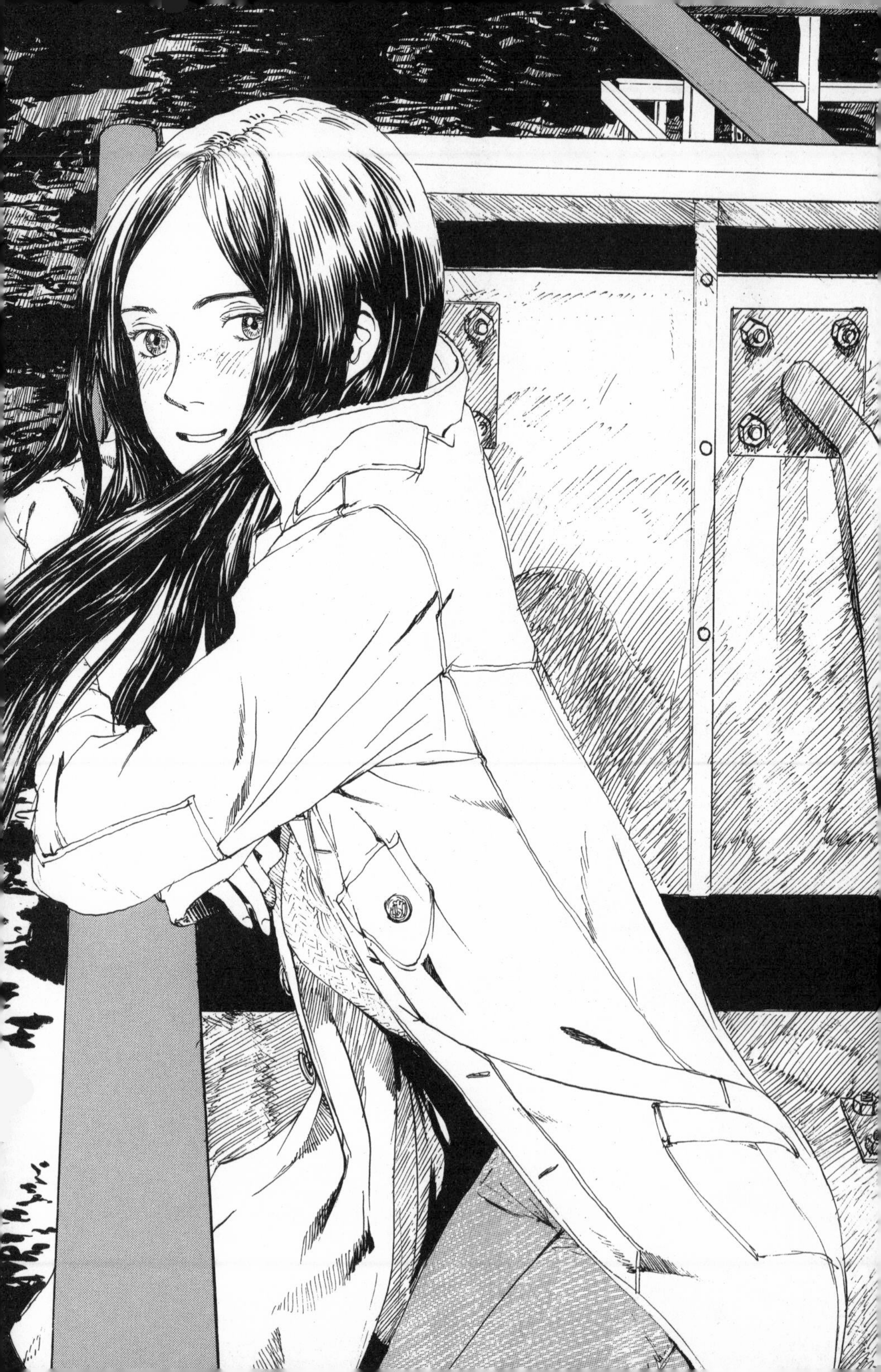

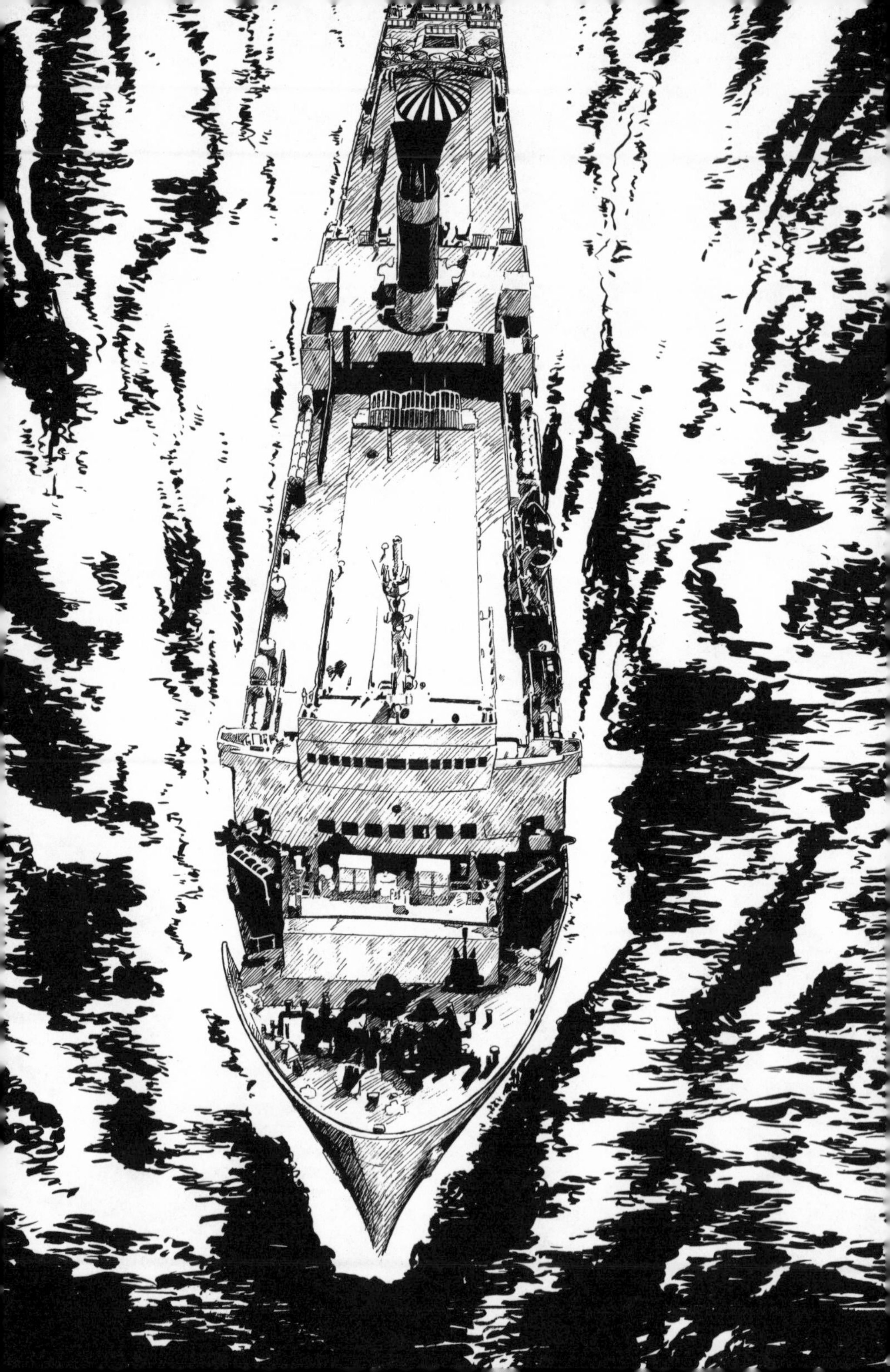

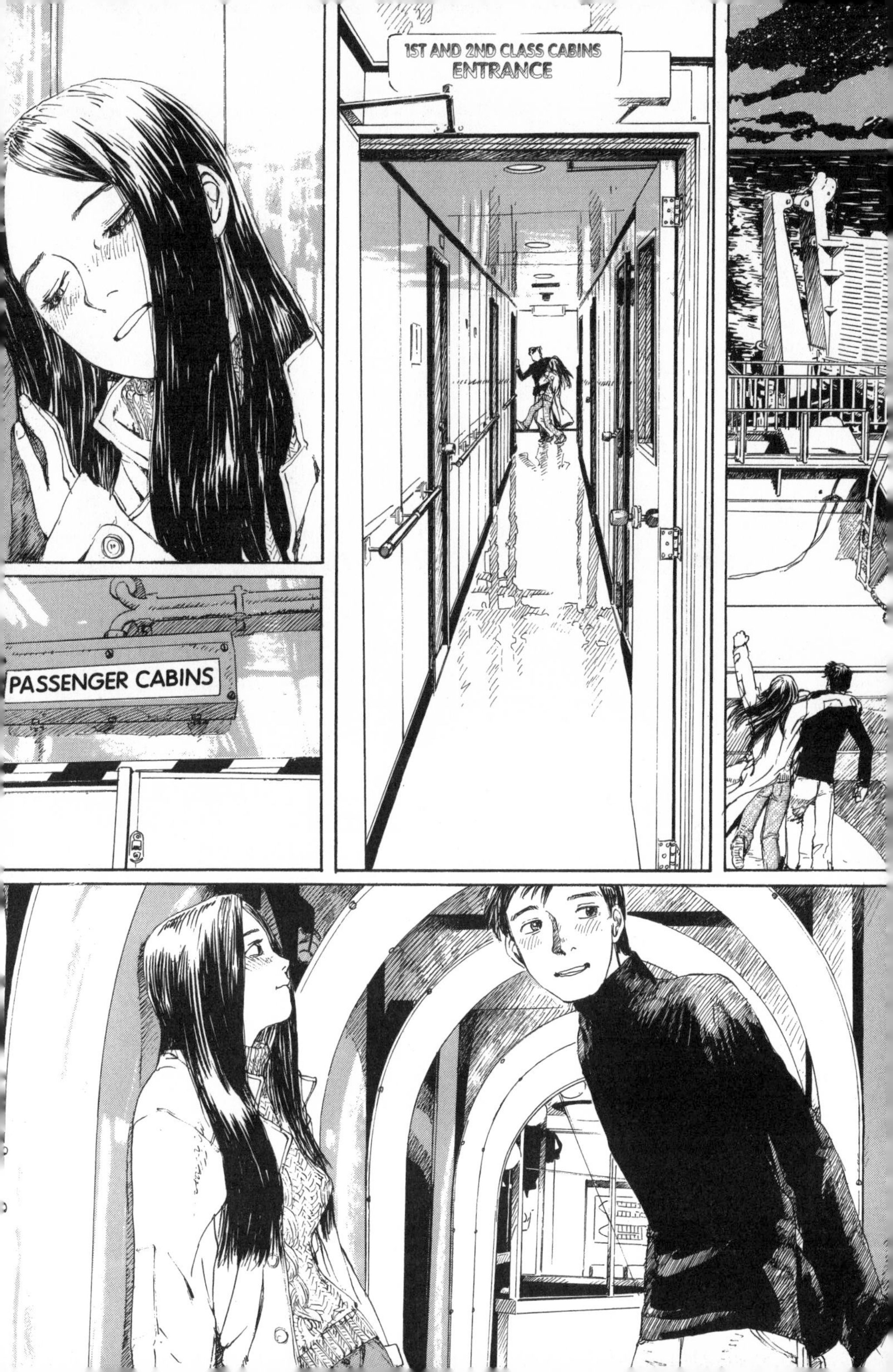
1ST AND 2ND CLASS CABINS
ENTRANCE
PASSENGER CABINS

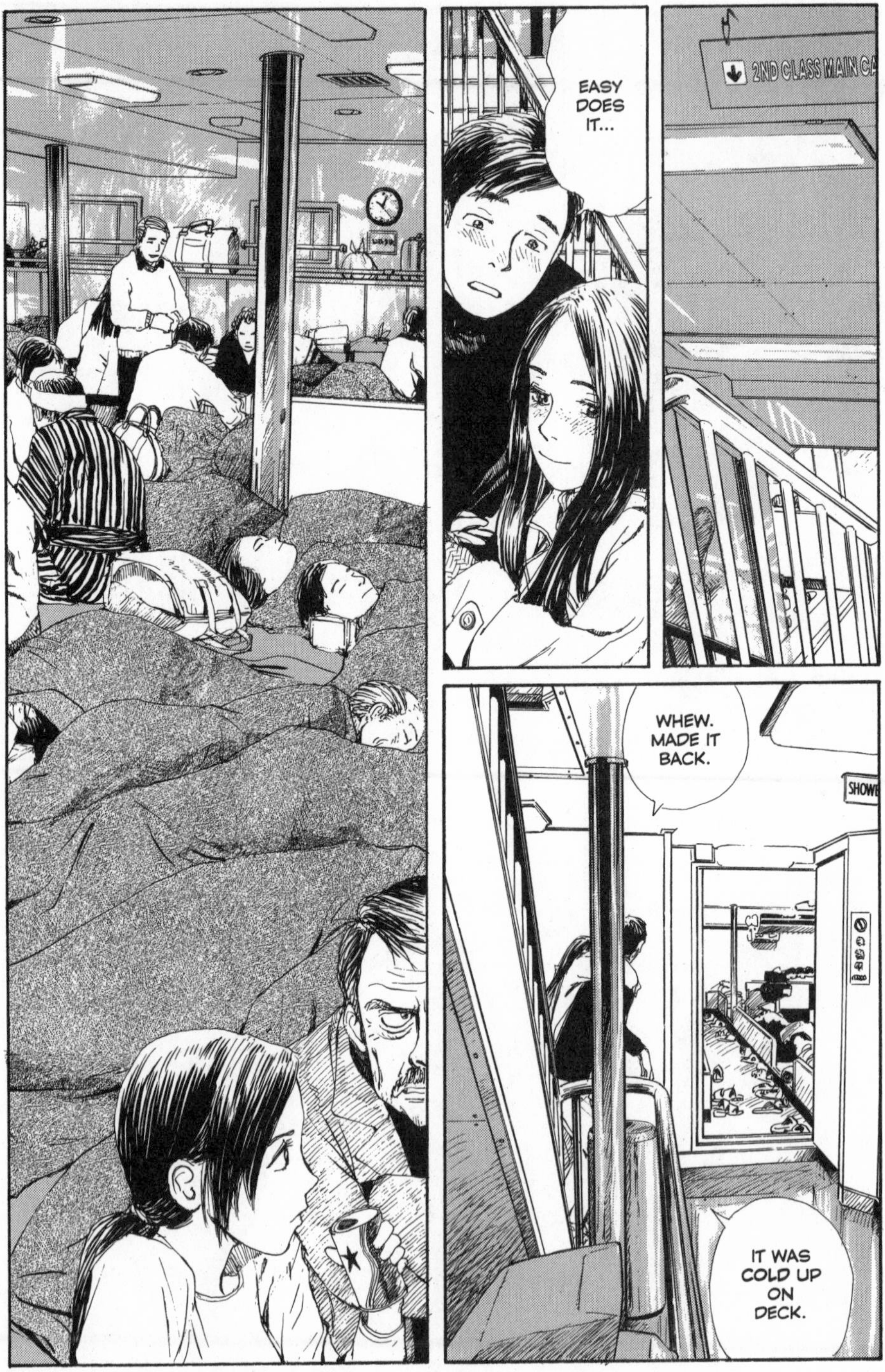
2ND CLASS MAIN CA
EASY DOES IT...
WHEW. MADE IT BACK.
SHOWE
IT WAS COLD UP ON DECK.

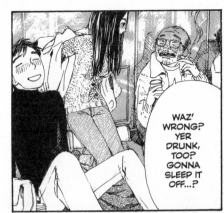

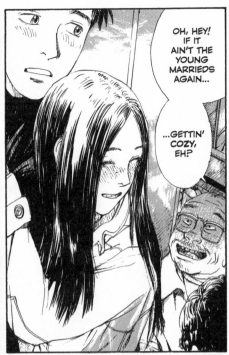

OH, HEY! IF IT AIN'T THE YOUNG MARRIEDS AGAIN...
...GETTIN' COZY, EH?
WAZ' WRONG? YER DRUNK, TOO? GONNA SLEEP IT OFF...?
C'MON...! YA CAN'T SLEEP YET...
...NIGHT'S TOO YOUNG! HOIST A NUDDER ONE WIT' ME...!
C'MON, SWEET-HEART...!
NAH! YER CONVERSA-TION'S STUPID!
GYA HA HA!
WA'Z YA SAY...?!

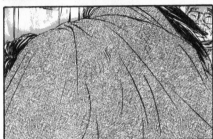

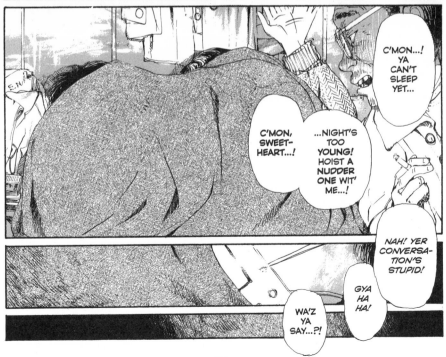

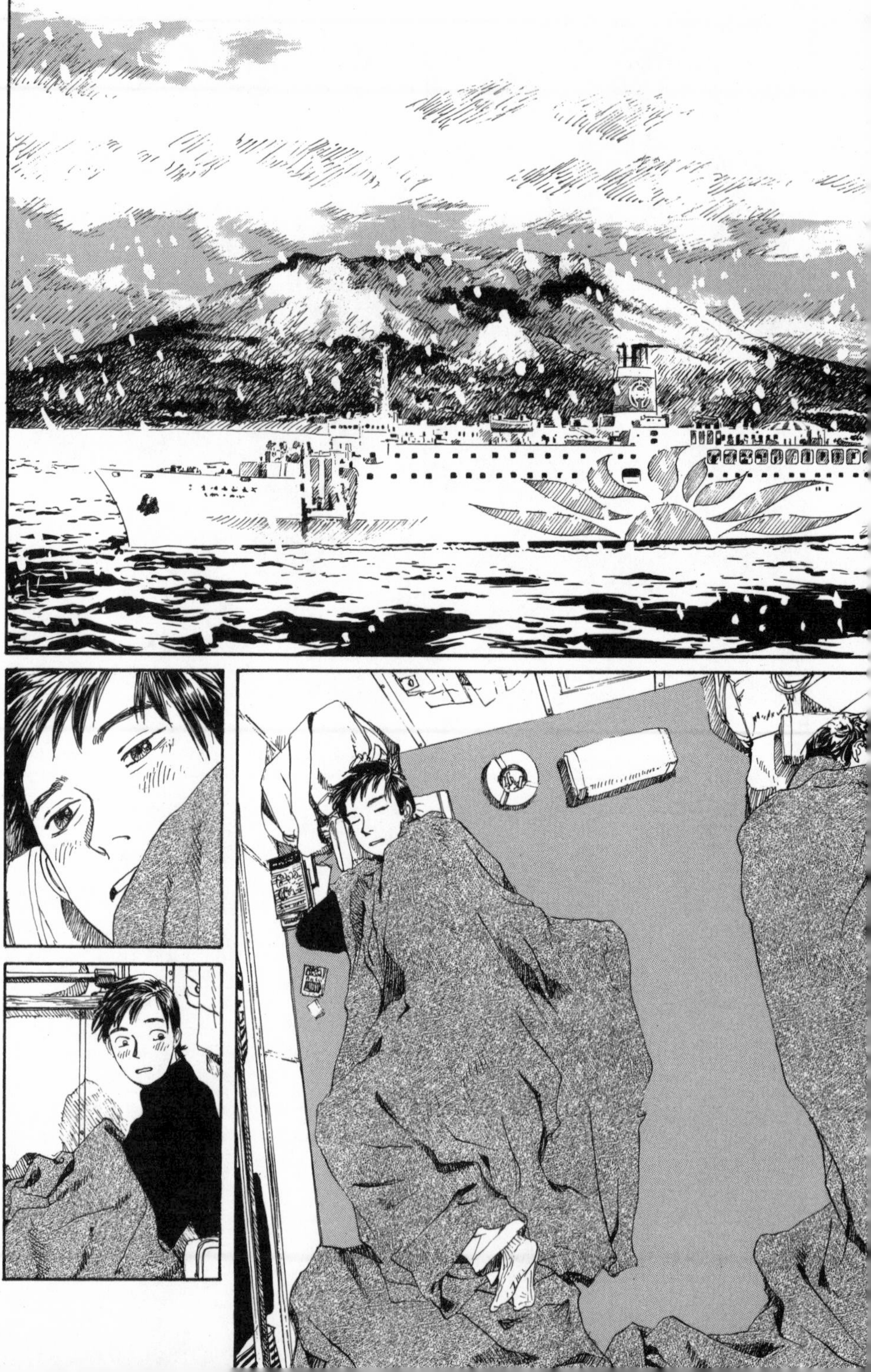

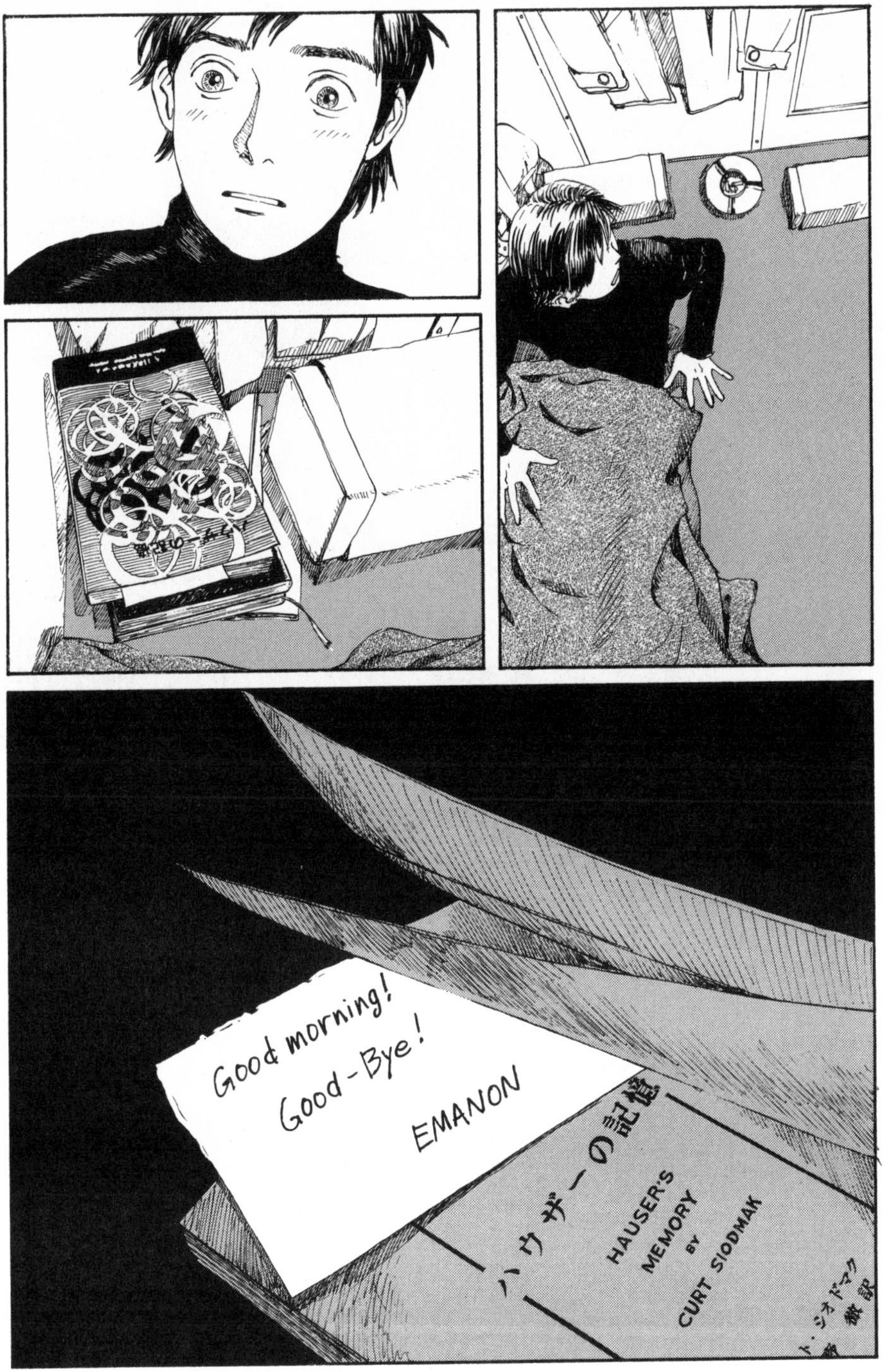
Good morning!
Good-Bye!
EMANON
ハウザーの記憶
HAUSER'S
MEMORY
BY
CURT SIODMAK

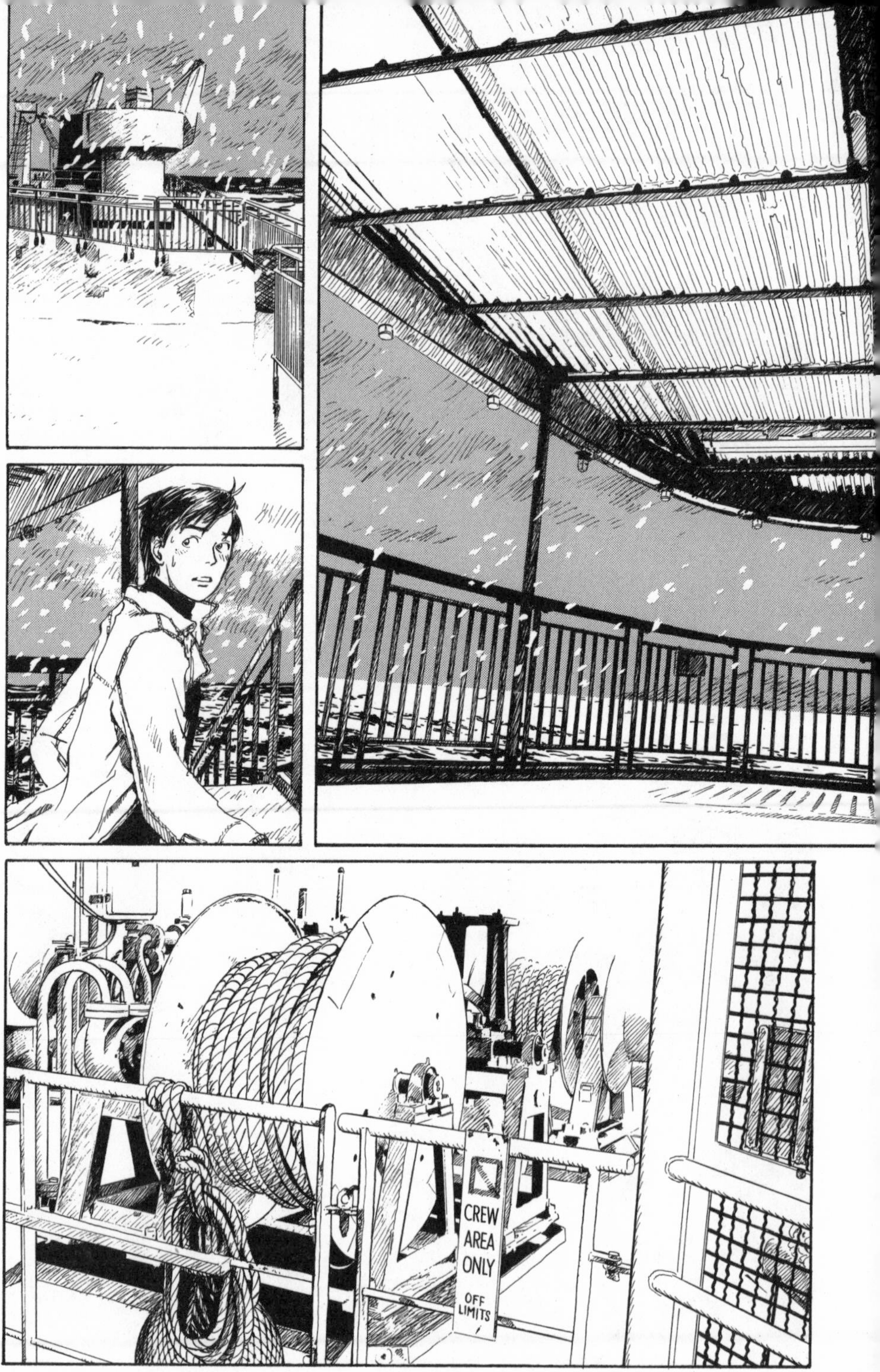
CREW
AREA
ONLY
OFF
LIMITS

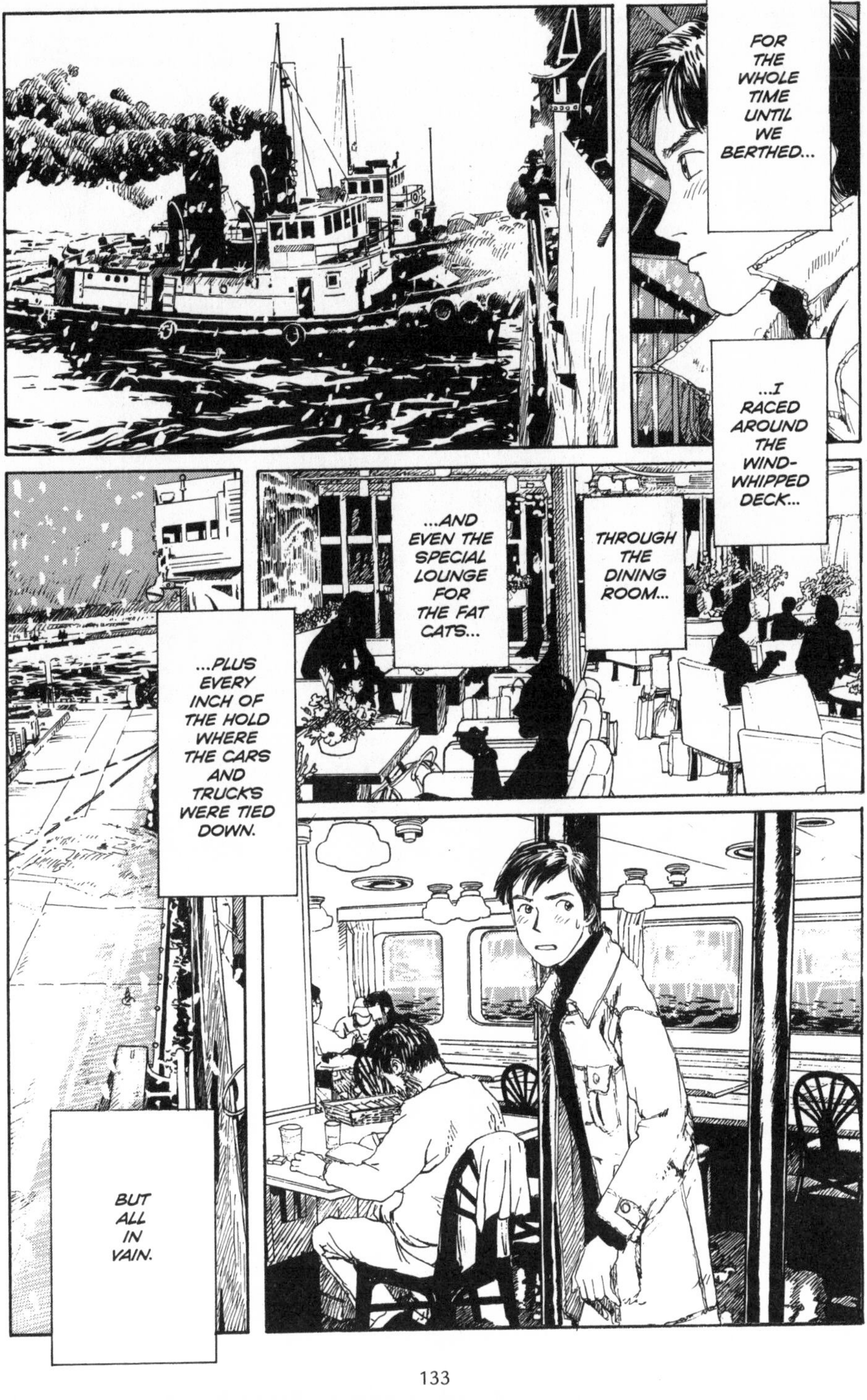
FOR THE WHOLE TIME UNTIL WE BERTHED...
...I RACED AROUND THE WIND-WHIPPED DECK...
THROUGH THE DINING ROOM...
...AND EVEN THE SPECIAL LOUNGE FOR THE FAT CATS...
...PLUS EVERY INCH OF THE HOLD WHERE THE CARS AND TRUCKS WERE TIED DOWN.
BUT ALL IN VAIN.

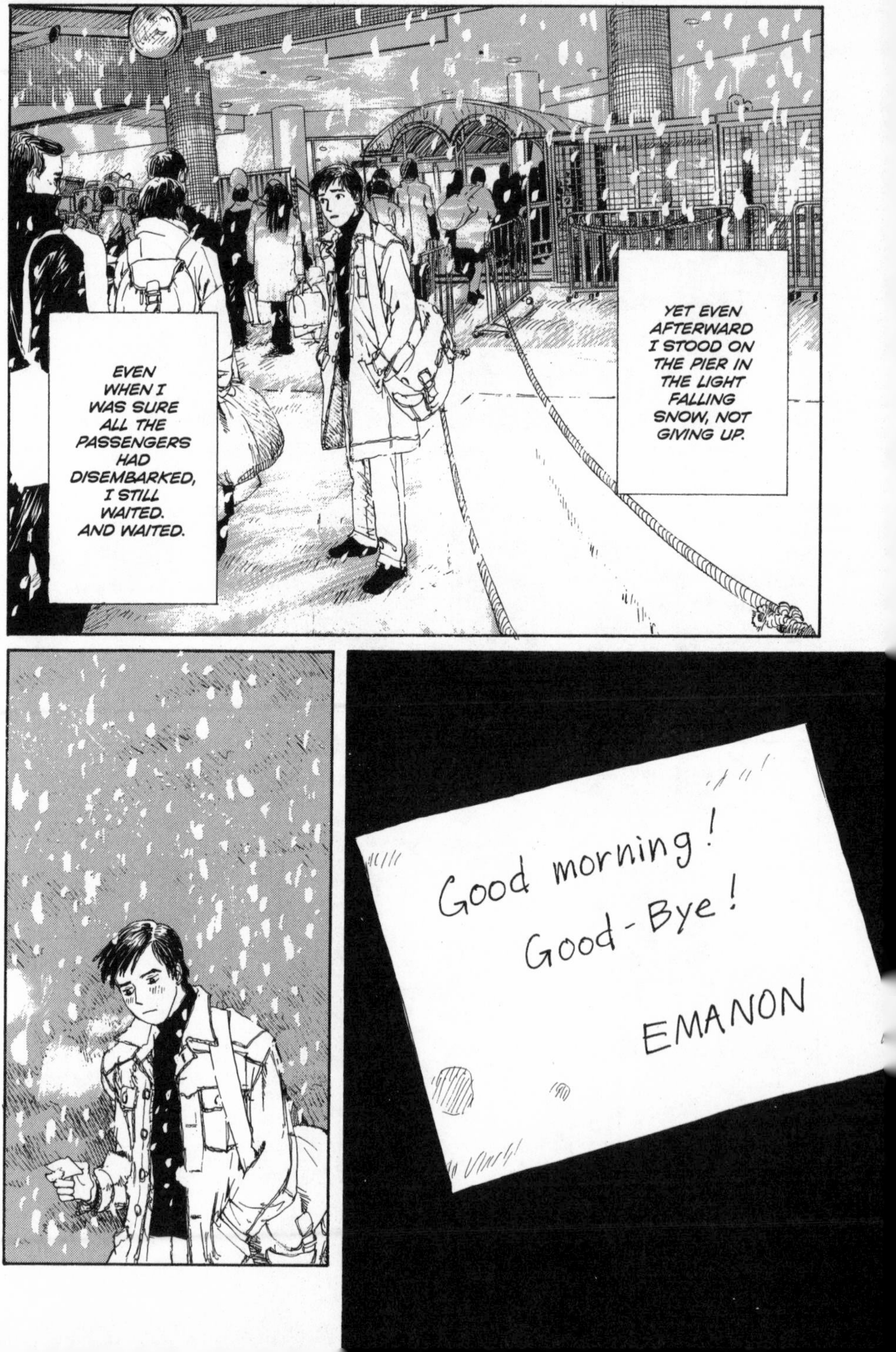
YET EVEN AFTERWARD I STOOD ON THE PIER IN THE LIGHT FALLING SNOW, NOT GIVING UP.
EVEN WHEN I WAS SURE ALL THE PASSENGERS HAD DISEMBARKED, I STILL WAITED. AND WAITED.
Good morning! Good-Bye! EMANON

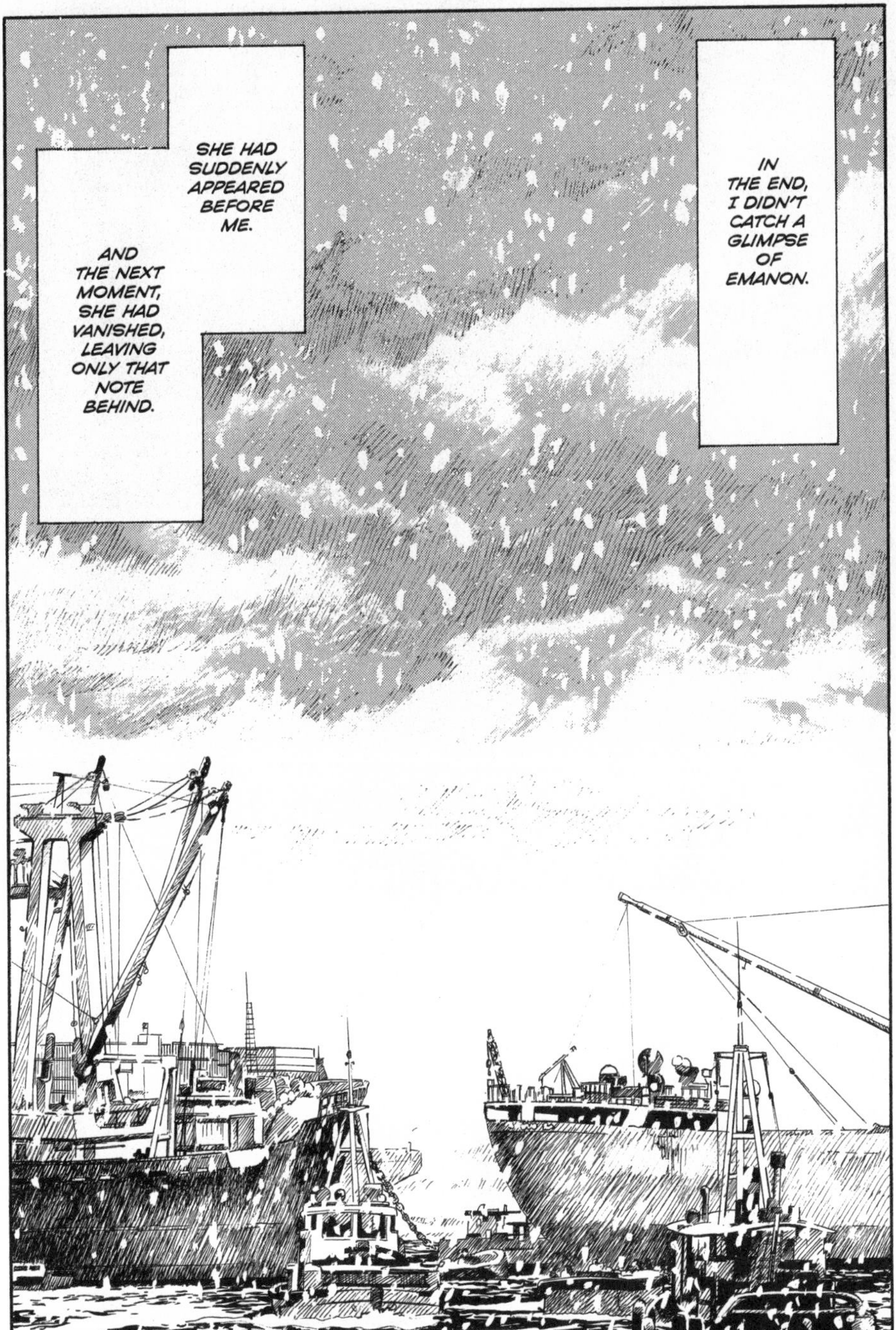
IN THE END, I DIDN'T CATCH A GLIMPSE OF EMANON.
SHE HAD SUDDENLY APPEARED BEFORE ME.
AND THE NEXT MOMENT, SHE HAD VANISHED, LEAVING ONLY THAT NOTE BEHIND.

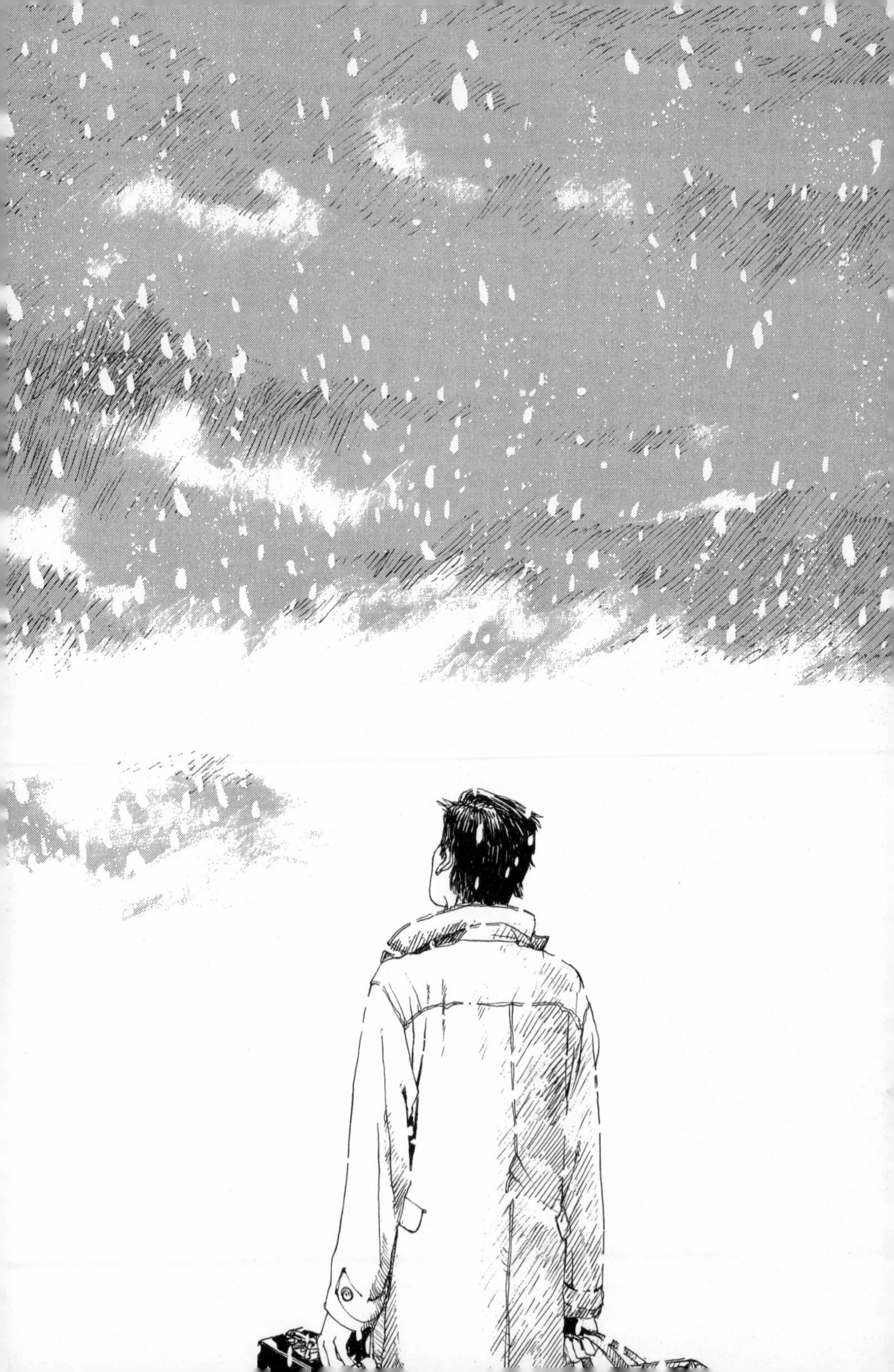

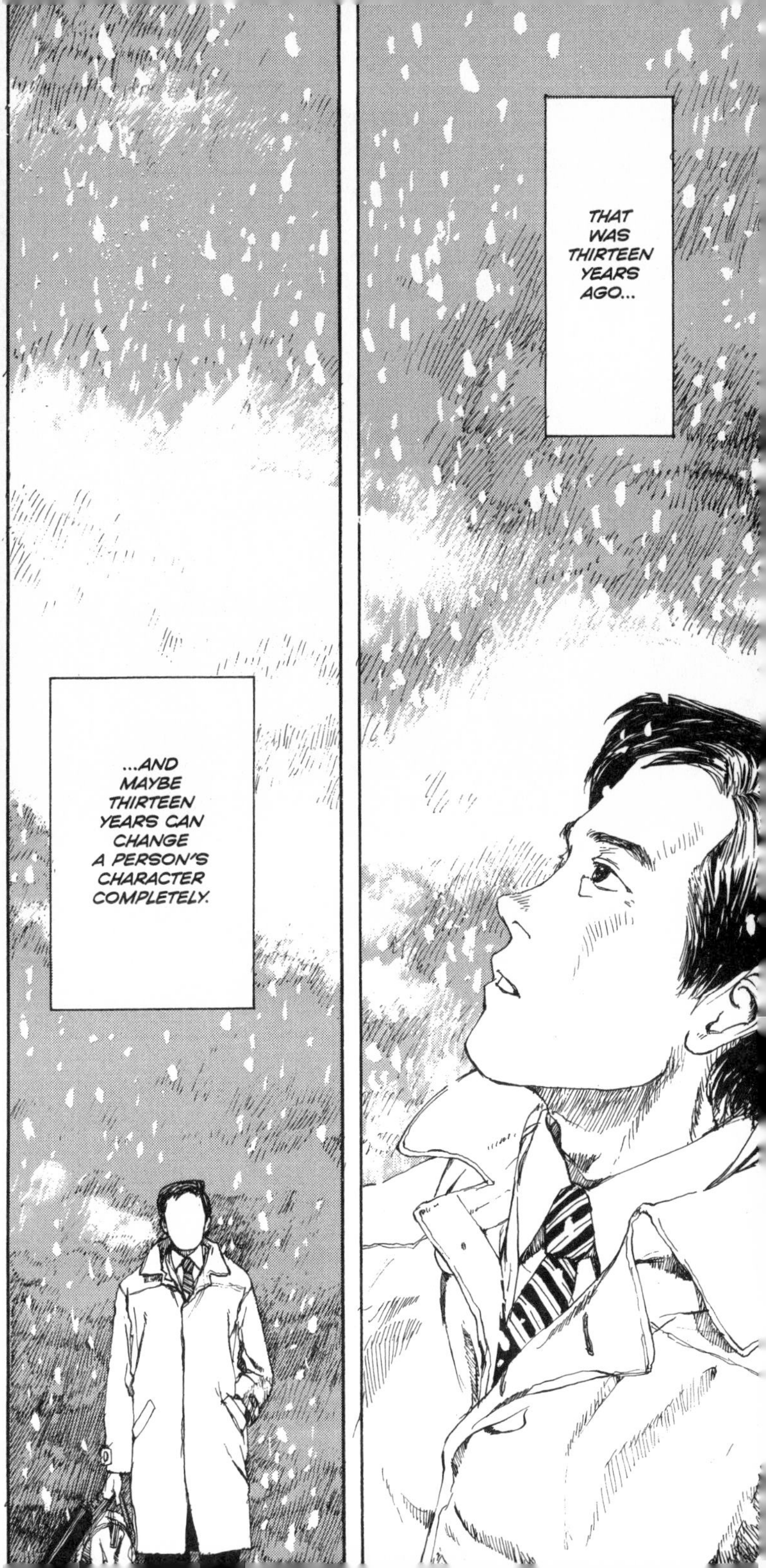
THAT WAS THIRTEEN YEARS AGO...
...AND MAYBE THIRTEEN YEARS CAN CHANGE A PERSON'S CHARACTER COMPLETELY.

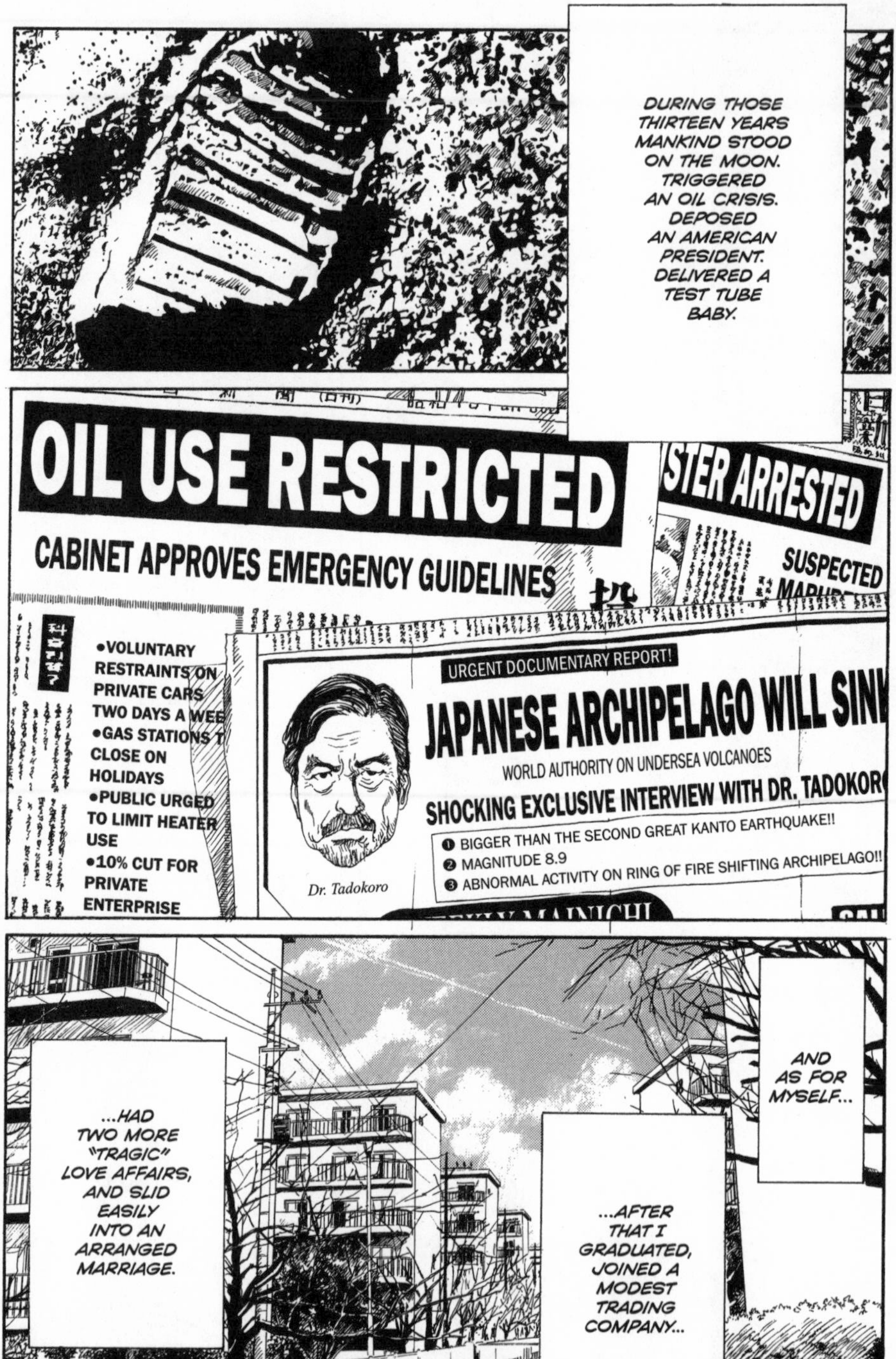
DURING THOSE THIRTEEN YEARS MANKIND STOOD ON THE MOON. TRIGGERED AN OIL CRISIS. DEPOSED AN AMERICAN PRESIDENT. DELIVERED A TEST TUBE BABY.
OIL USE RESTRICTED
CABINET APPROVES EMERGENCY GUIDELINES
•VOLUNTARY RESTRAINTS ON PRIVATE CARS TWO DAYS A WEE
•GAS STATIONS T CLOSE ON HOLIDAYS
•PUBLIC URGED TO LIMIT HEATER USE
•10% CUT FOR PRIVATE ENTERPRISE
STER ARRESTED
SUSPECTED
URGENT DOCUMENTARY REPORT!
JAPANESE ARCHIPELAGO WILL SIN
WORLD AUTHORITY ON UNDERSEA VOLCANOES
SHOCKING EXCLUSIVE INTERVIEW WITH DR. TADOKOR
❶ BIGGER THAN THE SECOND GREAT KANTO EARTHQUAKE!!
❷ MAGNITUDE 8.9
❸ ABNORMAL ACTIVITY ON RING OF FIRE SHIFTING ARCHIPELAGO!!
Dr. Tadokoro
AND AS FOR MYSELF...
...AFTER THAT I GRADUATED, JOINED A MODEST TRADING COMPANY...
...HAD TWO MORE "TRAGIC" LOVE AFFAIRS, AND SLID EASILY INTO AN ARRANGED MARRIAGE.

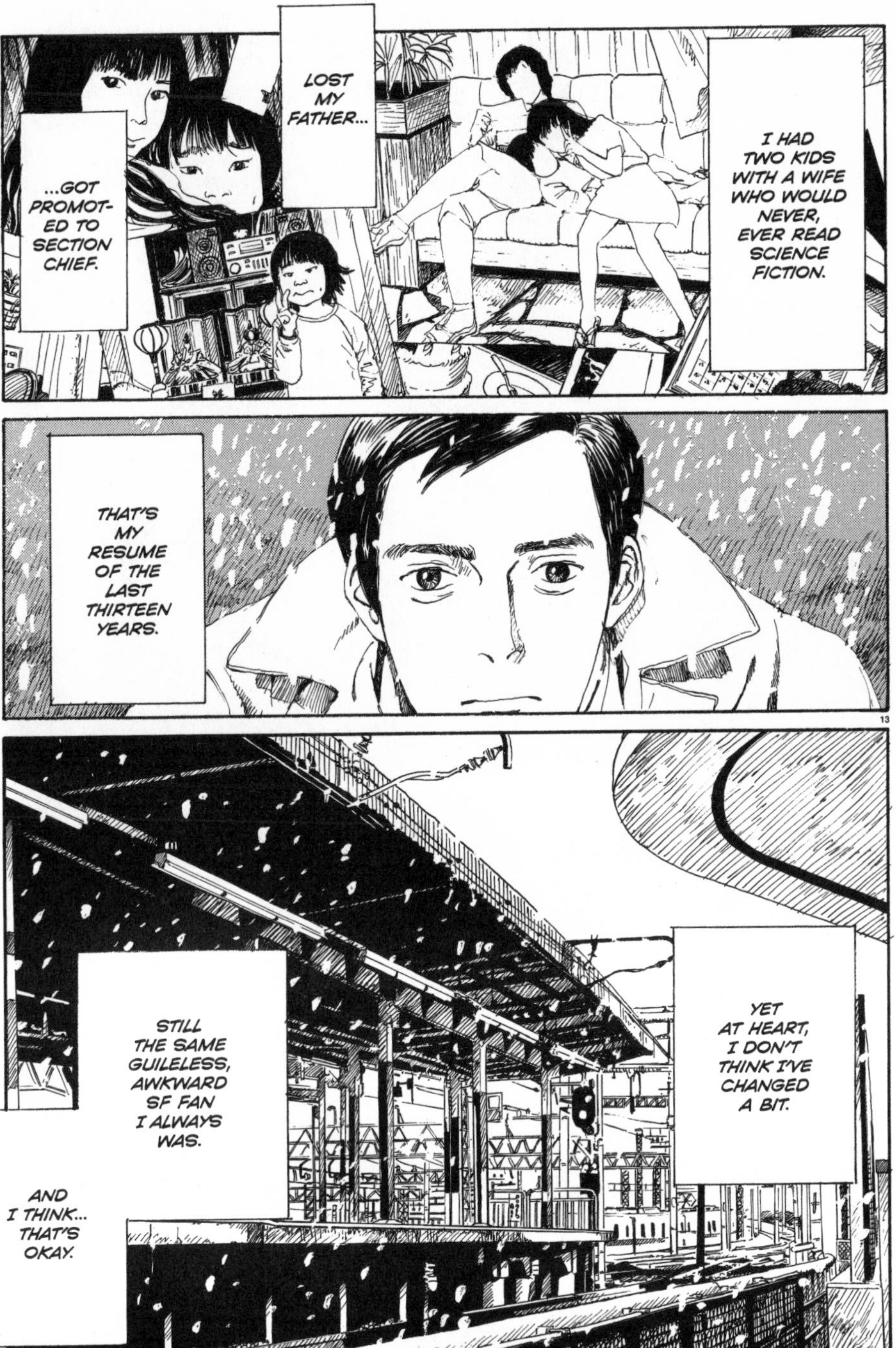
I HAD TWO KIDS WITH A WIFE WHO WOULD NEVER, EVER READ SCIENCE FICTION.
LOST MY FATHER...
...GOT PROMOTED TO SECTION CHIEF.
THAT'S MY RESUME OF THE LAST THIRTEEN YEARS.
YET AT HEART, I DON'T THINK I'VE CHANGED A BIT.
STILL THE SAME GUILELESS, AWKWARD SF FAN I ALWAYS WAS.
AND I THINK... THAT'S OKAY.

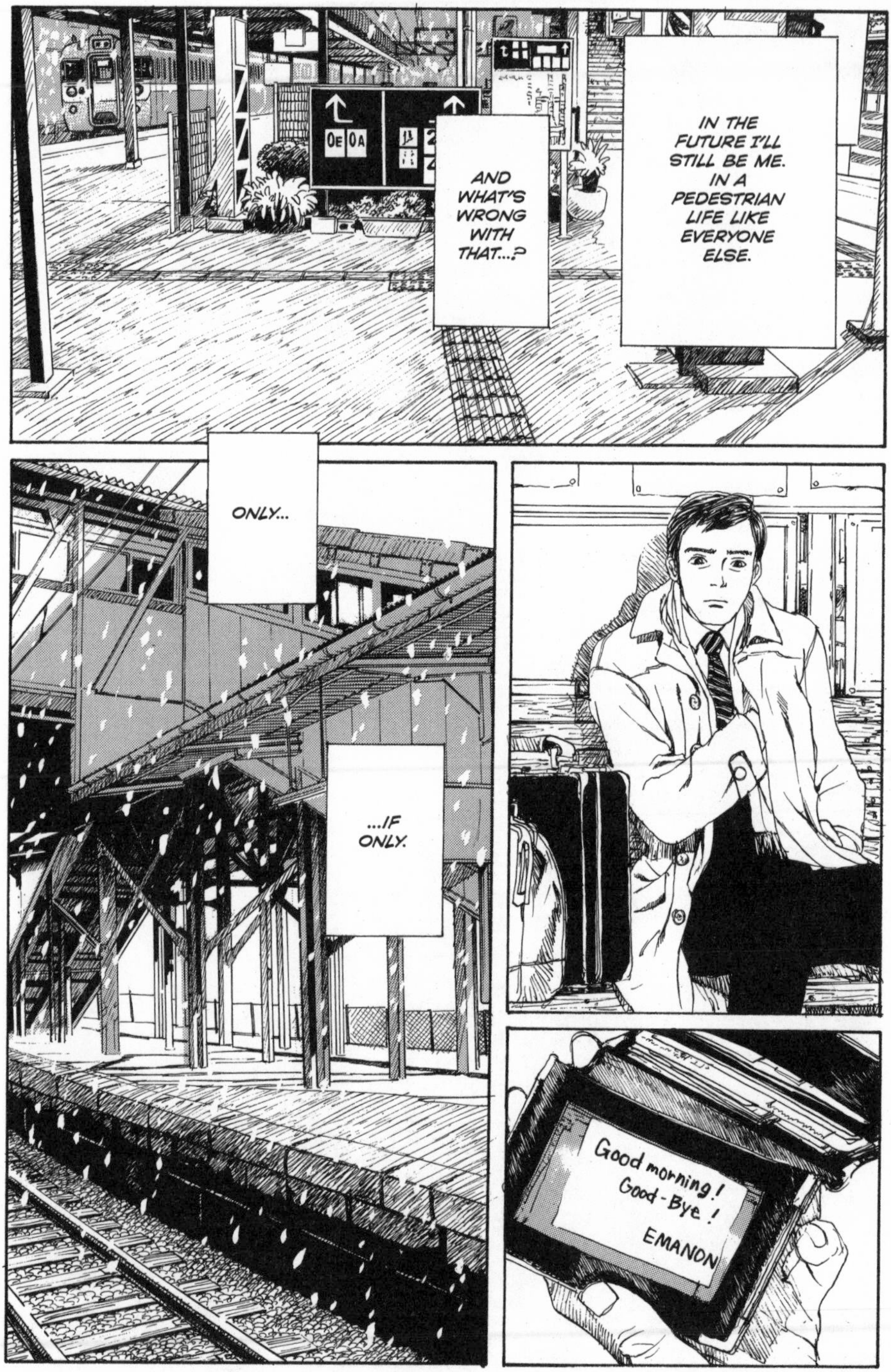
IN THE FUTURE I'LL STILL BE ME. IN A PEDESTRIAN LIFE LIKE EVERYONE ELSE.
AND WHAT'S WRONG WITH THAT...?
Good morning! Good-Bye! EMANON
ONLY...
...IF ONLY.

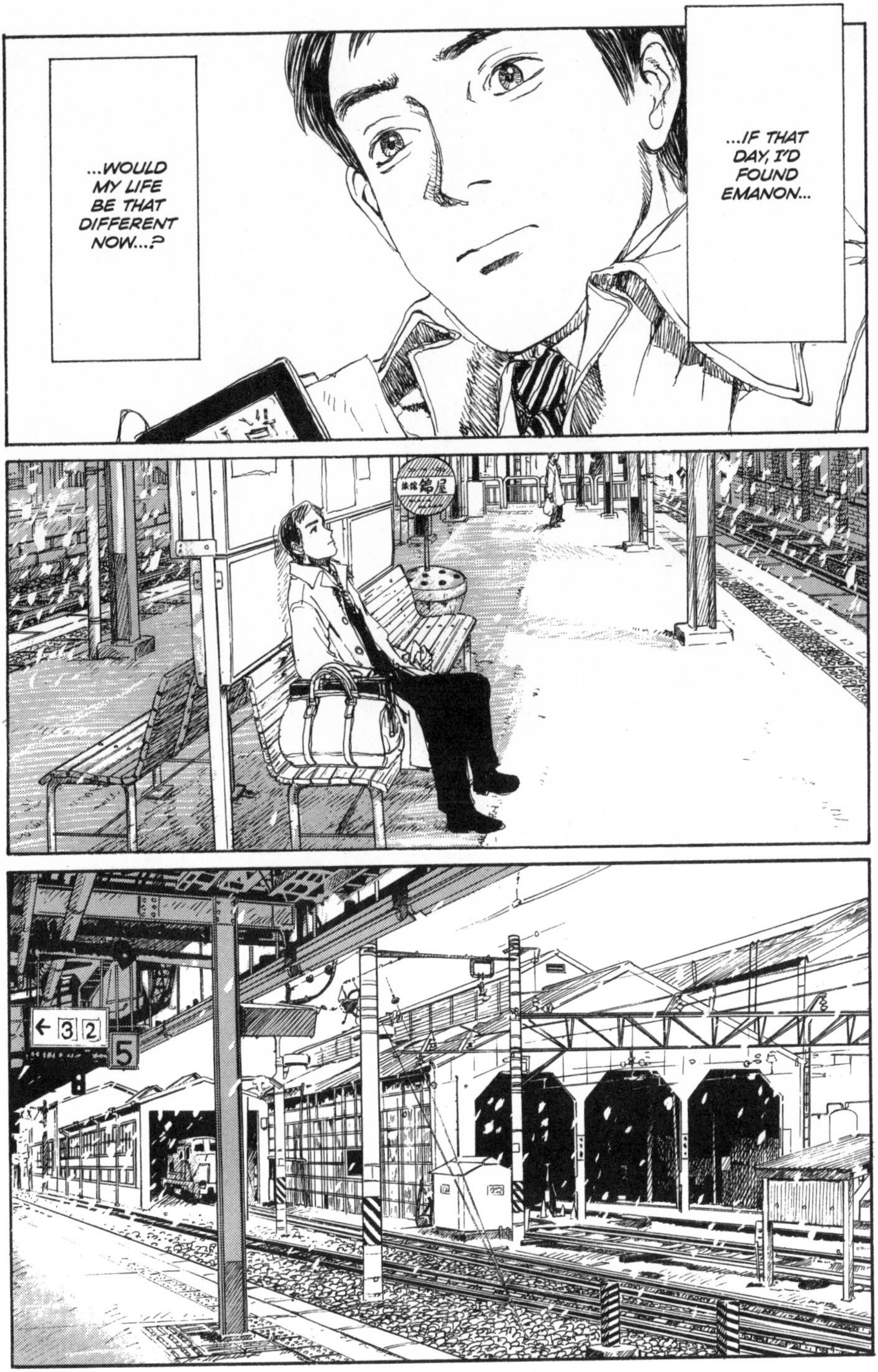
...IF THAT DAY, I'D FOUND EMANON...
...WOULD MY LIFE BE THAT DIFFERENT NOW...?
← 3 2
5

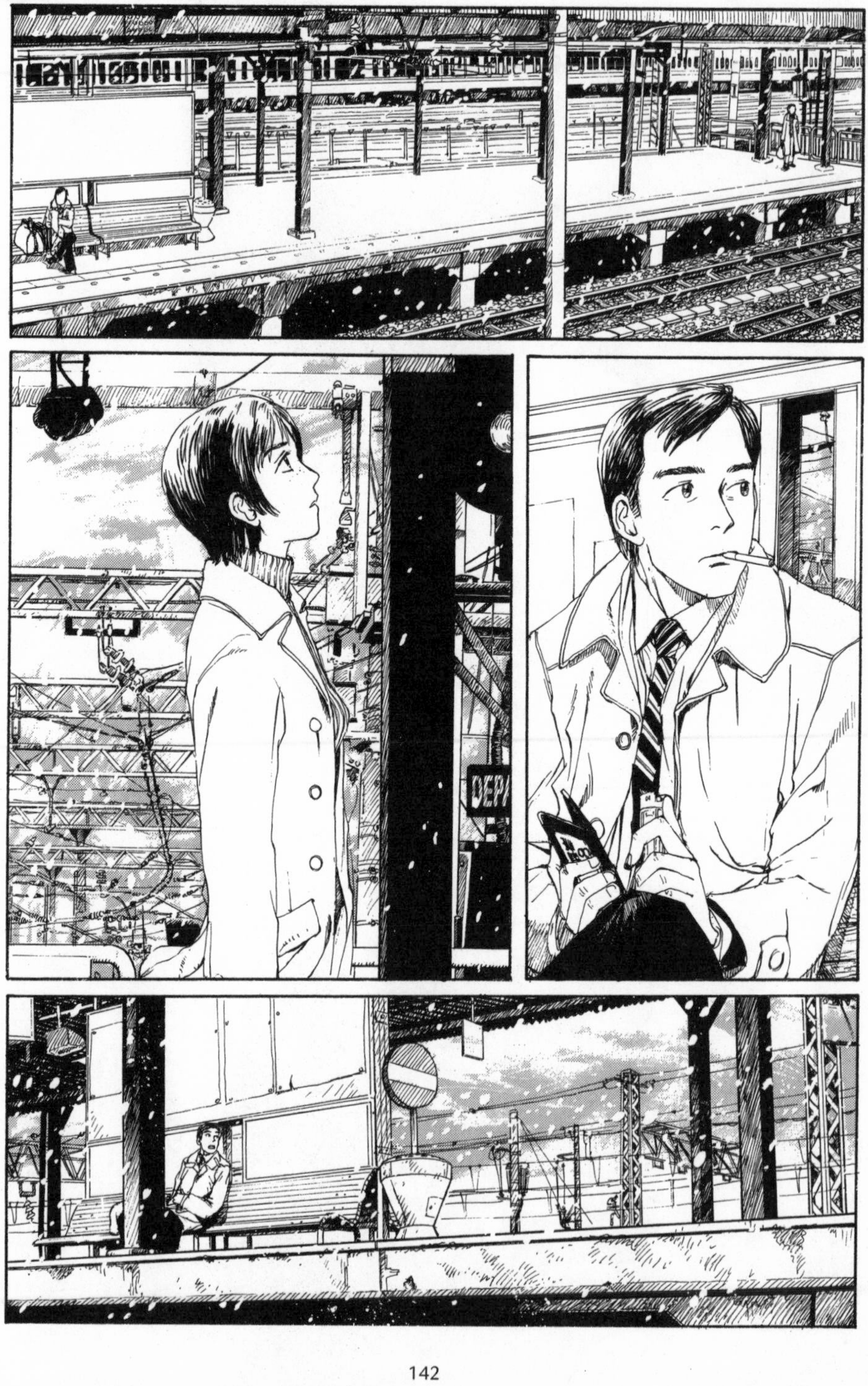
DEPA

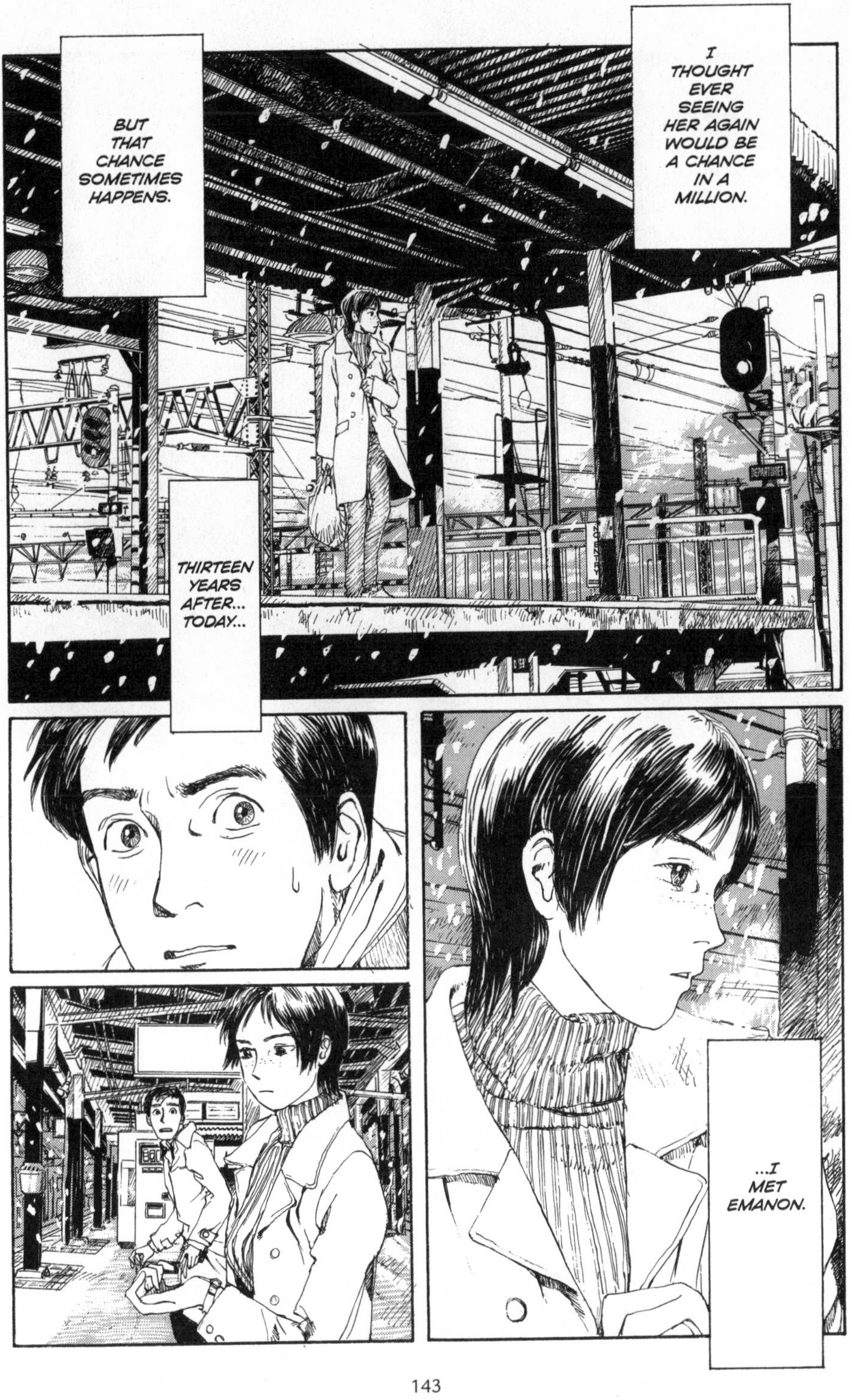
I THOUGHT EVER SEEING HER AGAIN WOULD BE A CHANCE IN A MILLION.
BUT THAT CHANCE SOMETIMES HAPPENS.
THIRTEEN YEARS AFTER... TODAY...
...I MET EMANON.

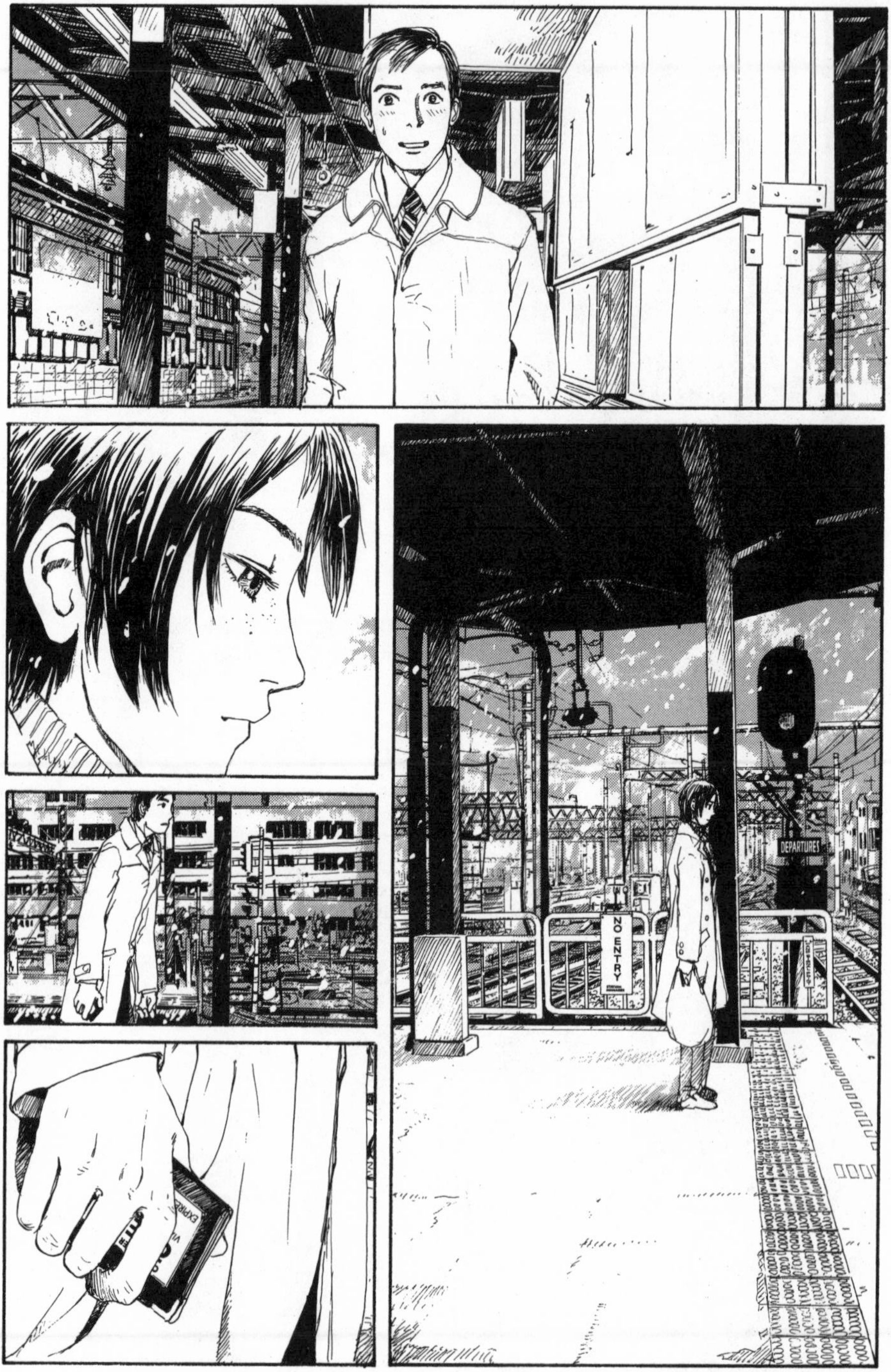
DEPARTURES
NO ENTRY

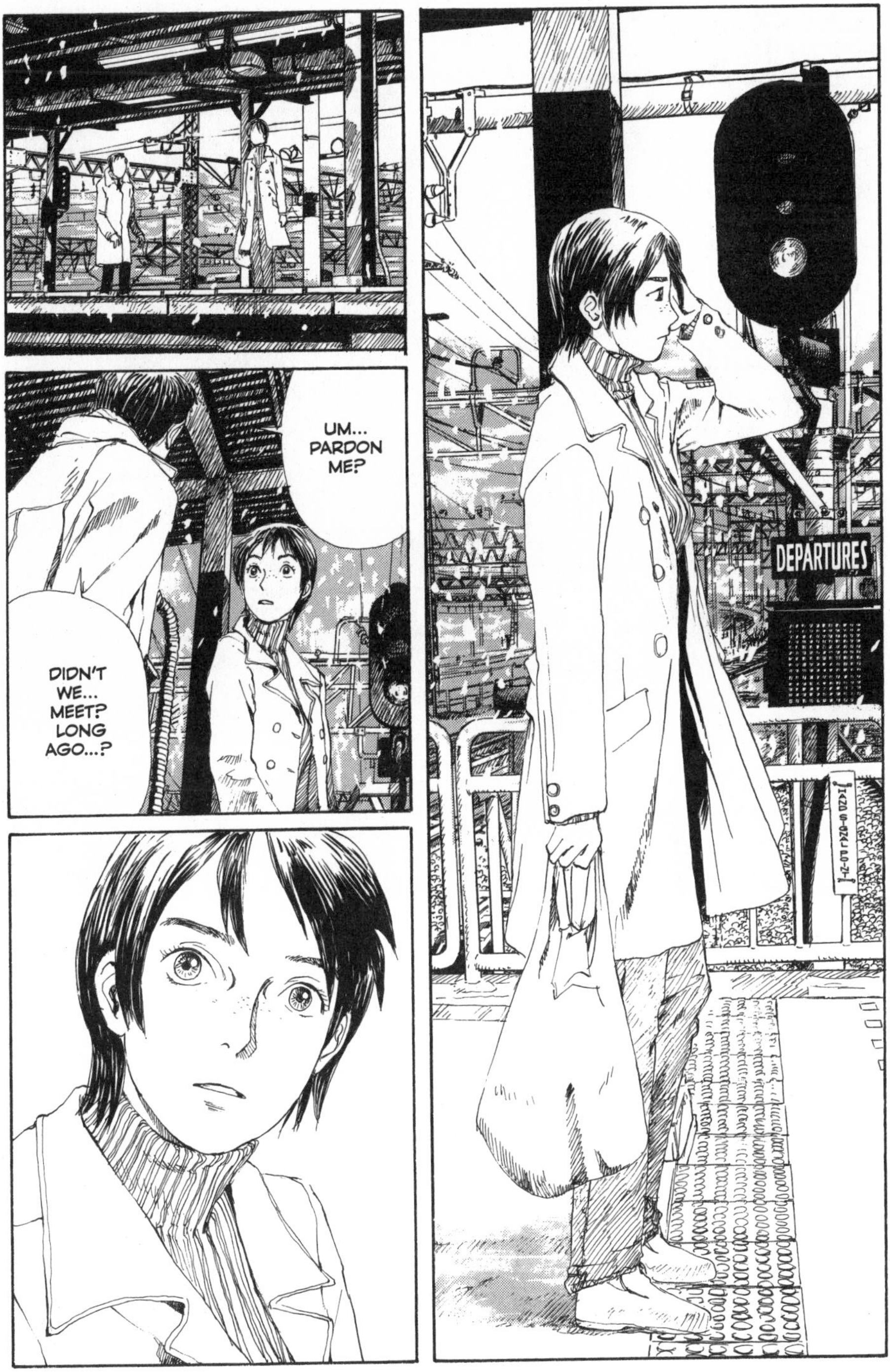
DEPARTURES
UM... PARDON ME?
DIDN'T WE... MEET? LONG AGO...?

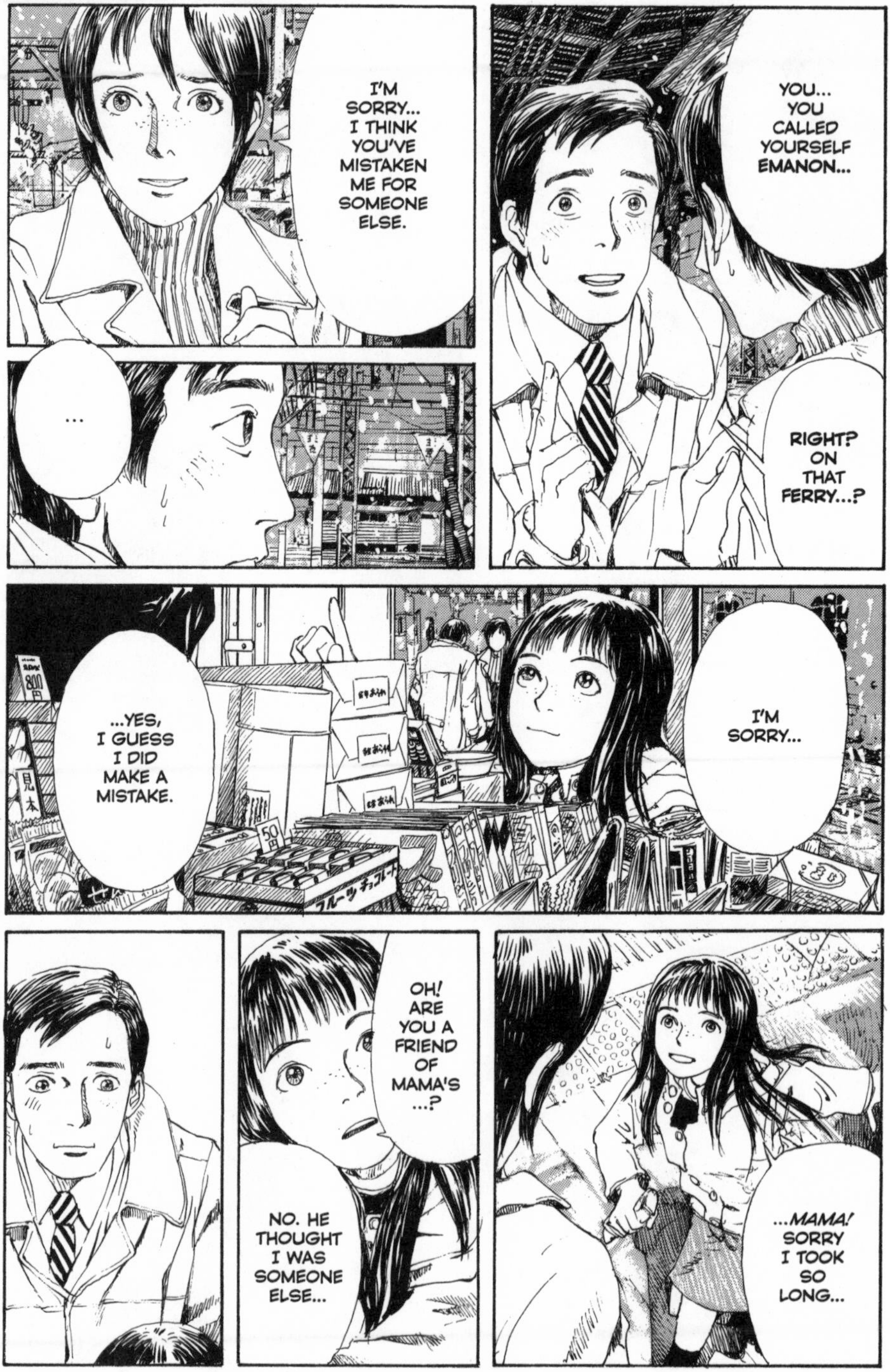
YOU... YOU CALLED YOURSELF EMANON...
RIGHT? ON THAT FERRY...?
I'M SORRY... I THINK YOU'VE MISTAKEN ME FOR SOMEONE ELSE.
...
I'M SORRY...
...YES, I GUESS I DID MAKE A MISTAKE.
...*MAMA!* SORRY I TOOK SO LONG...
OH! ARE YOU A FRIEND OF MAMA'S ...?
NO. HE THOUGHT I WAS SOMEONE ELSE...

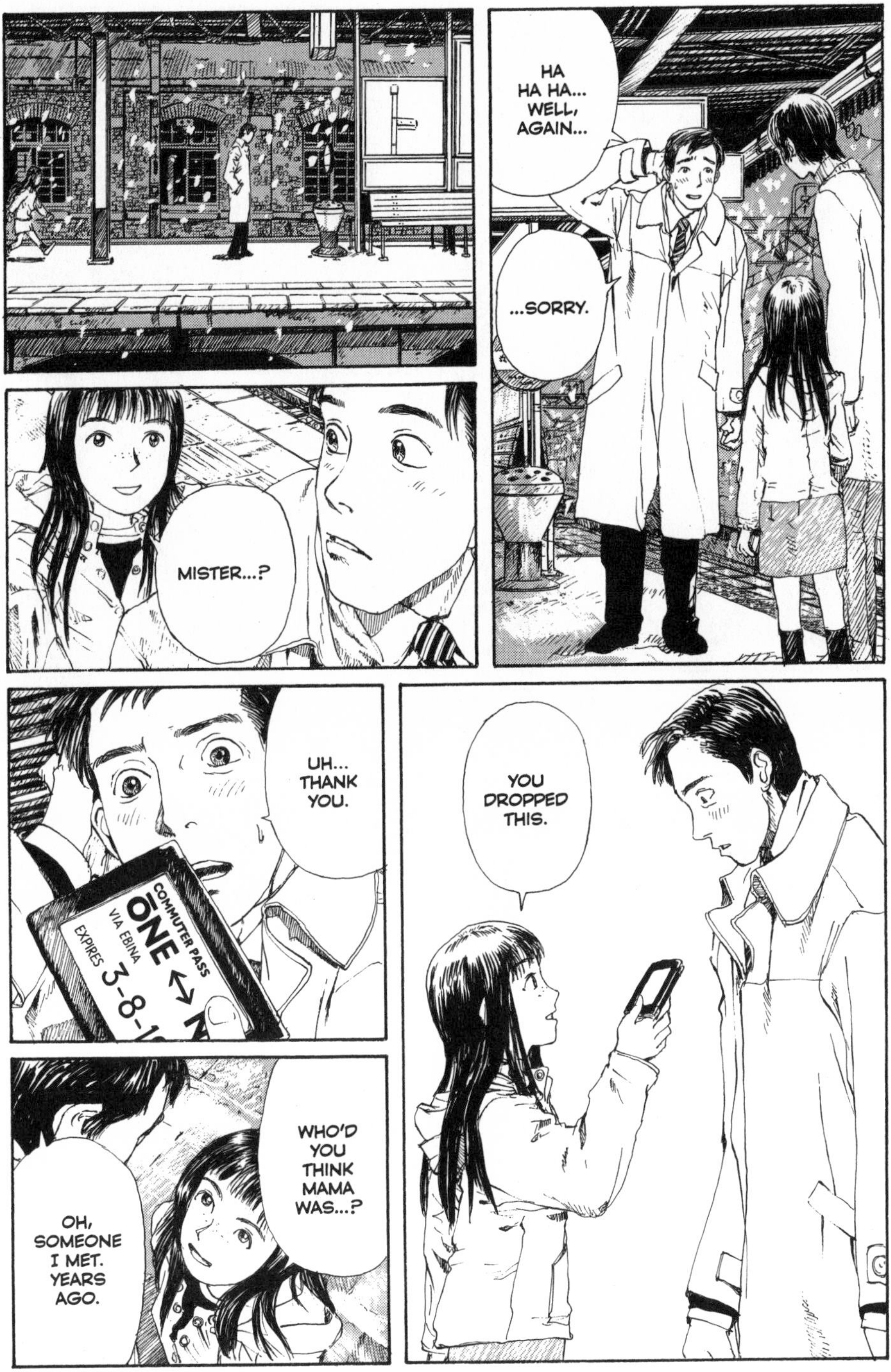
MISTER...?
HA HA HA... WELL, AGAIN...
...SORRY.
YOU DROPPED THIS.
UH... THANK YOU.
COMMUTER PASS
ŌNE
VIA EBINA
EXPIRES
WHO'D YOU THINK MAMA WAS...?
OH, SOMEONE I MET. YEARS AGO.

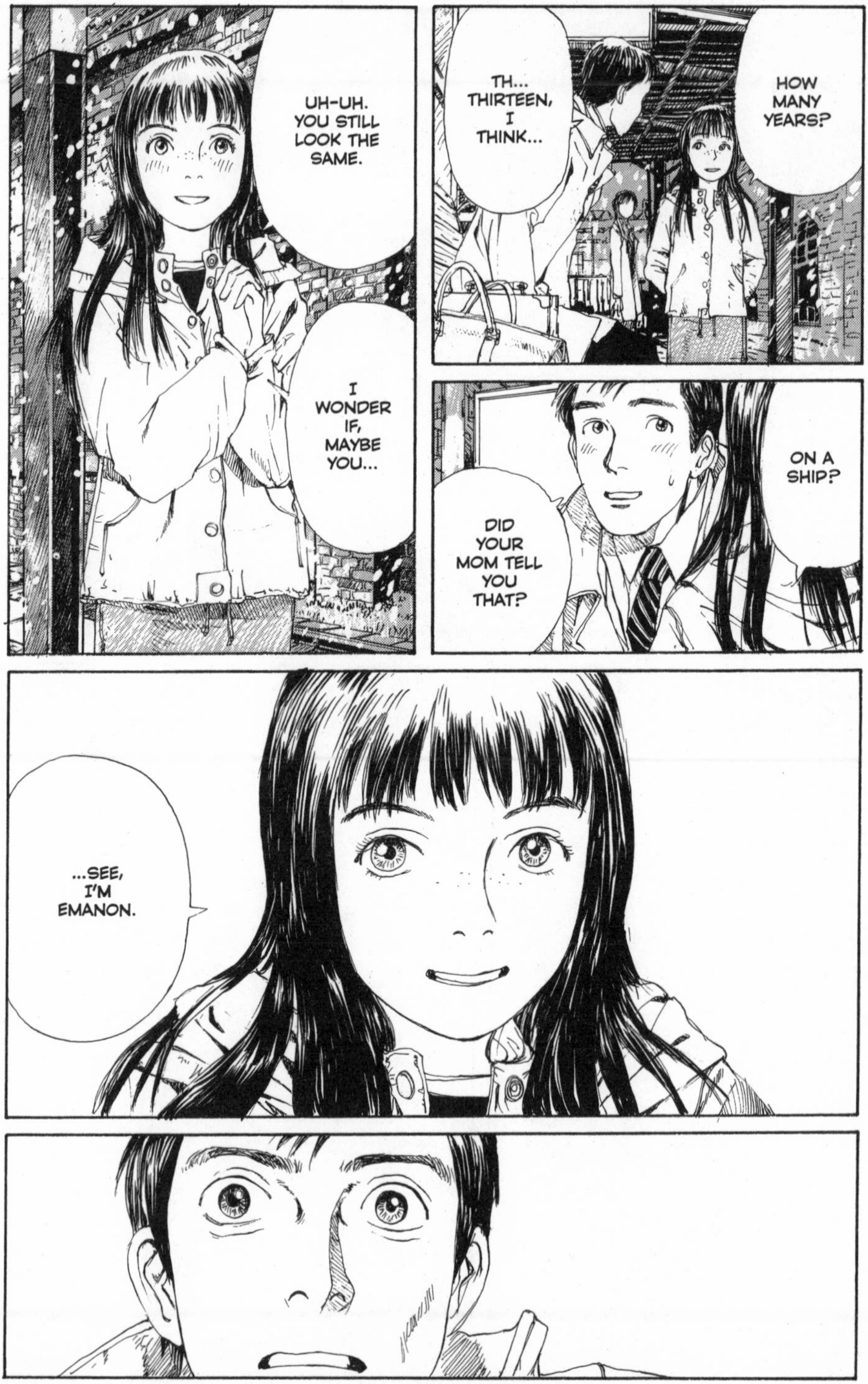
HOW MANY YEARS?
TH... THIRTEEN, I THINK...
ON A SHIP?
DID YOUR MOM TELL YOU THAT?
UH-UH. YOU STILL LOOK THE SAME.
I WONDER IF, MAYBE YOU...
...SEE, I'M EMANON.

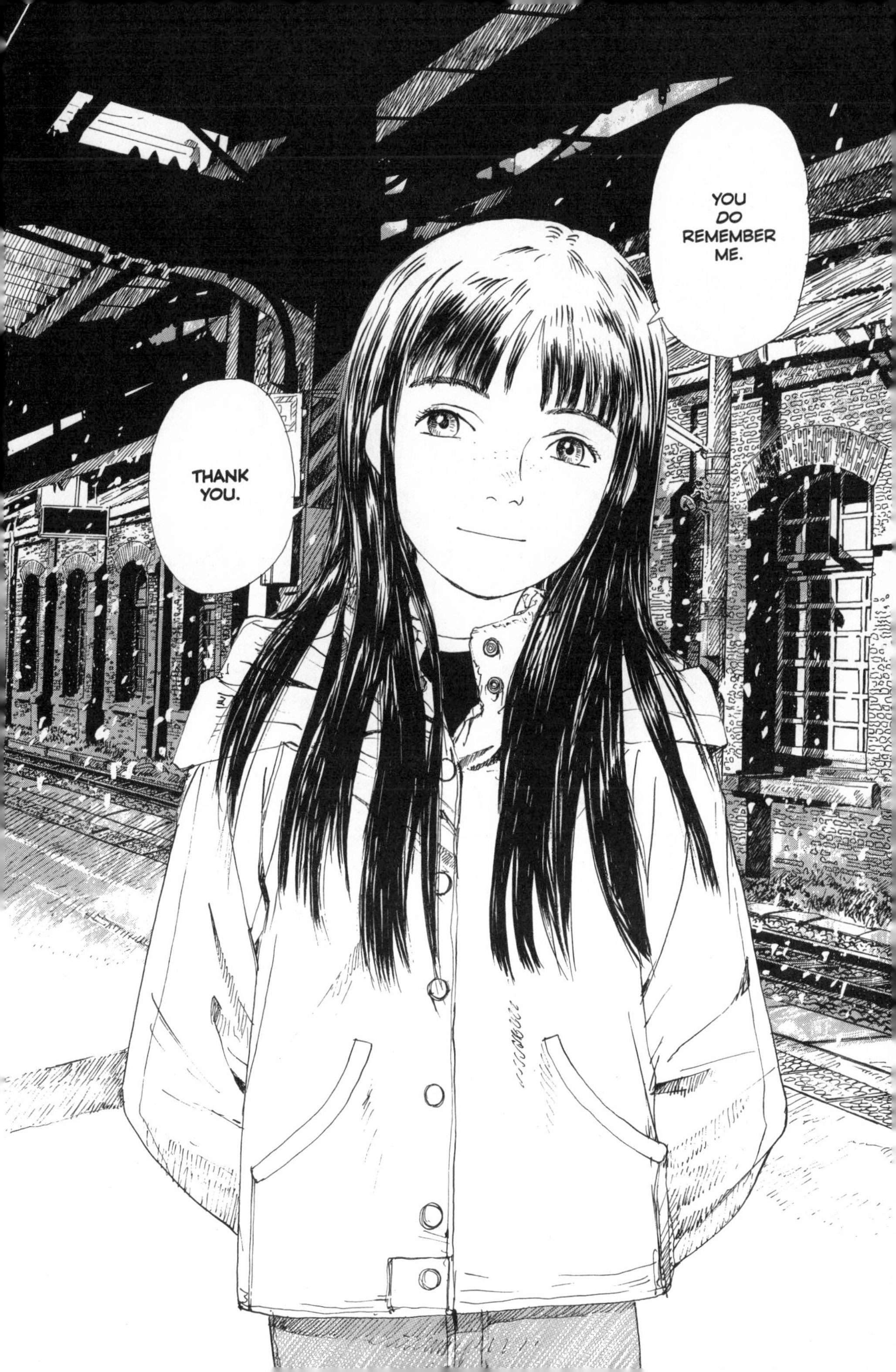
YOU DO REMEMBER ME.
THANK YOU.

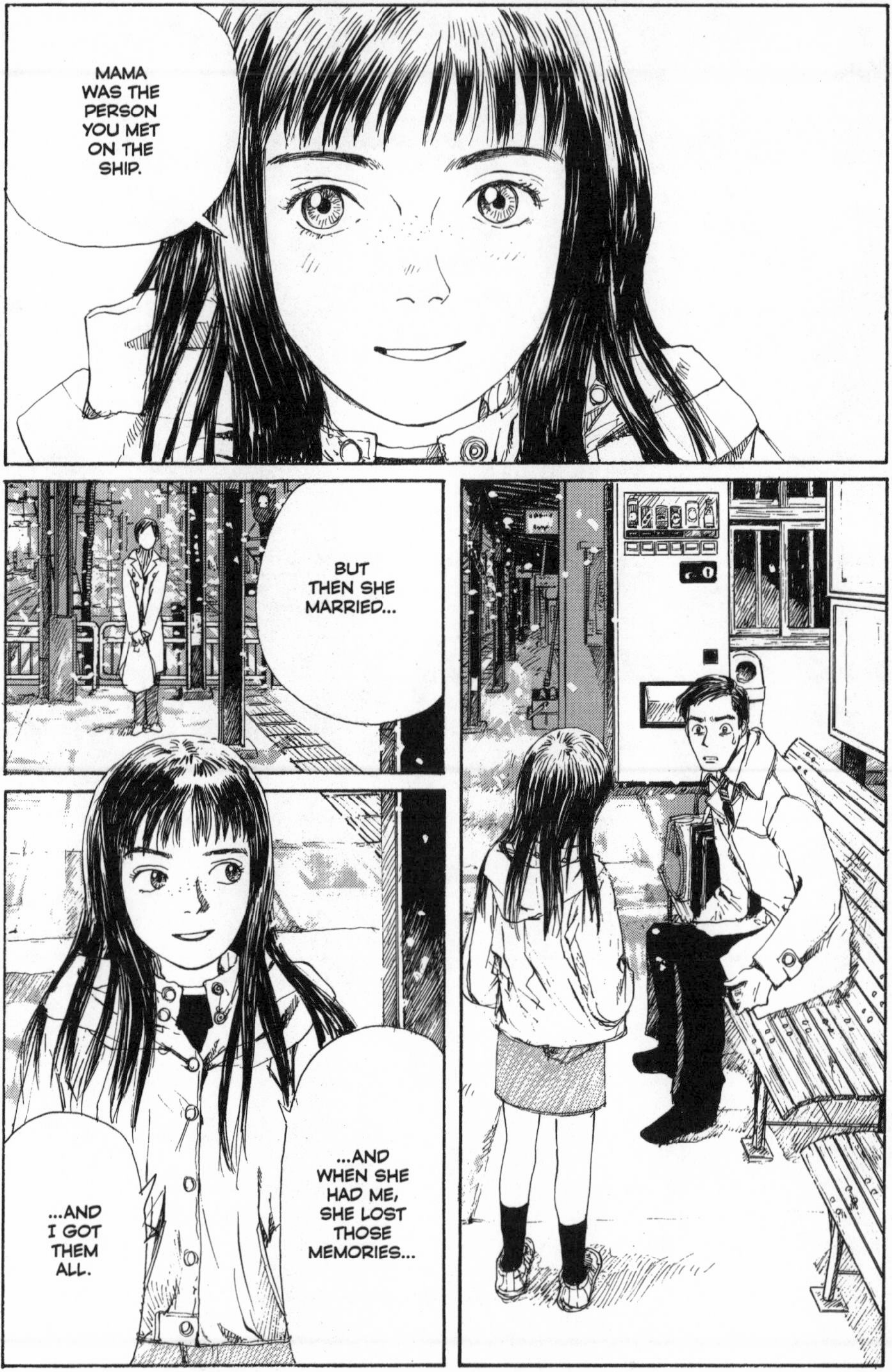
MAMA WAS THE PERSON YOU MET ON THE SHIP.
BUT THEN SHE MARRIED...
...AND WHEN SHE HAD ME, SHE LOST THOSE MEMORIES...
...AND I GOT THEM ALL.

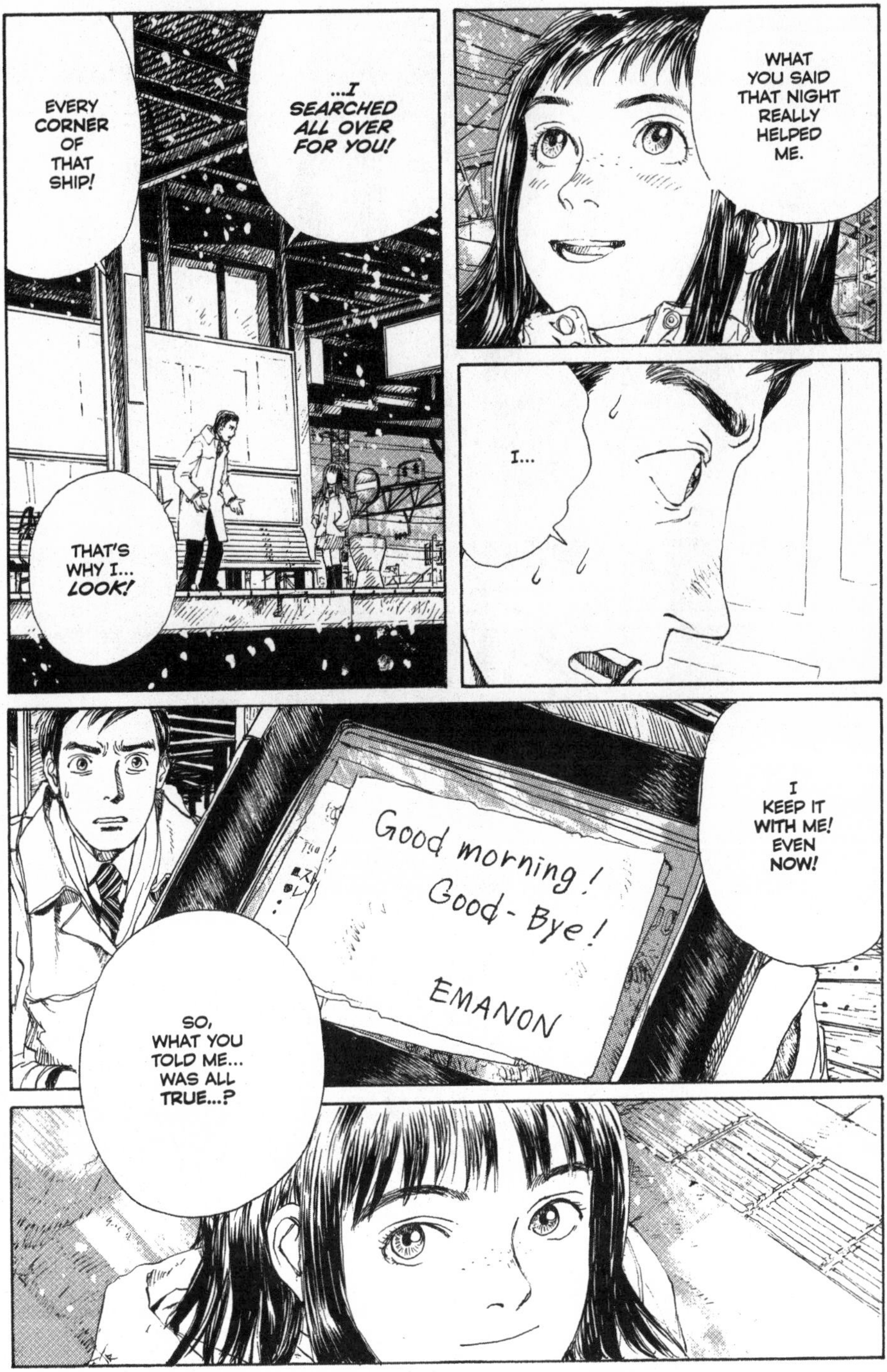
WHAT YOU SAID THAT NIGHT REALLY HELPED ME.
I...
...I SEARCHED ALL OVER FOR YOU!
EVERY CORNER OF THAT SHIP!
THAT'S WHY I... LOOK!
I KEEP IT WITH ME! EVEN NOW!
Good morning! Good-Bye!
EMANON
SO, WHAT YOU TOLD ME... WAS ALL TRUE...?

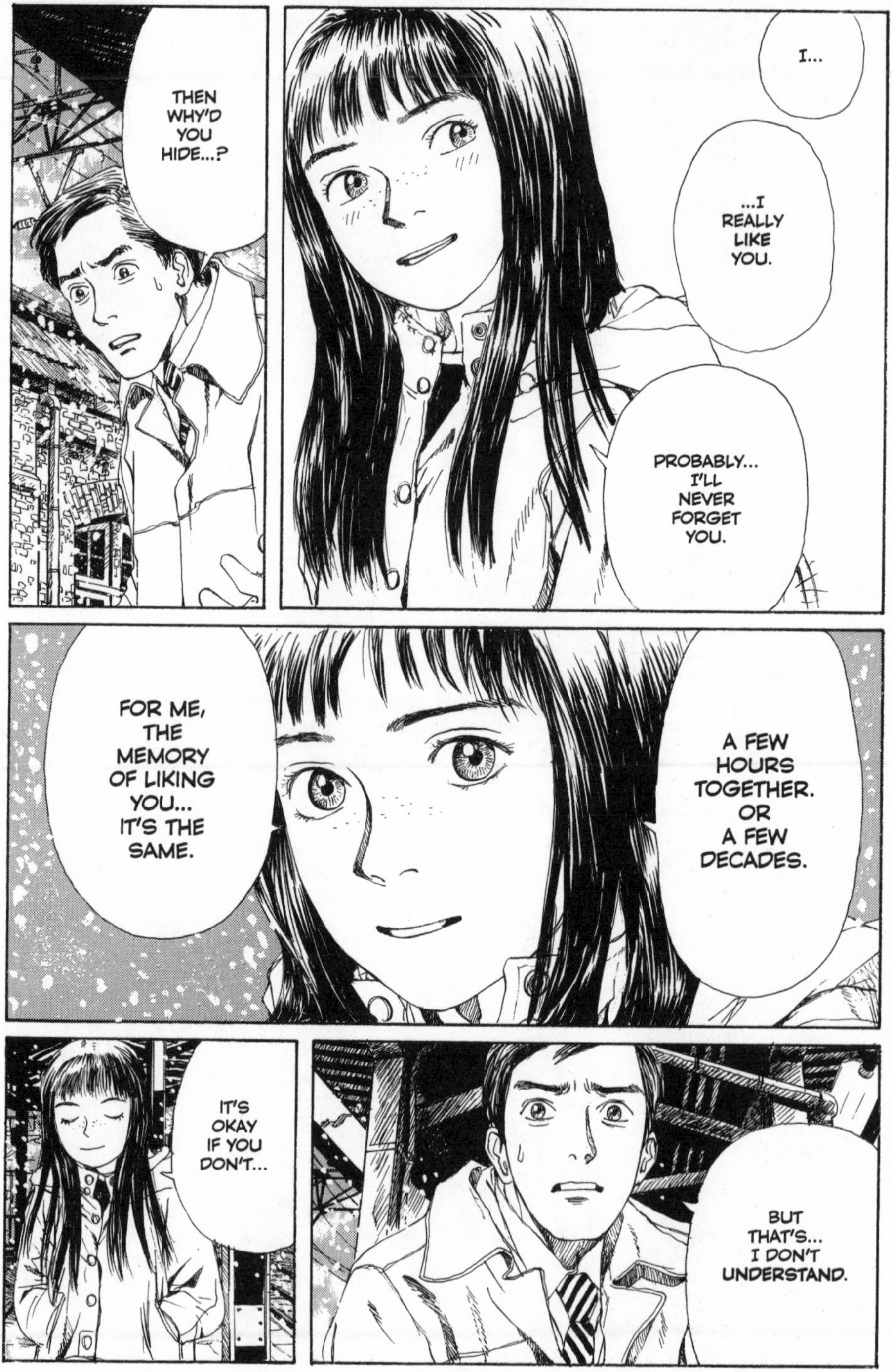
I...
...I REALLY LIKE YOU.
PROBABLY... I'LL NEVER FORGET YOU.
THEN WHY'D YOU HIDE...?
A FEW HOURS TOGETHER. OR A FEW DECADES.
FOR ME, THE MEMORY OF LIKING YOU... IT'S THE SAME.
BUT THAT'S... I DON'T UNDERSTAND.
IT'S OKAY IF YOU DON'T...

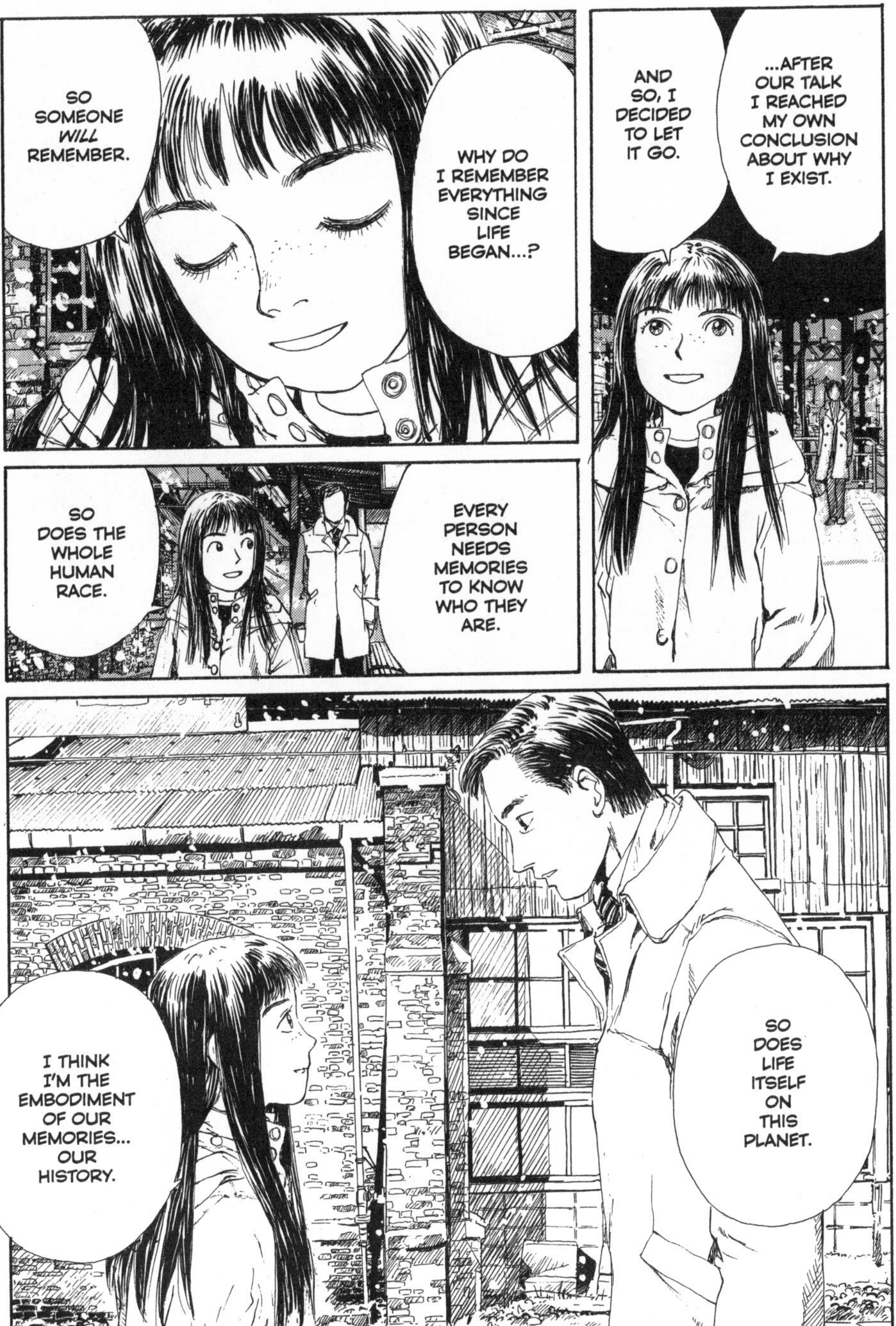
...AFTER OUR TALK I REACHED MY OWN CONCLUSION ABOUT WHY I EXIST.
AND SO, I DECIDED TO LET IT GO.
WHY DO I REMEMBER EVERYTHING SINCE LIFE BEGAN...?
SO SOMEONE *WILL* REMEMBER.
EVERY PERSON NEEDS MEMORIES TO KNOW WHO THEY ARE.
SO DOES THE WHOLE HUMAN RACE.
SO DOES LIFE ITSELF ON THIS PLANET.
I THINK I'M THE EMBODIMENT OF OUR MEMORIES... OUR HISTORY.

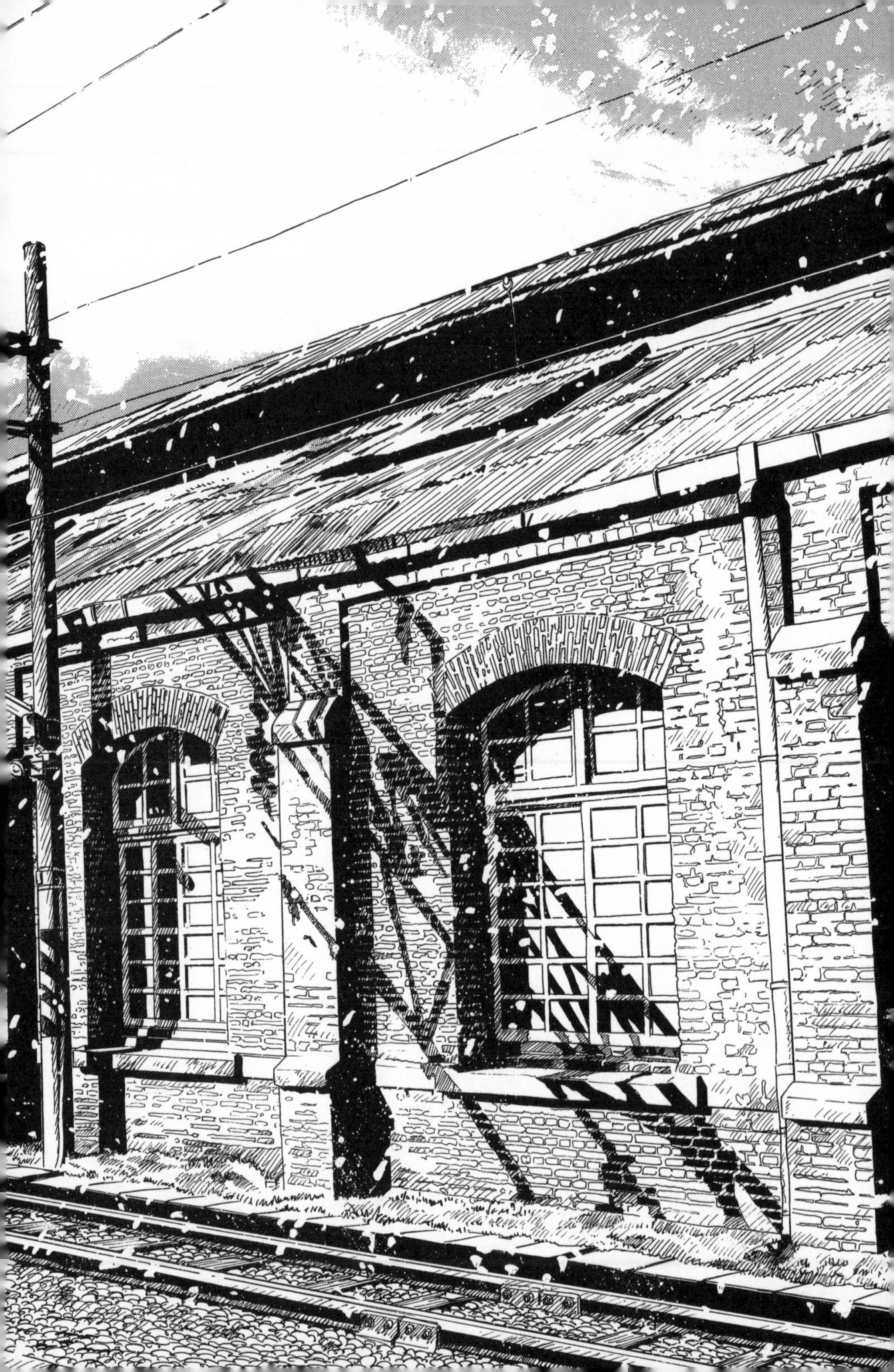

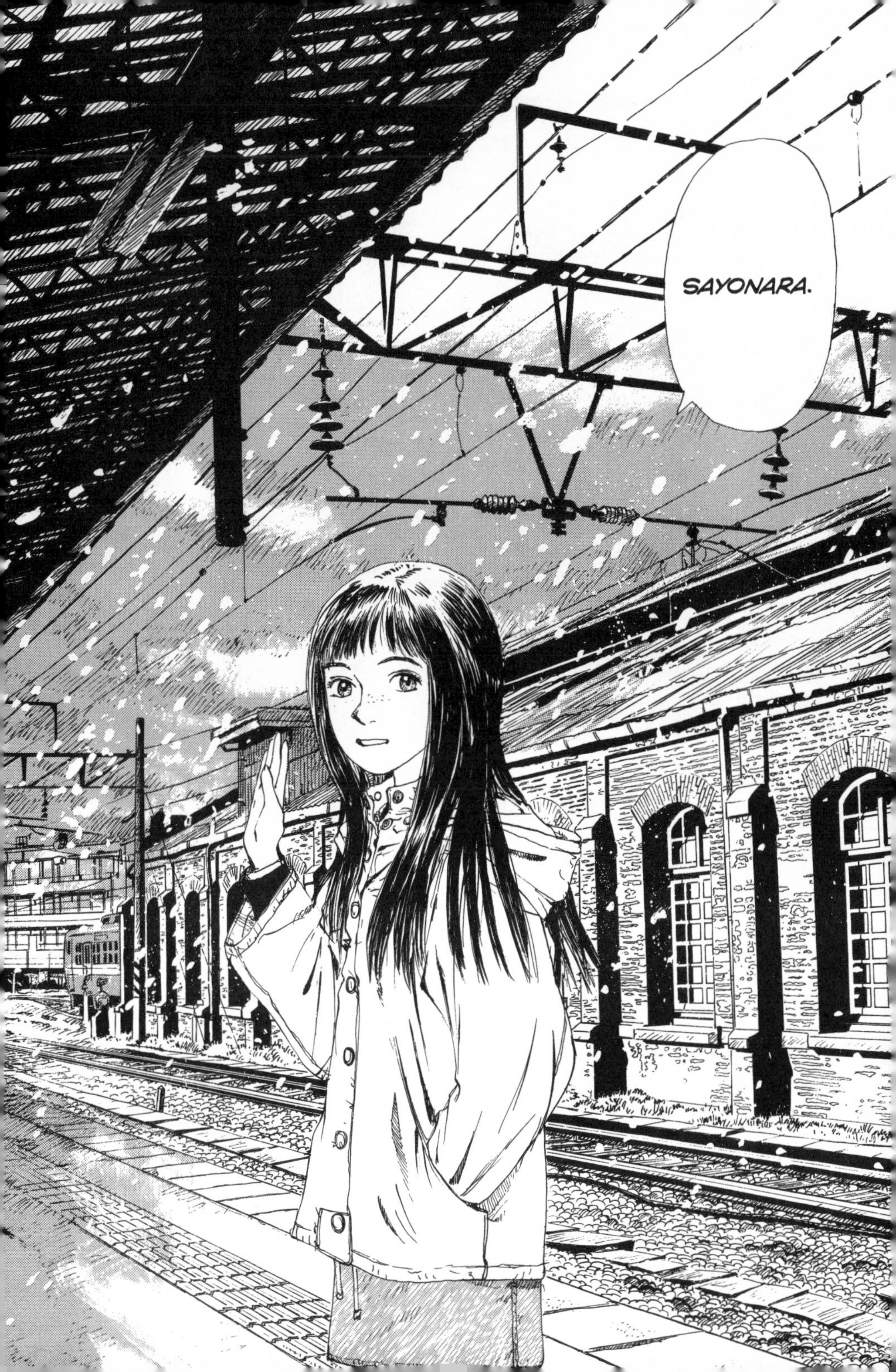
SAYONARA.

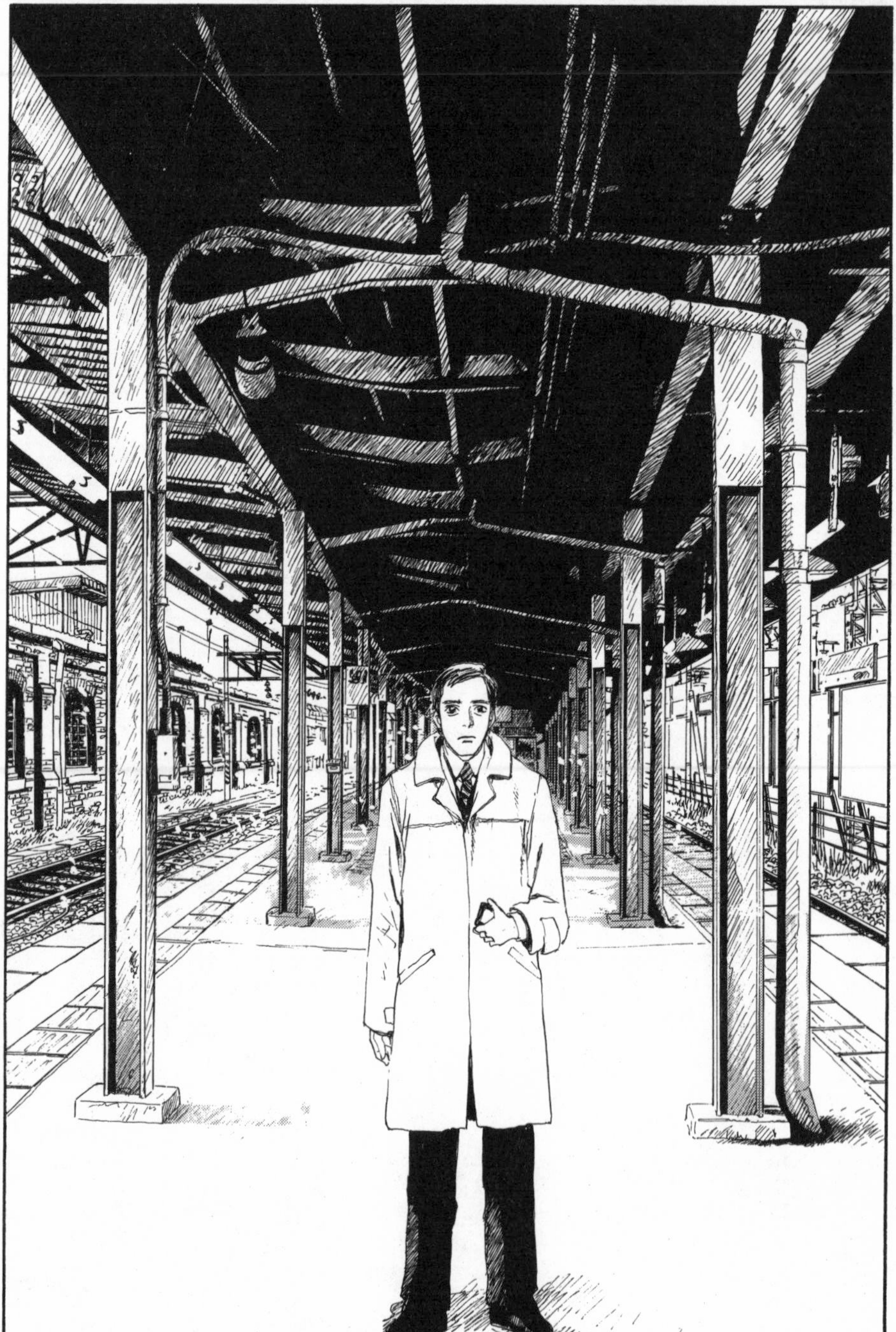

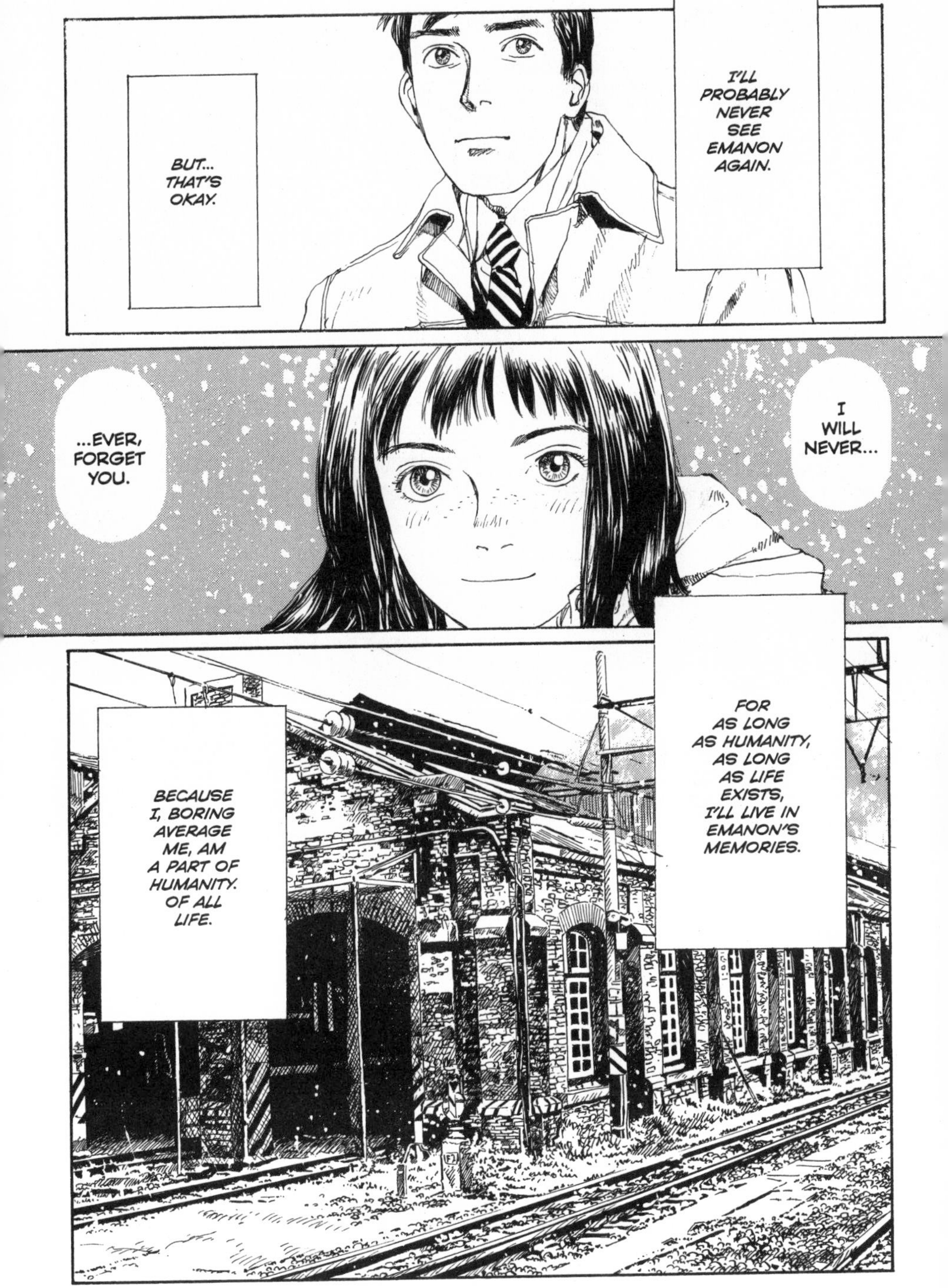
I'LL PROBABLY NEVER SEE EMANON AGAIN.
BUT... THAT'S OKAY.
I WILL NEVER...
...EVER, FORGET YOU.
FOR AS LONG AS HUMANITY, AS LONG AS LIFE EXISTS, I'LL LIVE IN EMANON'S MEMORIES.
BECAUSE I, BORING AVERAGE ME, AM A PART OF HUMANITY. OF ALL LIFE.

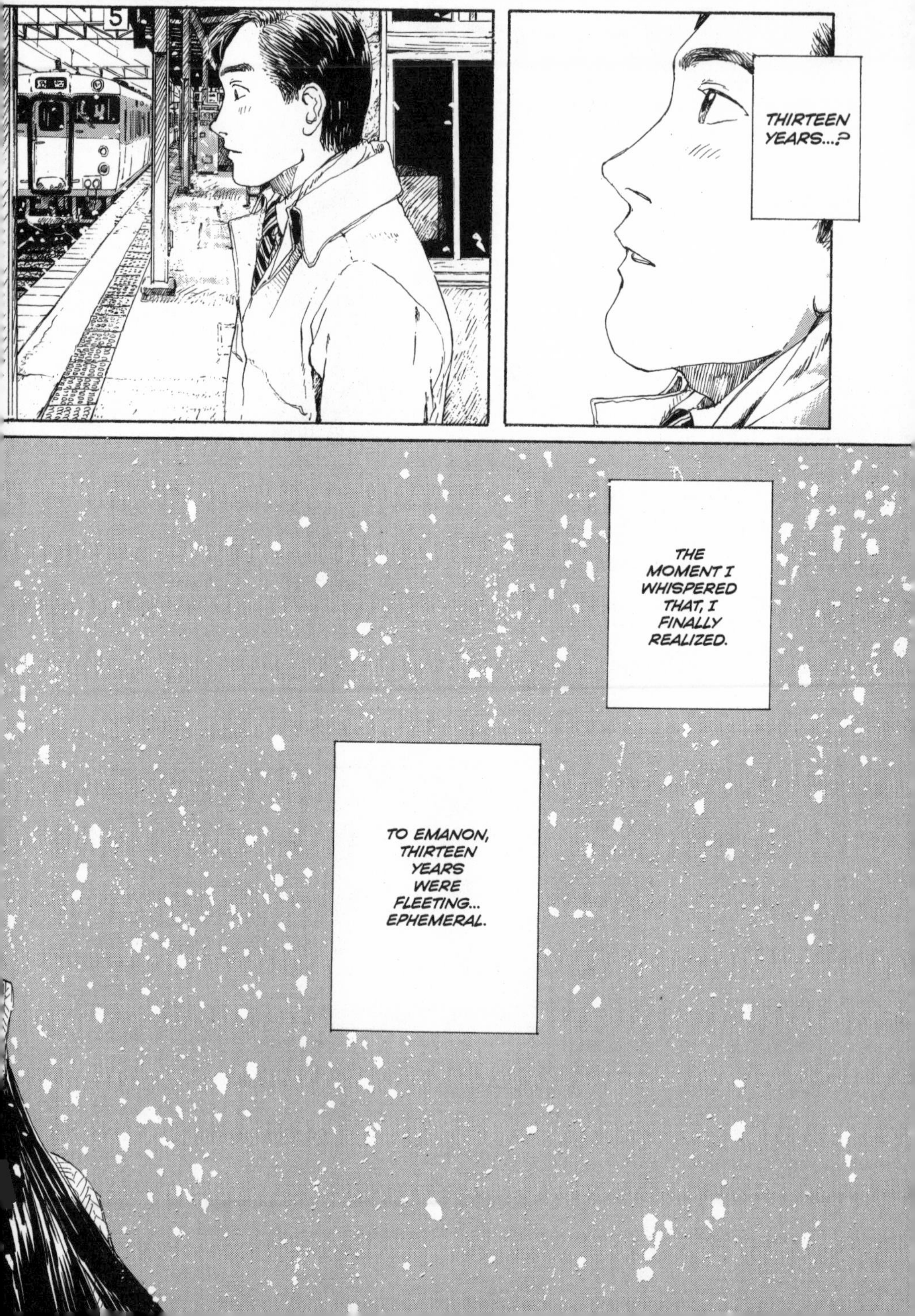
THIRTEEN YEARS...?
THE MOMENT I WHISPERED THAT, I FINALLY REALIZED.
TO EMANON, THIRTEEN YEARS WERE FLEETING... EPHEMERAL.

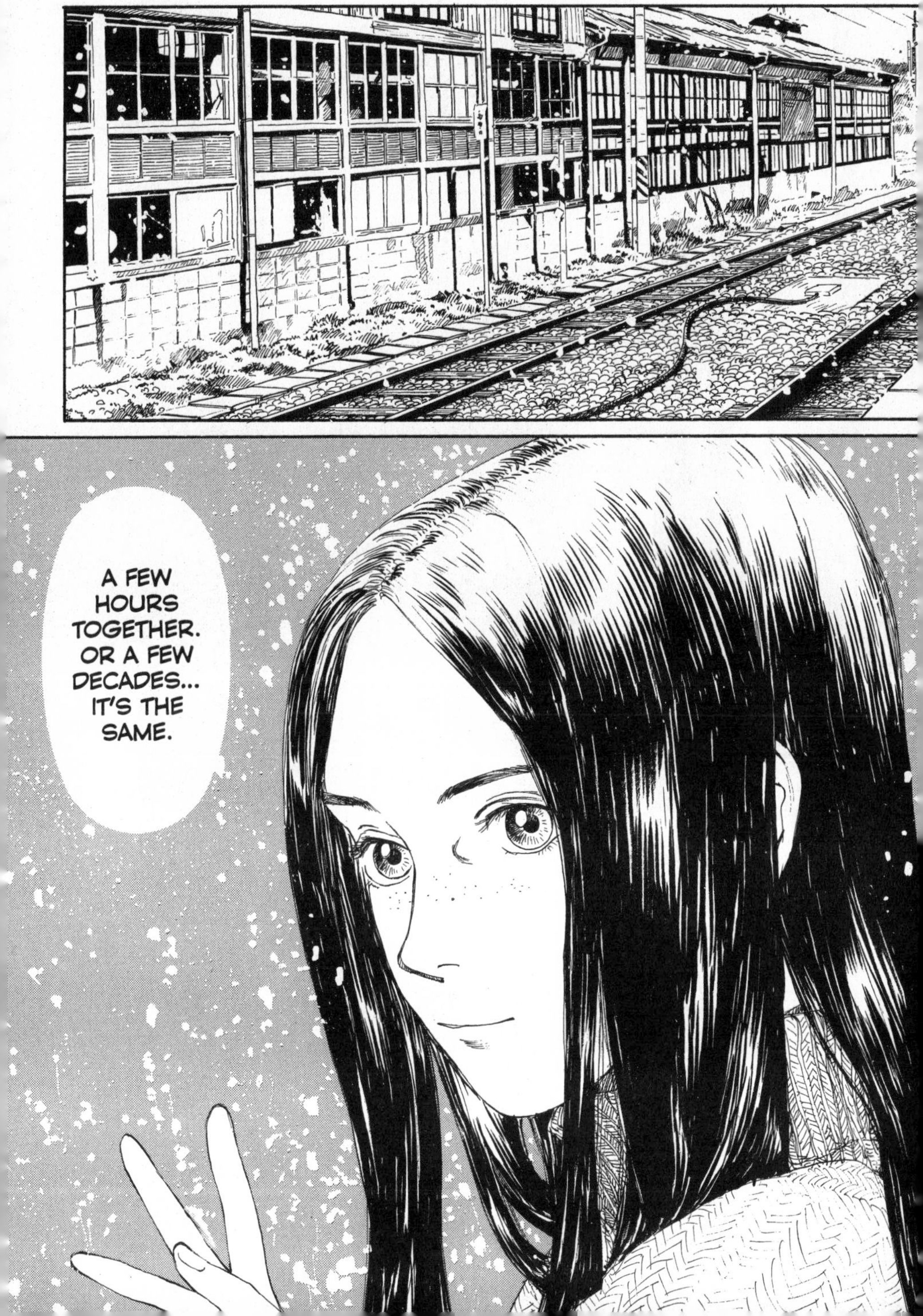
A FEW HOURS TOGETHER. OR A FEW DECADES... IT'S THE SAME.

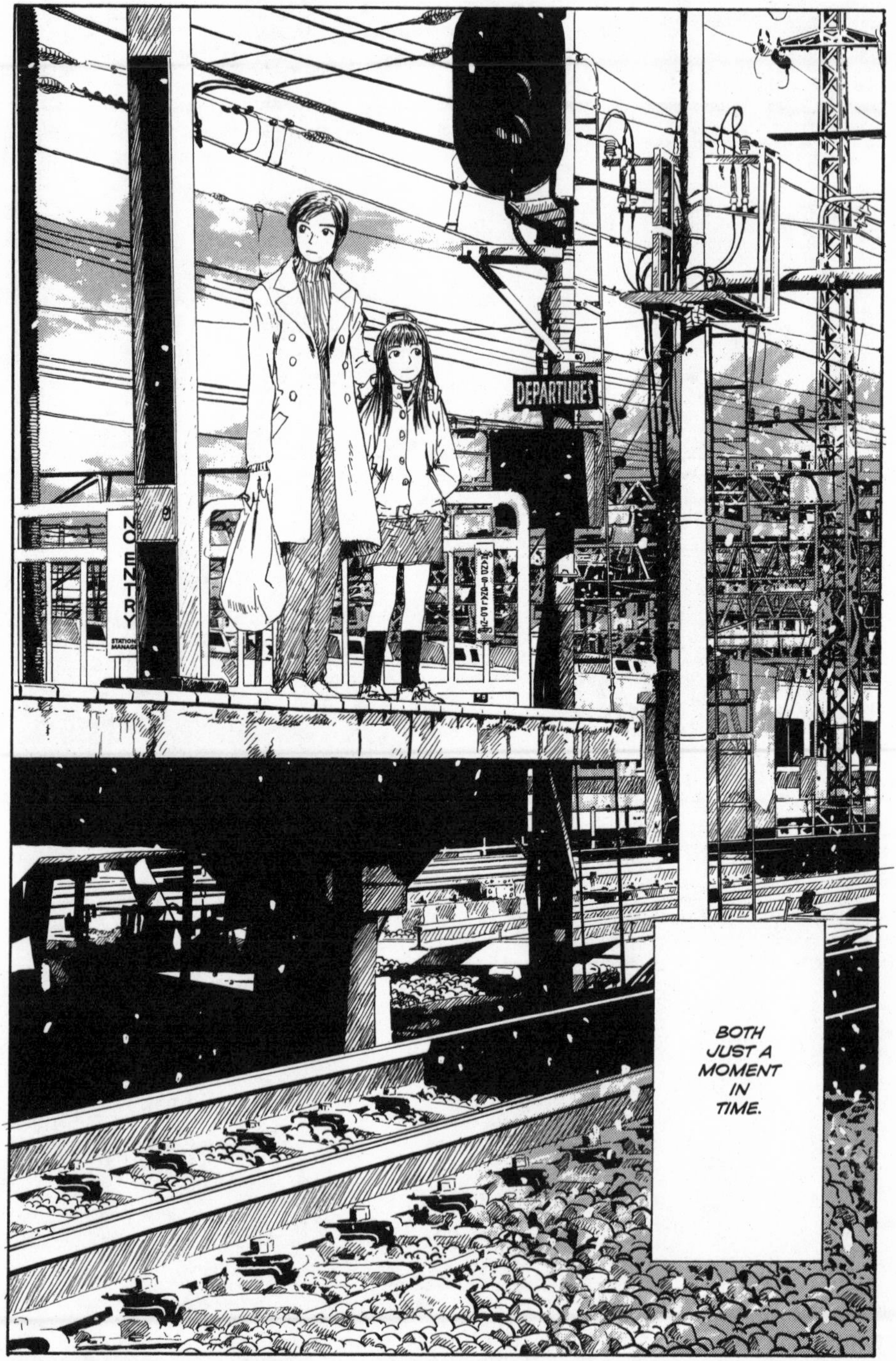
DEPARTURES
NO ENTRY
BOTH JUST A MOMENT IN TIME.

END VOL.1 THANKS TO KEISUKE HAYAMI & ATSUKO MUTO

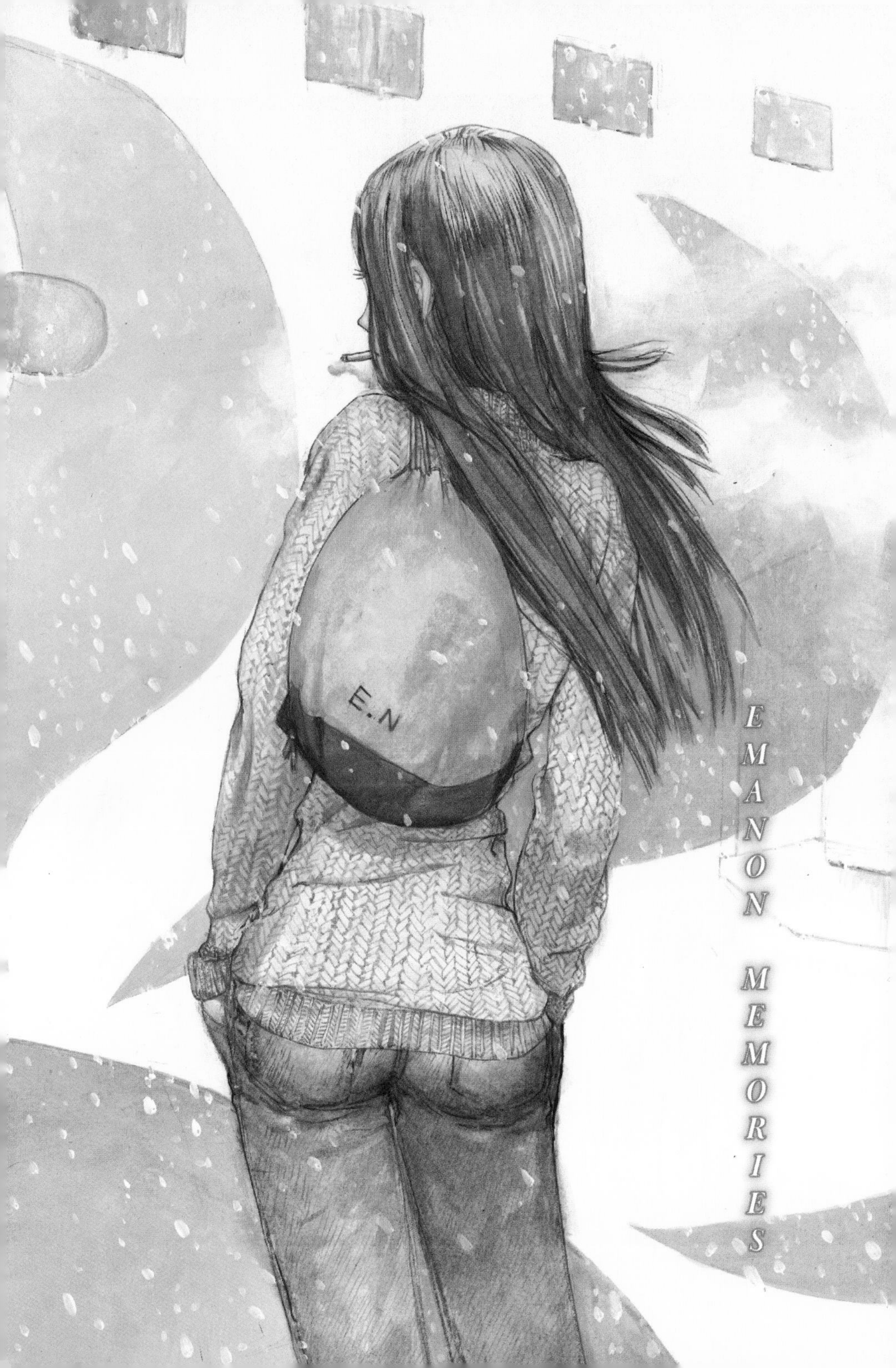
E.N
EMANON MEMORIES

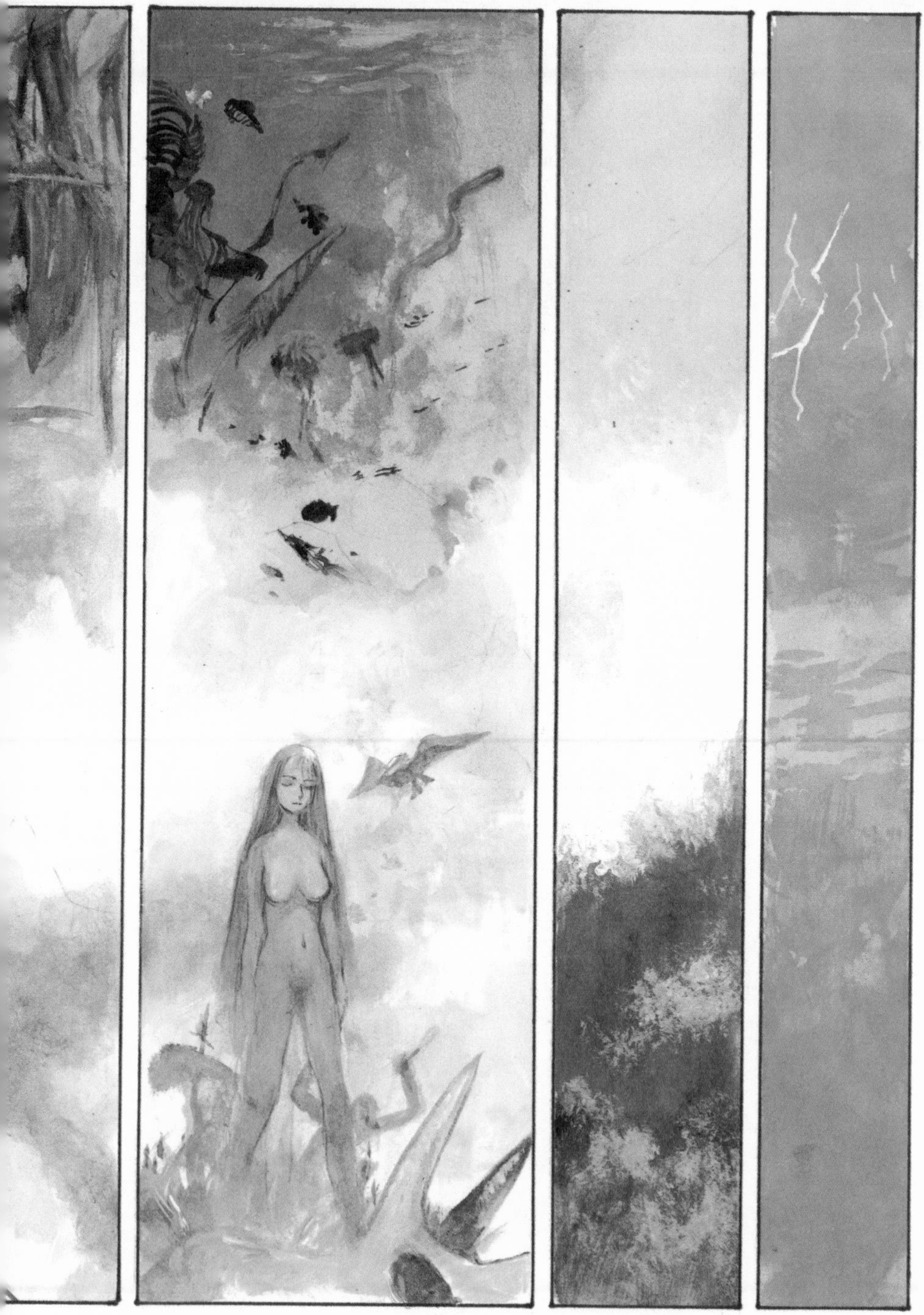

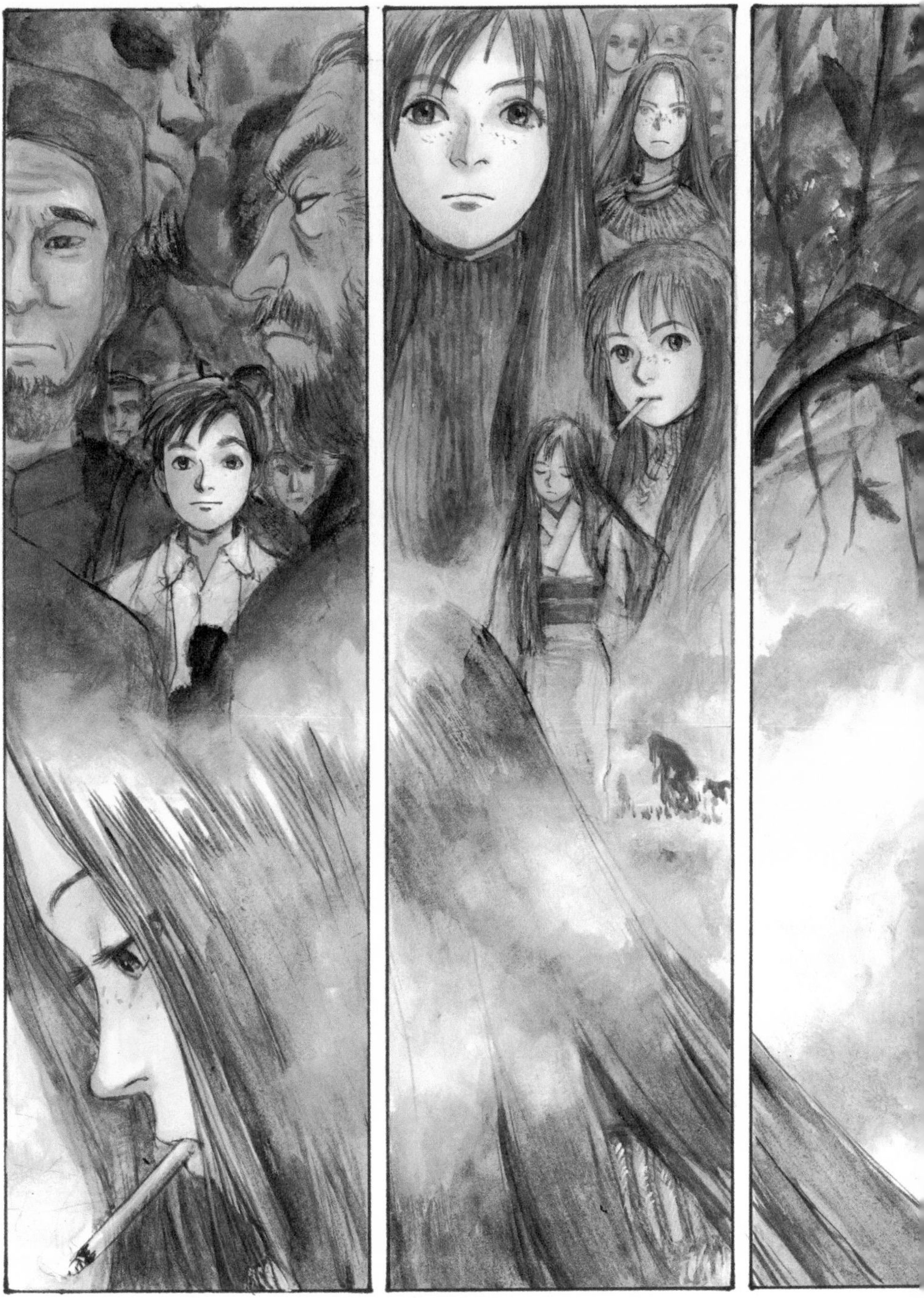

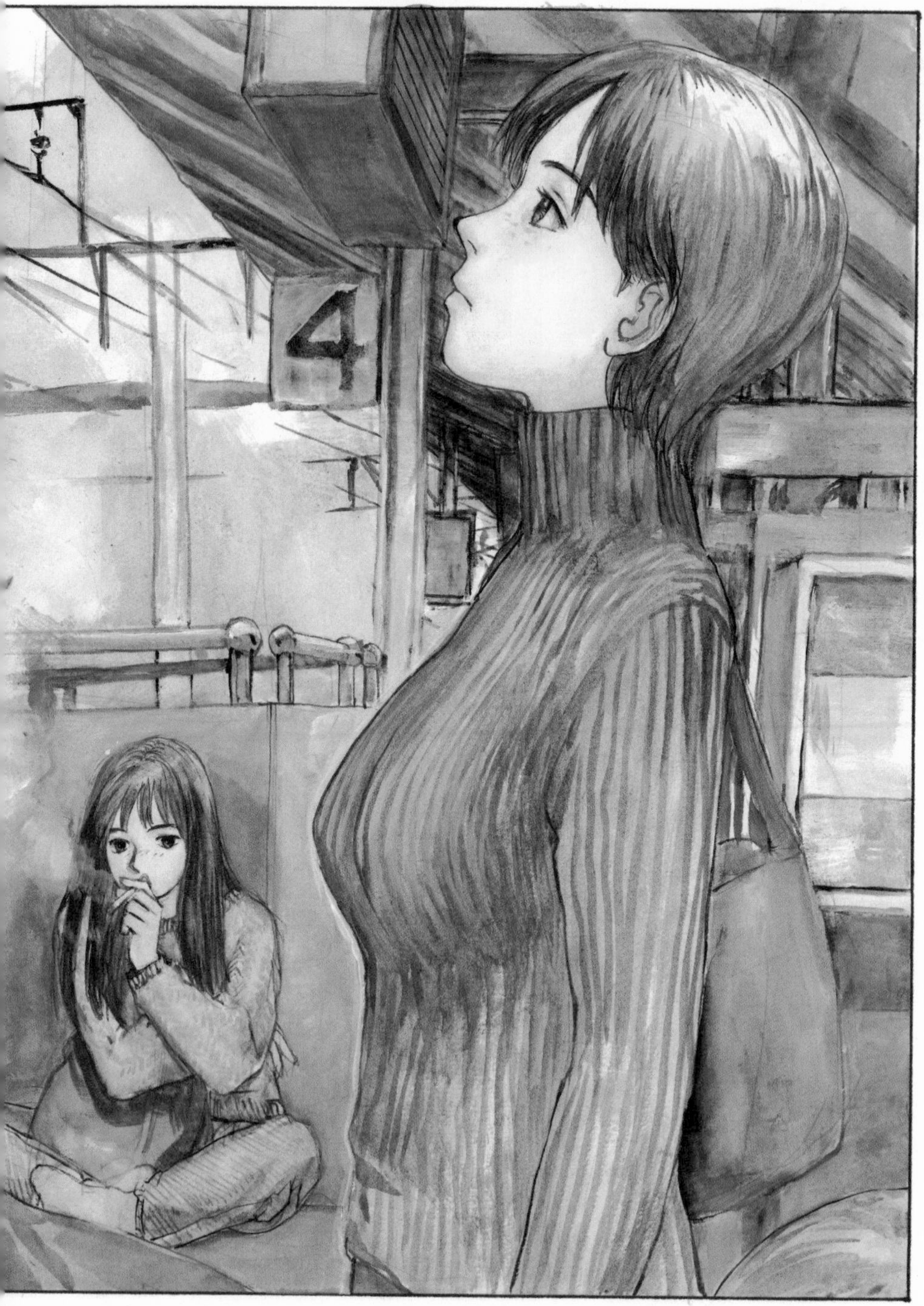
4

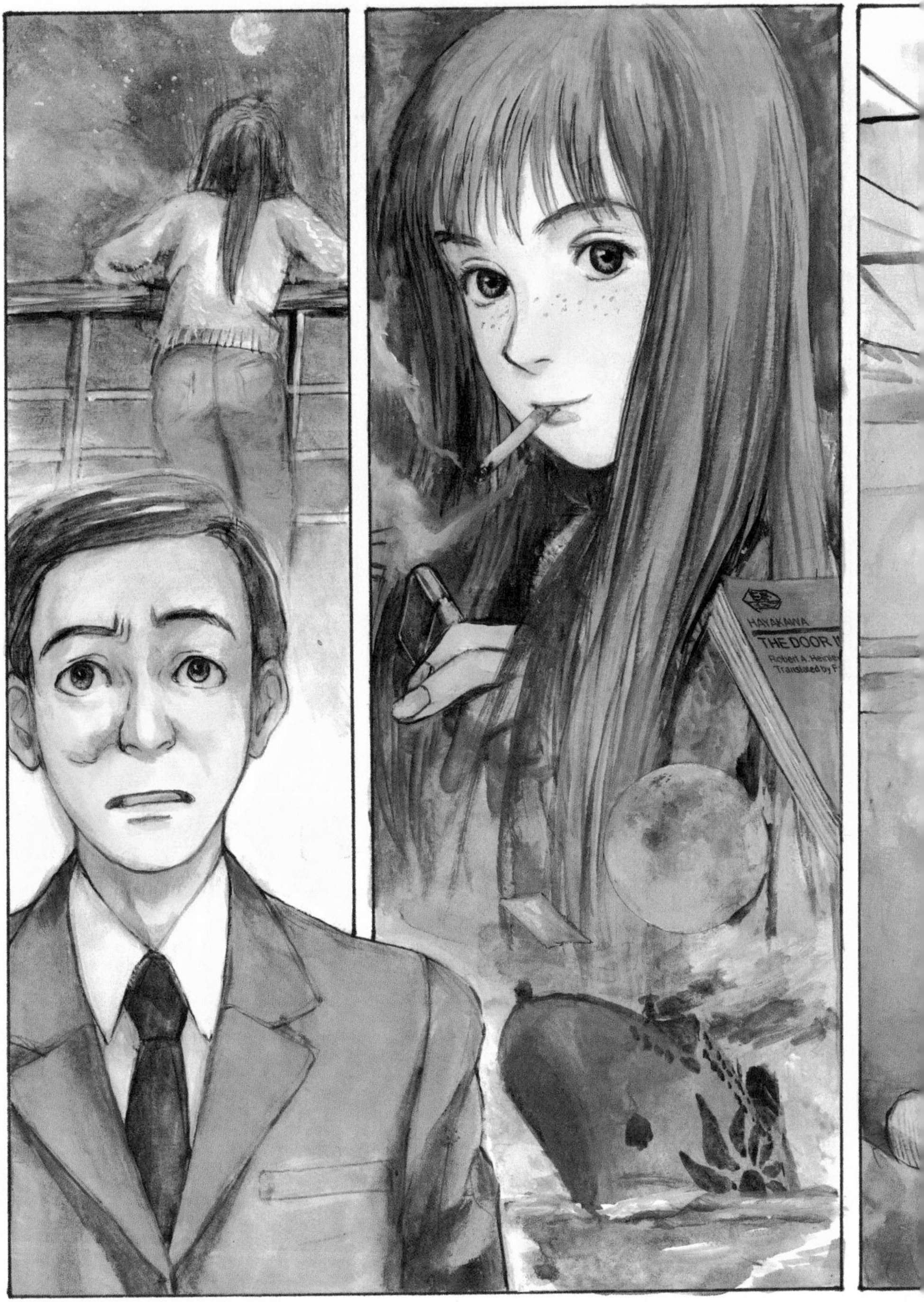
HAYAKAWA

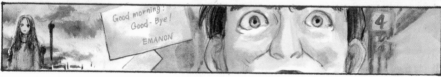

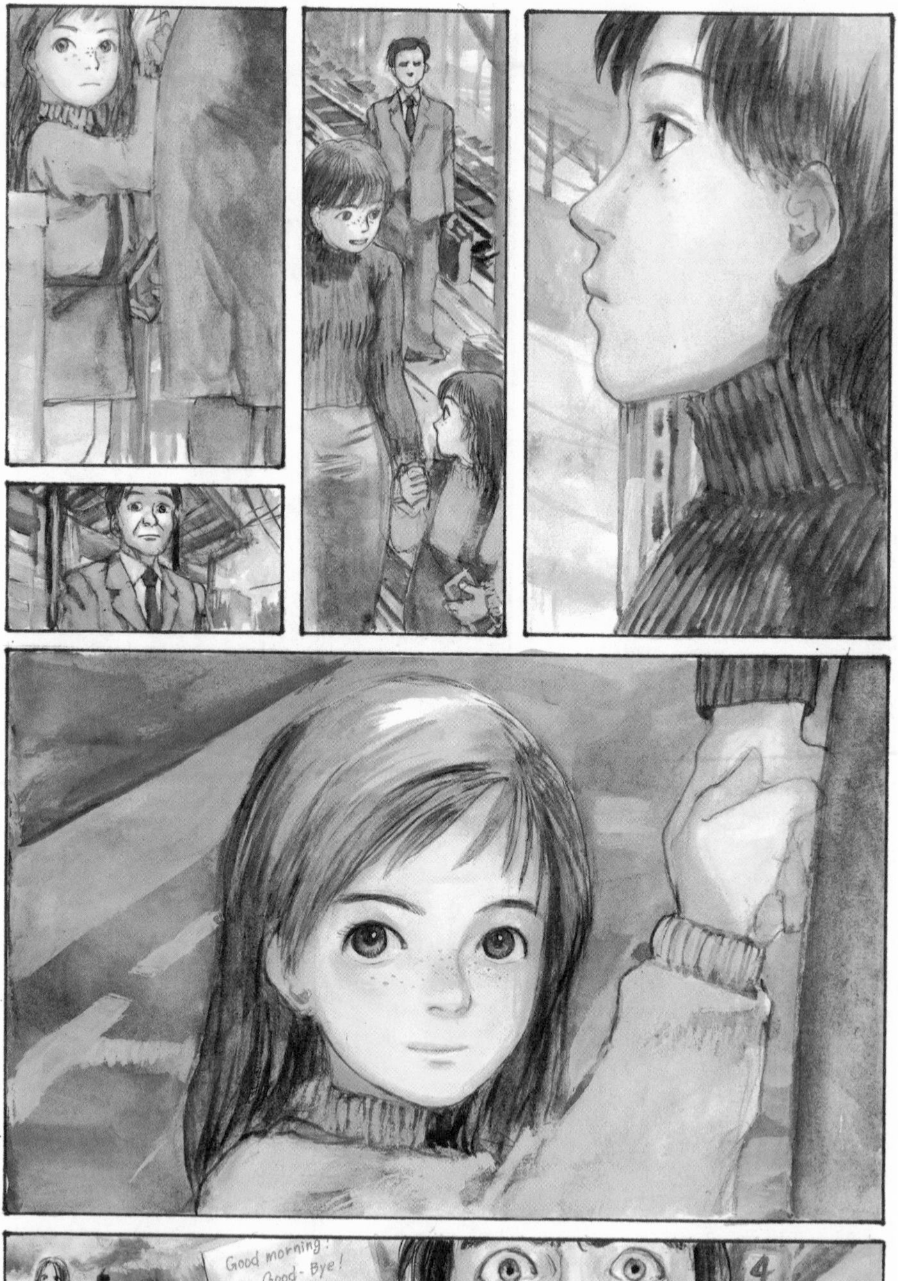
Good morning!
Good-Bye!
EMANON
4

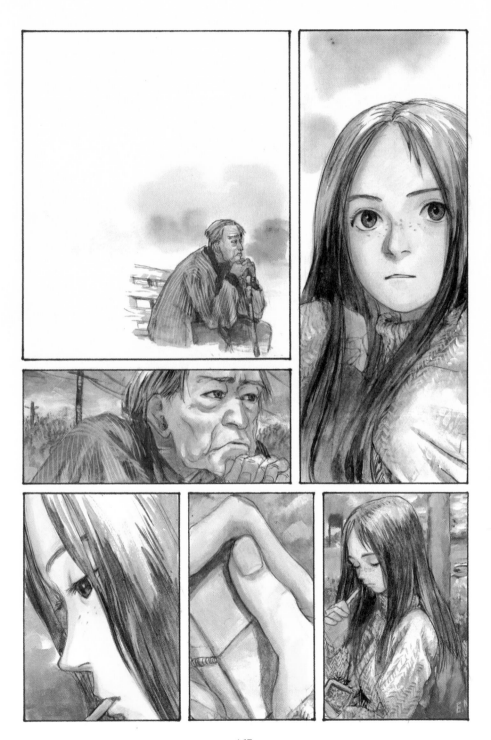

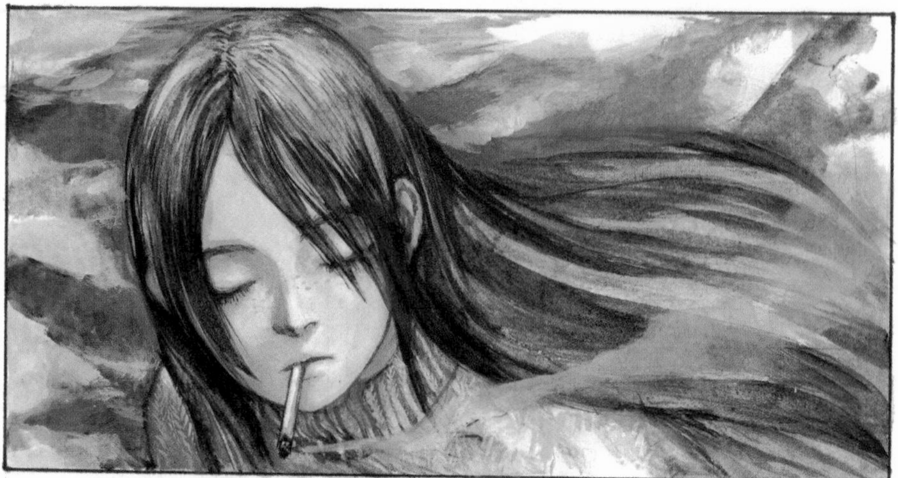

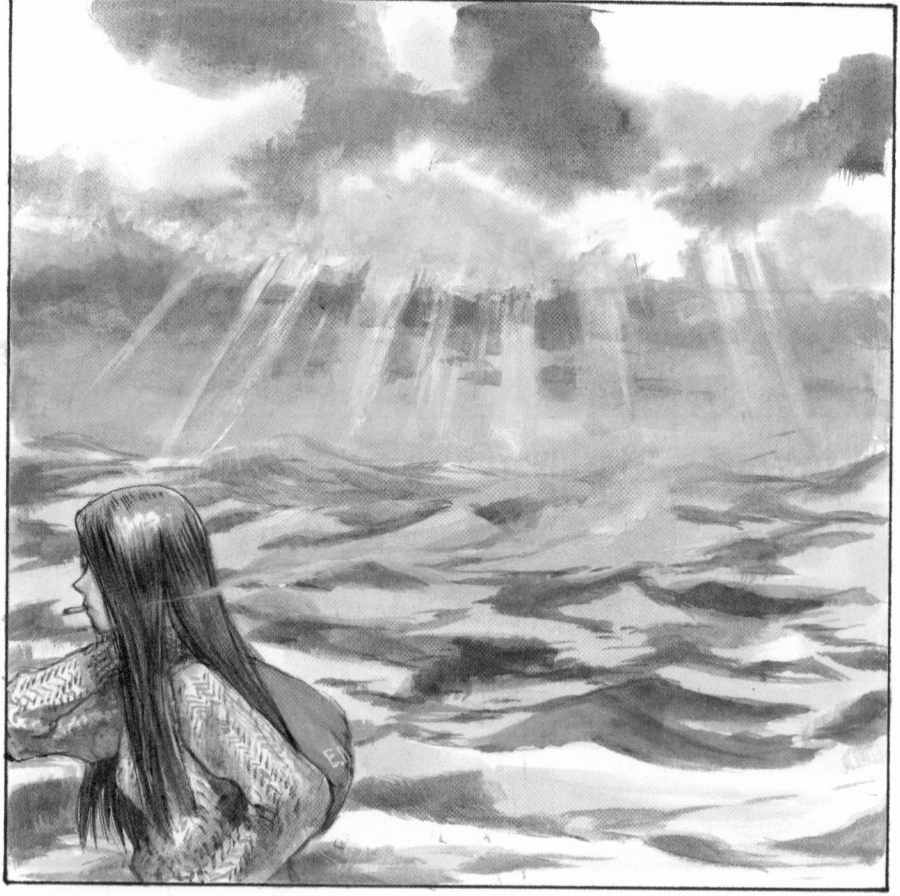

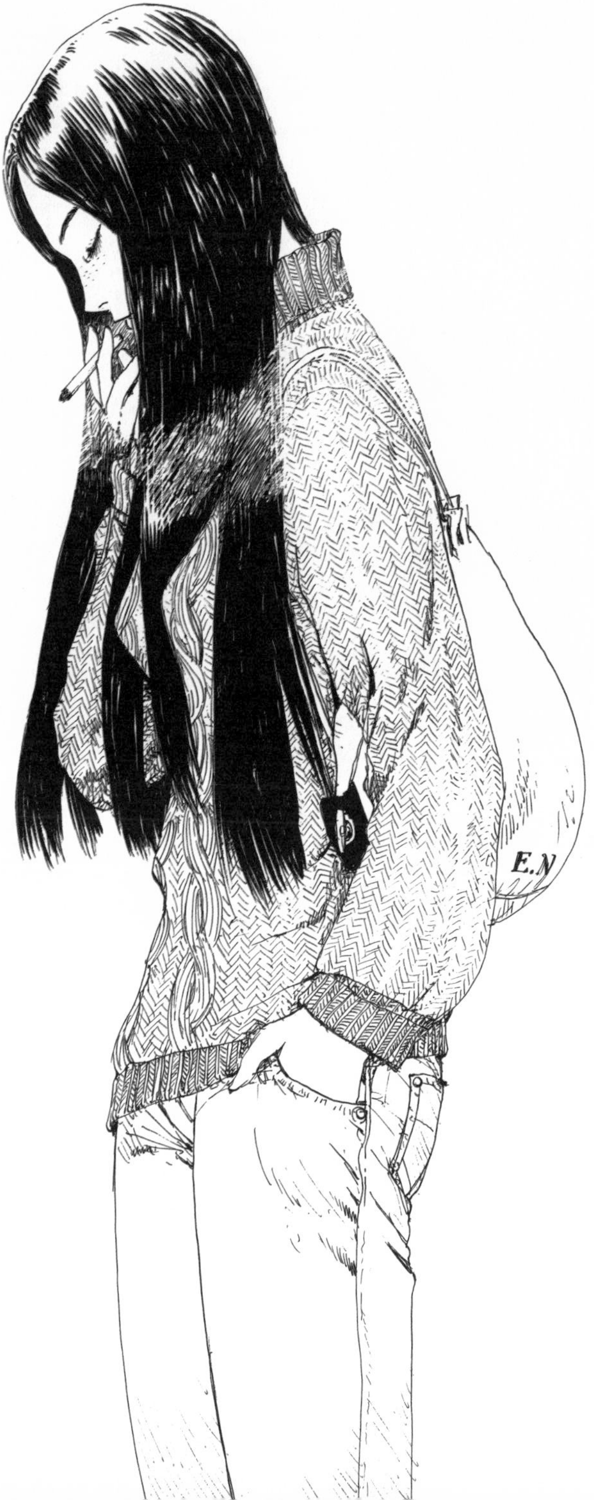
E.N

EMANON WANDERER

CONTINUED IN VOL. 2

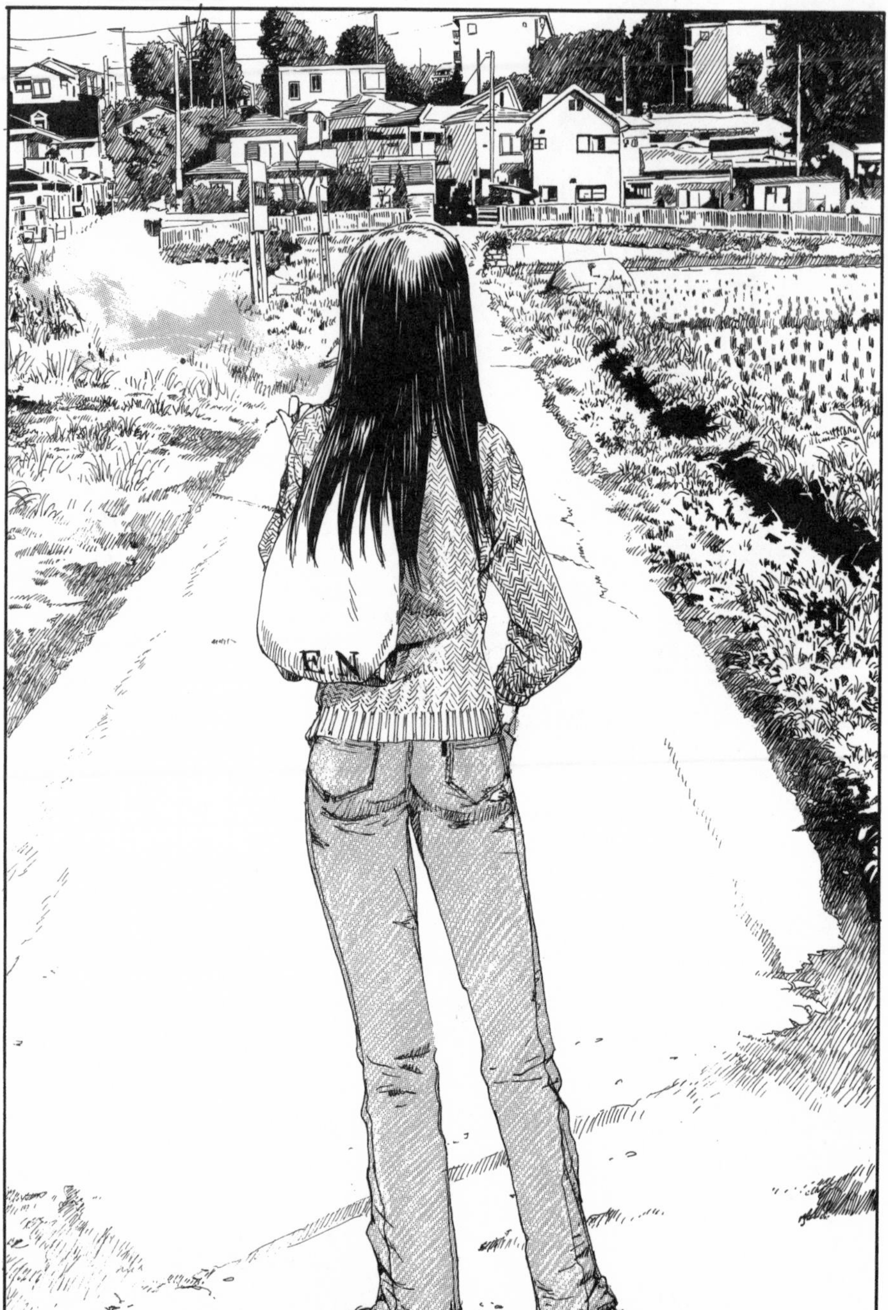
E.N

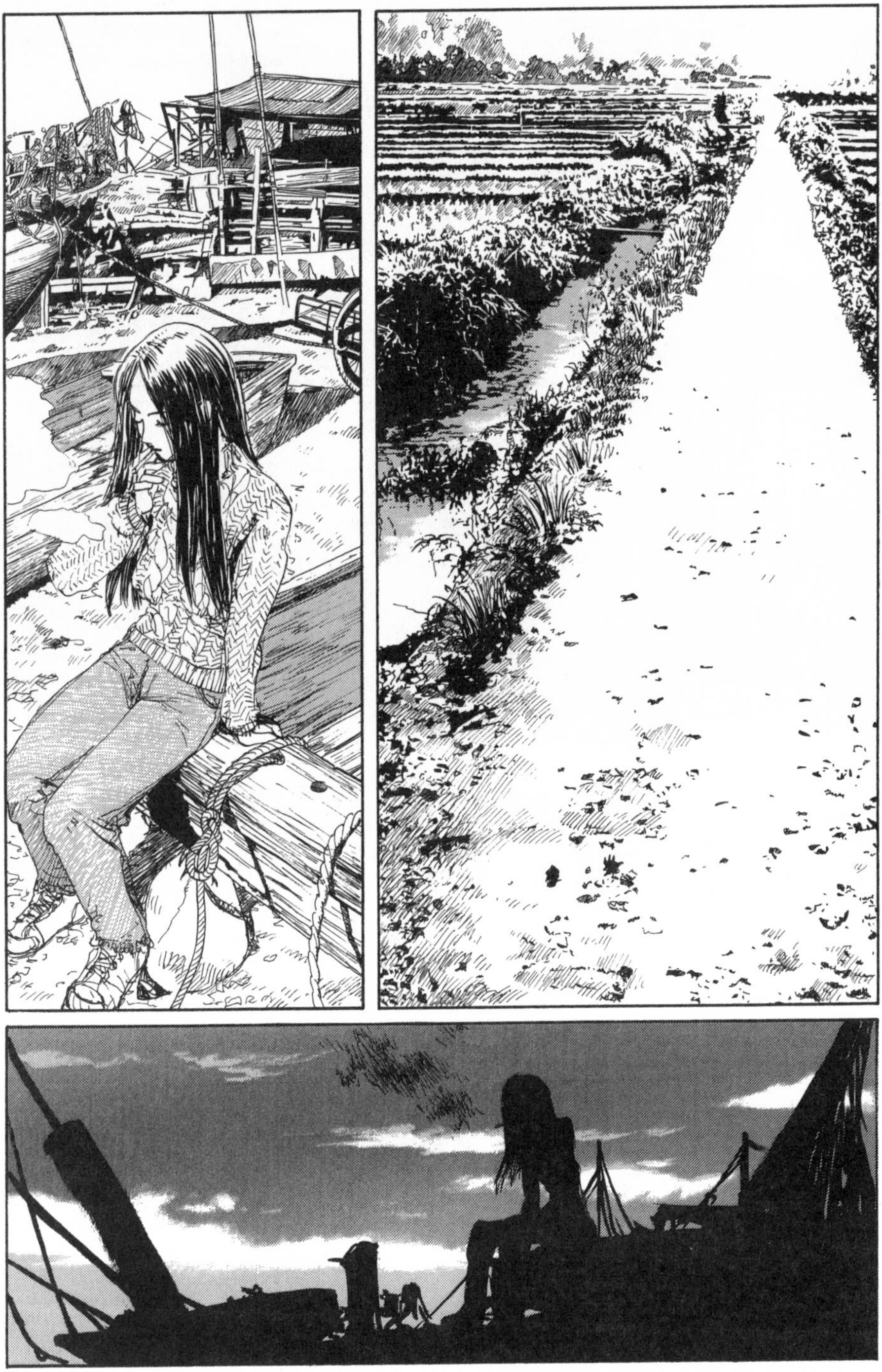

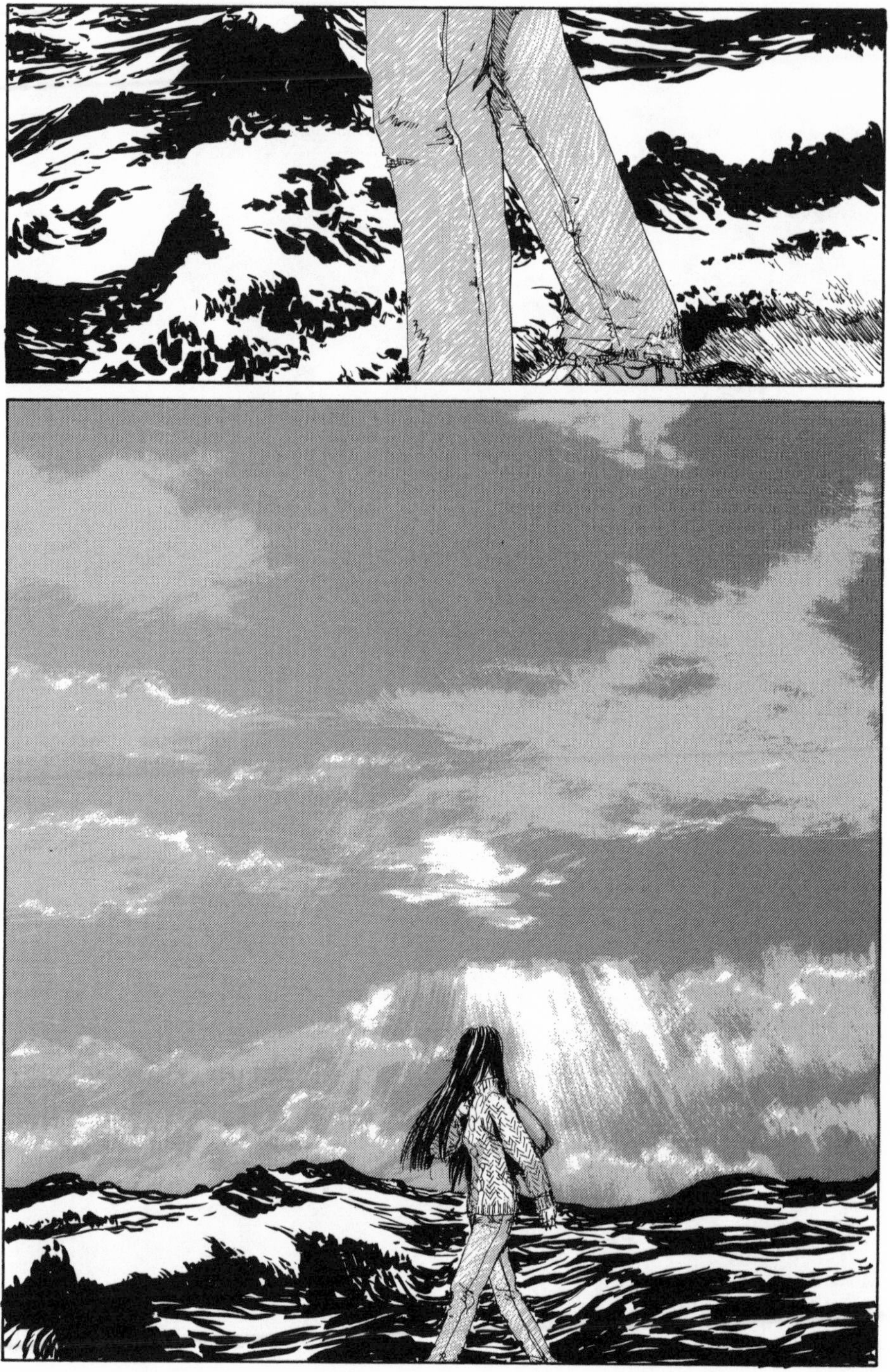

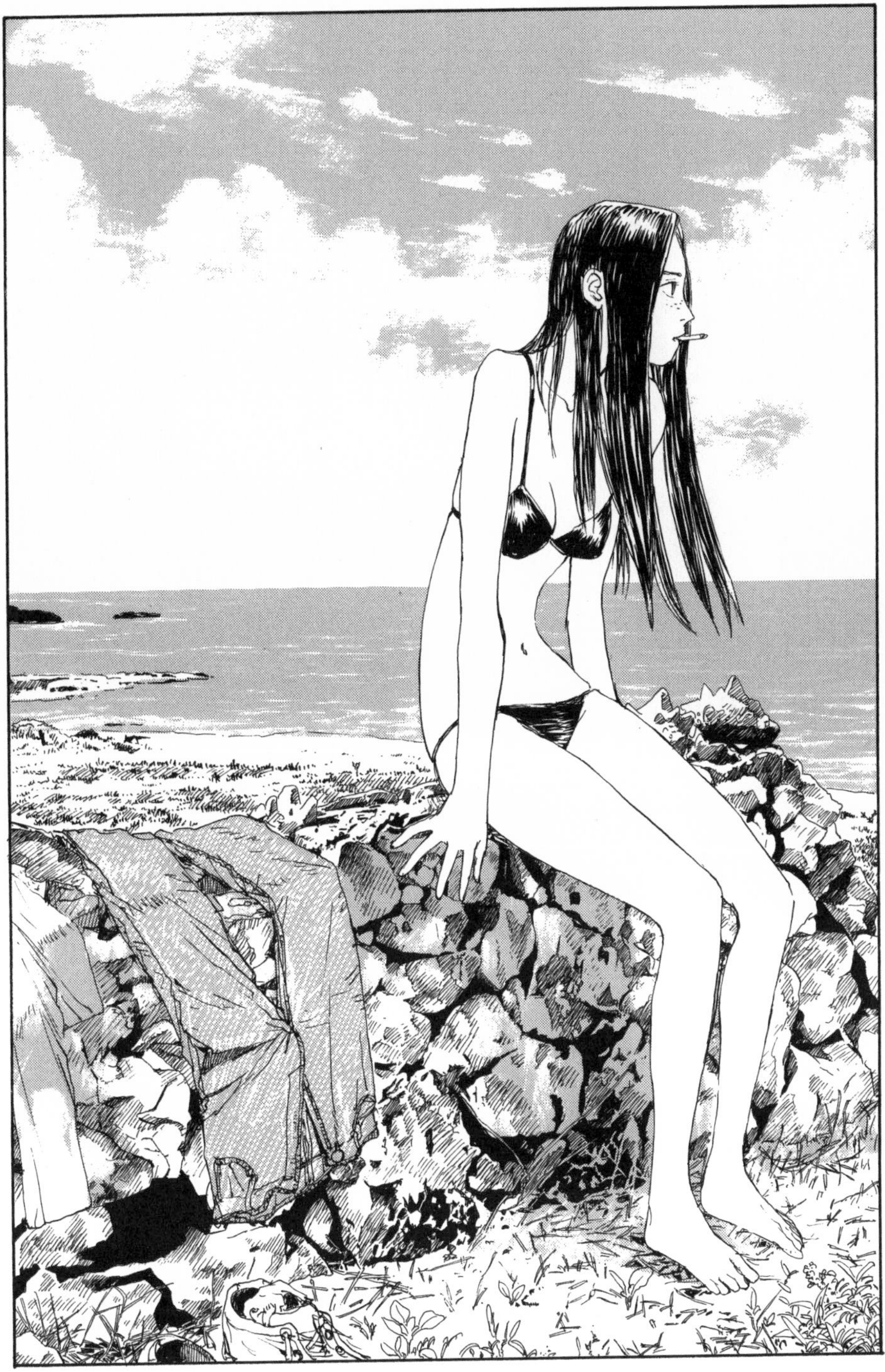

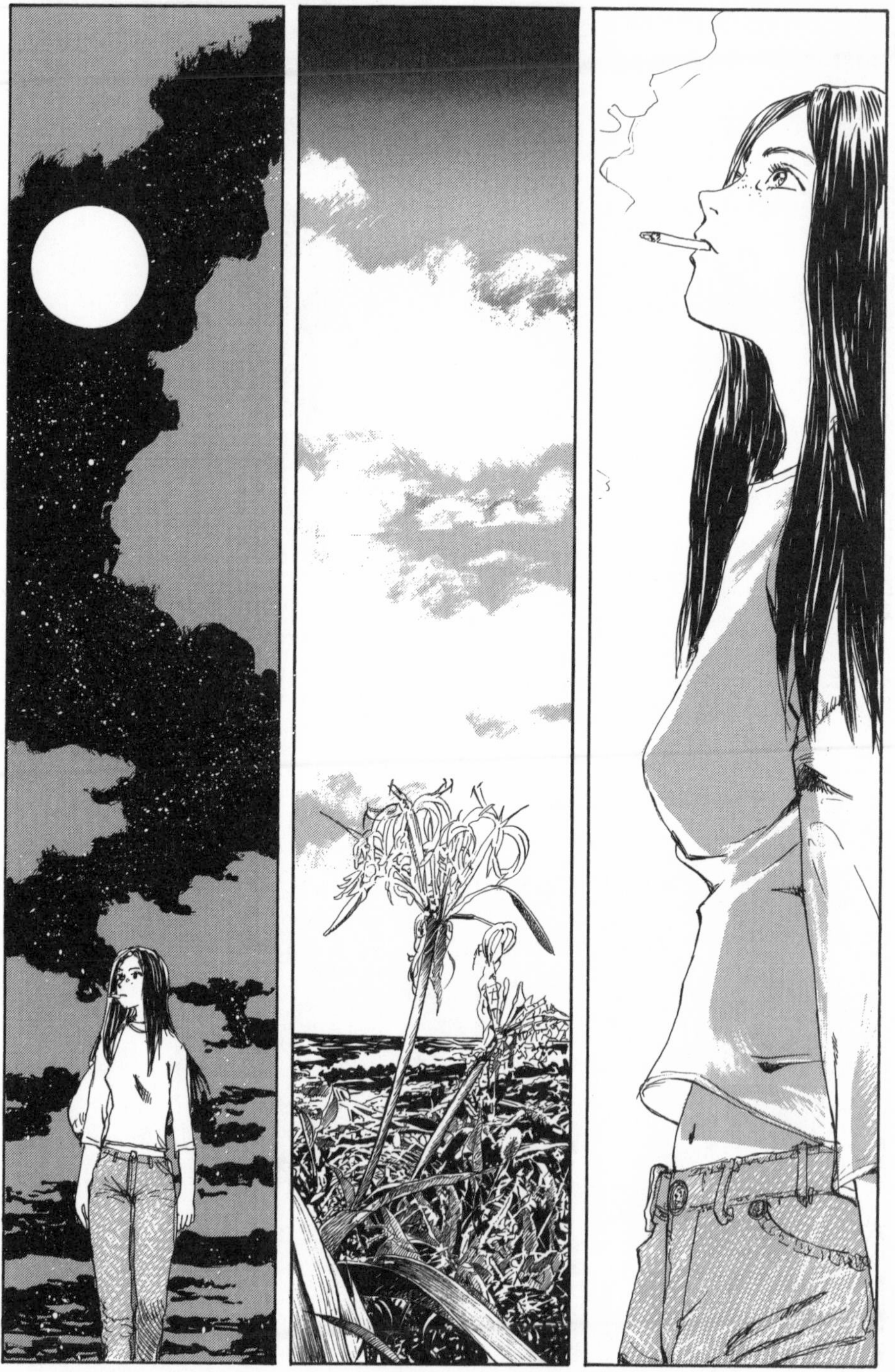

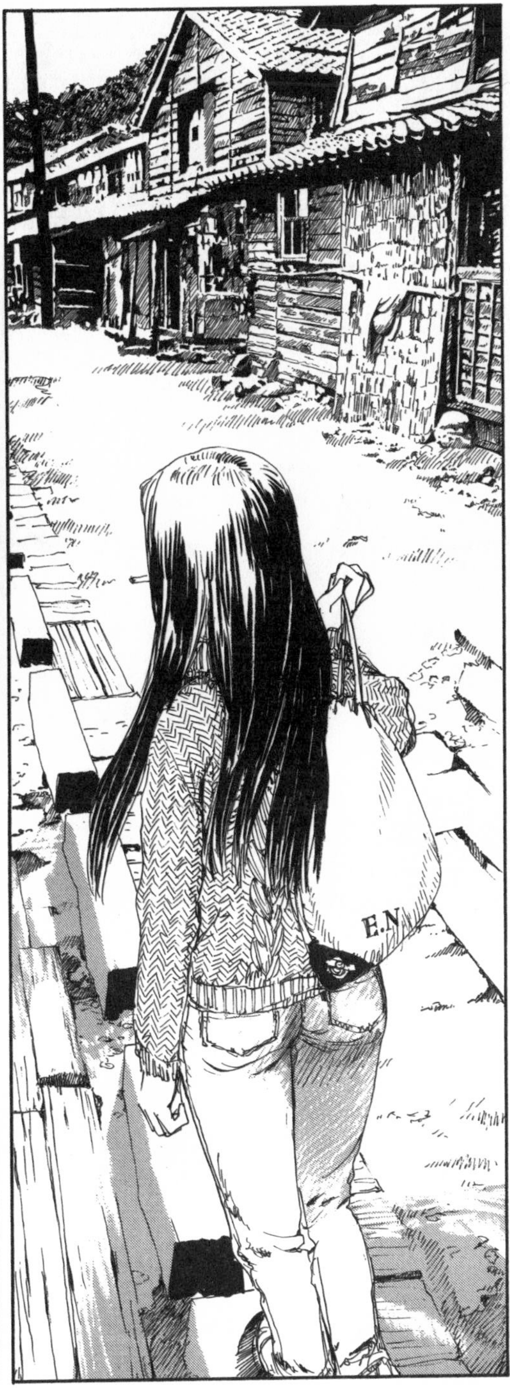
E.N

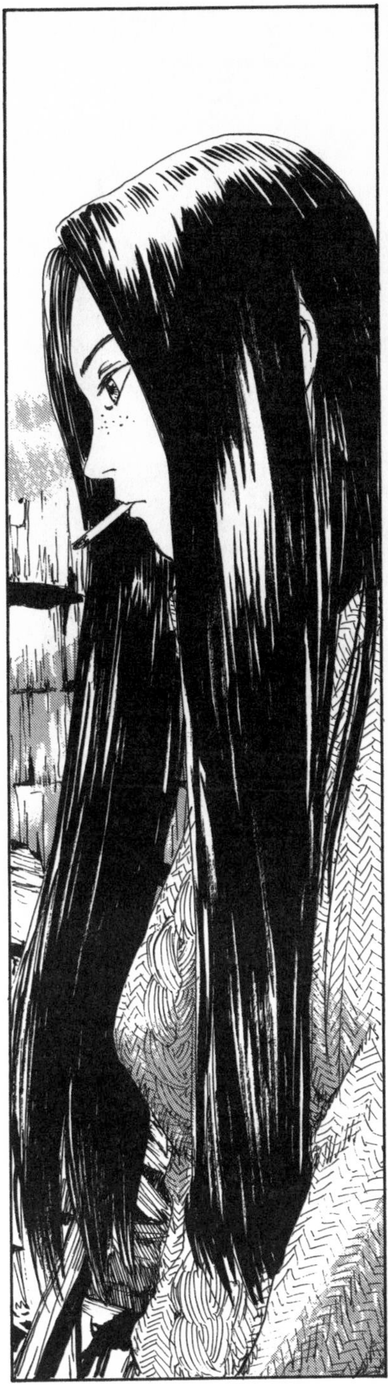

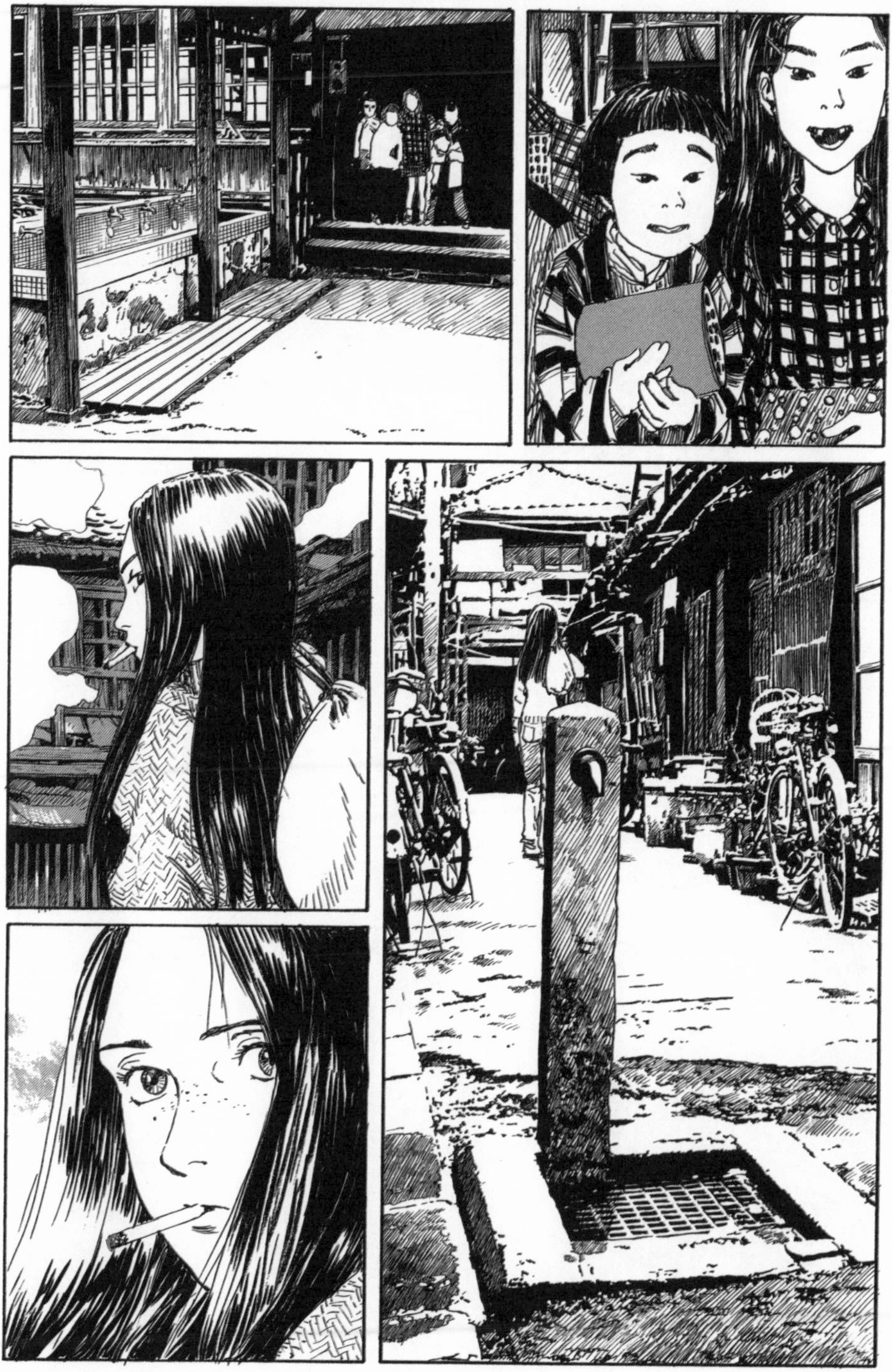

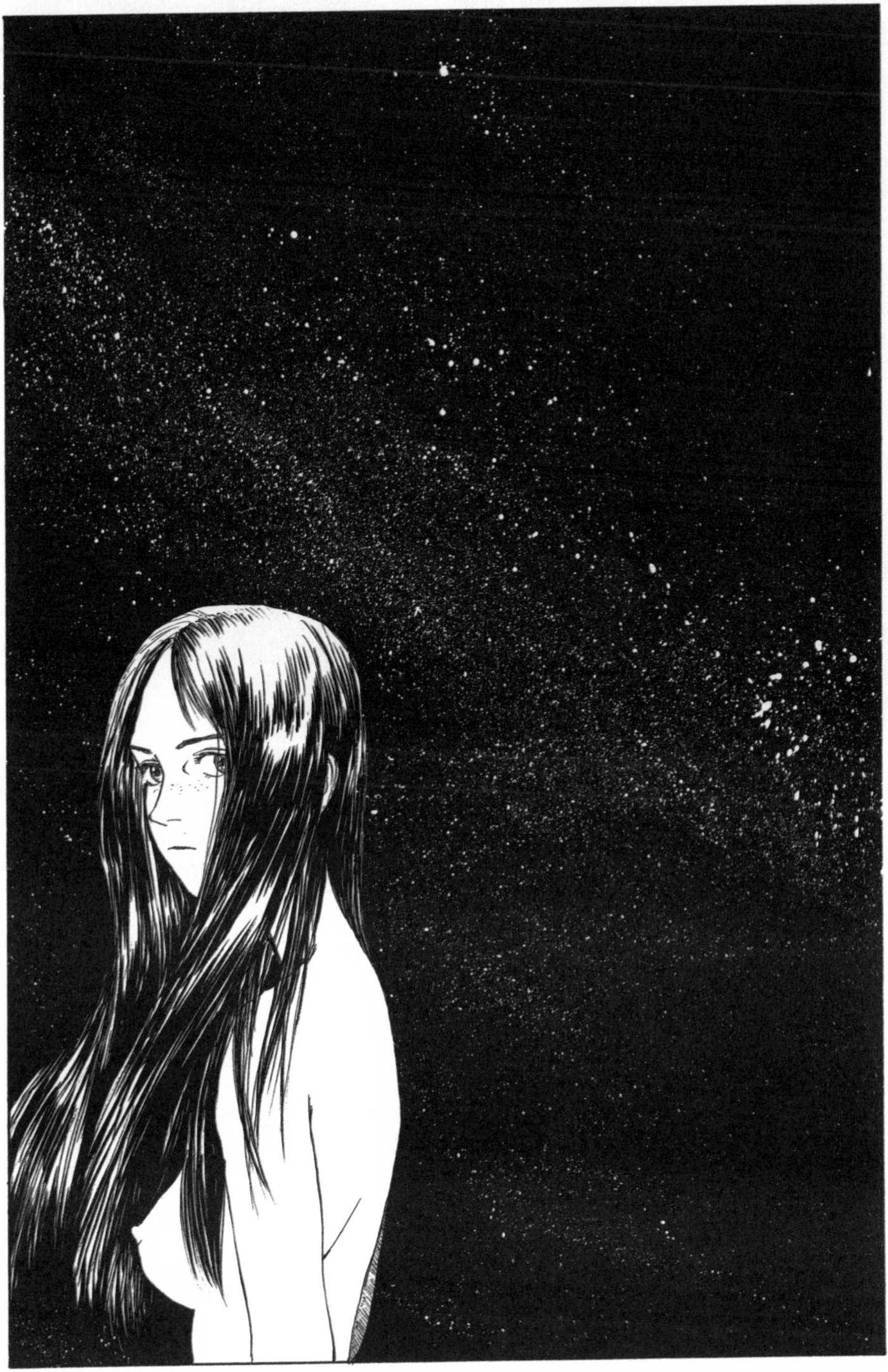

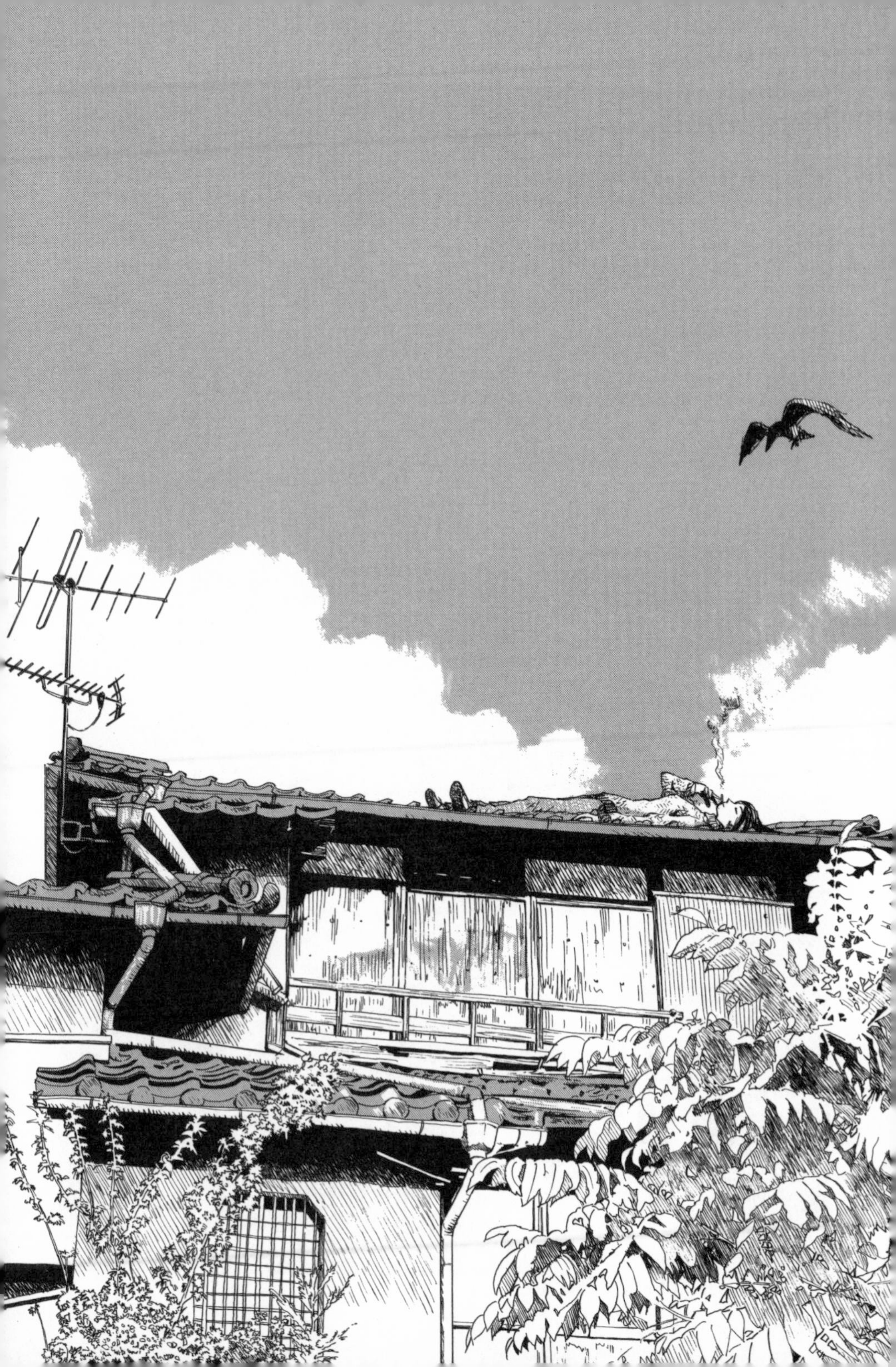

Shinji Kajio

The character of Emanon was born of a reverie. Thinking back today, it happened when I was traveling solo from Nagoya back to my home in Kagoshima on the *Sunflower* car ferry. This particular ferry service route had just been established, and for a day and a night I lay about the big economy-class cabin, devouring science fiction and losing myself in musings.

What kind of musings? Well, they were basically all variations on the same theme, namely: "What would it be like if an unbelievably beautiful young woman suddenly came up to me and we travelled on together, talking, just talking, about whatever silliness came to mind?"

In my fantasies it was better still if this young beauty was swathed in mystery. And as for her appearance? Well, I have distilled all of that into my character of Emanon. Long hair, jeans, dangling a cigarette from her lips.

And freckles.

Thinking back on that image today, I can see how much I was under the influence at the time of the so-called *fūten zoku*, those roaming vagabond kids who drifted through Japan in the early 1970s, and by the later hippies.

In those days I was also particularly captivated by two phrases

Kenji Tsuruta

For me, from way back, Emanon has always been my all-time favorite science fiction heroine. The key words to describe her are *fūten musume*, the early 1970s Japanese equivalent of "hippie chick."[1] I personally think it's a spot-on description.

My first "encounter" with Emanon came when I—like the protagonist of this story—was still in university. At the time there was a little bookstore along the way home to my digs that for some reason boasted a particularly deep collection of science fiction. It seems that, somehow, "Memories of Emanon" has come to be linked in my mind with that bookstore where I first met her, so much that every time I reread that initial story I recall with the greatest precision the shape of the stains on the plywood walls of the store, and the soft sound that the riser made whenever I stepped up onto it, to reach the shelves where the Hayakawa SF Bunko paperbacks[2] lived.

No such scene appears in the original work, of course. Yet buried somewhere in my desire to create an *Emanon* manga there was always also an element of wanting to bring that bookstore into the story as well.

Well, in the end I didn't draw it in.[3] But come to think of it now, when exactly was it that I spotted the young woman who

in Japanese: *yukizuri* (a "casual encounter") and *ichigo-ichie* (a once in a lifetime coming together of like minds)[1]. Both phrases evoke the image of a person or persons whom you come together with for just a fleeting while, who are imprinted deeply in your memory, but with whom you will never cross paths again.

Back then, whenever I imagined meeting someone who would make such an indelible impression on me, but whom I would never be able to spend time with ever again, I would be seized with the profoundest sense of loss...

Still docked to that sense of loss, my image of the fantasy girl of my dreams continued to live on inside me long after that ferry voyage was over. Somewhere along the away, I went on to invest her with yet another attribute, namely, that she possessed a "perfect memory of three billion years of evolution."

It would take eight more years from that first daydream of the beauty on the boat for me to finally give her form in a short story.

And as for that name? "Emanon"?

That sprang forth unbidden while I was putting her story on paper.

Once I finished the original short story "Memories of Emanon,"[2] I felt that "Emanon" was finally complete. Or she was in my own mind, at least. But then, several months later, I received a totally unexpected request from my editor.

Emanon was hugely popular with the readers, he told me. Please write us another story with her as its heroine. Since I had never once considered turning my dream woman into an ongoing series, his request was like water in the ear of a sleeping writer![3]

• •

looked exactly like Emanon aboard an express train on the Chūō Honsen mainline, running west out of Tokyo? Ten years ago, was it? That real (?!?) Emanon was in jeans and wearing a red sweater, and I had been intending to draw her that way in any case, yet, even so...

I think the first serious talk of creating a full manga version of *Emanon* came up after I had already drawn my first *Emanon* illustrations for the short stories in *SF Japan* magazine, some also drawn as inserts for the *Emanon* short story collections in Tokuma Publishing Co.'s (now defunct) Dual Bunko paperback line. Up until then, all my proposals to do an *Emanon* manga had been summarily dismissed. But this time Editor-in-chief "O"[4] of *SF Japan* was all for it, so much so that he traveled down to Kumamoto in Kyushu himself to get permission from Kajio-*sensei* face-to-face.

The initial concept was to produce a single manga volume that would contain two stories, the first a faithful manga adaptation of the "Memories of Emanon" short story, and the second a "title-still-to-come" *Emanon* tale that could play out any way I wanted it to. Then things shifted gradually in the direction of me doing just a manga version of the original story. Which was still totally fine with me, except for that bit about "gradually."

You see, at the time I was completely loaded down with any number of jobs that, for "this reason" or for "that reason" or for another reason or some other reason still, had all ground to a complete halt midway through, so much so that so that I moved ahead on the *Emanon* project as an undertaking that would probably only come to fruition in some distant future, like in a year. Or in two years. Which in publishing industry terms is the same as some distant, unpredictable eternity.

Eventually, though, I did get the "this" finished. That still left the "that," though, and all those "anothers" and "some others" still hanging fire, such that it would appear *Emanon* was perpetually either waiting in the wings.

180

And after that the number of Emanon stories grew and grew...

Eventually, however, Emanon's adventures did come to an end, marked by the publication of my second Emanon collection, *Sasurai no Emanon* (*Emanon Wanderer*), in 1992. Her story was done. Done, that is, until 2000, when Tokuma launched a new science fiction quarterly, *SF Japan*, and gave her fresh life. It was *SF Japan*'s editor-in-chief at the time—let's just call him "O"—who put me together with Kenji Tsuruta. And when I saw Tsuruta-san's visualization of Emanon, I was stunned.

It was too perfect!

Ever since then, whenever I have been writing a new Emanon story, the image of Emanon in my head has become Tsuruta-san's Emanon. His pen may move slowly across the page, but he has my unreserved confidence that he will give form to all of Emanon's allure in a way that justifies the wait. No matter how long that may be.

This "comics" edition[4] of *Memories of Emanon* is the happiest outcome of this collaboration yet. For years I had harbored an impossible fantasy of reading a Tsuruta *Emanon*. And now, for it to actually come true?

There are indeed miracles in this world!

1 The translator, Dana Lewis, included "of like minds" to reflect the nuances of this famous Japanese phrase, in that it refers to the need to cherish each encounter one has in life with those whom you find you share a common affinity or purpose. Yasuhiro Takeda of GAINAX used the phrase to reflect on the 2013 death of Studio Proteus co-founder Toren Smith.

2 Vol. 1 of the *Emanon* manga (that is, the volume you have just read ^_^) is an adaptation by Kajio and Tsuruta of this story. Dana Lewis notes that the original short story "has been masterfully translated under the title 'Emanon: A Reminiscence' by Edward Lipsett, in the anthology *Speculative Japan 2*, Kurodahan Press, 2011."

• •

Or abandoned completely. And in that way, four long years flowed by, while the number of Kajio-*sensei Emanon* short stories continued to grow.

And so it is that for that reason I am quite confident that, had Editor-in-chief "O" not been on such pins and needles to make the book a reality that he eventually ran out of patience and commanded me to start publishing *Memories of Emanon* piecemeal in *COMIC Ryu* even before all the main characters were present, then *Memories of Emanon* would still be unfinished to this day.

Did I say "unfinished"? I jest. It would probably have never even started! The real identity of the conjuror behind this miracle is Editor-in-chief "O." Thank you, Editor-in-chief "O"! And Kajio-*sensei*, forgive me, please!

My first, short version of *Memories of Emanon* ran as a complete story in *SF Japan* magazine. Drawn in 2002, you can think of it as a "pilot" version. The character designs weren't quite what I'd wanted, and the story itself wandered. Yet, out of respect for Editor-in-chief "O"'s obsession, it has been reprinted time and time again since.[5]

The simple truth is that, no matter how many times I draw Emanon, even today, I always feel as if her image keeps slip-sliding away from me.

And yet now, looking back over this story after all this time, I discover on p. 9, an Emanon that is **exactly** the image I have always had of her![6]

(Or...is she?)

1 The term Kajio used earlier, *fūten zoku*, refers to hippies as a collective group, whereas Tsuruta's *fūten musume* refers

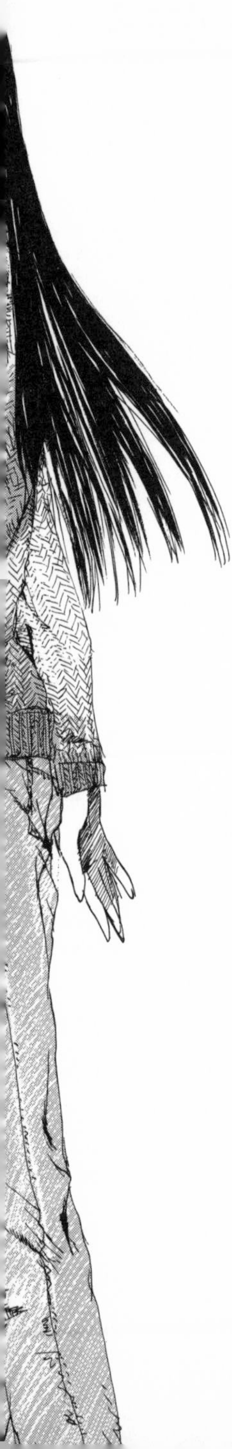

3 This simile is a direct rendering of the Japanese phrase. Dana brings up an interesting standard here about translation of which I had been unaware: "Using a Japanese idiom in a direct translation into English is nearly universally considered to be an amateurish, serious no-no in literary translation. However, anyone who has encountered *Hamlet* will also have an image of pouring poison in the ear of the sleeping king, and I personally like 'pushing' this proscription about idioms, when introducing a non-English idiom 'works' just fine and does no harm. After all, the writer could have also chosen a much more conventional was to say it, like: 'it was a total surprise.'...When my very first translation of a Japanese story was published in *OMNI* magazine all those decades ago ("Standing Woman" by Tsutsui Yasutaka) I did directly translate a Japanese idiom 'as is.' A Japanese reviewer writing in a Japanese magazine pounced on it, saying I had made a sentence that would seem totally normal to a Japanese reader sound 'strange and unworldly' in English. I guess he was right. When Ed Lipsett (the same person who translated *Emanon*!) anthologized the story in *Speculative Japan* vol. 1 some 30+ years later, he changed it into a normal English phrase without bothering to tell me!" As editor, this issue interests me because, while I can see the Japanese reviewer's point about how a literal translation can in fact change something that was meant to sound familiar to something that sounds exotic, the history of languages show that that one method by which they grow is by adopting loan words and phrases from other languages, even if these borrowings may at first be, or in fact remain, exotic. "Exotic" is a profoundly relative term, but nevertheless a concept that will retain real-world meaning as long as human cultures—and subcultures—differ from one another. It's issues like this that remind me (as I shouldn't need to be reminded...) that translation is not a mechanical or algorithmic process, but as complicated as human thought, for it is language that carries the burden of expressing it.

4 Dana notes that Kajio refers to this volume using the loan word *komikku*, rather than the Japanese word *manga*. We are not sure if this choice is intended to signify any distinction, but it is quite possible it does not, as the term "comic" or "comics" is freely used within manga culture in Japan—in fact the very magazine within which the *Emanon* manga is originally serialized is named *COMICリュウ* (*COMIC Ryu*), with the word "COMIC" written with all caps in the Roman alphabet, and "Ryu" written in Japanese katakana.

specifically to a woman who is a hippie. *Zoku* has for decades been a common term used whenever the Japanese media writes about pop culture, to refer to various different looks or trends among young people, and is not exclusive to any one of them; for example, *habitués* of the trendy 2000s development Roppongi Hills were called the "Roppongi Hills *zoku*" and even otaku have been called the "otaku *zoku*." The word *zoku* is often translated as "tribe," but perhaps "scene" might be a better English word to express it.

2 Hayakawa is a longtime publisher of both domestic and translated science fiction (see also the following afterword to *Emanon*) in Japan; as related in detail within Dark Horse's recent *Yoshitaka Amano: Beyond the Fantasy—The Illustrated Biography*, Hayakawa's *S-F Magazine* played a major role in Amano's career by giving him his first regular work as a freelance illustrator. *Bunko* refers to the small (105 mm x 148 mm; about 4 1/8" x 5 ¾") pocketbook size often used in Japan for print fiction and sometimes manga as well—perhaps the best-known use of this size in English was Dark Horse's original 28-volume edition of *Lone Wolf and Cub*.

3 Not in vol. 1; however, a bookstore does feature in *Emanon* in vol. 2.

4 The translator notes that the mysterious initial refers to Shūichi Ōno, editor of the regrettably also now defunct *SF Japan* (from 2000 to Spring 2011). Ōno also edited the "Dual Bunko" paperback line that was illustrated by Tsuruta; furthermore, he was editor and remains involved with *Animage*, Japan's oldest anime magazine—all of these projects (plus this manga's own home magazine, *COMIC Ryu*) being published by Tokuma Shoten. For more on Tokuma, a tremendously influential publisher (among other things, Studio Ghibli grew out of it—yes, that Ghibli), please see the afterword to Satoshi Kon and Mamoru Oshii's manga *Seraphim 266613336 Wings*, published by Dark Horse.

5 Tsuruta is evidently referring to the nearly textless eight-page color sequence "Emanon Memories" that occurs in vol. 1 on p. 161 through 168. The character designs are indeed a bit different, more noticeably so with the unnamed narrator.

6 Dana points out that this image is "the Emanon with the slightly exasperated frown beneath the full Earth!"

President and Publisher
MIKE RICHARDSON

Editor
CARL GUSTAV HORN

Designer
BRENNAN THOME

Digital Art Technician
SAMANTHA HUMMER

English-language version produced by Dark Horse Comics

Emanon Vol. 1: Memories of Emanon
© SHINJI KAJIO / KENJI TSURUTA 2008. Originally published in Japan in 2008 by
TOKUMA SHOTEN PUBLISHING CO., LTD., Tokyo. English translation rights arranged
with TOKUMA SHOTEN PUBLISHING CO., LTD., Tokyo through TOHAN
CORPORATION, Tokyo. All rights reserved. No portion of this publication may be
reproduced or transmitted, in any form or by any means, without the express written
permission of the copyright holders. Names, characters, places, and incidents featured
in this publication either are the product of the author's imagination or are used
fictitiously. Any resemblance to actual persons (living or dead), events, institutions, or
locales, without satiric intent, is coincidental. Dark Horse Manga™ is a trademark of
Dark Horse Comics LLC. All rights reserved.

Published by
Dark Horse Manga
A division of Dark Horse Comics LLC.
10956 SE Main Street | Milwaukie, OR 97222
DarkHorse.com

To find a comics shop in your area visit comicshoplocator.com

First edition: May 2019
ISBN 978-1-50670-981-9

1 3 5 7 9 10 8 6 4 2

Neil Hankerson Executive Vice President Tom Weddle Chief Financial Officer Randy
Stradley Vice President of Publishing Nick McWhorter Chief Business Development
Officer Dale LaFountain Chief Information Officer Matt Parkinson Vice President of
Marketing Cara Niece Vice President of Production and Scheduling Mark Bernardi Vice
President of Book Trade and Digital Sales Ken Lizzi General Counsel Dave Marshall
Editor in Chief Davey Estrada Editorial Director Chris Warner Senior Books Editor
Cary Grazzini Director of Print and Development Lia Ribacchi Art Director Vanessa
Todd-Holmes Director of Print Purchasing Matt Dryer Director of Digital Art and
Prepress Michael Gombos Director of International Publishing and Licensing Kari
Yadro Director of Custom Programs Kari Torson Director of International Licensing
Sean Brice Director of Trade Sales

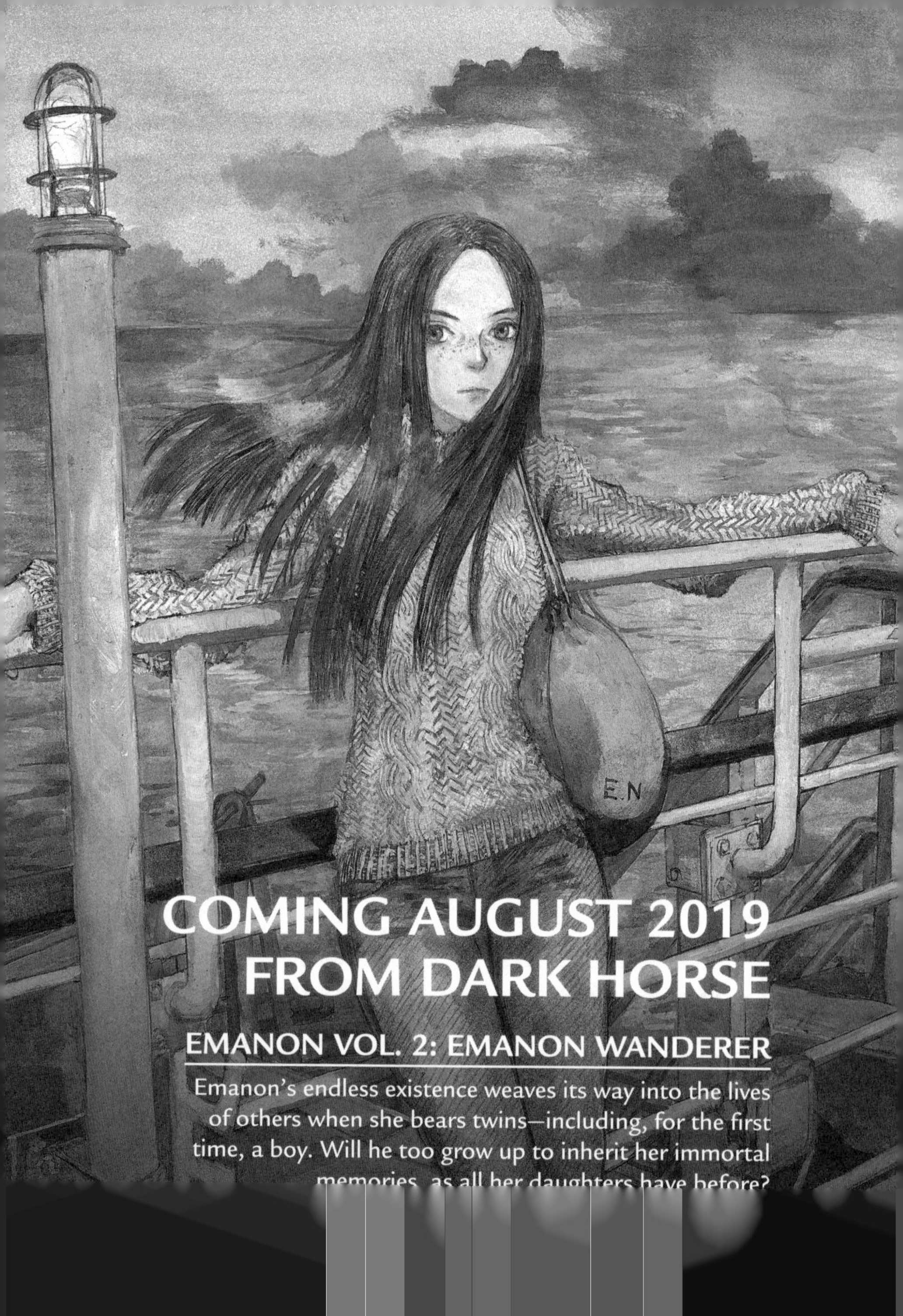
E.N
COMING AUGUST 2019
FROM DARK HORSE
EMANON VOL. 2: EMANON WANDERER
Emanon's endless existence weaves its way into the lives of others when she bears twins—including, for the first time, a boy. Will he too grow up to inherit her immortal memories, as all her daughters have before?

AFTERWORD TO *EMANON* VOL. 1

The first volume of *Emanon* comes in—and then takes its leave—with references to Robert Heinlein; to his 1966 novel *The Moon is a Harsh Mistress* on p. 17, and his 1957 book *The Door into Summer* on p. 165. Both works were published in Japan by the imprint Hayakawa Shobo, and, as William H. Patterson, Jr. recounts in his biography *Robert A. Heinlein: In Dialogue with His Century*, when the famed science fiction author and his wife Ginny visited Japan in early 1983, Hayakawa "laid out the red carpet for them," inviting the couple to be guests at a lavish wedding reception in Tokyo—that of none other than Go Nagai, one of the most influential manga creators of all time, whose works include among many others *Devilman, Cutey Honey,* and *Mazinger Z*.

Patterson writes that there were over a thousand other people who also attended, and that many "were science-fiction fans and writers, cartoonists... all evening long he was politely buttonholed by earnest men, almost all over forty, who told him he was their 'spiritual father.' Odd and very touching." This included Osamu Tezuka himself, who came to the reception on two hours' notice after hearing that Heinlein would be present (I wondered if this might imply anything about Tezuka's relationship to Nagai) and once there "told Robert his books had spurred him on for forty years," going so far as to loan the Heinleins his own car and chauffeur to use for their return trip.

An August 1983 follow-up letter to Heinlein from Tezuka is preserved in the SF author's papers, in which Tezuka says that almost the entire membership of Japan's science fiction authors' association had been present at the reception. As the snow fell about our unnamed protagonist at the end of *Emanon* vol. 1, now in 1980 and entering middle life with two children and a wife who "would never, ever read science fiction," I couldn't help but notice Patterson's informed remark in the biography's footnotes section, "Heinlein's visit was in the middle of the 'Wintry Age' decline of written-form science fiction in Japan, when public attention was shifting over to anime and manga."

Just like life, science fiction goes on (it would seem exceedingly strange if it did not) and I wonder if younger SF fans have a perspective on authors such as Robert Heinlein and Issac Asimov a bit like they themselves might have had looking back on Jules Verne—as a major science fiction writer, but someone before their time. Robert Heinlein died in 1988; one of Dark Horse's most recent graphic novels, from its Berger Books imprint, is *Laguardia,* written by Nnedi Okorafor, who won the Hugo Award for her novella *Binti.* She received it in 2016 at MidAmeriCon II in Kansas; exactly forty years earlier, at Mid-AmeriCon I, Heinlein had been the guest of honor.[1]

The aims, purposes, and effects of science fiction literature are complex, and SF is indeed a literary tradition as well as a genre—H. Bruce Franklin, emeritus Rutgers professor and pioneering Heinlein scholar (and, as both a former military intelligence officer *and* a former Maoist militant, surely the most Mamoru Oshii figure in American academia[2]) pointed out in his 1966 book *Future Perfect* that Poe, Hawthorne, Twain, Melville, and London had all written works that could be classified as science fiction.

If SF authors of the past often got the future wrong, it should be noted that their work is at least labelled *fiction,* whereas think-tanks, consultants, and pundits more respectable (and more highly paid) seemingly find an ever-forgiving corporate market for their oracles; meanwhile, powerful politicians court the favor of religious leaders who face the TV cameras and interpret today's events through the lenses of Revelation, Daniel, and Al-Kahf. To then go and aim any special ridicule at, say, the February 1940 issue of *Astounding Science-Fiction,* seems punching pretty far down by comparison.

It has become something of a cliché to say that science fiction stories ostensibly about the future (there are certainly other kinds, an obvious variety being the alternate history story, such as Philip K. Dick's *The Man in the High Castle* or Michael Chabon's *The Yiddish Policemen's Union*[3]) are "really" about the present. In a practical sense for the working author, this is always true. The author, after all, not only writes in the present but—if they want to sell their story—*to* the present; to have a viable career, they need to connect with the readership (and editors and publishers) of their own day. And often the future will be seen to include them, be of them—be for people like them, who think as they do. Those who had been made to feel as outsiders in their

1. MidAmeriCon has been the name used for the World Science Fiction Convention (or Worldcon) in those years when the event is held in Kansas City. The oldest fan convention still in existence, Worldcon is unlike many fan cons in that it is always held in a different city the following year, so that it may be years or even decades before it takes place in the same town again. Each year the con is known by both what number Worldcon it is, as well as by a local name, and so the 74th annual Worldcon in 2016 was also MidAmeriCon II, in recognition of it being the second time it had been held in Kansas City. Likewise, the 1967 event mentioned on p. 17 of this manga was known as Nycon 3; it was the 25th Worldcon, but only the third time the event had been held in New York City (the very first Worldcon was held in New York in 1939). True to its name, the host city each year is not always in the United States; Worldcons have been held in nine different nations, including Japan in 2007.

2. Excepting naturally Dr. Brian Ruh of Indiana University, author of the first book-length study of Oshii, 2004's *Stray Dog of Anime.*

3. Both of these works themselves won the same top prize referenced on p. 17; the Hugo Award for that year's best science fiction novel.

own time and place—or scene—will be known in truth, acknowledged; will recognize themselves in these visions, that they will in days to come be the protagonists, the heroes.

George Orwell, in a September 1941 essay within wartime Britain's *Horizon* (the same month Heinlein's "Elsewhere" appeared in *Astounding*)[4] emitted a strange inverted echo of those Japanese creators who would regard Heinlein as their "spiritual father," when Orwell said of his own favorite science fiction writer as a youth, "But is it not a sort of parricide for a person of my age (thirty-eight) to find fault with H.G. Wells?...I doubt whether anyone who was writing books between 1900 and 1920, at any rate in the English language, influenced the young so much." Nevertheless, Orwell could have been speaking of SF authors and their readers in general (and perhaps he himself, who wrote one of the great SF novels of the century, *1984,* cannot be spared this judgement) when he said of Wells that he was "always leaping forward to embrace the ego-projections (he) mistakes for the future."

But set aside the whole contentious history of SF a moment; the prosaic experience of our ordinary lives (as *Emanon*'s protagonist discovers) is enough to tell us that the actual future will be alienating—time will always make strangers of us as much as distance will. Even our progressivism, our critical wokeness, may end up looking somewhat cringy (in that term of the modern aesthete), and perhaps even reactionary in ways we simply cannot yet perceive from here in our roost, snugly confined within—however much we dislike to admit it—the past. Perhaps the stories that, in the end, better grasp the real future are exactly those that largely failed to find a readership in their own time, but which become rediscovered and praised by a later generation.

"Really" about the present, though—really? Not *Emanon,* and not most of us: most, both in sense of the majority of us, and in the sense that most of "us"—our lives as we experience them—is made of past, that antimiraculous substance. The present is right beneath our feet, a fresh coat spread thin over the strata we have accumulated and now stand upon, our own personal deep time. A less poetic way to put it is that we are mostly hoarders. On a cable TV show, we might watch the door of someone's storage unit begin to roll up, thinking, who knows what they kept inside it? But who (certainly not us) knows what we keep inside ourselves and don't ever throw away, a pile certainly heavier, more cluttered, and more disturbing? We say things like "live

4 Orwell's early death might now obscure the fact he was of the same generation as Heinlein, born only four years earlier. Patterson describes Wells as a "mentor" of Heinlein as well, noting specifically that he was "drawn to Wells because of the 'utopian socialist' idealism with which Wells burned."

for today" and "be here now," and speak of mindfulness, precisely because we grasp the problem.

We often feel we *should* approach the present, and most especially the future, afresh, so we can change for the better and make best use of its opportunities. But our current perspective was reached through an heap of years, years of both our decisions and the decisions of others, and of random chance. And, beyond ourselves, reached through the lives of our ancestors, whose memory we should cherish but not patronize. They were wise and foolish, just like us. The nameless narrator of *Emanon* vol. 1 would have been old enough to be my own father, and even the grandfather of many readers of this manga. What do you think he learned from his encounters with Emanon? Do you think there is something he might have learned that he perhaps didn't?

Before writing one word more ^_^ I need to praise and acknowledge the key people in this adaptation you have just been reading. As with the previous *Wandering Island,* they represent a classic team from Studio Proteus—the pioneering manga adaptation and licensing firm with which Dark Horse (not to mention Fantagraphics and the former Eclipse) have so much history, as well as present.

I am, of course, speaking first of letterer Susie Lee, who expresses not only the human warmth of the dialogue but the unusually involved signage and "scrap-book clippings" of *Emanon's* reverie. This, by the way, is a general stylistic difference between the English and the Japanese editions of manga—whereas English-language manga carry on the American comics tradition of dialogue fonts that look hand-lettered (until the 2000s, they generally *were* hand-lettered), Japanese manga dialogue is traditionally typeset; the closest stylistic equivalent I can think of in English is the look of many 1950s EC comics, even if manga gives you less fan service than Jack Kamen.

Second is translator Dana Lewis—formerly an editor at *Newsweek Japan* and former president of the Japan Society of Northern California—but before that, co-founder of Studio Proteus in the mid-1980s with the late Toren Smith. And already before that, as mentioned in the footnotes to Kajio-sensei's postscript, a translator of Japanese science fiction; Dana mentions as her first published work the English version of Tsutsui Yasutaka's "Standing Woman;" this appeared in the February 1981 issue of *Omni* magazine.[5] Those not familiar

---

5 *Omni*, originally published between 1978 and 1995, was a technology, science (and pseudoscience) magazine, but also perhaps the most widely-read venue for science fiction in English during its heyday. Far beyond the modest circulations and

with Yasutaka's writing may know two anime films from 2006 based upon his novels: *The Girl Who Leapt Through Time* by Mamoru Hosoda (whose *Mirai* was nominated for an Academy Award this year), and *Paprika* by Satoshi Kon.

Dana has been not only the translator of, but (as translators are often obliged to be) the detective of the manga's story. For example, the ferry *Sunflower* on which Emanon and our narrator have their meeting is a real ship (owned and operated by Mitsui O.S.K. Lines, whose logo you may have seen on transoceanic shipping containers). You could come close to taking their romantic voyage to Kagoshima even today; Ferry Sunflower's excellent English website offers a night cruise departing from Osaka (no longer from Nagoya, which is the route you see on p. 48). But although the manga's ferry route was in service in 1967, the *Sunflower* was not—its class first launched in 1970.

And so we cannot entirely rely on the narrator's own memory. 1967 was indeed "the year James Bond came to Japan," as he recalls on p. 20 of the English version of the manga. This refers, of course, to the film *You Only Live Twice*—invoked most recently in our era when its theme song was used for the final scene of Season 5 of *Mad Men,* concluding "The Phantom," an episode itself set in 1967. Today Bond movies are an institution, but in 1967 they were the most exciting film franchise in the world, a cultural phenomenon understood to be shaping the decade itself in real time;[6] the first Bond film, *Dr. No,* had come out only five years before. The fact *You Only Live Twice* was going to be set in Japan (to this day, it is the only Bond film shot in Japan) therefore had a thrill for Japanese people, and especially the young, that is more difficult to fully appreciate today.

But in the original Japanese, the narrator alludes to the film by saying 1967 was the year "SPECTRE turned Mt. Aso's crater into a fortress." As Dana, who is even more hardcore than I, observed, it wasn't Mt. Aso, it was Mt. Shin-

---

production values that traditionally characterize literary SF magazines, the unequalled resources of the slick and widely distributed *Omni* came from its peculiar status of being a project from the publishing empire of *Penthouse* founder Bob Guccione and his wife Kathy Keeton. Six of the early short stories of *Neuromancer*'s William Gibson first appeared in *Omni,* beginning with "Johnny Mnemonic," which ran in *Omni* just three months after Yasutaka's "Standing Woman" did.

6 In fact, the Bond films' box office had already peaked with the previous movie, 1965's *Thunderball* (to give some idea of how big a hit it was, when adjusted for inflation, no Bond film would make as much money again until 2012's *Skyfall*). As is so often the case with peaks, this was only realized in hindsight, which explains the worldwide frenzy with which *You Only Live Twice* was awaited. As *Mad Men* would par excellence, the Bond phenomenon by itself traced the changes of the 1960s. The decade had begun with John F. Kennedy expressing himself a Bond fan in *Life* magazine, but in 1969, the youngest actor ever to play Bond, 29 year-old George Lazenby ("Don't Trust Anyone Over 30" was a famous phrase of the time) decided not to continue after *On Her Majesty's Secret Service,* precisely because he believed movies like *Easy Rider* were more relevant to contemporary audiences, and that the Bond franchise was no place for a young actor's career.

moedake. You can hardly confuse them; Mt. Aso is much larger, and they're three hours' drive from each other. Moreover, the original writer of *Emanon*, Shinji Kajio, is from the region (Kumamoto prefecture) and lives there now. Similarly on that page, "The Drunkard Returns" is more often associated in Japanese pop memory with 1968 (it was the #2 best-selling song of that year) as the single made its debut only in the last week of 1967; *Sgt. Pepper's Lonely Hearts Club Band* had come out in May.[7]

Dana remarks that the narrator (and Emanon's) language sometimes reflects the academic sensibilities of 1960s Japanese college students, and so in the Dark Horse edition Emanon speaks of "semiotics" (in the original Japanese, *kigo*) on p. 42; Roland Barthes had lectured in Japan in 1966 and 1967, and would in 1970 release his famous *Empire of Signs.* The late director-general of the Cabinet Security Office, Sassa Atsuyuki, who as a senior officer in the Tokyo riot police was involved in the violent clashes with student activists evoked on p. 28, wrote that intellectually the struggle involved "a shift from German idealism to Anglo-Saxon pragmatism;" indeed, the German term for violence, *gewalt,* was fashionable in Japan to describe the violence.[8] The narrator's use of *gemeinschaft* (a concept from German philosophy which the Japanese word *kyodotai,* "community," was itself created to translate) on p. 26 to describe his fellow passengers, is such an affectation.

The personal and the professional, and the heritage of both SF and its translation, come together on page 20 and page 131, when the translator's credit of Curt Siodmak's *Hauser's Memory* is glimpsed, for the Japanese version was adapted through Tetsu Yano, perhaps best known in English through the anime version of his own novel *The Dagger of Kamui* (to which Satoru Noda's manga *Golden Kamuy* owes a debt). Yano served as a supremely prolific guide to Western science fiction for Japanese readers, translating in the course of his career some 300 novels and short story collections.

He was also the translator of many of Heinlein's works, and at the author's memorial service, Yano noted that he himself had been a sergeant on the Jap-

---

7 Capitol Records released "The Drunkard Returns" to the English-speaking market as the single "I Only Live Twice," evidently as a marketing riff on the Bond film, as both the song and the movie had been "from" Japan.

8 To the extent that a 1969 12-minute pilot film for *Lupin III* (the first anime adaptation of the manga) has narration which boasted that Lupin rendered "gewalt" in a cool manner. As Aoyama Gakuin University professor and scholar of 1960s Japan Chelsea Schieder has noted, Atsuyuki, in his memoirs, claimed genuine sympathy for the students and nostalgia for that lost era of struggle—again, a policeman/radical relationship strangely evocative of the works of Mamoru Oshii, himself a veteran of *Emanon*'s era.

anese side in WWII, but was proud to have been, "because Robert Heinlein dedicated his *Starship Troopers*[9] to all the sergeants of the world...His exhilarating tales gave me the will, hope and courage to go on living in the devastations of the postwar Japan." Of Yano, who died in 2004, Dana herself says, "Yano-san was one of my best friends, best guides, and greatest supporters in the Japanese SF world. He was a force of nature, who, when we all straggled down hung over and ragged after a late night 'SF Translation Workshop' at a hot spring hotel or downtown hostel, would whip out a bottle of whiskey, slam it on the breakfast table, and start us up all over again! He is sorely missed by all who knew him..."

If you'd like to read literary Japanese science fiction in translation—including 1960s novels that would have been read by *Emanon*'s narrator— an excellent imprint to discover is Viz Media's Haikasoru (a play on *The Man in the High Castle*), which traces its roots to Viz's 2003 publication of Koushun Takami's infamous novel *Battle Royale;* the 2014 Tom Cruise film *Edge of Tomorrow* was an adaptation of another Haikasoru book, Hiroshi Sakurazaka's *All You Need is Kill.*

As for the manga version of *Emanon,* it will return with vol. 2, and we'll hope to encounter you again there. I'll take my own leave by recalling a song that was a Top 40 hit when I was in junior high school, "I.G.Y. (What a Beautiful World)" by Donald Fagen. Born three weeks apart from Shinji Kajio, Fagen evoked the dreams of the science fiction of his youth with tender barbed irony; as the songwriter recounts in his 2013 autobiography *Eminent Hipsters,* he grew up a—you guessed it—Robert Heinlein fan, although he took him as a satirist. As Juvenal said, it's hard not to write satire. "We'll be eternally free, yes/And eternally young."

—CGH

---

9 Those who think they have Heinlein's politics nailed down should consider his 1980 story "Over the Rainbow—" in *Expanded Universe,* where the heroine is the first black woman president of the US, who, among her actions, has the fence between Mexico and the US *torn down,* cooperates in building a binational solar power collection zone, and eventually, a joint US-Mexico space colony, in which "knowledge of industrial Spanglish" is required to settle; *la raza cósmica.*

THE PAST IS PROLOGUE

This manga is printed in the common Japanese reading order (right-to-left). If you're not familiar with it, here's a quick guide to show the direction in which the story should be read. It also means this is the last page of the book rather than the first. Flip it around to begin journeying into the memory of *Emanon*!

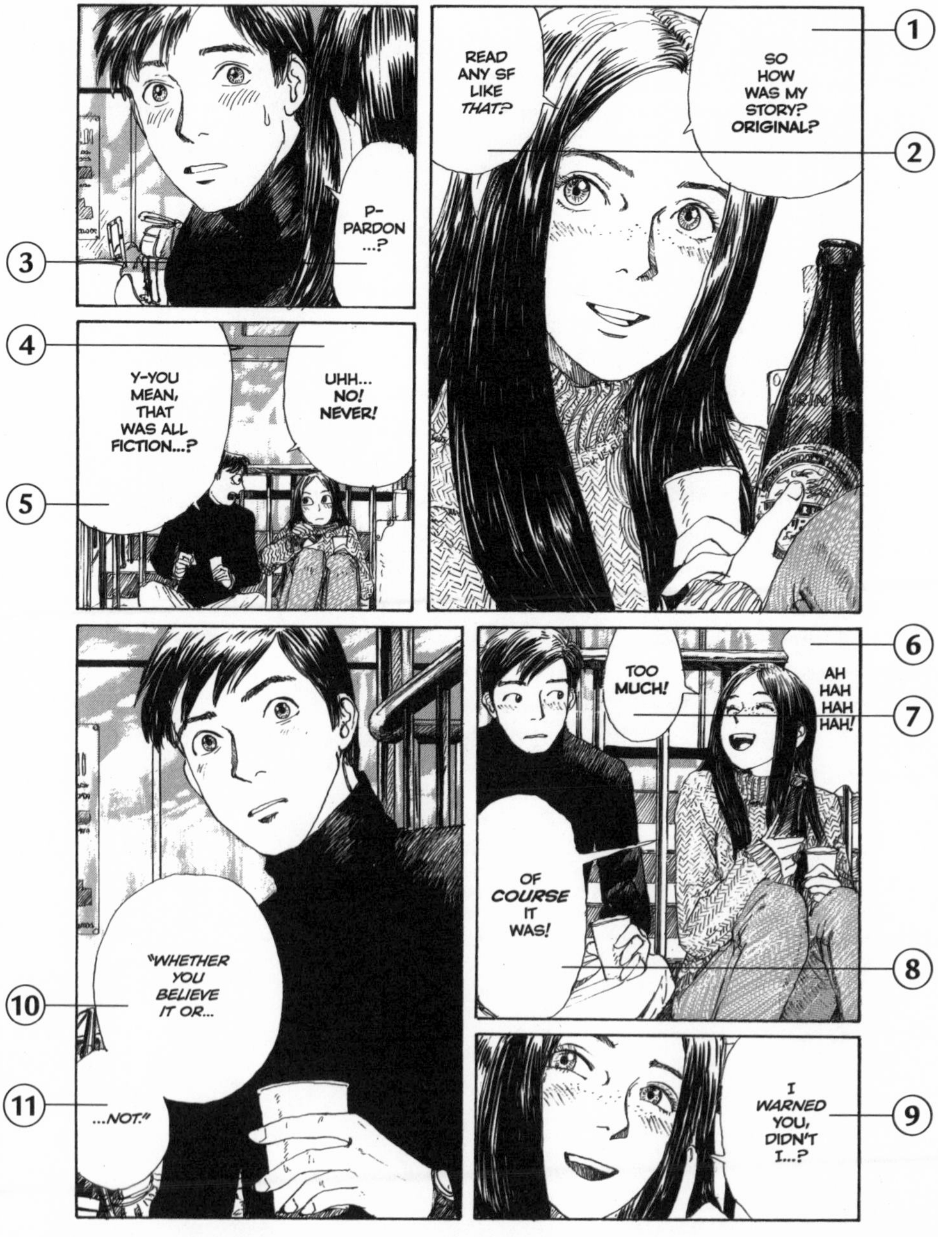
SO HOW WAS MY STORY? ORIGINAL?
READ ANY SF LIKE *THAT?*
P-PARDON ...?
UHH... NO! NEVER!
Y-YOU MEAN, THAT WAS ALL FICTION...?
AH HAH HAH HAH!
TOO MUCH!
OF *COURSE* IT WAS!
I *WARNED* YOU, DIDN'T I...?
"WHETHER YOU BELIEVE IT OR...
...NOT."